An Academic Lynching

MYTH, MISANDRY, & ME, TOO

By

Dr. J.W. Wiley

© COPYRIGHT 2019 by Dr. J.W. Wiley

All Rights Reserved

Published by: Amazon/& **X**amining **D**iversity

Permission to reproduce or transmit
any part of this book should be addressed in writing to:

Dr. J.W. Wiley (drjwwiley@xaminingdiversity.com)

ISBN - 978-1-09077-328-9

Acknowledgements

I could easily get lost in acknowledging those of you that made a huge difference in my transition from an academic to a writer. You know who you are, and fortunately for me there were so many of you that I would have to write another book just to acknowledge all of you. I know you know I appreciate you, immensely. Thanks for the energy you gave me when you called, came to visit, donated to my GoFundMe, defended me when I wasn't around to do it, and more than anything else, never ceased believing in me.

My intelligent, energetic, optimistic partner-in-life/ wife, Dr. Nesrine Hamila, is my spiritual doppelganger. She adeptly loves, supports, and pushes me to the extent I need it, oftentimes when I'm in denial that I do. Watching my soul mate, my Oomboogalah, my best friend, and learning from her daily, has been worth the price of admission. My ability and the quality of what I have to offer her and others has improved immensely from sharing my life with her. This novel is just one indicator of how wealthy I am because of her in my life. While my love may be obvious, my appreciation for my Mediterranean Mango has me at a loss for words, no small feat in itself.

Throughout writing this book Dr. Douglas Skopp and Kyla Relaford were often with me. I will miss and love you both, always.

CHAPTER DESCRIPTIONS

Preface - 1
Chris Rock; Susan Smith; Dr. Xavier Witt; John Lennon

Introduction - 9
JFK on Lies & Myth

Chapter 1 - The Angry Black Man - 15
A Casual Gathering or Strategy Session; Kathleen; Mythical Beginnings; Grinding An Axe through a Blog Post

Chapter 2 - The Myth of the Black Rapist - 42
Specific Steps; Denied Access to 'Woke Students

Chapter 3 - Misandry - 69
A Single Black Man; Women & the Cluelessness in Men; Inherited Ideals; A Conspiracy Perhaps?- Duh; In the Card Game of Gender Her Admitted Lack of Courage Somehow Left Him with Fleas

Chapter 4 - RSLM - 97
Romance is About the Possibility of the Thing; Consideration & Mindfulness; A Certain Type of White Woman; An Introduction to Interracial Dating; Michelle; When We Make Love; Fear Begets Misandry; Felicia; Jayne; One Evening; Peculiarities of Seeing and Being Black; Like a Nigger

Chapter 5 - The Lack of Subtlety in Lynching Niggers Tonight - 155
Inherited Ideals-Racism as Just a Way of the World

Chapter 6 - The Useful Idiot - 172
A Criminal and/or a Useful Idiot; Swimming with Sharks-Drowning with Dolphins

Chapter Descriptions cont...

Chapter 7 - The Investigation - 215
The Interview; FaceBook Post: Dreams of Reality; Slut Shaming; Confirmation Bias; Same Here/HimToo - Creating Male Survivors; Recipe for a Misappropriated Serving of MeToo

Chapter 8 - Allies, All Lies, Alibis, & Bye Byes - 256
Being in the House isn't Always a Privilege; Allies, All Lies, Alibis, & Bye Byes; Gangsta John Brown; Allies or All Lies; Mothburn - Opportunistic Ally; Posted Flyer; Student Government; Advice or Adverse; Embarrassed Himself; Allies; Student Excerpts; More Lies- More Alibis; Scarred Perspectives-Ally Objectives; Father & Son - Mutual Alliances; A Daughter's Love

Chapter 9 - A Hostile Environment - 334
Label Him, to Disable Him; Racism nourishes Sexism

Chapter 10 - The Twilight Zone - 347
Modern Day Hero; Dreams of Reality

Chapter 11 - In the Rear View Mirror - 368
Postscript

References – 373

About the Author – 376

PREFACE

Our lives up to this point could be described as an imbalance of power or privilege perpetually contributing to men furthering their socio-politically inherited dominance. From metaphorically if not literally owning women to situating them as objects to play with or discard, manipulate or deceive, anyone born with a requisite amount of masculinity would eventually have to decide whether to buy into the culture of masculinity, witness it silently, or contribute to dismantling it. Dr. Thomas Keith, filmmaker of *The Empathy Gap* and *Generation M: Misogyny in Media & Culture*, was poised to name his second film "The Bro Code" something much more reflective of the broad scope of that film, but was encouraged to change the title because supposedly it wouldn't sell. His original choice of a title "*The Manual for Making Dysfunctional Men, And How to Make Repairs.*" was symbolic of an attempt to get men to not just blindly and/or unwittingly acquiesce to inheriting or succumbing to masculinity as a culture. Instead, the original title suggests that men attempt to understand why we step in the directions we do, step lightly, with a lead foot, skip, tip-toe, or sprint. If there exist any type of a book, or manual that assists in breaking it down, men should fucking read it if it will help us understand how dysfunctional masculinity occurs. Like Dr. Keith's original title implies we can't fix anything we don't understand, and most people, or in this case men, have no idea to what extent we've been hard wired to believe we own women, have a right to play with them at our discretion, manipulate them, and when the mood hits, discard them. Glenn Close's famous line "I will not be ignored," from the movie *Fatal Attraction* notwithstanding.

From the chapter "The Lockdown" in "The New Jim Crow," author Michelle Alexander says *"Every system of control depends for its survival on the tangible and intangible benefits that are provided to those who are responsible for the system's maintenance and administration"* (p72).

It isn't difficult to argue that with the momentum acquired from the *Time's Up* and *MeToo* movements, on some level, as the above Alexander quote states, a new *system of control* has evolved and is dependent upon the benefits provided to those responsible for its maintenance. The ones who, logically, should be receiving the most benefit from this new system in terms of power are the survivors, and justifiably so. Unfortunately, some of that power is siphoned off, going instead to *no-proof needed survivors*, scarred by masculinity enough, or in different ways as to now be eager to wield a newfound, relatively unharnessed power, without the pain of not only having to look their accused in the eye, but probably not endure any consequences since the shaming that comes with naming a perpetrator is sufficient enough to do the desired damage.

A woman naming a male perpetrator, for years had the woman risking being slut shamed, amongst other things. Nowadays though, naming a male perpetrator situates the woman unequivocally as a survivor. It matters not that there exists a small percentage of cases where women lie. She is still, by default, identified as a victim, with the privilege of not having to name her alleged perpetrator. Not until she is emotionally prepared to do so, until she feels safe, with society ill-prepared to adeptly facilitate the possibility of her making a false accusation. Her telling a lie simply because it could be told, reaping whatever sordid benefits are available is a possible reality that some proponents of MeToo don't care to factor in.

Comedian Chris Rock offers one of the more entertaining ways to interpret lies. He chooses to explore the art of prevarication through relationships:

Relationships: easy to get into, hard to maintain. Why are they so hard to maintain? Because it's hard to keep up the lie. 'Cause you can't get nobody being you. You got to lie to get somebody. You can't get nobody looking like you look, acting like you act...sounding like you sound. When you meet somebody for the first time, you're not meeting them. You're meeting their representative. That's right.

Who are the biggest liars, men or women? -Men! -Women! Men lie the most, women tell the biggest lies. Men, we lie all the time. We lie so much, it's damn near a language. It's like, to call a man out for lying...is like playing basketball with a retarded kid and calling him for double dribble. You gotta let some shit slide. Men, we lie all the time. You know what a man's lie is like? A man's lie is like, "I was at Tony's house. "I'm at Kenny's." That's a man's lie. A woman's lie is like, "It's your baby." That's right. Who the biggest liars? Women the biggest liars. Look at you, all of you. You're a fucking liar! You're a liar! You're all liars. All of you, fucking liars! Masters of the lie, the visual lie. Look at you. You got on heels, you

ain't that tall. You got on makeup, your face don't look like that. You got a weave, your hair ain't that long. You got a Wonderbra on, your titties ain't that big. Everything about you is a lie, and you expect me to tell the truth?
— Chris Rock, Bigger & Blacker

All humans lie, often out of fear of consequences or to gain privilege. Children lie, learning how to do it from the very best, the adults around them. In the film "The Invention of Lying" lying doesn't exist until one man realizes the benefits that can be gained from telling a lie, and voila, the floodgates open when his moral ineptitude convinces him it's okay to stretch the truth if it benefits him in any way. The idealized model of behavior in the U.S. is putatively the President. Yet the current President, Donald Trump, is renowned as an inveterate prevaricator, perhaps exacerbating the possibility of any sense of truth having value. If humans, children, men, and leaders of our country can lie, how can women not? And if a survivor in any given instance is a woman, how is it she can be somehow seen as incapable of lying against a man.

Was Susan Smith--the White woman who lied about a Black man carjacking her, forcing her out of the vehicle, and thereby abducting her children still seated in the back--somehow more trustworthy because her lie was more easily seen as a truth when it featured a Black perpetrator.

Then the truth heaved up from the throat of Susan Smith: She had lied. There was no black guy. She put her two little boys -- one 3 years old, the other 14 months -- in her car and let the car roll into a lake, where they drowned. She would give her reasons -- she was depressed, her lover had abandoned her -- and a nation had to swallow hard. But for many blacks, it was another case blazing up from the embers of history. A boogeyman with black skin.

Price -- who returned to South Carolina for Smith's trial, in which she was convicted and sentenced to life in prison -- saw Smith as standing in the eye of a storm where sex and race converge. "You say a black guy did it, and it comes out so fast," says Price. "You don't even know you said it.

"I wanted to bring back why she had blamed this phantom black guy. People bought into it across the country." -- Wil Haygood, 2006

Was Fanny Taylor's lie in the film Rosewood (or in the actual true story)-- about being beaten by a Black man to hide an affair with a White man that ended with him beating her--more acceptable upon hearing it, though it led to the decimation of a Black township, because not only did it save her from possibly being beaten a second time hours later by her husband, but perhaps because her lie was also more easily seen as a truth when featuring a Black perpetrator? Aunt Sarah in Rosewood perhaps stated it best when she said, "Nigger, just another word for guilty."

Was Jussie Smollett's lie, that he was the victim of a hate crime, more acceptable because in telling his story in which he had been physically abused and humiliated, there was a rush to support him, and an immediate investigation to apprehend the perpetrators. Jussie, like Fanny and Susan mentioned above could be counted amongst that atypical two-ten percent that lie, for reasons that often don't make sense, that defenders of the MeToo movement somehow dismiss as collateral damage, until it is someone you know well, someone you love, a family member that becomes the civilian casualty in this never ending battle of the sexes. In Jussie's case he didn't make enough money, perhaps wanted more notoriety or fame, or is mentally ill since it is difficult imagining who would fabricate such a story. The parallel isn't a reach. Some women fabricate a lie for the infamous Andy Warhol 15 minutes of fame, out of envy, because of an underdeveloped morality, or because they are mentally troubled.

For many allies of the MeToo movement the men caught up in false accusations are guilty nonetheless for being susceptible to an allegation, not necessarily guilty of any actual crime. Their so-called inappropriate conduct possibly is irritating the wrong woman, or group of women, who are politically savvy enough to know how to make them pay. The *no-proof needed survivor* lie is real, and creates male survivors. Do the two-ten percent of men victimized by the *no-proof needed survivor* have rights all should care about, or are they just bystanders who stood too close by.

Women as a species are survivors. They have been second class citizens for an eternity, and then some. Now many of them are also designated MeToo survivors. Unfortunately, even under the auspices of an egalitarian upswing of women's rights, the lack of true power in far too many professional, as well as personal contexts, still finds women being manipulated, harassed, and abused. Yet there is something troubling as well as illogical about silently accepting every woman's allegation against someone just on the strength of circumstantial evidence at best, or an axe to grind, at worst. Without proof, how can she be right and him wrong, simply because women may be overdue an overcorrection or two, or five. There are stories that tell the tale of how problematic this can be. 'An Academic Lynching' is such a story, told against the backdrop of one of the most insipid times in American history, an era where MeToo intersects awkwardly at times with Black Lives Matter while someone is trying to make America great again.

Scholar Dr. Angela Davis, in her book "Women, Race, & Class" wrote:

"In the history of the United States, the fraudulent rape charge stands out as one of the most formidable artifices invented by racism" (Davis, 173).

The protagonist in this story—Dr. Xavier Witt—awakens everyday with the consciousness of a black man, as opposed to that of just a man. Dr. Xavier Witt awakens aware of the possible reality ahead of him just because the skin color he entered this world with is brown, though framed as black. Fortunately this shadowy consciousness doesn't occur in his sleep, so his internalized oppression gets some time off. As a university administrator and teaching faculty Xavier Witt spends an exorbitant amount of his time teaching with an underlying message about the privilege that is accessed through our dreams if we take the time to consider it. If we actively work against being naive, and somehow assist those whose dreams become nightmares, those who awaken without privilege, must return to their grossly underprivileged lives. The privilege unfolding within our imagination, unearned within our dreams, is only a bridge away from reality for some. Others dare not even dream.

A significant part of Xavier Witt's identity is linked to his ability to imagine a woman who awakens far too often necessarily exhaling in ways that differ from men. She knows what is ahead of her may be a day of second class citizenry, duplicitously cloaked as equality. She knows the probability of her being unheard and/or objectified is directly proportional to how many men she encounters that are unknowingly intimidated by her and/or clueless they are often contributing to the oppression of women. The fact Dr. Witt is defending himself against a veiled MeToo implication is counter to anything he has ever done professionally, and in his mind he struggles throughout this story with how anyone who knows him/his work could actually give such an allegation any serious consideration, and why? Nonetheless they do. This is that story.

Dr. Witt has no misgivings working to eradicate what he imagines as some white people awakening unaware of their racial privilege, unless they or a loved one has experienced oppression in some form. Maybe they are genetically predisposed to caring about something or someone other than themselves, in terms of race. Unfortunately White people don't come out of the womb racially sensitive any more than men who are not born gender sensitive. Of course, Black people don't enter the world racially sensitive either, but we aren't talking about Black people right now, so relax.

Xavier Witt, perhaps to a fault, imagines many people of color awakening preoccupied with the racial oppression they may endure throughout the day, without one thought though about the day that lies ahead of someone with physical or mental disabilities.

Growing up in an impoverished South Central Los Angeles neighborhood it wasn't difficult for Xavier to imagine poor people awakening hungry, perhaps not so much solely for food every day, but also for a lack of opportunities to transcend their limiting possibilities. Xavier knows that too many children whom become adults fit that description. As children they may dream impoverished dreams, only to become adults that sometimes awaken in a cold sweat from remembering having little and the fear of it becoming less.

Dr. Xavier Witt teaches that diversity & social justice begin with consideration of the other(s). Xavier's consideration enhanced his capability to imagine people born into bodies that have never felt appropriate to them. Furthermore, he could then imagine them necessarily awakening anxious about representing themselves in a world that will adversely critique them if they dare to be authentic, and that has already prejudged them as weird, strange, or any other pejorative imaginable.

There are some core beliefs that Dr. Witt believes. He believes that abolitionist John Brown awakened on the day of the Harper's Ferry raid, feeling alive with the hope it would go well, and hoping his actions as an ally would make a huge difference to millions of enslaved people.

Dr. Witt has never been shy about sharing his perspective if he thought it would further other's understanding. So, his ability to imagine Martin and Malcolm awakening to realize that they were essentially two different sides of the same coin was quite provocative while not being necessarily wrong. Both men passed each other as they morphed into more of a reflection of one another later in their careers. Xavier knew this and felt an understanding of this perspective helped lessen their demonization as well as minimizing undo saintliness. This is why he was comfortable painting a picture of Booker T. Washington-W.E.B. DuBois as the conservative-liberal forebearers of racial justice, with the torch being passed from a conservative Washington to a relatively conservative DuBois when he is juxtaposed to Marcus Garvey, with the once-upon-a-time younger liberal Dubois being made to look less cutting edge by a rambunctious Garvey, with then conservative DuBois-liberal Garvey, eventually passing the torch to a conservative Martin Luther King - liberal Malcolm X.

For quite some time after what is now infamously known as the "Lynching Niggers Tonight" episode it wasn't difficult for an emotionally, professionally, and morally wounded Xavier imagining far too many people falling asleep with an overwhelming sense of dread, only to awaken to deeply disturbing anticipation of what lies before them.

Dr. Witt's own drama undercut his ability to imagine Fox News TV hosts, certain Republican congressmen, and Vladimir Putin awakening, pondering what losing sponsorship and/or easily duped pawns would mean for their careers. Xavier imagined them at ease knowing that the culture of cluelessness most Americans are comfortable living in will allow them to spin any reality they choose, or shrug and not give a shit.

Dr. Witt was repeatedly warned by the editor of a newspaper--for which he wrote a column--that his diversity & social justice column was becoming "too political." Xavier would always reply by saying, "Unfortunately, all roads lead to—or eventually must go past—Donald Trump. His known obsession with ratings and propensity to seek attention has him inserting his nose in everyone's business, hence making it virtually impossible to escape the spectre he pathologically casts across everyone. As a result Dr. Witt often challenged his classes to imagine Resident Rump awakening without a concern for anyone that couldn't provide benefits to him.

You as the reader better understanding Dr. Witt's court case was something he imagined could happen if he chose to tell his tale, which reading this you now have a front seat to. Somehow Xavier as the protagonist in the story imagines a public consciousness that is wide awake, refusing to be fooled.

Musician John Lennon's awakened consciousness imagined this thought:

Imagine no possessions
I wonder if you can
No need for greed or hunger
A brotherhood of man
Imagine all the people sharing all the world,
You may say I'm a dreamer
But I'm not the only one
I hope someday you'll join us
And the world will be as one

Lennon's dream suggests that "imagination is only a bridge away from reality." It further implies that an awakened consciousness already knows or is receptive to discovering that no bridge is crossed without a series of steps in the necessary direction. Standing still only leaves the inactive immersed in a nightmare as they relinquish control. Inaction is always a threat to action.

INTRODUCTION

Dr. Xavier Witt always prided himself on being an ally. Being raised by a single mother trying to provide for her four children always had him appreciative of women. His mother being the eldest of eight children—five of them women—also was a great influence on his perspectives on women. Xavier was enthralled with his aunts as a little boy. They were so cool, so smart, caring and yes, beautiful. It was painful discovering that many of his female ancestors, like many women, experienced domestic abuse.

Xavier's natural father was allegedly a pimp at the time of his murder, when Xavier was just 15 years old. The lessons Xavier learned from knowing that, and continually self reflecting upon it, were powerful. Seeing more than his unfair share of unsuccessful uncles, pimps, and pushers, abused aunts, and derelict dads adversely affected Xavier's self image. Knowing his father lived his later life exploiting women made Xavier ashamed. So as you'll discover in the story when Xavier was publicly denounced as someone who disrespects women it was the worst badge of dishonor someone with his passion for being an ally could wear. Nonetheless, life is nothing if it isn't about how we perceive and communicate our perceptions. While Dr. Xavier Witt was perceived by a group of women on campus as a culprit, if not a criminal, he also recognized he must be cautious about how he perceived others whom most in his situation would consider enemies. In his situation it would be very easy for him to demonize someone.

Occasionally in Witt's career where he faced questions about his respect for women, to put it mildly. He was once questioned about his interactions with a female ex-student who interpreted some of his comments contrary to how he meant them, in response to a sexy conversation she initiated.

As a social justice educator Witt's understanding of political correctness is more than adequate, with an even more impressive feel for politically correct language. Nonetheless, he recognized that any seeming mastery of this/that could sometimes provide the so-called master with a false sense of security, making him or her even more vulnerable to inadvertently victimize someone.

Dr. Witt understands we live in a world where not only are mistakes not tolerated, but neither is the miscommunication that leads to them. We live in a world that should protect victims, though doesn't always. Witt is thankful to the "MeToo" movement. He fully appreciates that, because of the movement, actions that unjustly leverage power over the powerless were finally being met with contempt and swift justice.

Nonetheless consider his situation, a Black man rumored and eventually implied to have perpetrated sexual impropriety. Consider the possibility the implied accusation was aimed at him out of anger over a grade, or perhaps because he wasn't interested in potentially sabotaging his career with a sexual dalliance, or because he is resented for his success, or because he is suspected of something devious. How does anyone arrive at the truth from a distance? Imagine if the young woman's unsubstantiated, never filed claim were to become a whisper in the halls of academia. Are you—as the reader of this story—sure you would be socially just enough to default to giving a colleague the benefit of the doubt? Or would you succumb to your socialization, perhaps succumb to the pain of your own scars and participate in the whispering.

What is it about a black man, rumored and eventually accused of such a transgression, that makes it easy for some to unquestionably believe the whispers? What does it say about how people genuinely see him? More so, what does it say about you?

Angela Davis' concept of the *"Myth of the Black Rapist"* suggest Black men are seen as predisposed to sexually abusing White women because of injustices visited upon black bodies during slavery. It's seen as an anticipated form of racial retribution, as payback.

It's ironic that even when Xavier Witt was photographed with one of his male students many times that student one day revealed to him that his family wondered whether he and Dr. Witt were in an intimate relationship.

How does it become so believable that all men with power are predisposed to abusing it? However, if we allow, for argument's sake—that all men abuse their power, how can we not be capable imagining at least some women abuse their newly acquired power too.

In his lectures Dr. Witt often asks his students if they avoid eye contact--with someone rumored to have done something inappropriate--how socially just are they? Is it possible their posturing as an ally is a farce if a woman's accusation against a man has them believing that accusation to the extent of them taking retributive action(s) without ever having met the woman—instead of seeing the colleague whose work should speak volumes—as an ally instead of a perpetrator.

Ironically, Dr. Witt owns the fact that he has whispered. Early in his career, having been told someone's a racist, he didn't pursue any other possibility of truth simply because in his mind they fit the description. Professional basketball player Kobe Bryant fit this description virtually perfectly. Xavier subconsciously chose the side of Shaquille O'Neal over Kobe in their battle for leadership of the Lakers, prejudged Kobe as a head case who hadn't earned the privilege available to him, and whispered. Considering any other possibility only required a more profound commitment to social justice, a willingness to imagine someone else's truth. At that time though Xavier wasn't intellectually or spiritually mature enough to do it, no matter how much at the time he didn't realize it.

Dr. Witt struggled throughout his career at NYSU-Peru trying to understand why it is so easy for people to believe a whisper, or the whisperer? Allies usually work diligently to see people for who they really are. Or, allies risk becoming ill-informed whisperers, comfortably convincing themselves that they are allies by keeping alive what they may one day discover, to their chagrin and others dismay, was a lie.

"The great enemy of truth is very often not the lie--deliberate, contrived and dishonest--but the myth--persistent, persuasive and unrealistic. Too often we hold fast to the cliches of our forebears. We subject all facts to a prefabricated set of interpretations. We enjoy the comfort of opinion without the discomfort of thought. -- JFK

As you must have determined by now this extremely revealing and very personal story features controversial educator Dr. Xavier Witt, the protagonist in a timely academic tale. As an educator Dr. Witt unabashedly challenges people's perspectives by examining current day issues and topics in creative ways that most others would not dare to undertake. Dr. Witt challenges his students to unpack the myriad of messages hidden from *inherited ideals*. Wary in his classes of potentially, albeit only momentarily, losing his students due to his poetic license, Xavier is always attempting to demonstrate whatever educator's artistry he may possess. Unfortunately—while seldom hesitating to display some of his life experiences and philosophical acumen about those experiences and life itself—Witt left himself vulnerable. As one of the few Black men in a predominantly White environment, the North Country of New York, for many people he represented something akin to a pink elephant, if not a unicorn. Like the proverbial pink elephant he was a rarity for many students, staff, and faculty at the university where—until recently—he taught at since 2000. In terms of similarity to a unicorn, its most distinguishing feature is its protruding horn. As a Black man, for far too many, Dr. Witt's most distinguishing feature is assumed to be a perpetual state of horniness, exacerbated by sightings of Witt with a White woman.

Dr. Witt, an often controversial figure, consistently drops provocative pearls while avoiding or engaging unnecessary shit. This modern day tale of a Black man's journey--through the still racism ridden trail of what is often rightfully boasted as New York State's Underground Railroad--is a study in irony.

Oh, and of course this story is being told as much to reveal the complexities of workplace relationships. It reveals the practicality of having functional relationships, relationships of professional necessity that protect the vulnerability of underrepresented employees. In the process if it helps protect the innocent from those who would do dirt, creates self reflection in those who have done dirt, and perhaps if it inspires dirt-doers to one day discontinue doing dirt it was well worth it.

This story also needs to be told. It is a moral tale sorely needed at a time where across the country, and world, our ethical foundations are lacking. President Donald J. Trump's lack of action and inept reaction to the hurricane that devastated Puerto Rico, the Charlottesville protests and murder, and the killing of Jamal Khashoggi are all highly problematic within the context of modeling leadership. In all of these cases he provided a horrible example of ethical behavior--unless, for example, you have the ability to appreciate the far too often primitive utilitarian calculation that prompt most of Trump's reactions/inaction. Many observant of Trump's actions may have been appalled with his transactional approach--in contrast to the traditional, so-called American way of doing things. Regrettably we elected a transactional leader with no compunction, evident by Trump's endeavoring to protect a financial relationship with Saudi Arabia by attempting to reframe an obvious wrong. Trump justifying the brutal murder of a U.S. resident is symptomatic of the troubling world we live in. The U.S. under his leadership somehow can't afford to lose a relationship with Saudi Arabia, such a huge political benefactor. If it had been John Doelives from Oz, Wisconsin after some politically-correct posturing Trump's bottom line decision would have been the same. However, if it had been his daughter Ivanka---brutally murdered--the U.S. would have already bombed Saudi Arabia and would be on its way to lighting the fuse on World War III, if not global destruction.

Upon first glance of the title of this book it may appear as if this novel was written as a challenge to the MeToo movement. The fact that historically a well conceived morality was missing from any equitable interpretation of women's rights made the MeToo movement an idea whose time not only came, but was long overdue. Far beyond the glass ceilings, sexual harassment, and never ending micro-aggressions there have always been undue burdens carried by women that far too many men are clueless in recognizing. The lack of recognizing the plight of women by an excessive amount of men who have never been taught these lessons potentially exacerbates the reality of all women, including their daughters. However, most women who have suffered at the whims of men, or suffered due to a lack of real consideration about the realities of girls/women understand that a commitment to social justice means righting societal wrongs towards men as well. Anything less than actions discouraging or preventing ethical wrongs towards innocent men undercuts MeToo, ironically situating men to exclaim, *SameHere* along with women who want to protect these men by saying *HimToo*. Essentially and no less important this novel--while also an effort towards defending the MeToo movement against those that would misappropriate it--suggests some of the difficulties with reconciling gender intersecting with race.

Throughout Dr. Xavier Witt's journey he proffers "a perspective," never "the perspective." Musician Sting's song "Englishman in New York" has in support of its title a line in the chorus reiterating the song's overriding message, wherein he describes himself not only as an Englishman. As a result of ill-treatment he describes himself as a "legal alien in New York." One huge difference between Englishman Gordon Sumner (Sting) and Dr. Witt is that Sumner uses his music to metaphorically sting others, getting their attention about this or that social inequity. Dr. Witt, endeavoring to do similar things instead represents Black men repeatedly stung by a society that refuses to acknowledge the social inequities it unjustifiably allows to permeate its underclass.

Finally, the protagonist in this novel entertains, while also intellectually provoking you into different spaces, as well as places you seldom find yourself, wherein you're capable of considering this, that, or "the Other."

CHAPTER ONE
- *The Angry Black Man*

(In the NBA, the first foul often goes unnoticed)

"***Fuck that***!" stated Dr. Xavier Witt, to the packed house of faculty, staff, and students. "I'm not going out like that. I'm not crossing the street like I did anything wrong"

What would motivate an academic--a superstar to at least his infant children--to potentially risk his career by responding in such a manner? Some could overreach and speculate it was enduring another of the oftentimes violent winters this Californian sun child had been subjected to for now 19 years. Others more in the know might have surmised it was some of the political games being played at the expense of the academic center Dr. Witt had inherited, and successfully renovated upon his arrival at NYSU. And some could speculate that it was what W.A. Smith framed as exhaustion from "racial battle fatigue." Subconsciously perhaps, Xavier had decided he would not silently assent or acquiesce to someone's effort to make this moment the beginning of his winter of discontent. Xavier recognized that even though a storm may be looming on the horizon, yes, winter is coming, something he had been paranoid about ever since the MeToo movement had begun to take shape. Xavier's paranoia was justified considering the rumors he himself had heard were being told about him. He suspected this time though that the storm forming was man made, or more precisely, organized by women.

NYSU-Peru is a small college town nestled beneath the border of Quebec, Canada, approximately 90 min away from Montreal, if you have a NEXUS pass. The University enrolls approximately five thousand students in an area where the town of Peru and its contiguous neighboring towns combine for a total population of approximately 45 thousand residents. The demographic isn't racially diverse enough to slice and dice the numbers. Suffice it to say, somewhere around ninety-eight percent White with one-two percent everything else combined, on a good day. The community itself wasn't overly racist, no more than it was overly socially just, or aware. It just probably thinks it is better than it actually is, though unable to recognize this about itself until an event occurs that allows it to see itself in the daylight. Today was the beginning of such illumination.

Essentially, by exclaiming "Fuck that," Dr. Xavier Witt was declaring for all present to hear that he was not going to act like a criminal because--on some bizarre level--it may have been the expected behavior from him. Or, he wasn't going to be silent to make anyone feel better about them self for criminalizing him. Dr. Witt intuitively knew that his reaction would be processed very differently than the reaction of a White man to a similar allegation, especially at a predominantly white institution (PWI) in a predominantly white town/city in the eras of Black Lives Matter, the MeToo movement and the Trump presidency. Many of the White people living in the area had never seen an African-American emote in person if not having ever lived near one. Their conception of a Black person then would have been built off of media projections, music whose beats can have you singing lyrics that can get you killed, or books that sometimes at their best can only teach you about life on pages.

Considering that far too many people (in this case, White people) prefer to see themselves, what type of socially just programming can occur in a predominantly White community? Couple that with the fact that the face of crime in America is still--at the very least--non-white if not well tanned. While Xavier's thesis may be odd to hear, it nonetheless can be true. Since it isn't difficult or far-fetched to have an interpretation of one person based upon an ill conceived narrative from which that person derives, Dr. Witt--albeit for certain people--was now more easily seen as *the angry black man*.

Dr. Witt's temper had been provoked 10 min earlier by a glory seeking, center-of-attention desiring, fairly intelligent, marginally attractive Latina, Shalo Kloos. It would be unfair to paint her as unappealing, physically. She was probably about 22 years old, fit, athletically-inclined looking, and energetic. Upon first sight many, if not most, would call her attractive. She was competent enough to possibly accomplish most things she desired, only not necessarily adequately. She could also fool most people, convincing them that she was about something more than herself. She often tried to market herself as a leader to better present her pet projects as being about something more than advancing her own personal agenda, which was visibility if nothing else. However, a simple scratch of the surface and whomever was encountering her would get more than they anticipated, but not necessarily favorable in terms of a lasting impression. The expression someone is 'a mile wide but only an inch deep' describes her perfectly. On some level Shalo carried herself as if she was shallow, always in search of a beauty contest she might be capable of finishing third in. She was highly skilled though in projecting a modicum of sophistication and a requisite amount of intellect to further disarm an easy-to-dupe, not-so-discerning observer.

Shalo apparently had heard the rumor about Dr. Xavier Witt and decided to grasp the opportunity at hand. Like so many others of her generation—who don't know what to do with themselves when not taking a selfie with their ass protruding or lips pouting (or when not posting a not-so-subtle ass protruding photo)—she must have decided she would take full ownership of this masterfully crafted opportunity. Later Xavier would wonder if his never extending her the slightest bit of attention may have contributed to her seeming vendetta against him. However he rationalized it the bottom line was her comments preceded his provocative *"Fuck That."*

Shalo had approached the microphone saying, "Our university would be so much better if we didn't have to hear stories of our Chief Diversity Officer (CDO) disrespecting women."

Kloos' comments were totally unexpected by the standing room only crowd. Immediately thereafter it seemed as if the room collectively held its breath unable to anticipate what could possibly be coming next.

Up to that point the room had almost become a testimonial to the professional merits of Dr. Witt, the university's CDO. He had only recently been added to the list of administrators receiving a vote-of-no-confidence as a consequence of a perceived poor response to a highly offensive, politically incorrect social media posting. 15 of the 20 previous comments were ringing endorsements of Dr. Witt's worth to various student groups, as opposed to his three colleagues who also received no confidence votes. Perhaps the difference between so many students very personal defense of Dr. Witt versus the lack of student voices defending the other administrators was Dr. Witt's exemplary record as an ally to all potentially disenfranchised voices/beings and a perception that as one of the few Black professionals on the campus he could really relate to their experiences as 'the Other.'

Ironically, different voices followed the articulation of the allegation, some discussing specifically the brashness and potentially damaging accusation against a colleague usually respected as an ally, if not revered as a campus leader and mentor. Others tried to change the trajectory of the conversation, uncomfortable with what it was suggesting about the university's diversity initiative and its leader, true or not. And others relished the conversation that could possibly prove damaging to their political adversary.

There were many people present who had something to gain from undercutting Dr. Witt's career. LeAnn Prey and Judah Slate an interracial couple who were power hungry to the extent of even stabbing one another in the back to advance; Conan Labelle, advisor to the SG who surprisingly had an over-inflated ego considering he hadn't accomplished much; the Feminist Anthropology department who wouldn't have missed an event for which they had worked so diligently behind the scenes; Molly Mothburn the highly skilled President-whisperer; Linda Dewar the student version of a President-whisperer; and of course some who would never show themselves. However, whether this was the forum wherein most of them might be apt to weigh in against Dr. Witt was still to be determined.

Eventually the university president, Dr. Ian Utley, accepting a literal challenge from the student government for an administrator to speak, modestly approached the microphone. With an exceptionally weakened voice he spent less than a minute muttering something about respecting the student's voices and looking forward to more detailed discussions as to how he could begin to address their concerns. It was a combination of political correctness at its feeblest and feckless leadership at its most pitiful. Like the Sheriff in the film "Rosewood" who was supposed to be investigating the so-called rape of Fanny Taylor—a White woman—by a Black man, but instead was unsuccessfully preventing the wanton lynching of any Black person the mob encountered, Utley did nothing to challenge the votes-of-no-confidence against his direct reports and even less to mitigate the MeToo assertion against the CDO he himself had appointed, even waiving the traditional job search to make the hire. Similar to Rosewood's Sheriff's negligence wherein he only had to investigate Fanny

Taylor's alleged infidelity to perhaps uncover another possible suspect, Utley's negligence, his failure to take requested—if not obvious—action to once and for all put to bed the whispers about Dr. Witt would eventually take on a life of its own.

What no one in attendance knew was that two days prior to the social media incident Witt had received a phone call from Robin Kris, a woman who had been his secretary for a dozen years until she transferred to another campus unit. Even though their relationship was relatively cool now he knew that Robin may have left in silent assent of her two co-workers, Devin Greyson and Deidre Bright if she hadn't promoted out. Years before Dr. Witt had been in what seemed like a never-ending battle with Greyson, an impatiently precocious, eerily anxious employee. Greyson was a diminutive white man, often described as a poor man's Eminem, because he somewhat resembled the White rapper, minus five inches in height. Highly talented in his own right, the young man could articulate the problem of white privilege, and yet not recognize the scars he had yet to unpack because of his height. He was an angry White man, though not necessarily antagonizing people with his passionate perspective because most of the White people he would encounter, Dr. Witt surmised, had seen their fathers, uncles, grandfathers, male siblings and cousins at some moment in life passionately, if not angrily pontificating a position. So subconsciously it wasn't as threatening as when replicated by anyone who reflected the face of crime in America, as Dr. Witt couldn't avoid doing. Deidre Bright, a highly competent, elderly White woman, who along with Greyson left the Office of Pluralism, Inclusion, and Equity (OPIE) on not-so-good terms with Dr. Witt, for years had been close to Dr. Witt. She began her employment with Dr. Witt, despite being in her 50s, as his graduate assistant. Eventually she would become his Assistant Director and Co-teacher in the most significant general education course coming out of OPIE, Recognizing Otherness with Diversity Enlightenment (RODE).

Nonetheless, his ex-assistant Robin had called to inform him that she had been approached by a female student inquiring as to whether she had ever been sexually harassed by Dr. Witt. The student was Linda Dewar, a senior international student, 23 year old, short and squat in stature—known in many circles as an attention whore—had recently become an intern in the Title IX office. She joined another intern on the Title IX staff, Kelsey

Blak. Kelsey, a rather tall, shapely, and just as socially awkward Black woman with senior standing, was one of the students Dr. Witt respected immensely for her engagement of problematic campus or societal issues. Witt believed her I.Q. must have been exceptionally high because seldom had he seen a student turn a phrase or shoot from the hip as accurately as Kelsey did in impromptu academic workshops. However, Dr. Witt realized that in her case all the intellect in the world wouldn't allow someone to overcome their pettiness. Their relationship went south when just the semester prior she had taken a class from Dr. Witt and seemingly refused to adequately proofread her work. As a result, instead of an "A" she earned only a "C." It may have been Kelsey who briefed Dewar on the rumor that had been whispered throughout the hallways, propelled by what apparently was a never ending agenda that the two of them readily bought into. To thicken the plot, Kelsey had just joined a sorority on campus and Dr. LeAnn Prey, an adversary of Dr. Witt's was the advisor.

Dewar, a woman of questionable intellect to say the least, was an international student from Pakistan. Throughout her college days she was always leading. She led various initiatives on campus, led protests, and far too often led her constituents into meetings immersed in opportunities to eat, and eat, and eat. And she ate. Xavier struggled early on with whether he should either find a way to communicate with her, to see if she had some emotional problems driving her seemingly insatiable hunger, hoping to solve her oral fixation. The lies she told herself about her obesity, coupled with always seen eating junk food had to be profound. If you knew all this about her and looked for more than a minute at her you might surmise she lacked confidence. Nowhere near as readily visible were her attempts at being cunning, which always left you with the impression she was trying too hard. The bottom line though, Xavier owned, "is that in terms of the friendship between Blak and Dewars, they were as thick as thieves, with the thief description becoming more prescient considering how they would conspire, along with others, to steal Witt's career.

As a result of their sisterhood-of-sorts and the seeming politically savvy (though essentially inept) mentoring by Title IX officer, Molly Mothburn -- a Feminist Anthropology adjunct lecturer and sage to both of the two conniving students—Dewar embraced the whispering from her Title IX mentors, energetically believing the rumor. Shortly thereafter, perhaps in the spirit of the MeToo movement, they somehow decided to go after, arguably, the most vulnerable, high-profile administrator on campus. Dr. Witt doubted that they ever entertained the consequences it could and/or would have upon his life if they were wrong. The mere fact that any consideration about the consequences to this man's life may not have been considered speaks volumes as to how we see one another, or don't.

A Casual Gathering or Strategy Session

Dr. Witt--having for years seen them out and about enjoying a women's night out--imagined a casual gathering over drinks/dinner one evening amongst Mothburn, Dewar, Blak, and Kloos that resulted in a conversation not too dissimilar from this:

"So, what's been happening? Anything good to share?" Mothburn asked the other women between taking two good long sips of her drink.

"What has gotten my attention is how the MeToo movement is blowing up, everywhere," said Kloos. "It is impossible that we don't have a man on our campus who hasn't taken advantage of his position."

"I know. I was just thinking the same thing," chimed in Blak. "You know that someone on this campus has dirty hands."

"Rumor has it that Xavier Witt has a history," said Mothburn. "Over the years I have repeatedly heard that years ago he sexually harassed a student. I also have heard other things about him and his students that are also troubling if true."

I'm surprised to hear you say anything negative about him," Kloos said. "I got the impression you two were cool."

"We're not cool, and we're not, not cool." Mothburn said non-committal as possible. "He's suspected of some behavior I don't condone so my defenses are always up when he is anywhere nearby.

"Well, he carries himself as if he is above reproach," offered Blak. "I would have no problem seeing him humbled."

Linda, who up to this point had been quietly absorbing the conversation, finally contributed to it. "I start working as your intern next week Molly. I could start inquiring around campus as to whether the rumor is true."

Molly immediately responded to Linda, practically stepping on Linda's words. "If you start asking around about Dr. Witt be careful. He's popular and if you approach the wrong person it could get back to him, or President Utley. If anyone discovers what you are doing you need to take full responsibility for it." She then added, "I can't be associated with it."

Dewar, as overconfident as always, assured Mothburn that she had everything under control. Dr. Witt, now getting angry at the mere thought of such a conversation about him imagined asking her, "Do you have it under control better than you have your weight under control?" However, even considering the dirt they had already done, he knew he shouldn't even think like that. It's not cool and not him at his best.

Dr. Witt was not naive about being especially vulnerable because he was a Black man, a real-talking Black professional in a predominantly white college town. Only a few months back President Utley had told Dr. Witt that he was probably the most high profile academic at NYSU-Peru. This made him an easy target for in-the-closet racists and also one of the most vulnerable campus educators. Witt often passionately spoke truth-to-power to those unaccustomed to hearing it. As a result, it was much easier to frame Dr. Witt's passionate response as an angry outcry.

Regardless of the fact that Dewar had months earlier requested a letter of reference from him, somehow he was now enough of a predator, in her mind, that as an ex- President of the student government (SG) within NYSU-Peru—with an overinflated sense of worth—she would actually launch an unsanctioned investigation against him.

So that evening, as difficult and perhaps ill advised as it was, Dr. Witt approached the microphone. Moments earlier he had been shocked, and blindsided by Shalo's verbal attack against his character. Watching

President Utley follow her at the mic, essentially one step from groveling in response to his own vote-of-no-confidence, Dr. Witt knew he would need to specifically address what he surmised as the defamation of his character. What no one else in the room knew at the time was that the information Dr. Witt received about Dewar's unsanctioned investigation had incensed him and, oddly enough, somewhat prepared him for Shalo's insinuation, if anyone could ever be fully prepared for such antagonism.

"I'm almost impressed that anyone would have the audacity to besmirch someone's reputation as casually as we all just witnessed," Dr. Witt said to the room of approximately 850 people, comprised of students, faculty, and staff. In a very revealing moment of authenticity, interspersed with unresolved emotional anxieties, Dr. Witt continued, "I am fully aware of the rumors that have never ceased to exist on this campus, exacerbated by Feminist Anthropology."

The crowd collectively shifted its weight in anticipation of where this very verbal leader may be apt to go.

Dr. Witt then shared with the large audience a story. He revealed that years ago, well over a decade, a young woman, (Kathleen Klein was her name though he didn't disclose it to the crowd), disgruntled over two lower-than-expected grades (after receiving the top grade in two earlier classes) charged him with sexual harassment.

Kathleen

As if it were yesterday—though he didn't provide the audience with this level of detail either—while awaiting his turn at the microphone he recalled one of his conversations with the now infamous Kathleen during a horrendous snowstorm in late Jan, 2002.

"Well Professor Witt, have a great weekend," Kathleen said graciously.

"I'm going to try my best. Same to you/yours." Professor Witt replied. As he turned to walk away he got a glimpse through the window at how intense the storm was outside. "Do you need a ride?" he asked, trying to be considerate of the fact that it was late, cold, and stormy.

"Oh Professor Witt, that would be so nice," responded Kathleen.

"Not a problem at all," Dr. Witt reassured her.

Walking down the hallway they engaged in chit-chat until exiting the building and becoming overwhelmed with the inclimate weather. While cleaning snow off of his Honda Passport, Dr. Witt reflected upon Kathleen's tendency to remain after class until she was the last student. Once alone, her usually shy personality would surface enough where—though they were only speaking about an article assigned for class, a film clip viewed and discussed in class, or a current event that could be discussed in class—they sometimes would share laughter. She wasn't shy at all though when it came to letting Dr. Witt know his class was her favorite and that she hoped she could serve as a Teacher's Assistant (TA) in the future. She was his top student in the class, an excellent writer and a very strong academic voice, especially considering her shyness. She was a relatively tall, slender non-glamorous, yet attractive White woman. She was probably about 5'7 to Dr. Witt's 5'9, and a sophomore who appeared to have come from humble beginnings, which was further supported by perspectives she shared in class discussions. However, nothing prepared him for what would happen next.

After getting the car momentarily free of snow long enough to drive it in a steady downfall of snow, Dr. Witt returned to the car and what he anticipated as some more light banter.

"I really appreciate the ride Professor Witt," Kathleen said. "It would have been difficult making it back to my apartment on foot."

"My pleasure. Where am I taking you, exactly?" he asked.

"Straight down this road, on the right side of the road." she answered.

They only had to travel about a half of a mile to get her home, but the roads were so treacherous and this man from southern California who had purchased his SUV prior to knowing he would be living in Northern New York, was not driving a four wheel vehicle. So while Dr. Witt was overly preoccupied with avoiding sliding into a ditch Kathleen appeared to be speaking in somewhat of a stream of consciousness.

"Dr. Witt, do you smoke or drink. It seems like you would have to have a means of escape from this North Country living, especially coming from Southern California." assumed Kathleen. "I bet the marijuana in California is so good."

"Not really into smoking," he answered, wondering why she asked. He knew she was a chain smoker from more often than not seeing a cigarette in her hand and experiencing it on her clothes and breath when she came anywhere nearby. Dr. Witt's street instincts must have kicked in with this young woman early, on some level at least. While he didn't smoke cigarettes he wasn't above sharing a hit with his friends on rare occasions, though he did it so little he had never learned how to roll. Later in his career, more so when they became alums and now were personal friends he had smoked a smidgen of marijuana with one here or there. But he knew he would never be tempted to smoke with her. Perhaps it was because she always reeked of cigarette. He imagined she must have been asking only about cigarettes. Dr. Witt, in an attempt to maintain a light banter with her, tried to take the conversation somewhere else.

"Any good plans this weekend? You seem like it would be study/study. How else could you be such a good student, unless you study differently in my classes than your others."

"I'll study, but I can't wait to do some partying this weekend, she said. "I enjoy smoking weed to escape the drudgery of my existence."

Before Dr. Witt responded to her hard-to-reconcile comment, she continued.

"I had a dream last night that was so vivid," she said. "You were in it."

Anticipating he would hear something funny, and knowing she would be getting out of the car within ten seconds, Dr. Witt not knowing what to say naïvely replied, "Really."

Without a moment's hesitation Kathleen added, "In it we were having sex."

Dr. Witt went into immediate denial as to what he hoped he had not just heard. Speechless, all he could think of was getting her out of his car and never, ever being alone with her again. One thing he knew for sure, he needed to get her out of his car, immediately. Fortunately they had arrived at their destination.

"Well, here you go, home safely."

"Thanks for the ride, Professor Witt," she said, clueless about how much she had dismantled his sensibilities.

She exited the car before she could witness Dr. Witt hyperventilating. He asked himself what the fuck had just happened. Then and there he knew he needed to keep her at a distance. Unfortunately over time and a couple more classes her excellence as a student influenced him to reconsider his position. A year later she was taking Dr. Witt's most challenging course, 'The Philosophy of W.E.B. DuBois,' while serving as a Teacher's Assistant in his 'African American Realities' class, which resulted in her receiving her first two B grades from him. She was a good student in a demanding class that only generated a handful of A grades. She was a horrible T.A. though, often showing up to class tardy, sometimes appearing to be high, and very much intimidated by the superstar assemblage of students she was responsible for as a T.A. So, on some level the B was almost a gift. However, he couldn't begin to have anticipated what just happened, and its residual effects 15 years later. They would never have an alone moment again, with the sole exception being a brief moment after class as the classroom emptied.

Mythical Beginnings...

Upon hearing of Kathleen's filing of harassment charges against Dr. Witt in November 2003—six months after the last time he saw her—he encouraged her, through the administrator assigned to the investigation, Brenda Maims, to officially file and take whatever actions she deemed necessary to make her case. Witt said that he steadfastly refused to conform to suggestions that he avoid her, like crossing the street if he saw her coming his way. He emphatically expressed he would not consciously act out anything similar to an admission of guilt and/or criminal behavior. The disgruntled student eventually relented and didn't fully pursue an official claim. She graduated and for all intent and purposes the insinuated transgression should have died. However, It didn't.

This disgruntled young woman, posturing to assert sexual harassment against Dr. Witt, had been a double major between the Feminist Anthropology (FA) department and the Intellectual History (IH) program. Coincidentally the faculty chairs of those two academic departments—both who were her academic advisors— Dr. Sharon Winchell and Dr. Ronald Wiener, were also a romantic couple. So even when she graduated, the rumor remained, and its related whispering. However, it was five years later that the myth started by Kathleen would begin to take form, as evidenced by an email he received from the Affirmative Action Officer, Brenda Maims:

Brenda Maims wrote:

XW,
I have a formal, signed complaint from students in your RSLM course from Fall 2009.

Two things first:

1. I will talk with you and with anyone you wish me to speak with, especially students from the course, before any report will be made.
2. No contact between you and the complainant students, no retaliation of any kind, either directly or through a third party, privately or publicly.

The allegations are you established a hostile environment in the course based on sex, specifically by belittling particular students and mocking analyses of gender oppression. The concern was over two film clips you showed in the course, allegedly depicting coerced sex.

Lou Menard will sit in on the meeting between you and me. Note that is NOT a disciplinary process; we are attempting to arrange an informal resolution of the complaint, if there is any basis to it. I will give you a copy of the complaint at the time we meet.

The times that work are:
- *Wednesday of this week, the 17th, anytime*
- *Monday morning next week, 22nd*
- *Tuesday or Wednesday next week, 23rd & 24th, anytime*

Please let me know ASAP what time is convenient.

Finally, I will need two things, preferably before we meet.

1. Because the complaint concerns video clips you presented, please send a disk with /all/ the video clips you showed last semester. What we will need to do is put the two clips in question into the context of all the clips you showed.

2. A copy of the syllabus for the Fall 2009 course.

Thank you for your attention to this matter. (The entire complaint process is detailed at: http://web.Peru.edu/policies/affirmativeaction/policy.php)

Brenda Maims, Ph.D.
Professor of Sociology
Affirmative Action Officer
New York State University

******* Dr. Witt responded immediately.

Brenda,

Not a problem, any of it. I was actually wondering how long it would be before I received this correspondence from you. It will be difficult however for me to stay away from students whom I don't know as complainants, though I can imagine who they are. No worries though. I am about as eager to talk with students like them as they are probably anxious to talk with me.

I will inform some students that I imagine are not involved in the complaint to contact your office. There are some RSLM students who may want to speak with you unless you have some other method of contacting them.

You will need to get me a much smaller list of films to provide you than my entire film corpus. Providing you all those films would take me quite some time and I don't have it anytime soon. If you want to request four or five clips I can get that to you fairly quickly, if you provide me with a USB. I also don't mind providing you with the comprehensive list of clips I use.

Also, I am not interested at all in whether you and anyone else can put my film choices in some arbitrary context that you conceive from looking at a syllabus and a film list. If you attempted to do just this before we had a conversation I would be in shock.

I'm not running scared from this accusation Brenda. I welcome the fight!!! It is time students who abuse privileges they have acquired, who think they can bully someone who doesn't genuflect when they are near, were looked directly in the eyes. I am excited about doing that, even if it is only figuratively and not literally. I am really not interested in working too hard (busy work) on this matter and don't have a problem at all if these students make their charge formal. I am not one of these people who will run from egotistical students who think they can take over a class simply because they don't like the way certain conversations flow, or don't like having their voices challenged after they have disrespected the voices of others.

Lastly, and not to be flippant, but philosophical, I am wondering if you get tired of people wasting your time with trumped up charges because they are disgruntled? I would imagine, unless an individual herself/himself walks around with a chip on her/his shoulder and therefore can't see other's chips, this would have to get quite old for most people in your line of work... Anyway, I can see you on Wednesday at 3:30 pm if that works for you. I have an hour.

The syllabus for the class is attached to this response.

X.W.

P.S. Oh, and if my name is being dragged in the street don't think I'm going to walk around on eggshells carefully protecting their reputations. I'm not! If these bullies want to pick a fight, they chose the wrong person to do it with. The nice guy in me has left the room on this one.

****

From: "X.W. Witt" <wittxw@peru.edu>
Date: February 16, 2010 at 7:30:21 AM EST
To: "Brenda Maims" <maimsb@peru.edu>
Cc: Lou Menard <menardl@peru.edu>, "Blood, YG," <YG.Blood@umusic.com>, "Latrice Wiggins" <wigginl@peru.edu>, Helene Savoie <savoieh@peru.edu>
Subject: [Fwd: Re: Regarding RSLM Admittance]

Brenda,

The more I think about your investigation the more I wonder if you have inquired into the background of the students who are complaining. If I'm correct and one of them is Dick Satton, you should read the correspondences we had prior to his taking the class. What has occurred (with him complaining about someone else's behavior) was somewhat predictable, as you will see from the content of our early conversations.

As well, I am unsure if I should meet with you until after you have had the time to talk with some of the students from the class. I think it serves your investigation and my schedule best if you have a better profile of the class than that of disgruntled students with an agenda. Then our conversation might possibly be one where two people aren't sitting somewhat in judgment of me and my class based upon the accusations of two discontented students. Did you ask the students what grades they earned in the class? Did you ask to see their graded papers?

I didn't expect any professional courtesy from you because we don't do coffee, but your request for all my films before we have even talked is one of the most peculiar aspects of this entire episode, as echoed by many of my colleagues and attorney who I have apprised of this situation and your so-called investigation. The students assertions didn't take much to put you into the mode of me having to prove myself first, not them with their accusations. Well, with 45 students in that class I would wager a healthy amount of money that 85-90% of the students in that class would be/will be appalled by hearing these accusations. On the other hand, the logical trail that begins with these students runs through Feminist Anthropology (whom you have had an affiliation with and perhaps a predilection) all the way into another department that will be mentioned later when this incident becomes larger, and if I have something to do with it, it will. So, I am not going to sit quietly and compliantly and pretend that this doesn't involve Ramona Saphony (whom I have heard has discussed one of the clips in question), Sharon Winchell (who has an agenda that was recently made public) and perhaps others who have issues with the way people teach on this campus that doesn't reflect their pedagogy.

I know you are doing your job and expect you are trying to do it to the best of your ability with no preconceptions (though we both know that isn't possible for anyone to achieve). I am not trying to give you a hard time, but am very agitated by the pompousness of the accuser and your initial query that makes me feel as if I need to start with a defense, proving that I'm not guilty. I won't play that game to any major extent. So, be prepared to get Utley, and others involved in our conversation, because the solution to this won't be a Band Aid that doesn't even match my skin. I will use this accusation to explore some of the larger, but less visible politics playing out in the shadows of our campus.

X.W.

P.S. I have copied my attorney on this correspondence and will be copying him on all other correspondences from this point on.

Why would two students be so disgruntled with Dr. Witt? Discovering they were both FA minors started to provide clues. For now know that this rumor persisted just as much because there was no love lost between Xavier Witt and Wiener. Perhaps relative to his partner Winchell it was the friendship she had with a local White woman, Karen Rogers, who was interracially married to Tom Rogers, a Black man, exacerbating the rumor. Xavier and Karen had a past, but not an intimate one. Well, not really.

As a couple Karen and Tom Rogers somewhat resembled the comedy pairing of Laurel and Hardy, only with Karen as Oliver Hardy, though while their body shapes were similar, she was more of a bully than Hardy ever was. Karen would sell her soul for attention, and often inadvertently got attention she didn't know how to handle, while skinny Tom as Stan Laurel, more the laid back, clueless comic foil, would silently observe. Years earlier Karen, perhaps deprived, had literally, not figuratively, grabbed Xavier by the crotch in a crowd at her husband Tom's father's party. Xavier only meeting her that day, chose to believe her posturing that it was accidental.

"Excuse me," Xavier said (as tongue-in-cheek as anyone could say after having their testes cupped by a stranger). He even momentarily considered saying, "Sorry that my scrotum found its way into your palm." Instead, he took the high road and didn't say anything at all, offering up a dumbfounded expression.

"It's crowded in here, isn't it?" Karen said, as if to break the tension while offering an explanation. "It's no wonder that we would collide in some awkward ways."

"Wow," Xavier thought. "No, this woman, who unhesitatingly fondled my penis and testes, didn't really try to spin what she did as "collide in some awkward ways."

It was these episodes and more similar situations that convinced Dr. Witt she was sexually deviant, not for grabbing him in the crotch, necessarily, but doing it to a married man, with her being a married woman.

In 2009 Xavier had a hot and heavy relationship with one of the few Latina's living in the area, Sandita (Sandy) Ramos. Sandy was in her early 40s, gorgeous athletic figure, about 5'5. She had grown up in Northern New York, and coincidentally had never dated a Black man before. Sandy just so happened to be close friends with Karen, both of them having been reared in the area. With no shame around her prior outreach towards Xavier, Karen asked Sandy if she and Xavier were interested in participating in a sexual foursome with her and her husband, Tom. Sandy, a sexually liberated individual had no inhibitions about being sensually creative, including possibly playing with other couples they both considered sexy. Though she had never done anything like it, she was sensual enough to not freak out in a conversation about it. She brought the idea to Xavier, mostly as an opportunity for them to share a laugh at the audacity of the request. After all, there is no way Karen couldn't have known Xavier despised her. Just about a month prior she sexually transgressed Xavier again while knowing at the time he was dating Sandy. This time it was in a crowded bar. When this time she supposedly brushed up against his crotch he caught her lingering hand in his and wouldn't let it go. He immediately sought and got the attention of Sandy and more importantly--or at least he thought so--Tom, her husband. He managed to gain their attention while still holding Karen's hand, actually bending back her wrist with just enough pressure to prevent her from squirming too much or pulling away. Upon telling Sandy and Tom about it, Sandy gave her a look of disapproval, though lacking any real punch. Tom admonished her, but only still along the lines of a little fussing. The fact that everyone was drinking may have muted their responses. Nevertheless, considering this history, the fact that they wanted to have a sexual romp with Xavier and Sandy was surprising, and yet not really. Tom had been lusting over Sandy for years and would have probably slapped his wife into a coma for a chance to even look at Sandy's extraordinary figure, naked. Xavier could only surmise Karen's crush on him as desiring forbidden fruit.

Xavier, never beyond surprising someone with an unexpected response, told Sandy to tell the couple that if they came over and fucked in front of them who knows, perhaps something could happen. He didn't think Sandy would ever relay the message. More so, he damn sure didn't think that later that day, within three hours, Sandy and Xavier would be sitting on a couch across from a loveseat watching the 5'8, 155 lb. Tom being sexually ridden by the 5'6 240 lb. Karen, with no shame to their game whatsoever. Though Karen had an extremely obnoxious personality--evidenced by her wanton violation of Xavier's private space--she was still somehow lacking no confidence in herself as a sexy woman, in the sense that she obviously saw herself that way. Xavier's taste lent itself to a more petite/athletic woman, so while Karen's body wasn't his cup of tea, her face and attitude almost made you want to take a sip. It had Xavier wondering if it was only him that didn't get her sensuality.

Watching them essentially audition for a foursome that would never happen was amazing to say the least. Though Karen was abhorrent in so many ways it was just as obvious she was very much in love with her husband. A much larger person than her partner, Karen knew how to stylishly situate herself with her sexual partner. Xavier and Karen found themselves in awe of the couple's shamelessness. They let Karen and Tom finish their intriguing sexual show, quietly marveling at their confidence and passion. Afterwards, while the couple were getting dressed—obviously disappointed that their performance hadn't inspired the foursome they desired—Xavier and Sandy couldn't stop yawning to encourage the couple to leave, without making it anymore obvious that it was never going to happen.

Xavier was sure that evening—more than all the other awkward moments he had with Karen--had added fodder to her contributing to Dr. Sharon Winchell's animosity towards him. Karen and Sharon shared a mutual gossip locale that posed as a hair salon. It wasn't long before they would have a conversation about her interactions with someone who had a smidgen of celebrity.

Karen, standing behind Sharon while styling her hair, leaned over and whispered into Sharon's ear saying, "Guess who tried to flirt with me yesterday?"

"Let me guess," Xavier Witt?" Sharon replied.

"Yes!" "How did you guess that?" Karen asked.

"Because the last few times we have talked you have mentioned him flirting with you, that's why," Sharon responded. "I know you say he is flirting with you, but tell the truth. Do you really want to "do" this guy?"

"I don't 'REALLY' want to 'do' him, at least not especially so. I actually don't particularly like him. However, he is handsome, smart, and sexy," Karen said with mischief in her eye. "He would be an excellent hate fuck though. Also, my panties get wet just imagining fucking him, then afterwards seeing his wife, knowing I have a secret about her husband."

"You forgot to say he's Black. Don't think I don't know your fetish about Black men."

"I don't care if you know," answered Karen, dismissively. "Shit, you know I even married one to make sure I had my black dick when I needed it," added Karen with a twinkle in her eye.

"You are really sick, you know that," Sharon replied, with a smarmy smirk on her face. "And isn't he dating someone? Isn't she your friend?"

"Well, my philosophy has always been if you can't beat them, join them," she said in between a shit eating grin and a stomach hurting chuckle."

Suffice it to say that Xavier wouldn't have been surprised if Karen's interpretation of the animosity between them was more articulated to her friend Sharon as if Xavier was coming on to her, and not the other way around. Ironically, not once had he ever shared a moment alone with either of them. Whatever the reason, Winchell had an axe to grind with him that eventually became a spiel of hers about what she perceived as Dr. Witt's predatory propensity. She would reveal her animosity when in the midst of a spirited conversation with blog contributors, Winchell posted this.

"I cannot discern much of a difference between verbal and blog gossip. Your palpable disrespect for the "business owner," as well as your widespread reputation for disrespect toward, harassment of, and sexually predatory behaviors against women, makes the question of whether you call us girls or women a mere attempt to distract us from your more insidious, and infamous, misogyny."

The audacity of someone actually feeling comfortable enough to post such a thing was incomprehensible to Xavier. It spoke volumes about the environment he was in, especially after he shared her post with the administration, without consequences.

Grinding an Axe through a Blog Post

Winchell's posting was the FA clarion call against Dr. Xavier Witt, alerting him to the reality that he needed to have a healthy dose of productive paranoia to help protect himself, though in no way being able to anticipate the magnitude of the future storm.

Winchell's partner Dr. Ronald Wiener and Xavier worked in the same academic department. At the time Xavier was hired in July 2000 he and Wiener were the two youngest within the department, Xavier at 32 and Wiener at 38. The other five faculty were all at least 55 years old, perhaps even closer to 60, with one probably more like 70. The only woman in the department was the department Chair. She was married to another IH faculty member. They were outstanding, cool and socially aware. Two other faculty members were campus superstars who had outgrown any consistent activity with the department, but nonetheless supportively participated in departmental meetings trying to exhibit loyalty, and in their own ways some additional quality of thought.

The fact that Xavier was hired as an administrator at a salary of $70,000 without his doctorate while Wiener labored in a self-imposed obscurity at a salary of $45,000 with his doctorate, must have been hard for him to swallow. NYSU-Peru salaries, since it was a state operated university, could be found with a bit of effort. So it didn't require much effort to discover how much anyone was paid.

Two years later after the death of the wife of the married couple (the department chair at the time Xavier started teaching in the department) followed by a couple of retirements, when Wiener had no one to boss around other than the only person in the department younger than him (and without a doctorate), he really couldn't even do that. Upon deciding to also teach, since Xavier was initially only hired as an administrator, he was given the opportunity to choose whom he would report to, the V.P. of Academic Affairs, or Wiener, the interim department chair of Intellectual History. Prior to Wiener's ascension to the interim position Xavier had been tempted to choose the department chair as his boss. This was only because he viewed his administrative appointment as a necessary evil (preferring the classroom to offices and boardrooms), he nonetheless opted out of that scenario after imagining Wiener one day becoming the permanent department chair. He thought to himself, who wants to work for a Wiener. When Wiener finally did ascend to the position Xavier hyper-extended his elbow patting himself on the back in celebration of his clairvoyance. All this contributed to the rumor—initially told by the disgruntled female student—never dying. Winchell and Wiener were highly motivated haters with Wiener ironically never admitting to his misandry-filled partner that his real problem with Xavier was a social-economic class problem first, perhaps further exacerbated by what Xavier imagined was Wiener's dearth of experiences with Black people.

Wiener was short, shorter than Xavier who would never be described by anyone as tall, except Lord Tyrion on Game of Thrones. Wiener was about 5'5, balding, and with the way he was reported to intellectually flex on his students would never be mistaken as an athlete, though he was an intellectual bully. Lacking in creativity to make the teaching experience exhilarating, he was known as more of an overblown, bloviated bore during his lectures. Conversely, Xavier Witt's journey to become an intellectual went through his playing sports and growing up in the hood of South Central Los Angeles, though neither was mutually exclusive. Xavier at 49 years of age, at 178 lbs was literally only 7lbs. heavier than his high school football weight of 171. At 5'9 he carried the weight well. Xavier represented "fit," which was only a threat to someone frustrated with their inability to remain fit, or problematic to someone that couldn't see he would never flaunt his health privilege, nor his inherited DNA.

With all of those complexities in the backdrop, upon telling this story to the audience, armed with additional information no one else in the auditorium was aware of, Dr. Witt came to an emotional crossroads. He quietly acknowledged to himself that he had an option of responding patiently, trying to take the student's allegation in stride, naively hoping that the long arm of the MeToo movement couldn't grab him all the way up in the North Country of New York. He momentarily considered another option, perhaps he should attempt to remain philosophical, relying somewhat on whether his reputation—as an ally in terms of social justice, broadly conceived—was enough to withstand the onslaught of a character assassination. He considered saying: "*I refuse to act as if I'm a criminal simply based upon conjecture and prejudgment.*"

However, he didn't. He had made too many attempts at trying to rewrite the narrative already written about him to now intellectualize his response over his passion. So his other option, to verbally, passionately, perhaps even verbally-violently push back against it, loomed larger than anything else in his drop down menu of responses. With more in his head than most could imagine he instinctively chose the latter,

"Fuck That." Dr. Witt further added, "Why is it—as a Black man living in the North Country of New York—if I'm seen with a White woman we must be fucking?"

The crowd collectively shifted its weight upon Dr. Witt's use of profanity to accentuate his points. Not that the crowd in its entirety were new to Witt's creative choice(s) of words. He was known for punctuating points with what he likened to prophetic profanity. What is prophetic profanity? Witt always spun it as profanity that makes the powers-that-be pause, forcing them to acknowledge the creativity as well as power within the phrases turned.

Dr. Witt then offered, "I know why! It's the Myth of the Black Rapist. Regardless of any work I've done establishing myself as an ally to women, a student none of you know, with no insight into her reputation, can level an allegation against a professional colleague of yours and you choose to believe the student over a campus colleague known for doing exemplary work as an ally to you and many others. Why?"

Of course Dr. Witt knew that they couldn't really answer his rhetorical question. Most of them had never considered their implicit biases, or their need to have their biases confirmed. Unfortunately there was no way his self-defense would not be viewed by most in attendance as anything other than an irrational outburst, if for no other reason than they didn't know the behind-the-scenes shit going on.

He recalled once, while living in Southern California, having a difference of opinion with a female neighbor, his next door neighbor actually, over a parking spot on the street. After Dr. Witt's had a conversation with his wife Andrea who had brought the concern to him after she talked with the neighbor's husband—where the husband revealed that his wife had told him Dr. Witt had yelled at her—he became alarmed. Andrea asked him why he would yell at the neighbor's wife. Ironically, Dr. Witt had always been teased by his wife and other significant lovers about the fact that he never raised his voice in arguments. So, when Xavier asked Andrea to recall one instance where he had ever raised his voice at her, she couldn't recall one. Dr. Witt, in turn, asked Andrea how then she could believe he would be yelling at a neighbor. They both chuckled at how easily our implicit biases can be manipulated and/or exacerbated by others.

He also recognized that his sexuality may have been a curiosity to many in the region with some even questioning his sexual orientation as a result of the close relationship he had with one of his male students, Darren Schultz. Because Darren was single and they were often seen together eventually their relationship received speculation from those with too much time on their hands. People couldn't know that Darren adored women and was probably as far from being gay as Xavier was from starting on a roster with LeBron James and Kyrie Irving when the only position his short ass could play would have been point guard and neither one of them was going to give up the ball. Or Darren deserved an Academy Award. But what too many people without meaningful lives do is gossip. If they can't comprehend your reality, they'll create a reality in their minds for you.

In terms of the preponderance of women doing social justice work around gender identity that defaulted to accepting him as predatory he understood that many people firmly believe they are allies simply because they earnestly want to be. As if that is enough adherence to a criteria to justify being an ally. And/or some convince themselves they are allies because they always have been on the right side of issues, perhaps even history. Not too dissimilar from mothers as allies who disapprove of their children's romantic choices with justification it is in respect of the culture. Hmmm!

That same culture has women as less than second-class citizens. Or fathers as allies who—as boys and/or young men—wantonly promoted disrespect of women with their language choices, but now as more mature men and parents take umbrage against sexist language around their daughters. So on many levels Xavier's anger was often muted by an enlightened perspective and forgiving nature. However, this time was different from any moment he had ever experienced prior, in his life.

Dr. Witt had witnessed the destruction of many men's careers over the last year as a result of Me Too and the Time's Up movements. Bill Cosby as a perpetrator of sexual assault had been languishing in the wind for years until he finally got his comeuppance. Harvey Weinstein's demise appears to have been karma from his legacy of abusing women. Matt Laurer caught those without access to the inner workings of NBC off balance. Michael Kimmel a white male academic working within the SUNY system, appears to have a different situation unfolding for him in comparison to Dr. Witt's upheaval in a similar system, NYSU. As a man who has had countless profound, provocative conversations with all his students Witt recognized he could be vulnerable to an accusation. After all, a misread conversation, revenge over a grade, scorn from unrequited desire, someone seeking attention, light--perhaps once considered harmless--flirting, pick one. Therefore, the one-two punch of Linda's unsanctioned investigation and Shalo's not-so-veiled accusation could have been enough when not challenged by a leadership under siege with a vote-of-no-confidence. However, add to the mix multiple attempts to implore the college president himself to step into a leadership moment with his only action repeatedly being inaction, it was enough to make anyone lose their cool, blow a fuse, or pursue a lawsuit.

Witt also realized that his language, laced with snippets of profanity, and his tone, passionate, all would be packaged to suggest that at the end of the day he was just another *angry black man*, thereby providing his naysayers with the argument that he was not Chief Diversity Officer material. Witt had never lost sight of the fact that when he was promoted to CDO he had given up his permanent appointment and union membership for the far riskier status of serving at the pleasure of the president. Witt's response would be just what the doctor ordered, or in this case, what Dr. Utley could leverage to get him out from under his own vote-of-no-confidence.

Dr. Witt, knowing that anger has its place in any society, also knew that everyone in a society isn't granted the privilege to display their anger without being judged.

Witt's words had the room buzzing. No one could have anticipated what would happen next. Molly Mothburn followed Witt to the mic. Without an ounce of hesitation she said, "Don't let any earlier comments intimidate you into silence. My office is open and more than ready to entertain whatever stories you want to share."

Witt wasn't as blown away by Mothburn's comments as others would later indicate they were. Mothburn was a walking contradiction. She was a person who refused to accept that she had outgrown many of her dresses, instead always pulling and tugging at them to readjust their fit. Mothburn was a woman in her 40s, mother of eight, from three different fathers. Her second marriage had contributed to the word on the street being that their relationship had been rumored to have ended for all intent and purpose five years previously. Nonetheless Mothburn had birthed two sets of twins during that period, ages 4 and 2. For years she had been an adjunct professor in the Feminist Anthropology department. An attractive woman in many ways, and definitely equipped with a high intellect, she nevertheless always seemed fatigued. Her relationship with Xavier was never close, and Xavier had been warned to watch his back with her by his close friend Nyla Earlford. Nyla, the director of ALANA at NYSU-Peru saw Mothburn as a power seeker who appeared to be adept at playing campus politics. Nyla said it irritated her to see Mothburn cozying up to whomever she needed to align herself with to attain the power and position she craved. Mothburn, upon ascending to the Title IX Officer position, postured as if she was interested in being collegial with Xavier. She reached out to include him and his OPIE staff in their Title IX programming, as well as being receptive to collaborating with them. However, Xavier never let his guard down with her, knowing she was a faculty member in what for the last 14 years had been his nemesis, the Feminist Anthropology department.

CHAPTER TWO
- *The Myth of the Black Rapist*

"Hello cool students," Dr. Xavier Witt recalled welcoming his students. "On the board for all of you to see as you entered the class is the quote:

To incite the white workers against the Negroes, to further build the myth of "white superiority," the white ruling class has coined the poisonous and insane lie that Negroes are "rapists."
-- Haywood & Howard, *Lynching: A Weapon of National Oppression*

Dr. Witt had the quote up to support the primary conversation taking place in his Examining Dimensions of Cool class that evening, which featured a conversation about rape, and the often racist consequences that accompany being accused of it. The fact that some years later he would be fighting against a rumor that he sexually harassed a student, and an allegation of disrespecting women, was the epitome of irony.

He would always be appreciative in the most twisted of ways, that at least none of the women who contributed to his demise went anywhere near the penultimate lie, that he was a rapist. Though his daughter Autumn did share with him that in an online exchange with other students considering attending NYSU-Peru one of the young women in the group chat, not knowing she was talking about Autumn's father said,

"I'm not sure if I want to attend that college. I hear their Diversity Officer raped someone."

It is difficult to imagine how hearing this may have made Autumn feel. It's one thing to know your father has been terminated from the only job you ever knew he had. It's another thing to hear the alleged inappropriate behavior Daddy-dearest was accused of, escalating to rape. The Cool class itself was designed to address societal implications of what is 'cool,' in terms of acceptable, likeable, excellent, and any of its other synonymous meanings or social class markings. As well as what is deemed uncool. Rape and any form of abuse was unilaterally considered uncool. Lying that a rape had occurred or framing any group as predisposed to the act of rape was considered uncool. On the contrary, rape reframed in the way it was in the film Casualties of War, which was based upon the true story, the *Incident on Hill 192* can leave the perpetrators of a rape selfishly interpreting their actions as cool, justified by 'interrogating' instead of raping their female prisoners.

Beginning class, Dr. Witt said, "This quote was in your assigned readings last week, which you've all read for tonight's discussion. You were supposed to consider 'Storytelling' as you read your articles. In terms of 'cool,' what did you see:

"It was cool that she obviously wanted to fuck her professor, and did," he recalled Emily, a White female sophomore student, saying,.

"Why do you say that was cool?," Dr. Witt asked.

Emily answered, "She told her roommate she was going out looking to get her fuck on, in an effort to escape an evening of anxiety over the inadequately justified break-up initiated by her boyfriend. So it was cool she wasn't sitting around moping about it."

Patricia, a Black female senior student added, "She also endured a whole lot of shade from the professor when she approached him in the bar. More than I ever would have put up with. So, perhaps it was cool how she handled his rudeness."

"Are you saying he threw shade because he took forever to answer her questions?" Darren, a White male graduate student, asked, "Or because he answered her questions with brutal honesty, and as a result possibly curtailed any chance at sex with her that evening? In the latter scenario I painted it was cool that the professor kept it *100* with her, even answering her questions with integrity, especially when telling her she had no future as a writer."

Patricia raised the bar on the conversation when she added, "In the Chris Rock video we watched a few weeks back he said that a woman knows if she wants to fuck a man much earlier than most men imagine. Considering that thought, if she had earmarked him as someone she would make love with if he weren't her professor, encountering him that evening when she was despondent, and looking to have sex, he probably became quite fuckable. His shade probably meant nothing to her if she wanted her itch scratched. Sex isn't only just a fuck to men, you know. Women can have a non-emotional moment also. Men somehow have been convinced that it has to mean something to women to do it. Shit, really? A penis inside me doesn't mean love is certain because of it. I've never been emotionally attached to my Tampax, and only emotionally attached to my finger when it helps me achieve my goals."

Many in the class winced when Patricia got realer than real. Patricia was another one of Dr. Witt's superstar students. She knew intellectually that she was the truth in some circles, and the shit in others. Her intellectual game was extraordinary, moving in 0 - 30 seconds from shy and unassuming to bold and provocative. So her asserting, explicitly, her interpretation of the film clips from the movie 'Storytelling' and boosting it with a personal reference wasn't surprising in the least. Patricia wasn't above putting political edge or sexual tension into the conversation if she thought it would advance her point for her, if not add some proactive energy. Dr. Witt adored her mind for exactly that reason. However, him figuring out how and when to push back against the shoot-from-the-hip theories of this young woman was a work-in-progress itself.

"Now Patricia, we both know fucking isn't just sex to women, is it?" Dr. Witt asked in a more hushed tone, deliberately creating the intellectual space he desired by having everyone in the room have to lean forward to hear him. "While it obviously can be, and is to "some" women—some being indeterminable—to 'some other' women *fucking* is only *fucking* because *sex* means something different to different people."

Patricia, recognizing the game was on, replied, "True XW (using Dr. Witt's initials to let all know the depth of their connection as well as her lack of fear or idol worship, as well as her situational courage), but *fucking* can masquerade as just *sex* or just love as easy as the word *fuck* can exist as a verb or noun dependent upon its context."

Dr. Witt realizing Patricia was 'on' today had him wanting to avoid situating himself in any way as if he were competing with her, appearing to be striving for some nonsensical victory. His victory was her not hesitating to intellectually challenge him. Conversely, he was always hesitant to challenge her if it could not be done appropriately. He never wanted to take away her energy or anyone else's in his classes. Dr. Witt was never interested in disrupting any creative energy one of his students was bringing. However, shit happens, he thought. Before he could respond in any way someone else in the class found her voice.

"You may be correct in your assertion, Patricia. Nonetheless you just used the terms "fucking," "sex," and "lovemaking" without hesitation, at times impractically implying they were all equivalent," added Shawna, a White female junior, and one of the TAs, stating further, "when as we've discussed before, they aren't."

Patricia replied, "Shawna, I disagree that I did any such thing. However, to avoid being bogged down in an unnecessary defense, you should already know my game is tighter than that," which generated laughter throughout the class. She then added, "the author Robert Solomon wrote:

"Desire may (or may not) be 'natural,' but whom and how we desire is something cultivated and conceived through a culture and its ideas. But there are good ideas and bad ideas, creative ideas and self-destructive ideas, obscure ideas and clear headed ideas, ideas that tell us what to look for and ideas that make it impossible to find our way..." -- Solomon (18)

Dr. Witt chimed in, "Patricia, you need to unpack that quote within the context of the film clip under discussion at that moment, 'Storytelling.'"

"I know, I know," Patricia responded gathering to defend her use of the Solomon quote and its pertinence to the film clip. "The White female graduate student in Storytelling may have desired her Black professor, but he was theoretically off limits to her as her professor. Nonetheless in her fantasy about him she may have imagined something endearing, more akin to lovemaking, but then had to adjust that to having sex with him when they apparently decided to go to his place. However, when he asked her to say, 'Nigger, fuck me,' after he entered her body, they were not making love, nor was it your garden variety sex. When she acquiesced, giving him the 'verbals' he requested, they were then fucking."

Patricia exhaled as if she had straight dropped the mic. How well she represented her point became more evident from the fingers snapping in support of her point. However, in this class of academic superstars that Dr. Witt consistently attracted, it only took a moment before someone else stepped into the light.

"I appreciate Patricia's point even more when considering her quote," stated Erica, a White female junior. "When Solomon framed our desires as cultural phenomenon he open the door for the Black professor's White female student to act out Solomon's concept of the self-destructive idea of either having sex with, or fucking her professor. She may have been looking for solace, some type of escape from her immature boyfriend ending their relationship, but the notion of it taking two to tango doesn't guarantee that the professor's rhythm and hers will be sufficiently cool enough where both will be satisfied by the time the dance ends. Sexually, whether she was imagining fucking him, having sex with him, or making love with him, the professor was only interested in fucking her." The smoke he blew in her face at the bar and the eternity it took him to answer her questions were uncool, if not rude as fuck. So the social dimensions, as XW says (looking at Patricia as she used Dr. Witt's initials too) the little things all of the time that situates the sex act into one of the three coital categories eliminates it from being sex since, by definition, sex is relational and the professor in Storytelling doesn't appear to like or respect her, even though they have a relationship through him teaching her. They are not in love either, so lovemaking is out. There wasn't a tender or loving moment in their sex, unless she was into demeaning sex. In that case she would have been in heaven."

"I agree Erica," added Darren, cutting to the chase. "I doubt very seriously if her repeating "fuck me nigger," was ever intended as foreplay or a delicious segue for them to possibly make love."

Dr. Witt remembered placing a bow around the conversation by stating, "When someone is 'fucking' a person that views their shared intimacy as 'love making,' the person who considered the moment 'love making,' while trying to be endearingly sexual, may only be capable of actually fucking, not making love. Love making is as reciprocal as "fucking" with the difference being varying expectations in the aftermath. While all the coital acts must feature mutual consent, lovemaking stereotypically is relational, heightened desire inspired as much by emotion as by reason, when compared to sex with a friend, or consummated lust for a stranger. Love making is also highly considered and appreciated, and very unselfish" (Dr. Witt, always seeking clarity around our coital categories thought that even if she allows you to get yours, mindfulness should tell you to hide your glee, unless of course the glee itself gets her off). "Ironically, because someone may be holding onto the belief that the sexual moment just shared with a person was "love making"—when the other lover sees it as nothing more than a "fuck"—on some level the other person consentingly participating in shared intimacy and believing lovemaking was occurring essentially got fucked, twice."

Dr. Witt unnecessarily, most likely out of habit, tried to suppress his chuckling as he recalled the thinkers in the class trying to unravel the meaning in what he said while he was praying he had just made sense.

The details of his past classes seldom left him completely, especially the three hour evening courses, wherein the students were engaged, even floating in and out of conversations during their mid-class breaks, when some were not approaching Dr. Witt to further discuss his pre-break comments. It wasn't difficult discerning that these students liked each other and loved the class.

Dr. Witt could vividly recall his prompts to the class, "So let's discuss her implied allegation of rape against him."

"Rape? What a joke. She was relentless in pursuing that Black dick," offered Amanda, a White female senior. "Just because he flipped the script on her socially-just, Benetton posturing ass doesn't mean he raped her," she emphasized, which had weight amongst the class coming from this young white woman with a heightened level of consciousness, especially around her White privilege.

"She specifically told her roommate as she was leaving their apartment that she was going out to get laid that evening," added Marty.

"That doesn't mean she wasn't raped," said a frustrated Alyssa, a White female sophomore.

"It doesn't mean she was, either," Marty, a White male junior stated.

"She just freaked out when he told her to say, "Fuck me nigger," added an adamant Hollis, a Black male senior.

"Wouldn't you freak out if someone asked you to say, 'Fuck me white bitch?'" Alyssa asked Hollis, one of her best friends. "As a matter of fact, you may not have a problem with it at all, with your gangster ass."

The class erupted in laughter, with Hollis being a good sport, even winking at Alyssa, though not giving her any indication as to whether she could be right about how he would handle such a precarious situation.

Marty replied, bringing the class back into what for all intent and purpose needed to remain a serious discussion, "That's no more rape than a kiss on both sides of someone's cheeks is a kiss of passion instead of a greeting."

"This film clip and the conversation upset me tremendously," said Jayah. This Angela Davis quote sums up for me how upsetting this whole conversation is for me:

"If Black women have been conspicuously absent from the ranks of the contemporary anti-rape movement, it may be due to that movement's indifferent posture towards the frame-up rape charge as an incitement to racists aggression. Too many innocents have been offered sacrificially to gas chambers and lifer's cells for Black women to join those who often seek relief from policemen and judges" (Davis, 173).

Jayah continued, in her own voice, "Criminals must be punished to deter others from committing crime. I get that. But Black men have died as a result of the whims of some privileged White women who could easily cry rape just because they were confident they would be heard."

Obviously emotionally invested in her comments, Jayah continued, "There is a troubling racist legacy of rejected White women contributing in some way or another to innocent Black men suffering or dying. Even though the White grad student in '*Storytelling*' was somewhat 'woke' in being fully aware of the anxiety many white men have around black men, encroaching on what they want to believe is their territory, if not property, it didn't prevent her from playing the gender card--accusing him of rape--to negate his awkward introduction of a race card into their game of seduction."

"She knew that a black man's voice is grossly diminished," interjected Hollis, "when a white woman claims her alleged "no" was heard as "go," and then acted upon."

Jayah passionately added, "My family tree features a couple of incidents whereby my ancestors were rumored to have been lynched, over what my family deemed false accusations. So forgive me if I'm not too quick to put a noose around a Black man's neck."

Darren then added, "In the Davis article she references [Brownmiller's] examination of the Scottsboro Nine case as a revealing example. As Brownmiller herself points out, these nine young men, charged and convicted of rape, spent long years of their lives in prison because two white women perjured themselves on the witness stand" (Davis, 198).

"But why would anyone risk perjuring themselves?" asked Amanda.

"You don't think it is a measured move?" asked Taylor. "The persons willing to perjure themselves are doing it because they believe it will benefit them, somehow. They also know the society they are living in, their privilege, and how Black men are seen, and treated."

"You know there are some people out there who can't see how it benefits a White woman to falsely accuse a Black man of rape?" said Robyn, a White female senior student from Trinidad.

"It is her ultimate power play," added Erica. "As forbidden fruit in most societies the White woman's sanctity is sacred enough to be kept and protected, and sacrilegious when lost. This is why Davis said 'The *Myth of the Black Rapist* continues reflects the insidious work of racist ideology.'

Dr. Witt then said, "Perhaps the Myth of the Black Rapist would be more appropriate if it were changed to 'The Myth of the Nigger Rapist' though otherwise why is the racial adjective even necessary? Does a rapist rape differently across racial lines? A white man accused of rape is innocent until proven guilty, whereas a Black man accused of rape isn't just more apt to be seen as guilty, because of a rape accusation, but also must face the possibility the accusation against him may be him living up to the expectations his blackness creates in the minds of many, if not most whites. It begs the question are there extenuating circumstances that contribute to Black men raping that may be different compared to White men?"

Dr. Witt continued, "Davis coined the phrase consistent with how it has always played out in American society. Just like black women seldom being referred to as niggers especially not by black men--with the exception being Beatle John Lennon's song, 'Woman is the Nigger of the World.'"

"So are you saying 'nigger' is a gendered term, like rapist?," asserted Angel, Dr. Witt's top T.A, an African-Latino male senior.

"Yes, on some level, I'm saying exactly that," responded Dr. Witt. "Rapist in the minds of non-Blacks unaccustomed to breaking bread with Black folk--may be Black men. Rapist is seldom aimed at women as a descriptor for their acting out similar moral and legal transgressions. When "rapist" is aimed at White men, no adjective is necessary. Have you ever heard Caucasian Rapist, Cracker Rapist, Ofay Rapist, or White Rapist? Or heard of a Black Rapist, Mexican Rapist, Asian Rapist, Immigrant Rapist? Somehow there is no such thing as a White rapist, or an 'American' Rapist.

"As if in her own world of thought, Alyssa asked, "When Davis stated that "*racism nourishes sexism*" (177), was she paraphrasing what Dr. Martin Luther King said, 'injustice anywhere is a threat to justice everywhere?'"

Angel answered her before Dr. Witt could. "Yes Alyssa, and ironically, the sexism that racism often nourishes also unfolds towards black men--who in rapidly changing contexts lack the power to avoid criminal-like assertions that their sexuality is problematic--when a white woman decides to use her virginal sanctity against him."

The memories of that particular class would continue that evening, reoccurring often across the next few weeks, perhaps because having those very difficult, yet important exchanges of perspectives and ideas, enabled Xavier to better understand the difficulties people may be experiencing trying to understand his plight. The *Storytelling* film clips he used in the 'RSLM,' 'African American Realities' and the 'Cool' class provided more of a point of departure for those provocative exchanges. Dr. Witt, when he designed all of his classes had the goal of submerging his students in dialogues between one another that most likely they would never have elsewhere. However, if the opportunity to have one in real life--or weigh in on one in real time--ever arose, he wanted them prepared, not intimidated, and more so, knowledgeable about the topics.

Dr. Witt's reflections back on that class' conversation energized him. He knew he had probably improved his students understanding of the intricacies surrounding interracial sexual relations. When he shared with them back then the *Myth of the Black Rapist*, his battles with the Feminist Anthropology department were always in his mind.

Once in his office with his TAs, he was asked why the Feminist Anthropology professors didn't seem to care for him. He responded by sharing with them that adjunct professor Sharon Winchell—who Xavier had heard years earlier was an advisor to the young woman who started the rumor about him—in 2012 had posted this statement on his Wandering Witt blog.

"I cannot discern much difference between verbal gossip and blog gossip. Your palpable disrespect for the "business owner," as well as your widespread reputation for disrespect toward, harassment of, and sexually predatory behaviors against women, makes the question of whether you call us girls or women a mere attempt to distract us from your more insidious, and infamous, misogyny."

Discovering that none of them knew her, he shared with them that he had never once spoke with Winchell. However, he told them that if they've ever known someone that seems like life has given them nothing but lemons without the tools to make lemonade, or grapes with seeds in them, never mentioning there are seedless grapes, then they've met Sharon Winchell. A younger, less polished Xavier would have described Winchell as a sick bitch, but his evolution as an ally prevented him from being comfortable using such language. Ironically, like Black people using the terms nigger, nigga, and Negro as playful and passionate descriptors, some women can use bitch with no hesitation. Xavier was surprised when sharing the quote from Winchell with Kesi she responded, "That bitch shouldn't be teaching young impressionable women."

"I have never heard you refer to another woman as a bitch. I thought it was outside of the norms of your culture, you being Arab-Muslim."

"It was taboo until you started telling me about this bitch Sharon Winchell," she said mischievously. "Sometimes we must find just the right language to describe others."

How someone responsible for teaching young minds could brazenly post such unsubstantiated drivel and get away with doing it was always confounding to Dr. Witt. His informing the university president and other pertinent senior administrators of her posts on his blog wasn't enough of a warning for them to take action. Dr. Witt couldn't believe they couldn't see or didn't want to process the damage this emotionally immature professional, and others like her in that obviously dysfunctional department, could have on the impressionable psyches of young women arriving on campus looking for intellectual guidance and mentoring.

Dr. Witt never ceased thinking that those in the NYSU-Peru community who looked beyond the hype of the FA program--as a professional, morally sound safe space for impressionable young women newly arrived upon campus--would probably be quite disappointed. Xavier firmly believed that it was as much his moral responsibility to rip the lid off of the FA department, revealing them as mean-spirited, territorial, vendetta seeking, so-called allies, posturing as if they were socially just, while teaching racism and hate, as a result of having succumbed to the *Myth of the Black Rapist*. The use of the Myth of the Black Rapist is a racist tool that seems to never truly have gone away. NYSU-Peru as Goliath to Dr. Witt's David still felt it necessary to appropriate this unethical often unnamed trope. The fact that Angela Davis had equipped Dr. Witt to literally name it was beyond valuable.

Some of the newspapers in the region had picked up on what was happening at NYSU-Peru and sought to interview Dr. Witt as well as anyone from the college that would weigh in. Since Xavier had been removed from campus with little fanfare, no one knew enough to say anything. He had been admonished in advance about saying anything at all, with the consequence of him doing so being immediate termination. Fortunately, after he was terminated and able to tell his version of the story some of the newspapers eventually would articulate his version of the story adequately, trying to frame it fairly. However, Utley's Chief of Staff, Ben Judson's quote made it sound like they terminated Dr. Witt for something he did recently, or similar to what was in the posted flyers. The flyers--to anyone with common sense--were an obvious smear campaign. Nonetheless Judson said:

"Anytime a complaint is processed about an employee's conduct, NYSU-Peru has an established method to comprehensively reexamine and investigate those concerns," wrote Ben Judson, Utley's chief of staff, in an email statement. *"At any time during our process information comes to light, we take action."*

Judson, as the ultimate good soldier to Utley--unabashedly goose stepping in line and in sync with Utley's other minions--was trying to imply that something came to light, hence implying as to the reason why Dr. Witt was terminated. Judson's implication validated for those not in the know a mouthful about the investigation. Dr. Witt, serving at the pleasure of the so-called leader of the University was categorized as management confidential and with it not being a union position Utley could terminate him for scratching his ass in public. As a result the decision to remove him from campus because he supposedly posed a threat to the campus community, per the message inscribed within the flyers, could also be attributed to *the Myth of the Black Rapist*.

Ironically, he heard whispering that Utley was going to terminate him for defending himself in his reply to the infamous statement made by Shalo

Kloos. What Xavier eventually hopes comes to light is how Utley's lack of leadership in resolving the battle between OPIE and FA resulted in a series of dominoes falling that Xavier actually predicted could occur in an email he wrote to Utley in 2010:

I am not naïve enough to think that my not letting this incident slowly dissipate may cause me some consternation down the road, the least being that I am viewed as a non-team player or litigious. However, to the contrary, I have no interest in silently working at a university that would allow this type of dysfunction to continue on unabated. False accusations that continue to thrive and biased investigations that continue to contribute to the perpetuation of false accusations are what should be truly deemed a "hostile environment." If this matter isn't addressed or rectified in a more productive fashion, it is no idle threat on my part that I will endeavor to prove I have been working in a hostile environment, and I will start with whatever legal actions I must take against Sharon Winchell and Ramona Saphony.

The 2010 correspondence aside, Judson also said in the article, *"when a complaint is received about a faculty or staff member's conduct, NYSU-Peru has a 'set process to thoroughly review and investigate those concerns' and address them where applicable, in accordance with federal and state law and NYSU policy."* Interestingly enough Dr. Witt's documented complaints about FA faculty members conduct didn't motivate the *set process to thoroughly review and investigate his concerns,* nor were they addressed, not in 2010, nor 2018.

So Dr. Witt acknowledged, for the time being, that NYSU-Peru had won the first skirmish, but not the war. He believed that truth would surface and defeat the pettiness and ugliness of people that at best were knowingly teaching racism and hate while a cowardly administration looked the other way. At worst, Utley would fail to challenge the relationship between the FA department and Title IX Office, instead allowing the university to slowly self-destruct, even though back in 2010 in what will eventually be known as one of the two infamous 2010 memos Dr. Witt had provided the inept leader with specific steps to take:

Specific Steps

On some college campuses presidents and diversity officers have very open lines of communication...Since we don't interact much, I would much rather our interaction come about over many of the positive things that occur on our campus or within our community...That being said though, I'm hoping that you will respond to this email in the following ways:

1. Recognize that Maims may have a conflict of interest in her inability to put into perspective the frame Feminist Anthropology has situated me in and therefore should not be the one investigating the complaint against me.

2. Removing Maims from potentially investigating the forthcoming complaints by me against Winchell or Saphony.

3. Take or recommend someone taking a leadership role in sitting down so-called educators and redirecting our energies towards what should be all of our bottom lines, the students in the center of our efforts.

4. I would like someone to provide a list of students in Winchell' and Saphony's classes from Fall 2009 for possible interviews by unbiased arbitrator to determine the extent of the damage done to my character.

Lastly, in the year 2010 please tell me that our Feminist Anthropology professors on campus don't adhere to a double standard promoting our female professors developing close relations with all their students while male professors should know their place when it comes to female students? It can't be a rite of passage for male faculty members to either withstand accusations of this sort for treating young women with the same respect and dignity they treat their male students, or have to treat young women who represent a group of people that have been clamoring for social justice, differently.

This email excerpt showcasing specific suggestions to the university president generated no activity, though an inept Utley may think inaction is still some type of action. Not one student came forward to support the assertions made in the flyers. The closest date of an incident--from any of the flimsy allegations against Dr. Witt--was Dec 2016. The other incident was alleged to have occurred in 2011. Xavier knew both of those stories were frivolous and would collapse when the women were facing perjury.

Though rape itself was never alleged against Dr. Witt in any conversation, never a concern in his situation, Utley nonetheless utilized the sentiment within the Myth of the Black Rapist to cover up the fact that what he really did was retaliate against Dr. Witt's audacity in defending himself.

Knowing he was planning on writing a book about his experiences being railroaded, and forced into silence, Xavier was strategizing how he would one day reveal his version of the story. He had already begun his research, discovering a powerful quote that eerily paralleled his predicament:

"What is behind all this legal lynching? The answer has been given by Governor Ross Sterling of Texas. In January 1932, Barney Lee Ross, a Negro boy was executed after a trial which took less than two hours. In denying the stay of execution the Governor said, in words which no worker, Negro or white, should ever forget: 'It may be that this boy is innocent, but it is sometimes necessary to burn down a house in order to save a village. This statement brazenly admits two things. First, that Negro workers who "may be innocent" are being murdered not for any crimes, but to "save a village."

Substituting "a village" for 'lackluster leader,' Xavier saw himself as the innocent Negro worker being sacrificed to save *a lackluster leader*, one looking to get out from under a vote-of-no-confidence. Remembering Utley's telling him to *'tone it down'* when he posted a rebuttal of the SG's asinine articulation of his job performance, Xavier recognized himself and his situation in another bit of research he discovered:

"Other lynchings result from the refusal of a militant Negro worker or peasant to submit to every kind of social abuse and persecution. The lynchers themselves have admitted as some of the reasons for lynching, the following: trying to vote, accusing a white man of stealing, testifying against white men, being too successful, talking back to a white man' (Haywood & Howard, Lynching).

Dr. Witt had no doubt, due to his outburst, he was now the 'militant Negro worker' in the above quote who refused to submit to the *social abuse* (of an attention-seeking Shalo Kloos) and *persecution* (by Linda Dewar, an allegedly unauthorized intern). He wasn't going to 'tone it down' for anyone so that his character could be assailed, defamed, or defined. He recalled Utley's anxieties over him being given a monthly column in the *Democratic Perspectives* newspaper, perhaps anxious about Dr. Witt becoming "*too successful*" and subsequently uncontrollable. Utley's paranoia arose from the obvious comparison of OPIE to the Title IX office known for renting the ballrooms for events with only seven people showing up in contrast to OPIE's standing room only events, or Dr. Witt writing a book that was now being made into a documentary film. It is easy to imagine such pettiness not occurring on a college campus. Not the case though at NYSU-Peru. The last straw, which paralleled the quote was "testifying against White men." How convenient must it have been to launch an investigation on Dr. Witt after he threatened legal action against the university. How convenient it was for some fliers to surface that suggested inappropriate behavior by Dr. Witt, suddenly appearing the Monday after the Friday meeting in the ballrooms where he was accused of disrespecting women? However it wasn't until he stated his intention to sue the university that an investigation on him ensued.

The lynch mob in Xavier's situation will never admit their reasons. Instead they rely on the current zeitgeist of the MeToo movement and the publicly asserted rumor stated by someone unabashedly that she wanted a Chief Diversity Officer that she 'hadn't heard disrespected women.' If there is any truth to the saying, 'god don't like ugly,' the hideousness cloaking the deceitful antics of one of the two unethical cronies of ringleader Molly Mothburn is worth avoiding at all cost. Kloos, like snakes, from a distance may have often looked appealing, until you begin to feel the venom and realize you were fatally bit. And Mothburn, who lies as if it will make her smile more appealing until her teeth find out, claims that she knew nothing of their antics the same way Resident Rump knew nothing of the payments to Stormy Daniels, until caught red handed.

Perhaps in court, under oath, the rumor that surfaced publicly February 2018 will be revealed, along with the supposedly "unsanctioned" investigation by a Title IX intern two days prior to the '*Lynching Niggers*

Tonight' debacle, an intern who had just finished a class with Dr. Witt the previous semester, and asked him for a letter of recommendation. Yes, doesn't everyone ask for a letter of recommendation from a rumored practitioner of sexual misconduct? I guess so though, because the intern who allegedly took it upon herself to investigate Dr. Witt (a previous student body president and close friend of the current student body president) was rewarded with a seat on a newly conceived Social Justice Task Force weeks later.

Supposedly the Title IX Officer, herself a Feminist Anthropology adjunct lecturer, was clueless about what was occurring in her own shop. Upon questioning the president about his belief in the scenario of the Title IX officer not knowing, his response to Dr. Witt was "I trust Molly like I trust you, XW." Ironically, the investigation Dr. Witt asked him to do on Title IX never occurred. The investigation on Dr. Witt though, the guy that the president also trusted, probably encouraged by Mothburn, began thereafter. Xavier knew these types of mean spirited machinations were literary gifts, because you really couldn't make this shit up.

Xavier understood that what is happening to him now isn't anything new. Many powerful or politically situated men have been taken to task for misusing and abusing their position to sexually harass or engage in sexual misconduct. Because of a rumor about Dr. Witt being "that guy" the university hyper-extended its elbow reaching to find and spin tales that will not hold up in a courtroom, but that they deemed viable because it benefited them to do so.

Perhaps Xavier was naive to believe the students who actually took classes with him and got to know him, or spent any time with him would know that while he appreciates women, enjoys their company, both romantically as well as platonically, he would never leverage any acquired power or position to situate himself sexually with anyone. He also wondered if he was naive in thinking that anyone who took his African American Realities class, his Romance class, or his Cool class, or was a person of color in this still racist country of ours would know that this isn't new because men of color live lives (both personally and professionally) that unnecessarily have been deemed expendable.

Xavier asked himself why is it so easy for people to believe a whisper, or the whisperer? He couldn't reconcile why OPIE and FA weren't instead allies who work diligently to teach students to see people for who they really are? He thought that too many people were ill-informed whisperers, comfortably convincing themselves that they are allies by keeping alive what they may one day discover, to their chagrin, was a lie.

Dr. Witt saw America as guilty of peculiarly packaging its history to celebrate a reality that continues to recreate itself. Why is this significant? College students are arriving on campuses all around the country with preconceived notions that will be challenged when they attend college. Many of these collegians will receive new doctrines, consider them logically, and embrace them as new found truths that they have further intellectually armed themselves with. Others will encounter or discover thoughts that they have never been introduced to and will fight them with the very fiber of their being because accepting them as viable would be too damaging to their psyches—perhaps making them pause and ponder the validity of their very existence—if the epistemologies that they have intellectually departed from are grossly erroneous.

College students that refuse to recognize that their parents may have been mistaken in what they communicated to their children, misguided in supporting some of the educational processes that were made available to their children, and manipulated by a system disinterested in correcting itself will continue to purchase the same old brand. Ward Churchill, in his poignant essay, "American Indians in Film," eloquently referred to Josef Goebbel and Homi Bhabba's different, but yet similar takes on truth:

"The implications of this latter characteristic of the genre can be readily discerned in Nazi propaganda minister Josef Goebbels' famous observation, 'the more regularly a lie is repeated, the more plausible it is likely to appear.' On the other hand, as "postcolonial" theorist Homi Bhabha noted, "the compulsiveness with which certain lies are repeated can reveal not only the degree of their falsity but the extent to which their authors understand them to be false" (Churchill, 49).

As professors and administrators on university campuses who are tasked with the responsibility to intellectually challenge our students, Dr. Witt believed our jobs are to not only teach our students, but empower them to contribute to the ever shifting, ever changing, ever evolving world that depends on them for its growth. So, while the saying "those who are not students of history are doomed to repeat it," is definitely worth remembering, dwelling on the past doesn't do a whole hell of a lot for unencumbered advancement. That is why one of the many adages Dr. Witt always challenges students to consider is:

"Puppets on strings are not responsible for things."

Dr. Witt believed that at some point everyone is responsible for her or his actions and life. If we don't take responsibility for those actions we are nothing more than marionettes, puppets that can be manipulated to do whatever dance the one controlling the strings or who has her/his hand in our back designates we do. One of the most significant Affirmative Actions that we can undertake is the questioning of what we have been told. Once Socrates was accused of corrupting the minds of the youth, Jesus was charged with blasphemy, Harriet Tubman with slave insurrection, Malcolm X dared to threaten insurrectionary violence against a government that was built on that very same foundation, and the Reverend Dr. Martin Luther King, Jr. recommended love as his answer to violence and hatred. None of these people accepted the status quo. They all offered non-traditional, unconventional solutions to age-old problems.

Students aren't living in a vacuum. They recognize that the game has changed, as well as the rules of engagement. Somehow Xavier knew that we must get their attention, and develop or even devise a way to assist them in seeing that they themselves are immersed in a not to dissimilar struggle from those they think they are witnessing from afar. Xavier was forever working on a strategy that might convert many "students from dispassionate dupes of deleterious devices to conscientious colleagues committed to change" (Wiley, 250).

Xavier's mind once again wandered back to the infamous Shalo, who also succumbed to the Myth even though it doesn't negate the fact that she was an attention-addict when she referred to a rumor that Utley already was aware of. Shalo's accusation was totally predicated on a rumor, especially since she had no verifiable evidence of it. Perhaps in hearing the rumor she positioned herself for an opportunity to entice Dr. Witt to make a move on her, a move that never came. She had developed a close friendship with Lori Flee, once upon a time one of Dr. Witt's closest colleagues. As such she was often hanging around OPIE. Perhaps her venom towards Dr. Witt was that of a woman scorned. Probably seen as attractive to many men of her age, what Dr. Witt saw when passing by her or during Summer Orientations was someone trying to look sexy, reaching to be validated. This is why even if he had been a college student himself, a peer of Shalo's he wouldn't stoop so low. She couldn't have been enticing to Dr. Witt in an alternate universe because she thought she was hot. She was about as hot as an outside shower within Winterfell. Exchanging a passing look with her left him with the impression that while someone may be home, they weren't hearing the doorbell.

Dr. Witt had heard the word on the street. It was that Utley seldom takes action until it is politically expedient, like when in 2015 he offered Xavier the CDO position without a search. Then one week later when the Pigeon Messages newspaper incident happened he gave Dr. Witt $70,000 more in his budget, definitely $40-$50 thousand more than expected, just so he could appease the Black students by having given OPIE resources it should have already had.

With MeToo blowing up everywhere all it took was a vote of no confidence hanging over Utley, a Feminist Anthropology professor in the Title IX role whispering in his ear with a hand up his back, and Dr. Witt refusing to be quiet about his character assassination when Utley himself had no voice and he became as politically expendable to Utley as the student editors of Pigeon Messages once upon a time when sacrificed by him. NYSU then supported Utley's interpretation of the situation with them doing some things that are as questionable as they were problematic. They'll have to answer to it in court.

What was just as interesting to Dr. Witt is how some women clamor for equality and then when treated equally don't know what to do with it. An example of this is the many times Dr. Witt hosted students at his home, students who really needed to talk with him and he was already off campus. If the students visiting him were male it was not problematic at all what time they arrived, how long they stayed, or what Dr. Witt was wearing, assuming in all situations he was clothed with no intimate body parts showing. If they were female, unless it was someone like AnnaE, Jen, or Nyla, while not hyper-paranoid Dr. Witt knew to tread carefully.

Xavier also knew that it has often been stated a sign of higher intelligence is to not default into *inherited ideals*, nor succumb to innuendo or unfounded rumors. An intelligent person more often than not has intellectual curiosity. He emphasized exactly that sentiment throughout his career. Of course that would also mean that his assertions regarding the organized effort of a scarred, perhaps even a closeted-racist group of women, some whom sadly represent NYSU-Peru's Feminist Anthropology (FA) department as well as shockingly the Title IX office should be scrutinized as well. After all, some of the arguments that Xavier had made to defend himself wouldn't surprise him if they seemed far-fetched. However, he knew the letters he had in his possession that will come to light during the court case would dramatically alter the public perception of NYSU-Peru's leadership. FA student testimonials from students who refused to drink the Kool Aid—that for many tasted as if it was spiced with hatred of men—are more authentic than silly-ass indefensible public pronouncements about someone's character. And yes, attention addicts seeking to gain some modicum of fame at the expense of someone else since apparently they lacked confidence in their own potential are never surprising, though quite pathetic. Nonetheless Xavier knew he had to stop dissing Kloos, Dewar, and Mothburn.

Dr. Witt's biggest mistake was actually being naive. His success on and off campus was generating hate from haters, which would also include some of the men and women at NYSU-Peru. One of these haters at one time hoped to transcend the North Country, only to return positively spinning his experiences, while inheriting 'advising' some easily duped student organizations instead of achieving his own individual, perhaps even larger political dreams.

Denied Access to 'Woke' Students

It was 8:45pm on a Wednesday night. Dr. Witt, having been unceremoniously removed from the campus a few weeks back, sat in his living room gazing out the window wondering what his students were currently doing in his African American Realities class. Probably their final presentations, he guessed. Little did he know that they had been released early from class to begin their preparation for their semester ending presentations. One group in particular had chosen to focus their presentation on *"the Myth of the Black Rapist,* in an effort to not only highlight what they felt was currently and justifiably occurring to him, but to also better understand his predicament.

The students met one evening to discuss their movie recommendations. Each made a commitment to find a movie that would highlight the Angela Davis chapter of the same name, with an accompanying quote to accentuate the connection. As an additional dimension of the process they were responsible for selling the group on why their film choice should be used.

"Did anyone have a difficult time finding a film," asked Mitchell, a Black male senior. "I sure as hell did."

I didn't," replied Jasmine, a Black female junior. "In Dr. Witt's Romance class we use a film titled, 'Storytelling,' which feels like a companion piece to the "Myth of the Black Rapist. I'm suggesting we use that."

"Are you sure you can use that though," Abdou, a Black male senior asked. "I thought we couldn't use films that were in his classes."

"Not true," replied Yesenia, a Latina sophomore. "We just can't use films that were used in our class. We can use any films not used in the class we are currently in. I know because this is my fourth class with Dr. Witt and I reach back into his other classes for my final presentation film all the time."

"I agree," said Tess, a White female junior. "He actually told me once that he likes when someone does that. It provides him a different perspective when someone takes a film he uses in his 'Cool class' and articulates it through the lens of African American Realities, Romance, or Diversity.

"I've taken that class," Mitchell offered. "How does 'Storytelling' match 'The Myth of the Black Rapist?' No one is raped. It's consensual sex."

"Exactly my point," answered Jasmine. "You must have either been absent the day of that discussion or just not remember the debate that I've heard always takes place as to whether or not it was actually rape. I know we debated it in my RSLM class."

"Hey, don't start no shit now," Mitchell said playfully. "I recall the debate, but didn't hold on to it because it was so clear to me that it wasn't rape."

"Well, I'm using it more so because the protagonist in the film was falsely accused, which is the essence of the 'Myth' article."

"I don't remember anyone accusing him in that film," challenged Tess. "Oh, wait, the student he had sex with wrote about it in her final paper and alluded to it being rape."

"You'll eventually get tired of doubting me Mitchell," Jasmine said.

"I chose the Green Mile," Tess said, interrupting their irrelevant bantering. "The protagonist is a massive black man—6 ft 8 in tall and built like a bodybuilder—wrongly convicted of the rape and murder of two young girls and sentenced to death. At his trial, the prosecution contends that he lured the girls away from their home, having carefully planned the crime using abilities that most believed to be far beyond his reach. Eventually, after he is determined innocent of the rapes and murders too late, he allows himself to be executed because of his distaste for the cruelties of the world."

"Damn girl, that sounds good," complimented Mitchell.

"Who are you calling a girl, boy? "asked Tess, derisively, while trying to fight off an impending smile.

"Who you calling boy, woman," retorted Mitchell, knowing he fucked up by infantilizing the one woman who was not going to cut him any slack. Fortunately, in her retort, she opened a door he could easily walk through. "That was some racist shit," he said chuckling between smirks.

"Would you two stop the shenanigans," chastised Abdou. "To avoid the risk of sounding both sexist and racist, I'll just say that you are both acting like adolescents."

"Okay, but for the record, that's ageism. Anyway, what did Mr. Adult choose?" asked Mitchell.

"Well," Abdou responded, "I chose 'Freedomland.' There was no gray area there whatsoever. A woman claimed that she was carjacked by a Black man who then drove off in her car with her son still in the car. Later in the film it is discovered that her son actually died from her negligence as a parent when she would drug him with cough syrup so that he would sleep, freeing her to have a sexual interlude with a Black man . So, having to cover up her negligence she made up a convenient story that she thought would be believable. As a result of her lie many of the Black men in that community came under scrutiny."

"That is so fucked up," Mitchell said. "It almost sounds like some modern day Rosewood."

"It may be fucked up, but it's real," said Jasmine. "She made up such a story because she knew it could be believed."

"Would be believed, not could be," said Abdou. "It's not easy being a Black man in this fucked up country."

"Well, though I'm offended no one asked, I chose 'American Justice; The Susan Smith story,'" chimed in Mitchell, feigning hurt feelings. "It's about a woman who drowned her two sons so she could be in a relationship with a wealthy man disinterested in having any children. Ironically, like in your movie *Freedomland*, she lied about being carjacked by a Black man to cover up her crime."

"Mitchell, you can't use a documentary film, or television series. Unless I'm mistaken, and I doubt that I am, no major motion picture has been specifically made about Susan Smith. I hate to tell you that one film is based upon her story though. Do you want to guess which one?" Abdou asked teasingly.

"I have no clue," Mitchell answered, not interested at all in guessing games.

"Did you just call yourself clueless," asked Jasmine.

"Freedomland, my brother." Though they changed some of the details, the novel the film was made from was inspired by the Susan Smith story," clarified Abdou, somewhat impressed with himself.

"Nice choice frat. Now I have to use my other film, 'Birth of a Nation.'"

Almost in unison a chorus of 'no' enveloped the room.

"That's probably not even necessary with all the good films we have to choose from," said Yessi, rescuing the group. "We only need to agree on one film, and it definitely won't be the film that was propaganda for the KKK. I chose 'To Kill a Mockingbird.' It's set in the 1930s in a southern town. It's about a White attorney who defends a Black man accused of raping a White woman. When the trial begins, and the accused man is placed in the local jail, a mob gathers to lynch him, but the lynching is prevented. At the trial itself, the attorney provides clear evidence that the accusers, a daughter who is the alleged victim and her incensed father who discovered them in a compromising situation, are lying: in fact, the alleged victim propositioned the Black man. When the White woman's father caught her lusting after the Black man the father accused the Black man of rape to cover up his shame and her unpardonable guilt from desiring a 'nigger.' Despite the lawyer's impressive evidence pointing to the Black man's innocence, the all-white jury convicts him."

The students would eventually choose a film that represented what most of the films they chose had in common, false accusations levied against black men and their lack of having an opportunity at any plausible deniability.

It was just a matter of time before the class was going to broach the topic that was on all of their minds. Dr. Witt had been removed from all of his classes for some unknown circumstances that had all of them wondering what was up.

"Has anyone spoken with Dr. Witt?" Abdou asked.

"I spoke with him for about 5 minutes a few days ago," Tess offered. "I all of a sudden one day thought of him and wanted to send him some energy."

"How is he?" asked Abdou. "I have been meaning to call my big bro, but procrastination got the best of me."

"He's okay." Tess answered. "Just hurting that anyone could believe he would sexually harass someone."

"That is so much bullshit." Yesenia said angrily. "No one at this university has challenged the boys on this campus to become men more than he has. What fucks me up is after reading all of these articles and checking out all of these film clips I now fully understand how pathological *the Myth of the Black Rapist* can be. Think about it. Until video cameras on cell phones became the norm there was an unstated myth amongst White people that of course Black lives mattered. The cameras however showed us otherwise. Nonetheless, the socialization has been so profound around slavery being over, America now being post-racial, and all lives mattering that you can't convince some people otherwise. So as preposterous as it may seem that some people could be rushing to judgment about XW, it isn't really that far-fetched to believe their perspectives are nothing more than what XW identified as *inherited ideals*. Think about it. The flyers? Can you say smear campaign? Who in their right mind would believe that shit."

That's deep Yessi," said Abdou. "Doc's character has never been an issue though. I also agree these film clips and articles have given us not only better understanding but also the verbal skills to break it down to others who don't get it. I'm gunning for someone to push back on *the myth* as being fake news."

"I also spoke with Dr. Witt the other day. We talked about the flyers. He said Utley probably initiated the investigation on him out of necessity, to not take lightly the possibility that there was some truth to them." Mitchell explained. "He also mentioned feeling as if he was in the Outer Limits."

"He probably said '*Twilight Zone*,' you misrepresenting mother…" Abdou said chuckling. "I know that because I spoke with Angel and Mark the other day and they both mentioned it."

"I've heard Mothburn was dirty," said Jasmine. "Besides, it is hard for me to trust White women that think they have it like that with all Black people just because they have it like that with a few. Her Black assistant, I can't recall her name, is ghetto as fuck. I mean straight up hood rat. So if Mothburn isn't dirty, she's definitely stupid. Who would hire such an obnoxious person. And I was at the forum and saw what Mothburn did after Dr. Witt defended himself. She's an opportunist."

"When I spoke with him he said what saddened him the most was the effect *the myth* had on some friendships he had with women, whom he thought he was really cool with," Tess said depressingly. "I told him the women that know him aren't buying into the hype. Those that believe *the myth* are sheep who have allowed their own wool to be pulled over their eyes."

CHAPTER THREE
- *Misandry*

In the middle of going through his own Twilight Zone, Dr. Xavier Witt had to remind himself that the women he was fighting against, as demonic as one might act from one moment to the next, didn't enter the world hating men, or Black men for that matter, or even Black people. But inheriting the ideal of men as something to hate...is problematic.

As easily as some of the great leaders/minds of the past missed the mark on the social justice issue of their time, due to their blind spots, their implicit bias, or the prevailing socio-cultural norm of the time, a certain group of women at NYSU-Peru may not have gotten the memo either. Or perhaps they received a different memo. It seems as if, with all the dysfunctional treatment of varying people with different ideas, that an organization of women, some of them gay, would guard against leaning too far in the direction of prejudging a situation between a Black man and his White female student. The fact that some defaulted into an automatic belief in her story and requisite dismissal of Dr. Witt's story is as intriguing as it is disturbing. Perhaps it is the subtle messages these educators, many of whom teach about subtle messages, have absorbed.

Xavier thought, it's like watching my mother's impatience doesn't always keep me mindful of being patient, or at least more patient with others. What was that quote by feminist Susan Brownmiller:

"Black men's historical oppression has placed many of the "legitimate" expressions of male supremacy beyond their reach. They must resort, as a result, to acts of open sexual violence" (Davis, 178).

Perhaps many, if not most of the women in the Feminist Anthropology (FA) program and its closely connected program, Sociology, somehow subconsciously see *a certain type of man* this way. He wondered if he had a chance to ask a FA or Sociology professor why is it they believed a young White woman whom most of them didn't know nor were familiar with, over a Black man who many of them were at least somewhat familiar with. He already knew the answer. It was more comfortable for them to have their unknown implicit biases confirmed, than refuted. Not knowing Dr. Witt at all, it was much easier for the newly hired White female professors to absorb a rumor and allow it to grow into a truth, convincing themselves that what they were seeing was false when it appeared to have any value to their shared community, or convince themselves that what they were seeing was true, when seeing Dr. Witt interacting with any White female student.

A Single Black Man

"So do you have any words of wisdom to share about being a single, Black man in the North Country, Dr. Witt?" Tim, the reporter asked.

"Are you asking me what is it like dating White women?" Dr. Witt replied.

"Not really. Well, kind of. Okay, Dr. Witt, you've got me," he answered. "One of the editors told me to find a not-so-subtle way, if I was incapable of a subtle way to broach that topic."

"And so as a result of that encouragement," Dr. Witt said laughingly, "you chose to just say 'fuck it,' Dr. Witt's cool. I'm an ex-student and T.A. of his and we're cool like that."

"Well, when you put it like that," Tim said momentarily attempting to act innocent by looking towards heaven, innocently, "hell yes."

They laughed, then Dr. Witt answered with a philosophical challenge. "I'm curious Tim, would a White female reporter have been comfortable asking me that question, or trying to find a subtle way of asking it?" "What do you think?"

Tim took a moment to reflect before answering, then said "Probably very uncomfortable. Not just because of her youth, too."

"Did you just insinuate I'm an old-ass?"

"You know I would never call you an ass," Tim laughingly retorted, then said, "Also, like you teach in your Romance, Sex, Love, & Marriage

(RSLM) course--which for the record I both aced as a student and T.A.—most people are inept at talking about sex beyond what they learned in the street. Human sexuality isn't scripted when two bodies coincidentally enter one another's space and human chemistry takes over. It unfolds naturally. And don't you often say that most people hearing the title of the class only process the class' "sex" theme."

Dr. Witt replied, "You're so right Tim. Perhaps you have an idea of how many faculty/staff and students have initiated a conversation with me about the class by identifying the class as 'the Sex class.' The other three topics of the class reflected in the title are all ignored, with the romance theme even listed before the sex theme. Every now and then I'll hear people refer to it as 'the Romance class.' Never is it referred to as 'the Love class,' or 'the Marriage class.'"

Tim replied, "And keeping it real Doc, like we always do, there are so many little conversations always taking place about you. Everybody who knows our academic history probably imagines that I know you quite well. So I hear lame-ass questions or statements about you all the time. Darren and I were just rapping about some of the questions, or ponderings about you, that we hear from one day to the next, like "Does Dr. Witt only like White women?" "Does Dr. Witt fuck his students?' "I've heard that Dr. Witt is gay." "I've heard that he is a sex addict." "I've heard he is a freak in bed." "Never, 'I've heard that Dr. Witt is cool as fuck?'

I'm disappointed now. And nice Tim how you slipped the "dating White women" question in there again. Very nice. Of course, all of these questions have merit if there is a pertinent necessity to know, accompanied by an equitable approach to expecting answers from me on par with the answers of all the other faculty who of course would be asked these same questions." Why is it no one seldom, if ever, ask you is Dr. Witt a good father, or a nice guy?"

"Specifically though, 'Does Dr. Witt only like White women?' is a fascinating question. This is the North Country of New York. People who don't know what that means can almost get away with asking that question because of their ignorance of the demographics. In other words, where are the non-White women they would be curious—if not prefer—to see me dating? Other than students, the racial diversity in the city/town is a fucking joke. Not that there is anything necessarily wrong with the community, but why would the above average Black or racially underrepresented person want to move up here just to be the only one from their racially underrepresented group, or one of the few amongst the so-called far-too-often clueless majority who inconsiderately drop microaggressions like Dr. Dre intuitively drops gangsta-ass beats. While it is fairly cool here, that doesn't mean that some good ol' boys won't get liquored up and decide to treat themselves to a different type of evening at someone else's expense, like me."

"In terms of "fucking my students" my politically correct and instinctive answers align, no, emphatically." However, that doesn't negate people's perceptions, which are very much related to how we define, "students."

"Do we define students who aren't to be fucked only students currently taking a class from a professor? What about the 30 year old student who took a class in the fall, was academically exceptional, and propositions her professor the following spring? Are we only talking about male professors propositioning female students after the grading relationship has ended, or is whatever ethical code that fits this scenario without gender bias, preventing female professors from fucking their male students too after the grading relationship has ended?? How about same-sex fucking between professor and student after the grading relationship has ended? What about a student who is volunteering to T.A. the same class a second time for no academic credit since it can't be given twice for the same class? That student isn't receiving a grade and perhaps possibly looking to get paid in some other way. Should a professor deny those enterprising students another opportunity to be part of more perspective-altering conversations about diversity & social justice, power, privilege, and patriarchy because of anxieties that they could be, perhaps would be vulnerable to any situation that would pit their word against a students?"

"And for the record Tim," Dr. Witt said as he attempted to catch his breath from the lengthy response he knew could be considered a soliloquy, "I hope you noticed my paranoia. Darren and I once had a similar discussion where he named and framed that type of paranoia as productive paranoia, a necessary level of paranoia to protect oneself from mistakenly letting their guard down."

Exhaling, Dr. Witt said in a hushed tone, "I have never been able to win in this town when it comes to that. When I decided after a smidgen of local dating that it might not work out well for me to continue dating locally, I somehow then had gay added to the possibilities of my esoteric identity."

"The "am I gay" question fascinates me," Dr. Witt admitted. I always wonder, 'Why?' Are you asking because you want to fuck me? Or are you asking because that tidbit of information will get you paid, or laid? I never cease wondering what people get out of asking or wanting to know the answers to such questions."

Tim supportively replied, "The point I'm making here Doc is that people gossip, whisper, and run with rumors."

"It's a point well made Tim," Dr. Witt acknowledged. "Both my mother and my first wife warned me again and again to be careful, if not be wary of White women bearing gifts, requiring too much attention, extending too much praise, or even sharing a moment of alone time."

"Well, with that very real exchange I now think I have enough to put together something spectacular for our article," Tim said while apparently preparing to leave the office. "Thanks Doc for taking this interview," Tim added, while slipping his coat on, extending a fist momentarily until receiving one in return before exiting Witt's office.

Ironically, much of the situation that led to Dr. Witt's career snafu is inseparable from him being a recently singled Black man in a predominantly small college town. Dr. Witt often referred to this phenomenon by saying that the racially-underrepresented demographic presence in the North Country of NY was slim to none (and Slim just left the room). Arriving at NYSU-Peru in June 2000 as a married man and father he felt invisible, which helped him avoid temptations, something he knew he could possibly succumb to. As a married man, for the most part, he never felt the all-too-familiar smiles and/or lengthier glimpses (if not bodacious borderline stares) that sometimes occurred when Xavier had lived in larger cities with many people with similar paint jobs to Xavier's. In many larger cities his wedding ring didn't seem to curtail women outright flirting with him. Or perhaps he relaxed enough in these environments to know that light banter wouldn't necessarily have a default interpretation of him trying to get in someone's pants. In the North Country of New York in general and Peru, NY specifically he often felt imperceptible. Is it because the women he met in the North Country were more ethical and respected the state of marriage in some ways that city women don't? Doubt it. Could it be race? Probably, for how could it not be? Anyone living in the United States believing their perspectives on other people, including people of their own race, isn't affected by the racial politics that have played out for centuries--even worse for some racial groups in varying decades--has their head in the sand.

As a single man again, after his marriage ended, Xavier decided to enter the world of online dating. Beyond the fact that some of the women he met changed his life, profoundly, it also altered his perspective immediately. On the online dating site, Match.com, he knew his life was too hectic to get lost in that world. As a result of that awareness, combined with his practical nature, Xavier deliberately wrote a profile that would compete with any others for its lengthiness. Within it, he unapologetically spoke to his world view, philosophical perspectives on parenting, dating, and sex, as well as his previous marriage. Xavier's strategy in doing this was to minimize if not eliminate potential interaction with women with limited world views and no commitment to expand them. Not that there was anything wrong with such a person. He just knew they would not be compatible beyond the physical possibilities.

Xavier, when actually looking for female companionship was always in search of a woman with whom he could laugh easily, as much as intellectually engage, profoundly. On some level it felt to him as if he was always in search of a lover who could really hear him when he said if she was capable of seducing his mind it would take work on his part to emancipate his body from its self-imposed deference to her will.

He also realized—with a twinge of racial anxiety—that a majority of the White women who fit the personal description he sought were selecting every race except one as a preference, their sole exception being Black.

Granted, if they had an interest in Black men nothing prevented them from reaching out to one, unsolicited. But by clearly stating (by not checking the box) no preference towards Black men, they could better manage their online traffic.

This relatively costly online dating service featured men and women serious about finding a life partner. Otherwise why pay anything when there are so many less expensive, if not free dating sites available. Of course this doesn't preclude men, women too for that matter, who wouldn't hesitate to spend what they may view as a paltry sum in terms of their end result, a series of sexual encounters with romantic interests whom upon becoming disarmed by the potential of the relationship, or its ever increasing familiarity, could be worthwhile, if not hot and heavy, at least in the interim. Besides, Dr. Witt, like most things he involved himself in, treated these experiences as if they were somewhat research projects. He would not shy away from asking assistance in unpacking those things he didn't know. He saw this far better than assuming. Women who read his lengthy profile knew what they were getting in to.

One conversation he recalled involved a time when he called a woman out about her Match.com listing of racial preferences, except instead of asking her about it before they knew one another, he waited. Now, in the afterglow of an intimate moment, his confidence that he would be given the benefit of the doubt was higher. Xavier had only dated Bridget a handful of times, but from the beginning they were in never ending heat around one another. Xavier, not necessarily preferring one race of women to another, was more comfortable with Black women nonetheless. The shared cultural experiences notwithstanding, their flow/flavor was intuitively appealing.

Bridget was White, and blond. Xavier preferred brunettes followed by red heads. Bridget however was his type in so many different ways: smart, family oriented, athletically petite, witty, sensual in private moments, effortlessly sexy in public, and oddly important to him, intelligent eyes. Xavier somehow bought into the oft-mentioned suggestion that eyes are the windows to the soul. He was that guy who was seeking a woman whose soul had something to say.

Sitting at her kitchen table, bottomless, waiting for the coffee to finish brewing, Xavier decided to be even more vulnerable. They had just spent their first evening together and somehow, with no regrets apparently for either of them, they ended up horizontal. "Am I the first Black man you've ever been with?" Xavier asked Bridget.

Pretending she was invested in actually closing a robe that had no buttons to snap or belt to tie, Bridget replied as she took a seat next to Xavier, "That's a strange question coming from a man who seems so confident."

"How is that a strange question, just because I had the courage to ask it? It is an honest question, one of those questions that most people don't know how to ask, or won't ask for what they think it may suggest about them."

Mischievously she answered, "I'm not going to answer that question on the grounds it may incriminate me."

"How so," he wondered while unconsciously saying it aloud.

"Because if I admit that you are the first African-American I've been intimate with you may think your shit doesn't stink. We can't have that, can we?" Bridget said teasingly. "If I admit you aren't the first Black man I've been with you may relegate me to that category of White women who only date African-American men. I have no interest in being one of those."

Are you suggesting there is something wrong with a woman who only wants to date one type of a man, racially speaking?" he challenged her.

"I don't want to be judgmental, but yes, an interest in dating only one race of people seems peculiar to me."

Then why would you choose on your Match.com profile to not list as a preference Black men," Xavier curiously asked. "Are you suggesting there is a difference between your eliminating the possibility of finding your life's mate amongst Black men, and women interested in only dating the men you were so ready to disregard? It seems a bit counterintuitive to me."

Bridget was a high school teacher who would have had more of a connection with Xavier if her possible alcoholism didn't intimidate him. She was exceedingly quick witted and seldom missed an opportunity to flex her intellect. Upon witnessing her continually pouring herself glass after glass of wine, even long after Xavier had ceased to join her, followed by her staggering not just around her home, but in a restaurant one night too, he started to doubt any possible future beyond a sexual one. On the question Xavier posed to her about her seeming racial antipathy towards dating Black men in contrast to her disdain towards White women who only date Black men, she momentarily seemed as if she was at a loss for words. That didn't last long though.

"Let me answer your question with a question. Bridget replied. "Why did you wait until after we fucked to ask me that question. Why not before?"

"Wow," Xavier declared, "So what we did well into the morning was fuck, not have sex, which is what you initially invited me to have with you."

"It was downgraded to a fuck after you cheapened our intimate time together by implying I'm a hypocrite."

"Are you serious," he inquired, "Or just fucking with my mind now. You can't possibly be trying to flip the script for me asking a logical question."

"Just because you say it is logical doesn't make it so," she frustratingly replied. My logic tells me that you must have had that question in your head before today. What, did you hedge your bets to make sure you got me in bed?"

"Not at all," Xavier replied. "It was in my head the moment you reached out to me on Match.com and I saw you were going against your profile preferences when you reached out to me. I thought it was peculiar but wasn't sure I would ever ask you."

Looking as if she believed me, Bridget answered, "Your profile was written thoughtfully, and seemingly honestly. I was curious because of what I had read, or perhaps the story you told me about yourself. Your marketing of yourself was extraordinary. However, in general, I find most Black men too aggressive."

"Really," Xavier responded, realizing that he was bottomless while somewhat arguing with a White woman he was still in the getting-to-know phase with. "Which doesn't really explain how so many other White women may prefer Black men because they see them as more sensitive, if not more aware of their gender privilege than White men?"

For the next hour or so they would debate this back and forth. At times the tension was thick enough to write their name in the air, similar to writing on a dusty car. At other times they shared moments of frivolity. Sadly though, over the next few dates it became apparent to Xavier that Bridget and he had at best a friends-with-benefits thing, and not much more.

Ironically though Xavier realized that many White women were operating off of the same memo, either play with Black men, even fuck them if you dare, but don't marry one. No future in it. This type of socio-cultural response subconsciously reinforces in White women that Black lives don't matter enough to imagine a future with one. It made Xavier realize how fragile his reality could be from one possible encounter to another, an imagined encounter, and/or heaven forbid it, actually being bold enough or naive enough to spend private time with a White woman.

It was always unfathomable to Xavier how much a woman's fear of a black man they didn't even know could have them band together to destroy him. Author Tim Wise, an amazing white ally in so many ways relative to recruiting White people into favorably considering diversity & social justice, is nonetheless often viewed in a similar way, heavily criticized by Black people who indescribably don't feel him, regardless of his undeniable contributions to the cause. Dr. Witt has always been a staunch ally to any/all disenfranchised groups, still experienced being categorized and thereafter ostracized due to the labeling. So it isn't difficult to recognize when those who are apt to criticize others aren't familiar with their personal and professional philosophies, which to a large extent are often one and the same.

How the Feminist Anthropology department processed Dr. Witt's work in the community was always a huge curiosity when discussed amongst his peers. His presentations at local schools, columns and blogs in local newspapers, and his affiliation as a Board member with organizations like *Planned Parenthood*, *Boy Scouts of America*, and activists organizations like *John Brown Lives* seemed to conveniently be forgotten or dismissed whenever he was being scrutinized or depicted as lecherous, again with the scuttlebutt resulting from a rumor.

The diversity & social justice blogs, opinions, and columns Dr. Witt wrote for years, dating back to 2004 reveal much about him. There is no doubt that someone doing similar work to Dr. Witt can be perpetrating verbal and/or sexual abuse, inappropriate conduct, sexual harassment, or abusing their power and privilege. However, someone for years-on-end articulating social justice perspectives and positions like the column Dr. Witt wrote on men's lack of *really* understanding women is a funk that is hard to fake. Though Cosby fit that description and still pulled it off.

Women and the Cluelessness in Men

Dr. Witt, working diligently to stay afloat after being accused of disrespecting women, appreciated being able to return to his course, 'Reconciling Otherness with Diversity Enlightenment,' the following week wherein the majority of his students feeling as if they knew him better than most unhesitatingly gave him the benefit of the doubt.

Midway through that day's class he asked his students to articulate some of the strategies—that had been implemented before—which denied men access to women on men's self-serving terms.

"The Greek play by Aristophanes, 'Lysistrata,'" one student blurted.

"The movie 'Chi-Raq' by filmmaker Spike Lee."

"Good choices," Dr. Witt said, somewhat celebrating his student's contributions, "though Lee's Chi-Raq is based upon Aristophanes' 'Lysistrata.'" Dr. Witt continued, "So what was renowned soul singer

James Brown saying in the song "It's a Man's World." What is he really saying about romantic relationships when he said:"

"'This is a man's world, this is a man's world. But it wouldn't be nothing, nothing without a woman or a girl.' Your thoughts?"

Sarah, a brilliant Latina who challenges most things others would hesitate to even approach said, "While this seems complimentary towards women, suggesting they are vitally important to men, it really is an insult to men to suggest that a man would be nothing without a woman or a girl."

Before anyone else engaged Sarah, Edmund added, "It is also insulting to a woman or girl who essentially is victimized, often unknowingly, and thereby lives life as a second class citizen."

"With what must feel like the never-ending necessity of lifting fragile egos of men," added Sarah.

"Well now, Sarah and Edmund, aren't you two quite the impressive tag team?" Dr. Witt stated, with a mischievous smile on his face. "You two are practically finishing each other's thoughts. Didn't Plato and/or Socrates discuss people who act like you? Are you soul mates are something?"

This generated a big laugh from the class. Almost everyone in the class new Edmund and Sarah had just begun dating. Because they were both close to Dr. Witt and essentially had met in his class he knew he could tease them.

"So, back to our discussion," Dr. Witt insisted. "Legendary pop music singer/songwriter John Lennon once penned a tune titled 'Woman is the Nigger of the World.' In it he said:

"We make her paint her face and dance
If she won't be a slave, we say that she don't love us.
If she's real, we say she's trying to be a man
While putting her down we pretend that she is above us."

Dr. Witt then added, "Further on in the song he says:"

"We make her bear and raise our children

And then we leave her flat for being a fat old mother hen
We tell her home is the only place she should be
Then we complain that she's too unworldly to be our friend."

Dr. Witt challenged the class by asking, "What was Lennon conveying to his listeners?"

Ray, a White male with strong social justice instincts, answered, "Lennon was trying to say that women can't win. In the process he also sounds like he's saying what Edmund concluded, women are second class citizens."

Victoria, a high energy biracial junior added, "Lennon describes the plight of women, forever. Times have changed tremendously, but only in that the explicit bias is now often covert, while the implicit bias remains overt."

"Impressive unpacking of the lyrics meaning, class," Dr. Witt admitted. "However, in your upcoming weekend discussions I'll have the TAs all pushing you to consider what positive meanings Lennon could have had when he said 'Woman is the nigger of the world,' especially considering that within the Black community "nigger" isn't always viewed as an offensive term, albeit it is to some, in addition to being dysfunctional."

Dr. Witt continued, "Moving on, as you witnessed in the 2005 film clips from "North Country," Charlize Theron's character enters a room full of vocally violent men, her union brothers, along with some union women in the room. She had planned on challenging the sexist ways of the company. Theron's character's father attempts to ride to her rescue, taking the microphone from her after she was profanely silenced. On her behalf he admonishes the men. However, did any of you see anything problematic?"

Victoria replied, "At first glimpse we view him as an ally. However, his words in her defense reveal that he is really only the typical male. He says *"It's a heck of a thing to watch one of your own get treated that way."* He might as well have said *"If it wasn't my daughter being verbally abused I would just be sitting quietly like I always did."*

"Nicely expressed Victoria," Dr. Witt complimented. He then added, "Perhaps my perspective on women is different because of the fact that I am one of those men who fully understands that without women in my life the person many know me to be wouldn't exist."

Deciding to close out that evening's class with some personal sharing Dr. Witt continued, "The Tulsa Earth newspaper of Tulsa, Oklahoma recently featured Cary B. Bourne, the first black female attorney in the state. Attorney Bourne was my grandmother. Her great grandmother was a slave. I lived with her in Tulsa my last two years of high school." Dr. Witt openly acknowledged to the class that he was quite fortunate to recall many of the conversations he had with this pioneer who survived Tulsa's infamous Black Wall Street riots.

"If not for Mama Bourne in my mother's life the chances of my mother burgeoning as fabulously as she did would have been greatly reduced due to two often absent parents." (Instead Dr. Witt thought to himself, my mother, after retiring from the FBI as the highest ranking black woman in the Western region, was the founding president of 100 Black Women).

Xavier was never hesitant to acknowledge that his ex-wife, aunts, female teachers, female colleagues, female friends, and lovers all taught him invaluable lessons along the way. As a result of all of these lessons learned he had little patience for the hypocrisy of boys and men relative to women. He saw them all as our daughters, sisters, mothers, and potential friends.

Lao Tzu stated *"the journey of a thousand miles begins with a single step."* Xavier offered as a first step the simple premise that grown women should never be referred to as "girls," or groups of people comprised of mixed gender shouldn't be referred to as "you guys." Until someone can disprove the possibilities of scarred girls growing into paranoid women whose scars never healed how could men assert that infantilizing women is 'no big deal,' Xavier's responded with the popular social justice saying: *"When you're accustomed to privilege, equality feels like oppression."*

"So, as you leave class today consider that you live in a world where men have always been situated more comfortably, as implied by both the James Brown and John Lennon lyrics we unpacked earlier. Ironically we also live in a world where many men unfortunately are clueless about it. Men, don't be that man."

Inherited Ideals

Upon his arrival home from class Xavier decided to make himself a drink. He was trying to unpack why he was in perpetual denial about how anyone could think that someone who saw the world the way he did, and could articulate it at length in any given moment, with a history of friendship with every woman he's ever dated, and a bevy of brilliant female minds he at some time or another intellectually engaged in mutually beneficial ways, could ever be seen as disrespectful to women. He reconciled it some days better than others. He also recognized that 'disrespectful to women' was a non-committal code. It allowed the accuser to say something without saying to much. Today though, he found his perspective in focusing on Resident Rump. Just as some people may have strongly suspected Donald Trump was not all he postured to be, just like Cosby' turning out to be a serial something-or-other, at the end of the day, no one is above reproach. One could argue that people who take advantage of people with verbal deception simply because they can, are as much liars as men who take advantage of women are nothing short of misogynists. How can they not be? But then what effect does this have on the women of the world who are relegated to second class citizenship, voiceless, and always swimming upstream against *inherited ideals* that frame them adversely. What scars do they incur? Perhaps ones with the potential to remain if not treated early. To a Black man that grew up diligently fending off hating White people after he logically intuited that some good ones must exist, some women succumbing to misandry, a hatred of men, makes sense.

Unfortunately, it is virtually impossible to fully respect a woman who has—or women who have—no respect for you at all. Besides, scars or no scars, if a person is committed to not hearing you, Xavier thought, you won't be heard.

Some people have a problem calling a spade a spade, or deciding on whether to say tomato or to-maa-to. They are too wrapped up in adhering to protocol so as to score points. Or are afraid that if they actually speak their mind they may say something no one wants to hear. Never thinking that they may be saying something that people need to hear, even want to hear. Perhaps that was Xavier's problem, too real amongst fake-ass people.

Consider this example of how problematic being a Black man in the North Country of New York state can be. Approximately seven years ago Dr. Witt was invited to a summer barbecue at the home of an interracial couple who were colleagues of his at NYSU-Peru. The couple, a Black man (Dr. Judah Slate) and a White woman (Dr. LeAnn Prey), had arrived in Peru a few years prior. Xavier was excited about their arrival, figuring he had just acquired two new allies. He couldn't have been more wrong as time would eventually teach him a lesson he would never forget. It all began with Judah, the husband's first visit to Dr. Witt's office, a few days after their arrival at the college. Xavier remembered it like it was yesterday.

"Nice office, brother." Judah stated. "Looks like they're treating the Black folk well on this plantation."

"Plantation?" asked Xavier, somewhat perturbed by Judah's assertion. After all, it was Xavier's job to create a climate of inclusion and Judah's phrasing suggested otherwise had occurred under Xavier's watch. "What makes you describe your new place of employment—and the town in which it is situated—in such a demeaning way?"

Judah replied, "They're all plantations, on some level. If a Black person leads the institution, he is reporting to a predominantly White board or council, hence lacking the necessary power to make significant changes. If a White person leads the institution he or she is perfecting the *appropriate face* to wear around whatever diversity group they must appease."

Xavier was a bit caught off guard by Judah's frankness, though momentarily finding it refreshing. Nonetheless, he pushed back, testing the water with his new colleague. "Your wife is White, right? Xavier asked. "If she were leading the institution would she be wearing the appropriate face as well, or because she married you, her diversity street cred is validated and she intuitively knows her way around pressing diversity & social justice concerns? Is that what you are essentially trying to tell me? If not you should know that is what I'm hearing."

"Good point, though yes, my wife is the exception to the rule," Judah said in defense of his marital partner.

"And she's the exception because she is your wife?" Xavier responded, "Somehow marrying you punched her ticket to ride?"

Xavier saw the discomfort rise in Judah. He had witnessed this type of oxymoronic behavior before. A glib Black professional who felt his Blackness, perhaps his height too, allowed him to say whatever he wanted, while having the audacity to be hypersensitive to receiving any variation of criticism. The combination of being Black, intelligent, and very, very tall could be quite intimidating to some. White people in the Black Lives Matter era, who consider themselves allies, will be uncomfortable harshly critiquing a Black person, unless provoked.

It was at this point that any future possibility of a burgeoning friendship between Judah and Xavier hung in the balance. Unfortunately it didn't hang there long. Judah shrugged off Xavier's question and redirected his energy towards getting to his bottom line, trying to take a shortcut towards advancing himself instead of paying his dues and earning his opportunities.

"So, what do you think about bringing me in on some consulting I hear you are doing? asked Judah. Everywhere I go in this town when a conversation comes up about my desire to consult eventually 'Xavier Witt' comes up."

There are moments where you want to extend thanks to someone for revealing their dark side to you. After all it provides you the opportunity to really see them as they are. This exchange with Judah, a political scientist, was one of those moments for Xavier, making him curious as to whether Judah's height equipped him with a false sense of security. It was a no-brainer for Xavier. In no part of the universe would he pitch a specific project to someone he just met, putting them on the spot to say yes, or clown him. Judah had no shame to his game, whatsoever. Xavier knew what being the only light eyed Black person felt like. In his youth he had also often been 'the only' with a speech impediment, and always one of the shortest men amongst his towering male cousins. So Judah could be overcompensating, and/or Xavier could be tripping too. Without saying anything rude, or as inconsiderate as he felt Judah's question was to him, he answered as diplomatically, albeit directly, as possible.

"I don't really know you, and would be very foolish to think because we are both Black that we are, or will be, on the same page." Xavier said sincerely, "At best I can say we may have a chance to collaborate on some projects in the future."

This was a conversation with the Black male of the legally sanctioned interracial partnership. At the time Xavier saw it as assuming, premature, and an insult to his intelligence. Didn't this extremely tall man have a more convincing argument to challenge/nullify Xavier's instincts about him? Probably not, Xavier surmised. Judah apparently chose to be as much a bull in a China shop, at least in that moment, as he was old school in every sense of the phrase. None of this necessarily suggested the end of the world was underway. However, considerations of Judah's entitlement paled in comparison to his life partner's savvier-than-thou disposition.

Dr. LeAnn Prey taught in the English department. From the time she began her tenure her perception of the policies/procedures put in place prior to her arrival was that they were grossly inadequate. More so, with somewhat of a Trumpian disposition they both postured as if they either had the answers, or were the only answers to the university's problem. LeAnn, like Judah, was not shy about playing the race card, knowing that any pushback against them could leave those doing the pushing as susceptible to being perceived as racists. However, as a Black man pushing back against them the race card was to a large extent nullified. Labeling another Black person racist is an extremely difficult argument to make. In her specific case though she postured almost as if she was chosen by the race gods to determine who was worthy enough to accompany her on what was akin to racial crusades.

So then why would Xavier have validated this couple by accepting their invitation? Because beyond the politically correct thing to do he really did want a relationship with them. However, he realized quickly that they were not, as Dr. Lee Jones was apt to say, *energizers*, people who always left you with more energy than you had before your encounter with them. They weren't even *energy stealers* that you could see coming from a mile away and take action to prepare yourself to fend them off. No, they were *energy impostors,* poised and packaged as panaceas, though upon discovering how bereft of energy you were after they exited the room you were left understanding how it felt to have Pandora's box uncovered in your immediate presence.

Nonetheless, Xavier attended their barbecue with high hopes. It was at their home that he was introduced to a newly arrived English department faculty member, Dr. Michelle Boone. You will meet her later.

A Conspiracy Perhaps? - Duh...

Kesi--while reading the comments section of the article on the Democratic Perspectives website about Xavier's termination--had a stroke of genius. One of the comments by a pandering Feminist Anthropology professor posturing as an ally to survivors that didn't exist, never left her. Nonetheless she solicited survivors to come forward and get free help. Kesi posing as a survivor named Nicole followed this thread to see if she could discover who is really behind this fishing expedition. So she created an anonymous account. Below is what it generated:
(The person corresponding with an incognito Kesi writes under an apparent pseudonym: *justice4survivors*. Eventually she identifies herself by name, while continuing to provide information)

On Sun, Jul 22, 2018 at 11:08 AM, Nicole Unknown <metoo@usa.com> wrote:

Hello,
Since I read your message, I hesitated to send you this email. Who tells me that you're not X.W. (or one of his friends) trying to find which one of his victims is reporting him...? Anybody can hide behind your email address.

That's hard to believe that somebody is offering to help his victims for free. So how will it help me to let you know my story or who I am. And if my identity is discovered who tells me that I'll still be safe?

So how can I trust you and let you know who I am or how to contact me or know what happened to me and what is the effect on my life till today. Because every story is unique (I guess); then by hearing the facts, the identity of the teller will be known.

People know him as the high figure who did a lot for the community and the students. Look at how many people still trust him and support him everywhere even after the video!!!

And I am just a woman who tries to recover and survive. I don't have money to pay an attorney. But still, I want Real Justice. But I guess it's the case of everybody.
RealJustice.

On 2018-07-22 at 2:26 PM, justice survivors wrote:

Dear Nicole,

Thanks for trusting me. This is Ramona Saphony, the former chair of the Feminist Anthropology department at NYSU Peru. He has been attacking me as well. If it feels safer, please feel free to give me a call at 518-666-6996. There is a group of former students who filed complaints earlier on that are working with me to provide support. I am no longer at NYSU-Peru but am one phone call away!

First and foremost, I wanted to make sure you know that you are not alone. I work with Faculty Against Rape (FAR), if it comes to it, we will make sure you get an attorney that would represent you for free. You were very brave to post your story. I know others will follow.

Looking forward to working with you!
warmly, Ramona

On **Sun, Jul 22, 2018 at 10:54 PM, Nicole Unknown <metoo@usa.com> wrote:**

Ho! yes! I think I saw your name on a post!!! I will go back and try to find it again if I can.

Thank you for your support. And thank you for giving me your telephone number. That feels good to know that I'm not alone. I will call you for sure, but I need time to really think about it.

You told me that he attacked you too? I'm so sorry to hear that. I know how traumatizing it is. I can imagine that you still try to recover. And I understand your offer now. But you were in a position of power, why didn't you report him?! I guess it's like me. I couldn't report him. I didn't trust anybody there. He was a superstar and everybody was on his side. You certainly know how smart he is. Look! Even after they investigated him, he's still free! I can't believe after all that, the investigators didn't find something!!! Otherwise they wouldn't have fired him. But since they couldn't prove it, he's still free. I don't want to go through an investigation myself. Especially if they ask for details.

You know, I was following that for months, since it started. You can't imagine how much it was a very stressful period for me. I really thought that they will have something that they will be able to prove. Because, on my side, it's my word against his. I can't prove anything. That's why, if I charge, I need an attorney who can guarantee to me that that will work. I'm not doubting you but, I have the perception that attorneys who work for free aren't the best. I don't want to dismiss them, but it's my name that will be place on the stage. So how can I make sure that I will win? Will the attorney be able to answer my questions before I reveal my identity? Or maybe you can tell me since you have the experience with the Feminist Anthropology department, which is impressive.

I'm seeing him in my dreams every night, and the idea of seeing him in court makes me hesitate a lot. And look at how he's doing with all the posts, the articles, the videos. What will he do after he discovers who I am? All that is so frustrating and stressing!

****

From: "Justice Survivors"
Date: July 23, 2018 at 7:55 AM
To: "Nicole Unknown"
Subject: Re: Me Too

Hi again,
First, I am sorry you are having nightmares as this case is re-surfacing. This is known as re-triggering. For most survivors, speaking up and getting

support and then becoming part of a community of survivors and working on this issue helps ease those moments when one is re-triggered. I know this as both a survivor and someone who has been working with survivors and researching gender-based violence for three decades.

I am a survivor of several sexual assaults in academia since earlier on in my career, so I stayed away from XW. As a professor, I defended and supported students whose education has been interrupted by violence since i began teaching in 1994! My involvement at NYSU-Peru began when I started to hear unsettling accounts from students attending his classes, especially the Love, Sex and Marriage class where is showed several clips of sexual assault and rape, including one of a black professor raping a white woman who was is graduate student. I had several students who are survivors who walked out of his class. That's when I felt that I had to speak up. I went to the Dean and Provost, the President knew. There was a Title IX complaint filed by students and supported by me. I filed a follow up years later when I found out he is still using the same disturbing materials.

Now to the bad news: I am afraid he'll remain free, unless there are multiple survivors who come forward with allegations and demand damages. That would then become a criminal case. It took over a decade to get him fired because the institution covered up for him, so I doubt there'll be an attorney that will take on a criminal case unless we have multiple survivors with detailed stories showing patterns of abuse. the problem as you know is that survivors are scared and his tactics are designed to prevent others from speaking up. The MeToo strategy was to publish anonymous accounts and hope that they will give others courage. The hope is if such accounts surface -- we could find someone to publish them anonymously, he will think twice about suing individuals. Now he says he will sue the university but he has insinuated that he will also sue the students that exposed him this year, so everyone is being careful.

To be clear, if you want to help, we need you to recount your story in as much detail, including how the re-opening of this case is impacting you and your wellbeing. We will disguise anything that would identify you and try to get the other survivors to add their stories before we make them public. Sadly, no lawyer I know would give any guarantee about winning or speaking up. Those who take these cases without being paid a retainer do so as a service to the movement and it is difficult in this case because it involves race. So, at this point PR is essential as we watch his attempt to sue the college, which may go nowhere because he doesn't have enough money and most likely no attorney to represent his pro-bono, which is good news for survivors.

Hope this clarifies things. let me know when you want to chat and I will clear up some time. In the meantime, please take good care of yourself.

Warmly, Ramona

Kesi, to say the least, was infuriated. She was in disbelief that Saphony admitted a ten year agenda against Xavier, which included ceaseless character assassination while undercutting the agency of the administrative office he led. She admitted creating anonymous survivors who supposedly participated in the sullying of Xavier's reputation, without a concern as to her being unable to undo the damage done if no survivors surfaced, with the impact to his reputation and career nothing more to her than collateral damage. She even admitted to endeavoring to turn her misguided intuitions against Xavier into a criminal case, though she had not one iota of evidence of any wrongdoing. She was willing to do all of that because she didn't concur with his pedagogy. And she is so relentless that even without a presence on NYSU-Peru's campus any longer, she continues to stick her wicked, unclean nose in their business.

It clarified quite a bit for Team Witt. Saphony's eagerness to recruit the seeming one true survivor her campaign against Dr. Witt lacked had her throwing caution to the wind. Her manipulation of students over the years, infusing the impressionable ones with much-too-much misandry, and encouraging as well as supporting the back-alley tactics of her colleagues were now documented. Saphony had just stupidly admitted to an ongoing campaign against Dr. Witt that would possibly eliminate her voice as any longer pertinent to the movement she claimed to value, but misappropriated for her ill-gotten gain.

Saphony's strategy is best portrayed--if not revealed--in this conversation between LeAnn, Michelle, and Felicia, walking back to LeAnn's home immediately after the votes of no confidence forum where Molly Mothburn for all intent and purpose was looking to recruit.

"Can you believe what just occurred? asked an excited LeAnn. "XW just completely walked away from his career here."

"What makes you think that?" replied Felicia. "Utley doesn't have the balls to take action against him. XW is too well connected."

"No one is that well connected," Michelle said. "You heard Molly almost begging women with anything on him to come forward. I think when he said 'Bring it' it she took it personal, almost like a challenge."

"I agree," Felicia said. "I hope someone comes forward. He fucking thinks he walks on water."

LeAnn, recognized that Felicia was still angry about losing her office due to budget cuts. She also figured that Michelle was possibly still feeling scorned about XW not pursuing a relationship with her after their one meal together, even though it was seven years ago. Thinking about Mothburn's solicitation she concocted a plan in mid stride.

"Didn't you and Xavier go out one evening for martinis?" LeAnn asked Felicia.

"We sure did." answered Felicia. "But as much as I hate to admit it, he was very cool and we actually had fun."

"I see where you are going LeAnn," Michelle said appreciatively. "We can't afford to rely on others to come forward who may never do it. Who may not even exist."

LeAnn, with a gleam in her eyes, added, "If enough women come forward with accusations of misconduct against him, it could cause him some serious problems. I mean, I'm still in disbelief that Senator Al Franken resigned with Kirsten Gillibrand leading the charge against him. What he did was wrong, but he wasn't shown any mercy, not even by his fellow Democrats. What makes XW any different?"

"He's Black, responded Felicia. "That's a huge difference."

"So what, he's Black. Bill Cosby is Black. Russell Simmons too," replied Michelle. "This is our time. Accusations from enough of us can do real damage."

"Well, considering all of that, when he and I hung out that evening we did smoke some weed," Felicia offered in support of a plan beginning to hatch. "When we smoked he passed the hit to me by mouth."

"You probably enjoyed that," said Michele laughing. "Besides, I've seen you greet him with a kiss on the lips a couple of times at campus events, where many others probably saw it too."

"That's beside the point," LeAnn cautioned. "The point is you have something you can assert that you can say made you uncomfortable. You are a survivor of his sexual misconduct."

"Well then, since you put it that way," Michelle said with a smarmy smirk on her face, "He shared a poem with me that was sexually inappropriate."

"Didn't you tell me you liked his poetry," asked LeAnn, playing the Devil's advocate while wearing a shit-eating-grin.

"Oh, did I?" answered Michelle. "Was that before I also told you about him hugging me inappropriately on our one and only encounter."

"Did he really?" Felicia asked naively, missing the obviousness of their well woven web of deceit. Michelle and LeAnn both looked at her as if she needed to stay in step with them. LeAnn then added, "I should probably call Deidre too. She might have something to add. When she left OPIE her and XW were not as close as they had been. She just might have something. Oh damn, and Devin would definitely want to help take him out. I'll call them both tonight."

In This Card Game of Gender Her Admitted Lack of Courage Somehow Left Him with Fleas…

Xavier saw sexism as an intriguing thing to unpack and consider. He was convinced that people should be able to see this in the way many people responded to posturing politicians Sarah Palin, and Michelle Bachman back in the days of Barack Obama's first presidential campaign. Both of these women were often mocked as intellectual lightweights, as if all men who are seeking forms of higher office are intellectual giants. Somehow Hillary Clinton avoided the complex criticism of her aptitude to gain the respect that both of her female Republican counterparts avoided. It could be related to her ability to answer both complex and simple questions with a level of clarity that the other two often appear to struggle with. It could also be that she actually had political prowess. However, no matter how you see what should not be seen as the phenomenon of women in politics, the evaluation of a female candidate will always require teasing out sexist views. But the thought preoccupying Xavier was to what extent does unpacking our potential sexism benefit a racist society? Simultaneously it would be just as necessary to consider to what extent does unpacking our potential racism benefit a sexist society? After all, the intersectionality of these two identities may be the most problematic of any identity combination, though the intersection of race and class are stiff competition.

Xavier often used as an example NY State politician Senator Liz Small, who at one time appeared to be so invested in entering the good-old boys club that once upon a time she threw a disenfranchised group under the bus—in terms of their civil rights to marry the one they love—even though she herself belongs to a group (women) whose civil rights were denied along similar rationale (it's always been this way). Another example Xavier often used is how some feminists with scars from their interactions with some men (not all) still default to seeing most men (if not all) as overtly oppressive/sexist while they try to convince themselves they can't be racist, classist, etc. because of their level of sophistication/expertise with one 'ism.' Is this just an instance of the pot calling the kettle black? Regardless, the sexism card, like a similarly powerful card—the race card—often is played as a wild card when it serves the purpose.

Some time ago Xavier dated a woman named Bea who was quite brilliant in her own right. Foreign born and reared, she was one of the best communicators he had ever met, actually quite the linguist, having literally mastered five languages (German, French, English, Italian, and Spanish). Seldom was there a joke, quip, conundrum, or display of wit from anyone within her range of hearing that she didn't totally understand and/or have a response to. This woman was quite the social commentator having a familiarity with so many cultures she could easily juxtapose the best/worst of any culture with another. As a result, her intellectual depth was unparalleled relative to the people that Xavier had met thus far in his lifetime. But she was still a woman in contemporary society who carried scars that were quite surprising to witness, admittedly, even to her.

Once when Xavier traveled to Quebec to see her they spent an evening together. They had wine at her place, then went out to a nice dinner and practically closed the restaurant, staying there so long, chatting one another up in a dark corner. The next morning Xavier left her place early to return home to attend to some time-sensitive family commitments. They didn't talk later that day at all, nor the next day, or the next. Xavier did however, text her once during that period to wish her well on her son's first communion. She responded with a thank you, and nothing more. He should have recognized her very brief reply as a harbinger of things to come. Xavier actually thought about calling her many times, but also thought she could have taken the initiative to contact him just as much as he could her. Up to that point, he had seen her twice and both times he had made the effort of driving to her town. Both times he had picked up the tab. Following the first meeting he called her afterwards. So, he decided he would wait to see if she would take some initiative to acknowledge their evening. Well, after a few days she finally broke the ice and sent him a text message that had no amicable salutation within it. It simply requested that he return a film to her that she had loaned him. Xavier then responded to her that he was curious about her tone and wondered if the undertone was in response to their lack of conversation after a romantic evening. She acknowledged she was perturbed from his lack of contact with her immediately after such a great evening. He then asked her was it not the case that he had driven over an hour to see her, brought her a bottle of wine as a gift, took her out to an expensive dinner and picked up the entire bill. With that effort, was he still obligated to also be the one to make the "morning after" phone call? If so, why? Her response was that it was inexplicable to her, she actually owned the fact that she didn't know why. She honestly stated she just felt bad having shared an intimate evening with him and not received a call from him for closure on that evening.

After pressing her a bit further, she admitted she was a bit nervous about contacting him afterwards, a bit uncertain how he would process the romance that had occurred that evening. They eventually laughed it off because they were both cool with the fact that they were finally at least talking. However, Xavier couldn't get past the fact that somehow—in her mind when she hadn't heard from him—he had become a "dog," the stereotypical designation many men receive when they don't conform to some women's expectations. He had become just another typical male whom after the so-called conquest (from her perspective) that had taken place was over he must have moved on. At that point in his mind, somehow, due to her lack of courage, he had acquired fleas. Xavier then pondered what dysfunctional amorphous stereotype could be affixed to women who also don't acknowledge an exhilarating evening with a man, and then label that man something that they themselves must logically resemble, if all things are considered equally.

At what point will women—claiming to want equality long denied them—put away the "gender card" and step into equality by moving beyond the hypocrisy of certain realities that continue to undercut their movement. Or is it acceptable for a woman in today's society to continue to believe it is okay for her to be the victim when it serves her purpose. While women should not be held to a higher standard, they should not be held to a lower one either. Neither should my engaging companion be able to suggest that Xavier is carrying fleas that she isn't.

Ultimately, or perhaps ironically, if the deck of cards that represent life is full of certain cards that one must play, if we don't play the ones that fate has dealt us, do we have a chance of winning? After all, how many of us are ever truly in the privileged position to deal, or even cut the cards.

CHAPTER FOUR
- *Romance, Sex, Love, & Marriage*

"Okay, you know the drill," Dr. Witt said, challenging the 45 university students in his Romance, Sex, Love, & Marriage (RSLM) class to elevate their focus, to prepare their intellectual game for the start of class activity. Dr. Witt then academically challenged the students, asking, "So what are your thoughts about this quote from the film clips we watched of 'Love Jones,' relative to romance and/or sex?" Dr. Witt then motioned to Gabriel, one of his Teacher's Assistants for the RSLM class, who then brought the quote up on the screen:

People with profound insights on life know not to get married. And those that do, ought to know marriage is what you make it.' – Savon Garrison

Immediately hands went up. The reaction to the film clips had been extremely favorable and Dr. Witt already had anticipated a lively discussion, especially since every semester he had taught RSLM the Love Jones clips and its ensuing conversation were always well received.

"It sounds so simplistic in its assertion of the obvious, but somehow it feels like a warning," offered Erica, a White graduating senior who previously served as a TA in Dr. Witt's Ethics class. "He's bitter, maybe hurt, and cautioning his friend to not expect only smiles and hugs."

Dr. Witt responded, "No doubt Erica, but it doesn't negate the truth he spoke, though he does imply people who are married lack profound insight on life, as well as those that weren't smart enough to avoid it need to live up to their 'until death do we part,' vows."

"The quote pushes me to imagine a lack of intimacy in the relationship, possibly after a romantic and steamy courtship one or both of their libidos died," said Kim, a White female, and an amazing voice in this class of superstars, especially considering Dr. Witt allowed her to register for the class as a first year student amongst juniors and seniors. Kim continued, "The profound insight is that marriage often imprisons lovers creativity, especially if those lovers aren't aware that it can happen to them too, not just to others."

Nicholas, one of the coolest White male students Dr. Witt had ever taught, who also previously served as a TA in two of Dr. Witt's classes, had a shit-eating, mischievous look on his face as he answered, "It can also suggest that lovers with creative imaginations would be well served by discussing if not negotiating their fantasies of public displays of affection, threesomes, foursomes, and yes, fivesomes or more, in advance of exchanging 'I do.'"

The class erupted with energetic desires to reply, to which Dr Witt contentedly chuckled. His thoughts somehow led to the fact that he had never planned on teaching a class on *romance, sex, love, & marriage*. He had no extensive academic training on the subject matter. However, he had been academically trained as a philosopher with a research interest in Applied Ethics, and Existentialism. He also acquired experience facilitating large and small group discussions from the consulting business he had virtually accidentally launched. So the two came together to form the perfect storm.

Witt realized that the ethical dimensions of romantic relationships are far too often overlooked when many couples embark on sexual and/or loving relationships. Existential crisis arise—more often than not—from not revealing and negotiating who we are, what we mean, and what we want from our romance(s), sex, love, and marriage. Dr. Witt realized early on that true learning could be elevated by more conversation(s) and consideration about all of these topics. Witt's academic journey had revealed to him that unfortunately these two things aren't always present simultaneously in relationships. He understood that people talk about their feelings, and obviously think about their romantic other. But consistently considering what you are going to say to your partner before you say it (with thoughts about the consequences too) is done sporadically by the best. And the corollary of consistently discussing anything/everything on one's mind that is relationship-effecting is done even less. Hoping that he was talented enough to create and facilitate an atmosphere for young minds—to not only learn, but want to learn about topics that individually as well as collectively led to their literal creation—energized him.

It was in an Intellectual History class he taught at NYSU-Peru wherein the seed was first planted that students enjoyed conversations which centered upon their sexuality, needed them, and could immensely benefit from them. The textbook he used in his Morality and Social Dilemmas course had a chapter in it titled, 'Sex, Love, & Marriage.' Within this chapter the author explored many of the highly problematic philosophical questions involving morality, relative to sex and sexual situations; what it means to love, be loved; and why we marry, divorce, or choose to be/not be monogamous, as well as how people are taught to disdain open relationships.

Dr. Witt also realized the necessity of his speaking their language, or speaking a language they would want to learn. Dr. Witt was a younger professor than most on the campus. Being from one of the major U.S. cities, as well as being Black, he had half the battle won if they could intuitively feel him, and were curious enough about this brother from a very different mother to trust him to help them unpack some perspectives they had unwittingly inherited as ideals.

Perhaps the pivotal moment in which Dr. Witt realized the importance of these conversations was after two of his White female students, both juniors, AnnaE and Amanda, used the song by Eminem, '*Superman*' for their final project, to demonstrate the complexity of moral problems. "The song starts off with what seems like an endearing relationship between a man and woman," explained Amanda, "only to quickly and sharply turn astray, with the man revealing an inexplicable anger towards the woman."

AnnaE added, "Also, while the song's repetitiveness hammers home Eminem's point--that he is not anyone's Superman--the gist of the lyrics we're sharing essentially represent a man who is scarred by the reception of "some women" to his stature as a burgeoning rapper."

Pointing to the elevated screen in the smart classroom Amanda then said, "These are the lyrics we'll be unpacking."

Eminem: You high, baby?
Baby: Yeah
Eminem: Ya

Baby: Talk to me
Eminem: You want me to tell you something?
Baby: Uh-huh
Eminem: I know what you want to hear

Eminem:'Cause I know you want me baby
Baby: I think I want you too
Eminem: "I think I love you baby"
Baby: I think I love you too
Eminem: I'm here to save you girl
Come be in Shady's world
I wanna grow together
Let's let our love unfurl
You know you want me baby
Baby: You know I want you too
Eminem: They call me Superman
I'm here to rescue you
I wanna save you girl
Come be in Shady's world
Baby: "Ooh boy you drive me crazy"
Eminem: Bitch you make me hurl

[Verse 1]
Eminem: They call me Superman
Leap tall hoes in a single bound
I'm single now
Got no ring on this finger now
I'd never let another chick bring me down
In a relationship
Save it bitch, babysit
You make me sick
Superman ain't savin' shit
Girl you can jump on Shady's dick
Straight from the hip, cut to the chase
I tell a motherfuckin' slut to her face
Play no games, say no names
Ever since I broke up with what's-her-face
I'm a different man, kiss my ass

Kiss my lips, bitch why ask?
Kiss my dick, get my cash
I'd rather have you whip my ass
Don't put out, I'll put you out
Won't get out, I'll push you out
Puss blew out, poppin' shit
Wouldn't piss on fire to put you out
Am I too nice?
Buy you ice
Bitch if you died, wouldn't buy you life
What you tryin' to be? My new wife?
What you Mariah, fly through twice

But I do know one thing though
Bitches, they come they go
Saturday through Sunday, Monday
Monday through Sunday yo
Maybe I'll love you one day
Maybe we'll someday grow
'Til then just sit your drunk ass on that fuckin' runway ho

'Cause I can't be your Superman
Can't be your Superman
Can't be your Superman
Your Superman, your Superman

Don't get me wrong, I love these hoes
It's no secret, everybody knows
Yeah we fucked, bitch so what?
That's about as far as your buddy goes
We'll be friends, I'll call you again
I'll chase you around every bar you attend
Never know what kinda car I'll be in
We'll see how much you'll be partying then
You don't want that, neither do I
I don't wanna flip when I see you with guys
Too much pride between you and I
Not a jealous man, but females lie

But I guess that's just what sluts do
How could it ever be just us two
I'd never love you enough to trust you
We just met and I just fucked you

The conversation that ensued—led by his two stellar students—over dysfunctional versus healthy relationships was one to behold, and never forget. It was surprising how many men, provoked by AnnaE, Amanda, and Dr. Witt's facilitation, owned the fact that many of their male friends, if not themselves, viewed relationships similar to the way Eminem articulated them, as transactional. It was just as much surprising to hear many of the young women defending Eminem's position of having no responsibility for rescuing the women he shared intimacy with.

"Okay, we've exhausted shooting from the hip to unpack the hell out of Eminem's meaning," AnnaE mentioned, "what quotes from your assigned readings can you share that further accentuate Eminem's reasoning?"

Derek, a White male junior, replied, "This quote captures aspects of their relationship:"

"And if if we insist that love must be reciprocal, is there not very real danger that our model of love may have built into it a ferocious form of competition, summarized in the almost always destructive comparison: 'Do I love you more than you love me?'"
-- Solomon & Higgins

"Solomon & Higgins would argue that their verbal expressions of affection in the song were socialized sentiments, not actually real," Derek offered, "but appropriately rhetorical, until Eminem heard himself placating her, saying what he knew she wanted to hear."

Adam, a White male junior, added, "Eminem no longer was interested in feeling like a hypocrite, so he decided to get real and end the competition often imbedded in the reciprocity of who can say the most endearing things. Their amorous exchange of the sentimental phrase 'I love you,' brought this quote to mind for me:"

"Why is this phrase so significant? Because it signifies a decision and presents an invitation, perhaps a dilemma, which may well change the whole of one's life. The phrase, like the emotion, is at its very heart reciprocal, not that it cannot be rebuffed, it often is, but in that it is essentially a plea, even a demand for a response in kind" (Solomon, 37).

"That is an excellent quote as a companion piece for Eminem's '*Superman*.'" exclaimed Dr. Witt. "Amongst so many other things the quote in conjunction with the song hints at how difficult it is to be authentic, to be real in our romantic conversations from fear of hurting the feelings of our romantic interests. The courage to be told 'I love you' by someone you care a great deal about—when they are uncertain you are prepared to verbally reciprocate it is, AWKWARD to say the least. Nonetheless, though Eminem initiated the 'loving' exchange, it isn't difficult to imagine he was just saying it to score points, or believing it was what she was waiting to hear."

"And if she did love him," Amanda added, "then he fed her lies, feigning the vulnerability that accompanies such a declaration."

"And if she didn't love him," AnnaE surmised, "then she is an emotional coward for lacking the courage to say—instead of '*I love you*—something similar to '*It warms my heart to know you feel that way about me.*' It may hurt to hear it but not as much as it will later when someone admits to not loving the other, as Eminem does in the song."

Later in the class discussion Professor Witt was surprised to discover how many of the young women had already encountered a lesser version of the young man depicted within Eminem's '*Superman*' lyrics. The class' theories of how such a person is created had everyone leaning in. How and/or why women stay in such verbally abusive dysfunctional relationships was just as pertinent as it was poignant. It never failed that after the two weeks of discussion on the topics of Sex, Love, & Marriage students would always approach Professor Witt with the push for him to create such a discussion based class. Little did he realize it was this class itself that would contribute greatly, perhaps as the most significant catalyst, to his career challenges as well as professional demise.

One thing he did realize was that teaching a class on Sex, Love, & Marriage made no sense without exploring and unpacking the concept of 'romance.' The Judeo-Christian ethic insists that to be a fully developed moral person within a relationship one must evolve in a sequential way. Hence, romance to whatever extent practically allowable didn't necessarily serve as the ideal place to start, especially followed by marriage, sex, and then hopefully love. The Judeo-Christian route towards ideal marriage begins with a supervised conception of romance, followed by what is usually considered the ultimate goal of a relationship in contemporary American culture, marriage. In the Judeo-Christian sequence of relationships the marriage is thereafter consummated by sex with the hope that familiarity, if not compatibility, will culminate in a shared love. However, the typical American college student's pathway to marriage begins with romance, followed by sex, and depending upon how emotionally/spiritually connected they find themselves with a romantic partner, love occurs. It all theoretically culminates in marriage, ideally forever, though only lasting as long as the romance itself did, or does.

Recognizing that most people experience romance without ever having any academic engagement about it, Witt decided the order for his class on these topics would be consistent with how the average American college student approached their relationships. Hence, *romance, sex, love, & marriage* was the order in which the concepts would be philosophically undertaken.

Consistent with his use of film as a point of departure to access pop culture and make the subject matter more user friendly for his students Dr. Witt would begin every semester of his RSLM class with excerpts from a little known Black cultural film titled "Love Jones." In the early moments of the film, while in a conversation with some friends in a jazz club that featured spoken word that evening, the film's protagonists Darius Lovehall, defines romance this way:

Romance is about the possibilityof the thing. It's about the time between when you first meet the woman, and when you first make love to her; When you first ask a woman to marry you, and when she says I do. When people who been together a long time say that the romance is gone, they're really saying they've exhausted the possibility."

Immediately after this provocative statement the protagonist, Darius Lovehall encounters a woman at the bar named Nina Mosley, who captures his attention. Thereafter, Darius is invited to the stage to share some spoken word. Ascending to the stage he surprises Nina when he tells the audience that the spoken word he is about to drop on them is titled, '*A Blues for Nina*.'

"Say, baby... can I be Your slave?
I've got to admit girl you're the shit girl
and I'm digging you like a grave.
Now, do they call you Daughter to the Spinning Pulsar...
or maybe Queen of 10,000 moons?
Sister to the Distant yet Rising Star?
Is your name Yemaya?
Oh, hell no. Its got to be Oshun.
Oooh, is that a smile me put on your face, child...
wide as a field of jasmine and clover?
Talk that talk, honey.
Walk that walk, money.
High on legs that'll spite Jehovah.
Shit. Who am I?
It's not important.
But they call me brother to the night.
And right now... I'm the blues in your left thigh...
trying to become the funk in your right."

"Who am I?
I'll be whoever you say?
But right now I'm the sight-raped hunter...
blindly pursuing you as my prey.
And I just want to give you injections... of sublime erections...
and get you to dance to my rhythm...
make you dream archetypes... of black angels in flight...
upon wings of distorted, contorted... metaphoric jizm."

"Come on slim. Fuck your man. I ain't worried about him.
It's you who I want to step to my scene.
'cause rather than deal with the fallacy... of this dry-ass reality...

I'd rather dance and romance your sweet ass in a wet dream."

"Who am I?
Well, they call me Brother to the night.
And right now I'm the blues in your left thigh...
trying to become the funk in your right."

"Is that all right?"

Their romantic relationship began that evening, somehow unencumbered by the obviousness of Darius plugging Nina's name into a poem he had already written, and probably previously named something different, like '*A Blues for Cynthia*' three days earlier at another spoken word event. Their burgeoning relationship provided those viewing the film with a unique, non-stereotypical depiction of Black romance, unfettered with racism. For many of the students in the RSLM class, especially the non-Black students, it was their first extended look at a healthy Black relationship and Black sexuality, often invisible in movies outside of Black themed films that many White students may not have had available in predominantly White enclaves. The film clips also provided other moments of conversation that were worthy of unpacking:

'God is a woman ... if you ever kissed a woman you know that women have a certain power. A certain sexual thing that renders men totally incapable of functioning.' – Darius Lovehall

'You fucked him, didn't you? And you weren't even going to tell me. You ain't slick! You can't keep that kind of shit from me. I can't believe you fucked him on the first date. Ho!' – Josie Nichols

"I gather up each sound you left behind and stretch them out on our bed. Each night I breathe you and become high. - Nina Mosley

Perhaps none of these isolated snippets of conversation was more pertinent than this exchange the two lovers had later in their relationship:

Nina Mosley: You always want what you want when you want it. Why is everything so urgent with you?

Darius Lovehall: Let me tell you somethin'. This here, right now, at this very moment, is all that matters to me. I love you. That's urgent like a motherfucker.

Dr. Witt recognized there needed to be a similar *urgency* in providing students with conversations they never had, but should be having. He also knew he could build a class around examining and unpacking conversations and concepts of romance, since theoretically as well as practically romance intersects with sex, love, and marriage, sometimes and perhaps ideally, all at once. More so, creating a conversation about these non-taboo, or perhaps somewhat taboo topics could be even more profound if the class were to also address some of the possible intersections along the way. So in Dr. Witt's class gay couples were also considered for their differences along a socio-economic reality, or relative to their physical and/or mental ability, always attempting to normalize relationships of that type, de-centering heterosexual relationships as standard. The differently-abled person in a relationship with a temporarily-able bodied lover or the differently-able couple having sexual orientations that possibly go unnoticed by those who are more preoccupied by the gawking, gaping, and staring they receive.

Romance is about the possibility of the thing

It was in reference to this class that Dr. Witt often would ask and answer the question which came first, the chicken or the egg? He would ask his students does a fascination or fixation by their generation regarding romance necessitate the creation of conversations, if not a college class to explore it further? Or did the creation of the class provide them with the intellectual acumen and confident voices to philosophically explore it. Dr. Witt recognized also that like a coin seemingly offering two realities—heads and tails—the side, often overlooked in conversation, provides the necessary separation for the other two to exist. He warned his students that they may experience something perspective-altering if not life-changing if they would only open their minds to it. Ironically creating and facilitating these conversations would make it impossible for him to not actively and consistently ponder the merits of his relationship(s), no longer meandering about in them.

Ultimately, in this class it would lead to the pivotal moment where even as a well educated, paid professional *the Myth of the Black Rapist* would eventually have to meet the *MeToo* movement, to Dr. Witt's detriment. It's the moment where because of 'the Myth' a Black man that isn't cognizant of his movements, actions and words, is susceptible to any and all allegations. Xavier was cognizant, though unfortunately not overtly.

Xavier experienced the marriage part of *Romance, Sex, Love, & Marriage*, practically first, and in retrospect philosophically. His first wife Andrea was, and is still, one of the most beautiful people to ever walk the earth. She was/is intelligent, gorgeous, cool, witty, charming, family-oriented and unfortunately reflecting poor taste in her choice of one man. This is no attempt at modesty but in Xavier she married a man who hadn't learned yet how to fight for his relationship. Their relationship never had a chance. She would also own on her part that she had constructed some walls, with an unfair expectation that he would try to climb them. When Xavier realized he had no interest in climbing agenda-laden walls essentially constructed to measure, perhaps even test his love, he emotionally bailed. Because Andrea believed that a healthy relationship is about meeting shared expectations she emotionally left as well. As two loving people Xavier was sad for quite some time when considering how he and Andrea lost their rhythm, and went their separate ways.

As a single, albeit divorced, Black man in the North Country of New York, teaching the RSLM class once per week for 15 weeks out of the year while also actively interested in romancing as well as being romanced, sexing in terms of fucking-sex-lovemaking, loving in all ways applicable, and marriage in terms of ethically, necessarily, philosophically, and socially, Xavier was looking forward to 'livin la vida loca.'

Xavier seldom discussed the Romance, Sex, Love, & Marriage course he taught at NYSU-Peru. Self reflecting upon this he couldn't avoid asking himself, 'Why the reluctance?' He knew the reason was because those topics are so personal that just being a part of those moments are worth their weight in gold, and the moments are metaphorically heavy. More importantly, he was hard wired about wanting everyone to feel comfortable putting their voices out there, knowing it is a safe space. Hence, talking about romance, sex, love, and marriage with a stranger, especially romance and sex across gendered lines, may have been tougher than actually asking a complete stranger--who may even be attracted to you--for a French kiss.

Recently the class had just watched two women flirting with one another in the film 'Bound' and Darren Schultz, TA extraordinaire, asked the students what did they like about the film clip we had just finished watching. Asher, a Black male student answered 'lesbians.' The room chuckled at his wit and excellent timing, though he was exemplifying atypical maleness by overtly asserting a far too often mentioned male fantasy (as if it couldn't be one for women too). Dr. Witt's response appeared to throw him off balance for a moment.

"So the scene with the two women was hot for you?" asked Dr. Witt.

"Yes!"

"Would it have been hot if it were two men?"

"No," the student retorted as if insulted by the question and what his answer could imply about him.

"Have you ever seen two men 'frolicking,' or for those of you slang impaired 'immersed in coitus,' or for those of you lacking vocabulary, 'fucking?'"

"Never."

"Then how can you be sure it wouldn't be hot for you?"

He didn't reply, possibly thrown off his game by being challenged about his seemingly blind conformity to male supremacy, possibly induced by irrational fear, probably adversely affected by the dominance of enough testosterone in the room to make him feel uncomfortable saying anything at all. Yet, he was still quite cool. He didn't verbally or with body language disrespect the gay lifestyle, and was quite mature in the way he received Xavier's questions.

"You're right Doc, I couldn't be sure."

"Thanks Youngblood, but I'm not trying to be right. I'm trying to make you think. What we just experienced was the beginning of a philosophical argument, that should never become personal as long as it is entered into as a fact finding adventure. No winners, and perhaps more importantly no losers. Unfortunately too many people argue to win, instead of arguing for clarity. If we aren't arguing for growth, why are we even exchanging opposing opinions?"

Dr. Witt figured Asher had endured enough and it was time for him to be let off the hook so he turned away from Asher to the entire class, but addressed the men only, saying:

"I have a challenging homework assignment for the men in the room who are taking this class to go deeper on these topics. After all, it is an elective and we are all adults. I challenge you to watch this weekend at least 30-45 min of a movie featuring a gay romantic relationship leading to a sexual encounter, or gay male porn, ALONE. If you do this please eliminate all distractions, and open your mind. Watch it while earnestly looking for something positive to get out of it, instead of with a closed mind, dreading the entire experience."

Dr. Witt told them to keep in mind that American women live in a culture where they see images of themselves with other women and no one blinks, probably because some of them are staring, titillated. Why should that be 'the norm' when it is really no more normal than two men. Dr. Witt also told them that he didn't need to know the results, nor anyone else. They could keep it to themselves whether they were aroused by it. What is important is they will know, and will also know that they took a step beyond their socialization, faced whatever fears they may have consciously or subconsciously been succumbing to, and will probably emerge from it a better ally for the LGBT community.

Dr. Witt then said, "For those of you wondering if I practice what I preach, I do. Years ago I challenged myself this way and watched a film titled "Grande École", before I eventually added "Brokeback Mountain" to the class."

Lastly, as you leave class today I want you thinking even more deeply about the complexities of romance, sex, and love. So instead of four articles this weekend, you will only have three to read along with the following quotes that we will email you, which will need to be unpacked against clips from the following films (*He's Just Not Into You; Legends of the Fall; Braveheart; Bound; The Notebook; Monster's Ball; Lust Caution*) that will all be in Google Drive this weekend:

"Berglar argued that people often fall in love with someone in order to be able to replay things from their childhood" (Solomon 88).

"A relationship does not start the day two people meet; it starts in the childhood of each partner. For it is long before they meet that the template of their relationship is established. We learn to love as children" (Armstrong 91).

"When we fall in love a massive effect is worked by an apparently slight cause. You see her walking down the street and you turn weak at the knees. He smiled in a sweet way when you waved; you are delirious for the rest of the day. Without imagination there would be no such thing as love" (Armstrong, 71).

"What we call love is not a universal phenomenon but a culture-specific interpretation of the universal phenomenon of sexual attraction and its complications" (Solomon 35).

"Isn't it possible love could be a disruptive force in human society, an idle entertainment appropriate to only idle aristocrats, a neurotic obsession that impedes healthy self realization, or even a conspiracy by men to keep women in subservient roles" (Solomon 1)

"We have lost the idea that love takes time, that love is a process and not just an experience, that love is a lifelong development not something found and enjoyed, ready-made" (Solomon, 19).

Sexual attraction, unlike love, presupposes no prior experience together, requires no mutual interest (save one) and can be oblivious to

questions of personality/character. Sexual attraction, unlike love, does not look far into the future, need not care about compatibility as a couple, and makes very limited plans together (Solomon, 144).

Sex with a stranger may be exciting, but it can also be humiliating, foolish, guilt-ridden and filled with anxiety--which may ironically serve to momentarily bolster the thrill of the experience (Solomon, 139).

Dr. Witt then said, "Again, this assignment is to help you engage these quotes outside of the context of the articles they have been taken from, and placed by you in a context you can articulate, and if necessary defend. This is due next class. Have a great weekend."

Consideration & Mindfulness
- 2 Sides of the Same Coin

After class Dr. Witt, reflecting back on the discussion wondered how many of the thirteen men in his class, including three male TAs, would actually watch it? Knowing that women can also be homophobic about gay male images he wondered how many of them may have accepted the challenge too, though it wasn't extended towards them.

Dr. Witt also mentally revisited Asher's attempt at wit at the expense of lesbians. That momentary slice of homoerotic rhetoric brought to mind the nature vs. nurture debate relative to same-sex identity. He thought of Robert Downey Jr.'s character in the film "Tropic Thunder" who posed something profoundly provocative for people to consider when responding to a gay rapper's denial of his homosexuality. Downey's character replied, "everyone's gay once in a while." He thought of what he often told his students to consider, what if both nature/nurture are wrong? We all could have been born bi-sexual and moved to our sexual predilection by the unceasing perpetuation of heterosexuality over homosexuality modeled everywhere in our society. If so, those who gravitate towards bisexuality have ceased fighting their nature and won the battle over their nurture while everyone else living heterosexually or homosexually are waging a never-ending war against themselves.

In terms of social justice for our transgender sisters and brothers Dr. Witt often told his students, readers, and audiences that beyond people transcending their self-absorption and self-centeredness, even a smidgen of consideration aligned with basic common sense—as a result of a desire to not be a hypocrite—could be game changing. It takes both consideration and mindfulness—first cousins in terms of differing stages of cognizance—to help us imagine ourselves born feeling internally incompatible with our prescribed gender, contrary to what we may be projecting externally to know we would all hope to be accepted by allies.

More so, challenging people to imagine that our gendered realities at birth weren't necessarily our choices is paramount. While many are content with the decisions their parents may have made in choosing their gender there are others whose parents got it wrong, deciding their child should be a boy when inside that child was a girl, leaving the children vulnerable, mandating that they must live with that decision until they find the courage and/or means to change it.

So then the question becomes "How do we scoff or ridicule someone that easily could have been you or I?" Dr. Witt always marveled at how various actions and decisions in our so-called land of the free are a result of our identity rules, and just how much our identity, rules.

A Certain Type of White Woman

"A Black woman would have handled that entire 'Storytelling' situation differently, Doc," exclaimed Habiba, a Black female senior, and one of Dr. Witt's more vocal female students.

"Specifically, how so?" Dr. Witt replied.

"Well, a Black Woman with any dignity wouldn't have stood there awaiting an answer to her question, with him taking forever to respond and blowing smoke into her face as she awaited an answer." Habiba offered.

"But a White woman would," asked Carla, a White female junior, seemingly insulted by the racist, over-generalized assertion.

"Let's just say that a White woman is more apt to accept that type of behavior from a Black man, having grown up outside Black culture and possibly having a dysfunctional monolithic perspective on Black male behavior," Habiba replied, defending her earlier assertion. "And a Black woman wouldn't have been ruffled by his desire to hear his sex partner say, "Fuck me Nigger," or "Nigger, fuck me." Between two Black lovers it isn't racialized. It's equivalent to "Baby, fuck me, with some edge."

"I agree!" chimed in Jasmine, a Black female junior. "The moment she heard him request her say "fuck me nigger" she was thrown off her game, unable to win whether she said it or not."

"Does it make sense that we assign behavioral characteristics to racial groups?" Dr. Witt asked the class, rhetorically. "My fiancé is White when you first perceive her, until you hear her speak. Upon noticing her accent, you realize she isn't your garden variety American White woman. Couple that with her being from North Africa and you're left with the oxymoronic consideration that while she isn't Black, she is more African than most African Americans you'll meet with little understanding of their African heritage beyond originating from the so-called dark-continent." This means she is White in complexion but not necessarily White in reflection."

Carla, one of Dr. Witt's daring students jumped all over the opportunity to respond to Dr. Witt's conceptualization of White females, "Are you saying White women think White?"

"No, I'm saying most American White women who didn't grow up physically or intellectually connected to the Black experience can't see pass the racism they've been spoon fed since birth. My fiancé doesn't default to an expectation that all Black men will exhibit a typical or stereotypical behavior. She may end up interpreting some Black men negatively but only as a result of an interaction with them, not simply because they have darker skin."

The question that Dr. Witt really wanted to ask his 'African American Realities' (AAR) class was '*How Are White women different from Black women in terms of how they romantically respond to Black men?*' He decided against examining such a provocative question as class was ending, nor sharing a story with his AAR students may have been too revealing.

On his way home that evening Xavier recalled during his college days in the eighties working at a black-owned barbecue restaurant in Hawaiian Gardens, California with an older Black man named Jack. Jack was what is commonly known as old school, with the old school designation implying someone who holds onto perspectives or values that for many have changed. For example, once Jack told Xavier that Black women were too argumentative and that he only dated White women. Xavier was blown away by this older man's unapologetic dissing of the women of his own race. Dr. Thomas Keith, in his book, Masculinities in Contemporary American Culture identified this "Moya Bailey coined term as 'misogynoir,' to mean a hatred of Black women. It is a type of misogyny that denotes the cultural fact that blackness has been placed at the bottom of the cultural hierarchy in America as a matter of white supremacist policies and practices" (11). Xavier had just taken a psychology class and had just been introduced to the concept of internalized oppression/self-hatred. It was good he had learned about this because he was able to recognize it in Jack. He also realized that he had encountered it before. He even self-reflected, asking himself if he had ever succumbed to self-hatred.

Jack affected Xavier more so in that he raised Xavier's consciousness about why he may like/dislike certain types of women as well as why he may be dismissed or not seen by some racial groups and not others. Most importantly though it eventually prevented Xavier from elevating any race of women over another. This would be vital in understanding a Black man that seemingly ceased to date Black women. After all, how does it happen that anyone of a certain race or culture could/would/should be incapable of finding something romantically attractive in most every race/culture other than their own?

Xavier's divorce from one of the few Black women in the North Country of NY would seem to be an answer. Many people who wanted to see this upscale Black couple continue to represent highly functioning blackness were daunted by their separation. Xavier almost felt as if the dating gods had met and unanimously decided there would be no dating black women for him. Like the television comedy Seinfeld's Soup Nazi's "no soup for you," it was to Xavier "no Black women for you," though perhaps aided and abetted somewhat by his specific physical preferences with Black women. There were no viable Black women available to date in the entire region of the North Country of New York other than those already taken, or those existing in a completely different world from his. With what seemed like less than a handful of Black women in the city of Peru, it was rare to encounter a professional. Xavier knew the book on him was he had high expectations for himself and as a result couldn't always see his expectations of others as sometimes unrealistic, if not subconsciously unfair.

Xavier has no problems dating women of different realities, including social class. However, ironically across the span of his life thus far many Black women talked themselves out of relationships with Xavier. Within an early conversation or two he would eventually begrudgingly have to hear "you're intimidating." It seemed as if Black women with less education than Xavier had no problems owning their insecurities.

Xavier couldn't recall one instance of a White woman ever identifying herself as out of his league. Perhaps by living in societies that often default to whiteness as the norm how could these White women see themselves as less than anyone non-White, especially a Black person, and even sadly, albeit subconsciously, a Black man who just so happened to be a romantic possibility. Many White women walk around clueless as to how the deck has been stacked for them, as the symbol of beauty in the United States. Those who Xavier had more education than were still White, and he wasn't. If a superiority complex wasn't the case with most of the White daughters Xavier dated, it was definitely the case with most of their fathers and ex-husbands. Imagining losing your daughter or ex-wife to a Black man, romantically, had to be one of the most difficult, if not also fearful things to encounter in life if you're White, especially while living in a predominantly White neighborhood situated within a predominantly White country. After all, with the racial privilege White men have, nothing is more embarrassing to the extremely fragile ego of an insecure White man than to feel as if you've been one upped by a once-called Negro.

An Introduction to Interracial Dating

Xavier reflected upon his once upon a time direct encounter with a White father's racism. It was meeting with the father of the first White woman he had ever really dated. He had kicked it with the cheerleaders in high school, smoked a joint with some of his White classmates. However, it was in Los Angeles when Xavier was 19, working at a jewelry store in the Del Amo Mall in Torrance that he met the first White woman he would actually date.

There were always groups of young women moving through the mall. On one such occasion Xavier fell into a conversation with a 20 year old White woman named Allison. Allison was blonde, 5'7, and very athletically fit, with a heightened emphasis on the "very." She was more than just average or even "kind of attractive," looking something similar to Brittany Spears in both face and fitness (when Brittany was at her peak). She was obviously into Black guys because she didn't even seem to notice White guys, but a brother couldn't step anywhere within the vicinity of Allison without her noticing. So, Xavier never allowed himself to believe she was into him in any way other than a passing fancy. Xavier nevertheless liked her because she was very smart. She also was what his good friend Craig Little framed as 'noice,' which was nice to the next level. She was also "nicety." She was exceptionally nice most times, and sensually nasty when she appropriate. Allison had a look whereby if she told you she played tennis you would have thought she was not only on the tour, but highly ranked. The fact that she was street smart, kissed wonderfully, moved her lower body against his imaginatively, and gave him tremendous romantic energy didn't diminish the effort they both spent trying to connect.

One day Allison invited Xavier who lived in Cerritos, Ca, 45 minutes away, to come over to her family's home in Torrance. Allison was living in an apartment with her father. It wasn't hard to see they were a lower middle class family. Xavier originating from a upper-lower class family situated him to not be judgemental. After all, it takes one to know one. Besides, there was no reason for Xavier to expect the worst, or anything less than cordial behavior. Instead what he got was a few strategically placed "*niggers*" unabashedly stated by the father in conversation between him and Allison, with Xavier possibly the not-so-veiled inspiration for his tirade, though it wasn't difficult to also imagine the father was dropping *nigger* more often than not when Xavier was not around. For some reason he didn't aim a single one at Xavier, but Xavier nonetheless felt their sting. Perhaps it was growing up in tough streets that had Xavier always ready for whatever comes. He did wonder if the shit hit the fan whether he could physically take him. He convinced himself this slowly-softening human being, probably around 40 years old, couldn't take him. Allison succumbing to the tension in the air--from a father who just realized his daughter could be on the verge of getting fucked by a Black man-- eventually ushered Xavier into her bed room. Xavier, still upset at the White fathers racism wasn't given the opportunity to initiate romance between he and Allison, perhaps subconsciously wanting to fuck his anger out of him. Instead Allison, more perturbed with her dear ol' dad than Xavier realized, was bound and determined to get her fuck on, after having played some hardcore grab-ass with Xavier during their other two tete-a-tetes. This time, almost as soon as the door closed, she was suggesting fucking as the panacea.

"I thought he would never shut up," Allison said, as she leaned against Xavier, pressing him against the wall in her bedroom, the very same wall that separated them from Daddy dear. Practically sticking her spicy-tasting tongue down his throat, she added, "Every ignorant thing he said made me want to open my legs that much wider."

"Really?" Xavier questioned, somewhat in disbelief as her lips and hips met his, very much uncaring as to the reason this hot ass woman wanted his body. Whispering he added while she sensually placed her mouth against his, "So we're about to hate fuck, is that it?"

Allison, who already had perfectly aligned her below-the-waist intimacy with his below-the-waist intimacy, and her--more than a mouthful is a waste--breast against his chest, slowly brought her hand southward from his neck, moving it through his upper back downward towards his ass, pausing there to let him know she believed he would have no problem with her sexual trespassing. He didn't have any real problems with her armed assault on his masculinity, but did have a philosophical concern. If he brought it up now it could kill the mood and with life being what it is, who knows, it may never happen. If he waited though, he would be bringing it up after the fact, putting himself at risk for being scrutinized for partaking of her delectable offering first, hence undercutting him acting as if he questioned whether to have sex with her. He was considering whether it would be more advantageous to discuss his intellectual hesitation with her until her hand left his ass and moved from the back of his body to the front, where it finally arrived at what may have been its predetermined destination. Her hand momentarily rested in peace, altering the moment by holding that piece of his anatomy as she apparently planned on not giving a moment's rest.

"Are we really going to do this with him in the next room," Xavier asked rhetorically while having his pants unzipped.

Allison knelt before him, a few seconds later mumbling, "I can't answer you with a full mouth."

Xavier lightly laughed, far too entrenched in passion to give a shit about anything but escalating their moment. He knew he was flirting with disaster. Allison's racist-ass progenitor would have probably tried to kill him if he knew Xavier was serving her the chocolate she apparently craved, and now deserved from the game she brought. Nonetheless he also knew they had no time for lovemaking. Of course them not being in-love would be one reason their sexual moment would be difficult to consider "lovemaking." But when lovemaking usually invokes thoughts of tender touching, ample time, long kisses that are easy to get lost in, and two lovers endeavoring to become one, while both arrive at the same destination, preferably simultaneously, a fuck is often as much a statement as a quick fix to horniness. So, in response to all she had done, he flipped both the script and Allison, deciding that while it was a fuck that had to be a quickie, he had time to eat a little something, an appetizer before the main course.

15 minutes later, pulling their clothes in place to be deemed appropriate just in case Daddy dearest barged into the room, Xavier decided to go there. "So, did that fuck, beyond our well coordinated conclusion, make you feel better about your Dad's racism?"

"Did it make you feel better?" she replied, answering a question with a rhetorical question.

"It didn't make me feel worse, though if he had caught us who knows what would've happened," Xavier answered, still fixated upon the risk he took to enter this sensual human being's body. Appreciating the moment they shared he realized that the father's racism had given them an opportunity to have a conversation they had never had before. He had partied with a few White girls in high school, but being only a fling meeting parents was never part of the equation. In this instance they both knew that they had just shared a moment that neither would ever forget. So, with that thought in mind, he wanted to further explore what had just transpired.

"Seriously, did our fuck make you feel better about your Dad's racism?"

"Yes, he's a dinosaur who I fucking hate. He can't control me."

"But one could argue he did control you anyway. After all, you fucked me in response to him fucking over you." Xavier challenged her to consider.

"True, except that I wanted to fuck you the moment our hands touched in the jewelry store, maybe even the moment I saw your big brown eyes."

Blushing, Xavier stumbled for words to address her sexy compliment. Eventually he found them and said, "And don't get it twisted, I want nothing more than to really have some time to work your hot ass into a frenzy. It doesn't negate the fact that what we just did was fucking crazy.

"That was some crazy fucking," Allison wittily replied.

"You're changing the subject woman," Xavier asserted.

"I know I am," Allison admitted. "It hurts for me to become too preoccupied with it."

"Seriously though, where does your Dad's hatred of me or people who look like me come from?"

"I really don't know. His parents, my grandparents have never shown me they are racists. His brothers and sister, my uncles and aunt, are a mixed bag. My aunt has dated Black men, and one of his three brothers and him had issues with it. Maybe he lost a job opportunity to a Black man. He's always talking negatively about affirmative action."

"Maybe he or a friend he is close to had some negative experiences growing up around Black people." Xavier added. "Maybe he got his ass whipped by a Black guy back-in-the-day and begrudges all Black people any sense of normality, or respect?"

Allison then asked Xavier a question he could have never anticipated. "Did you cum better knowing you were doing the one thing to his daughter he didn't want you to do?"

"Well, first I think I did a few things to his beloved daughter that he would have problems with, and hoping to do more if, or when you walk me to my car. All that said though, yes, it was better because it was me partaking of the forbidden fruit. It was him not knowing that his worst nightmare came true when you '*came*' with me. Not only did you fuck a Black man, but you thoroughly enjoyed it. You know the saying, once you go Black you never turn back."

She laughed and said "I must admit if the next Black man I am with treats my body the way you did, that saying may become my anthem. Now, let me walk you to your car and perhaps you'll be the next Black man."

Allison, on various levels taught him lessons about interracial dating that he would never forget. Even after all of these years, just from reminiscing, 30 years later he could still almost feel her warm mouth and active tongue sensually interacting, sometimes moistly, gently colliding with his when not alternatively exploring other places.

Now, as a single man in a predominantly White community Xavier chuckled to himself thinking "Now that I've gone White, I realize my societal plight may never feel right, but if her game is tight it may be worth the fight." After all, they don't lynch Negroes anymore, aight!!!

Michelle

Dr. Michelle Boone was a single mother, White, and attractive. Since Xavier was recently divorced and they were the only two unattached people in attendance at the Prey-Slate barbecue they naturally gravitated towards one another, though not necessarily romantically.

"Are you excited about the start of your first semester at NYSU-Peru?" Xavier asked Michelle, knowing it was a rhetorical question that might reveal he was reaching for conversation.

"Most definitely," she replied. "I have no idea what to expect from Northern NY students."

"Well, you can expect to teach much more than just local students," Xavier answered. "The recruitment effort by this campus brings in a surprising amount of racially underrepresented students. So mixed in with the local, predominantly White students will be Black, Latino, and Asian students though representation of Asian students comes from the International student population more than it does NYC."

I'm happy to hear that. My research interests involve unveiling prevailing White privilege and the accompanying mentalities further perpetuating it. My research provides answers to questions on the impact of transcending strongly held beliefs in our desire for growth and ability to love.

"You do all of that within the context of teaching English too. Impressive."

"I wasn't trying to impress you," she responded, with what Xavier interpreted as more edge than was merited.

Observing she was wound tightly, Xavier said, "I didn't think nor say you were trying to impress me. Nonetheless, in an attempt to extend an authentic compliment your way I admitted that you did impress me. Did I somehow insult you?" he genuinely inquired.

"Not really," she reluctantly replied. "It's just tiring hearing men imply that a woman's actions all point to an end goal of gaining favor with men."

"Wow!" Xavier said. "You actually heard all of that in what I said?" Collecting himself a bit Xavier continued, "An implication is always subjective. However, at the risk of incurring your wrath once again I'll go out on a limb and say "thanks" for sharing with me one of the often revealed foibles of men."

With that said it was all that Xavier could do to eventually move on from this conversation with whom he surmised was a Negative Nancy. He knew too much affiliation with someone very comfortable articulating the glass as half empty would increase the possibility of his being seen as a Negative Norman. Surprisingly, a few days later he received a text message from Michelle following up on his casual suggestion about finishing the conversation (she started about him contributing an essay to a book she was editing) over a meal. Though he wouldn't have initiated it, he figured why not? Apparently, their initial conversation was cool enough from her perspective to warrant another one. For Xavier it was a no-brainer. As the director of the diversity effort at NYSU-Peru it was his responsibility to try to build relationships with as many faculty/staff as possible. Her research interests were not too dissimilar from his own, so the potential for future collaboration loomed large. They exchanged some small talk texts, more endeavoring to finalize a time for their lunch meeting. Eventually they set a date/time to meet at a local high profile restaurant.

Meeting inside the Ground Round restaurant their conversation didn't really start until they were seated and beyond the server's greetings.

"So, your first week went well, I presume. You're here and I don't see any visible scars," Xavier said in an attempt to start their conversation.

"It was okay," Michelle replied with a total lack of enthusiasm. "I'm a bit disappointed in the quality of the student in my classes," she added.

"Really, Xavier replied. "Have you ever taught at a state university before?"

"No," she replied, almost as if she was irritated by either Xavier's question, or what he may have been alluding to. "And I know that the occasionally inadequate student should be expected at a state college. Nonetheless, its okay for me to be disappointed. I allow myself to feel that way."

'Okay,' Xavier asked himself, 'Did she just third-person me?' Fuck it, if she apparently has no problem being real why should I hold back.

"Do you," Xavier reassured her. "However I must admit that I take the often stated low quality of our students as a challenge. After all, if it were easy anyone could do it, and we possibly wouldn't be in the jobs we are in due to lower hiring standards as a result of its easiness and its subsequent competition. The one thing the students don't need is anyone teaching them who doesn't necessarily believe in them."

"I didn't say I don't believe in them," Michelle insisted.

"I didn't say you said it," he unhesitatingly replied.

"Are you ready to order?" asked the server, catching them by surprise, bringing them both a modicum of relief. The moment of negotiating with the server when he might return to take their order gave Xavier just enough time to wrap his mind around a few possible topics of discussion.

Xavier was thankful about the interruption, noting that it couldn't have come at a better time. What was supposed to be an amicable midday meal was morphing into a Cold War. And with her disposition, seemingly poised to attack anything he said, he wasn't experiencing heightened levels of confidence about her receptiveness to any conversation he might initiate.

"So you mentioned something about a book project," Xavier asked.

Michelle's reply was detailed and as such, lengthy. Xavier decided midway through her articulation of the book project to resist all temptation to play to his name and be witty. It didn't seem as if this angry person could perceive anything coming out of his mouth as worthy of hearing it. As an often angry Black man himself, Xavier's ability to recognize undercurrents of anger in others was a virtue. Removing any possibility of antagonizing Michelle resulted in a much improved shared ambiance. Perhaps she considered Xavier an academic lightweight, especially since he wasn't on a tenure track. Perhaps she didn't want to be rude and the discussion that evolved around her book at the barbecue took a turn she wished it hadn't, which led to her being painted into a corner. Whatever the case, upon Michelle concluding what was one of the oddest invites into a project he had ever received, Xavier informed her that he appreciated the opportunity, but because he was in the formative stages of writing his first book it wouldn't be prudent, nor feasible.

Somehow, that bit of information seemed to disarm her even more. Consequently, some of the ice between them earlier had melted away. Somehow they had found an adequate intellectual space to coexist in. From that point forward Xavier tried to imagine her wearing an occasional smile, imagining more so what happiness might look like for her.

An interesting moment arose when he shared with her he was planning on including within his book some of his original poetry and published columns and In My Opinion articles. Upon discovering that Xavier not only wrote poetry, but could also recite most all of it from memory Michelle inquired further, curious about how he expressed himself in that medium. Xavier decided to share two very different poems with her to display his range of interests as well as hopefully his depth. Gathering himself for the moment at hand, Xavier stated,

"The first poem I'll share with you, he said, is:

'Coach King'

Martin,
Where is it that you placed your dream
and why is it
that as a team
we always appear to be in a game
we cannot win.
How badly we need you to return
and coach again.

Our squad needs direction
Some type of game plan.
We have yet to learn
how to score on "The Man,"
who blitzes us often
and stunts quite a bit,
intentionally roughs the passer
and doesn't give a shit
as to the penalty flags
that might be thrown on the play.
He knows all close calls will be called his way.

With the referees on the take
the commissioner too,
it's no surprise player loyalty
may not remain true.
Many feel that a victory
is just a momentary thing.
It hurts me how soon
you are forgotten
Coach King.

I have faith that we'll discover
the plays you would have called,
that we'll pick up the fumble
and run with the ball,
where even if we don't score,
the yards we will have gained
will at least tell the world
you coached not in vain!
-- Xavier Witt

Michelle politely acknowledged his poem with an appreciative, lightly demonstrated table-for-two applause. "What inspired the poem?"

"The oftentimes feelings of hopelessness relative to the struggle of Black people, and our need for competent, talented leadership," he replied.

"Changing the subject slightly, I like asking this question when I meet people. What bothers you the most about meeting people the first time?"

"People's pretentiousness and their often unrecognized or duplicitous reasons for being fake," Xavier responded. "I've known people who would wear what they deemed as the appropriate face to win someone over, perhaps effecting a cool persona when what was needed was more in line with whom they usually are when no one is around."

Michelle replied with a non-committal "I agree that pretentiousness is troubling."
Xavier thinking something different might breathe some life into her, asked Michelle, "Would you like to hear one of my relationship and/or romantic poems for dessert?

Sure, she replied, "Who doesn't make time for a good romantic poem?

From that point on they exchanged light banter with far less edginess attached to it. Their meals were served, eaten, and plates removed while they chatted away about their previous professional experiences at different places. They talked about the similarities of their experiences as single parents. After asking for their checks and paying them, Xavier was surprised Michelle requested for him to recite the second poem he had earlier offered.

Okay, said Xavier, per your request, here is that second poem. It is titled,

"When We Make Love."

I love the way that you undress
when you know what I want to do
I could easily rip your clothes to shreds
in my haste to get to you.
When fully clothed, you are so sensual
that you keep me in the mood.
So, I hope you forgive my eagerness
to see you in the mood.

I love to see you lying there
innocent, yet such a tease.
Your body, beautiful and bare
simply brings me to my knees.
To close my eyes and anticipate
how delectable you might taste,
the scent of you, the things you do,
accelerate pulse and pace.

I love the foreplay that we share
for that is what lovemaking is all about
and just when I've acknowledged you've done it all
that is when you turn me inside out.
You blow my mind, open my nose
and make me want to scream.
Is this reality I'm experiencing
or some fantastic dream?

I love the way you try to satisfy
by giving me all of you.
And the liberties you allow me to take
to do what I've so longed to do,
like licking your body up and down
as I would an ice cream bar
wasting not a single drop of you
for that's how precious I feel you are.

How I love to look into your face
when our passion is on the rise
to touch you in that special place
or kiss you on the thigh.
To run my fingers through your hair
and gently down your back.
Why it's the very sight of you
which compels me to attack.

And I love the love we make
For you love me with such style

And when I feel your body quake
It really drives me wild
Like the way you softly speak
and sigh into my ear
when we are reaching for our peak
and know that it is near.

I love to wrestle in bed with you
and let you think you've won
for it's the second time around
that is really all the fun.
Yet I must admit the third time
is nowhere close to bad
for I would take you a million times
if a millennium of time I had.

I love the conversation after
as much as holding you so tight.
and I would just as soon converse all day
as make love to you all night.
But that instant that we unite as one
does hold the upper hand
because when I'm not a part of you
I'm a fraction of a man.

I'd love to love you tonight my dear
or better yet, right now.
Let's put everything we have into it
until sweats upon our brow.
for there is nothing that has ever been more right
under the beautiful stars above
than that time we take to hug and kiss
those times when we make love."

Michelle wasn't ready for the unbridled passion within the poem, no more than she was able to handle Xavier reciting it word-for-word, flawlessly, and with unflinching eye contact, inadvertently flirting with her on the strength of the topic itself, without any conscious effort.

"Now, I must admit, that was very nice. A tad revealing, but then that is what poets do," Michelle exclaimed. "What prompted you writing that sexy poem?"

"It was inspired by a song titled, 'Say Yes' from a group called 'The Whispers.' Just as much it was inspired by my conversations with women who described what making love, ideally, would be like," Xavier answered. With that all said, Xavier then asked, "So, are we out of here?"

"I guess so," Michelle answered.

Together they exited the restaurant. After verbalizing farewells they went their separate ways. On his way home Xavier asked himself what, if any, potential there was for a relationship with Michelle. She was overly-cautious, perhaps from prior relationship scars. That wasn't so much a problem until the spectre of past incidents adversely might affect their current reality. He had already been there, done that. She had something sexy going on, a fit, shapely hard-body in her mid to late thirties. But her face, on the rare occasions Xavier experienced it, was far too often vacant of any semblance of happiness, positivity, or even energy. He doubted if he was the person who could contribute enough to help her find any consistent happiness. Xavier knew the best thing he could have with Michelle, if she were even interested, would have been a friends with benefits situation, with a high probability that the friendship wouldn't last any significant period of time. It didn't. Over the years Xavier's growing distance from the Prey-Slates and their ongoing friendship, perhaps better stated, mentoring of the much younger Michelle created an inexplicable chasm between these one-time dining partners.

Seven years later, as one of LeAnn's closest confidants, Michelle would offer her own version of what occurred inside the restaurant during their meal, and immediately after their lunch meeting in the parking lot dramatically alter its tenor and tone. Her version suggested an inappropriateness regarding the reading of the poem she specifically requested hearing. Her version also stated that Xavier tried to make physical moves on this blonde, unhappy woman in broad daylight outside of a high profile restaurant. Later, when the NYSU investigators asked

Xavier questions about his one encounter with Michelle he was flabbergasted. How did 90 minutes, one time only, sitting across a table from one another become an incident of misappropriate behavior? Hell hath no fury like a woman scorned, perhaps? Or perhaps blind allegiance to a cause whose time had come, letting the chips fall where they may.

Fear Begets Misandry, Resulting in Bigotry

Xavier, reeling from discovering that Michelle had come forward, thought to himself what is it that actually creates misandry? Knowing that misandry defined is 'hatred of men,' Xavier was very familiar with various definitions for hate. Hate more often than not itself is defined as 'an aversion usually deriving from fear.' Considering those definitions Xavier wondered if it is too much of a reach to interpret many people's misandry as just as much a fear of men as opposed to simply a hatred towards them.

In Xavier's "African American Realities" course he often created the opportunity—with significant assistance from his Teacher's Assistants (TAs)—for his students to unpack racism and classism. One of the many things these two 'isms' have in common is promoting hatred of the other race or class, justified by their xenophobia, their fear of "the other," predicated as much on a fear of the unknown, or fear of strangers, unknown cultures, fear of people that for some reason, somehow unbeknownst to them, threaten them. In a racist, capitalist society racism and classism necessarily intersect quite problematically, in addition to having instances of cloaked classism that when fully unpacked can be misinterpreted as racism only. Not at all dissimilar to Chris Rock's "I love Black people, but I hate niggers."

Rumors, lies, and half-truths--relative to race--contribute to stoking our fears and legitimizing our hatred based upon our fears. This is why poor Whites in the antebellum South and extending throughout Post-reconstruction easily developed a contempt, better yet outright enmity for disenfranchised, recently emancipated sons and daughters of once enslaved people. They feared the unavoidable competition with Black men if they ever became equal.

Xavier knew, as his employment situation gradually evolved into a legal situation, women waging war against him saw him as much the enemy as some U.S. soldiers during the Vietnam war saw some Vietnamese citizen capable of being their enemy. Too much misandry can leave the man-hater open to being interpreted as a bigot, or someone succumbing to bigotry.

Xavier wasn't as surprised when he discovered that a woman named Felicia Priest had come forward with a supporting allegation of improper conduct against him. She had sat on his OPIE Task Force for about two years and in that time he had a chance to witness her extremely immature behavior first hand. To not underestimate it, it was appalling. Upon being notified in Jan 2017 that the Administrative office she coordinated was being eliminated due to budget cuts she morphed into one of the ugliest professionals Xavier had ever seen. She would attend OPIE Task Force meetings devoid of any professional pretense that she was a team player, instead scowling, pouting, and silence became her trademarks.

Ironically, when times were happier for her back in September 2016 Felicia and her partner Mikaela had double dated with Xavier and Kesi. After months of doing the *'let's get together for drinks one night'* they actually made it happen. In terms of social evenings it was an interesting one. Dr. Mikaela Priest was an enigma to a large extent on campus, primarily based upon the fact that Mikaela was gender fluid to the extent that many were not comfortable around them as a couple. As the Chief Diversity Officer at NYSU-Peru, Xavier was expected to welcome new faculty into the academic community. Having more experience with people from different backgrounds Xavier was cool about an evening with what many around the campus interpreted as a unique couple.

Arriving at the restaurant Kesi and Xavier were joined a few moments later by the Priests. Kesi knew neither of the Priests so as everyone greeted one another individually Kesi noticed a kiss on the lips between Xavier and Felicia. Later she would ask Xavier about it, with him contextualizing the 'greeting kiss' as something some of the White people do in the North Country. With Kesi having lived in Morocco, Paris, Germany, and Belgium she put the kiss in perspective and never gave it another thought, especially after Xavier jokingly added, 'she had a breath mint in her mouth that she shared with me,' to which Kesi laughed.

Over dinner Dr. Kesi Mahila was her usual self, attentive to the conversation at hand, always present no matter what the topic, and visually affectionate towards the love of her life, Dr. Xavier Witt. It made sense that she was because those who knew Xavier well knew something magical had happened for him upon meeting Dr. Mahila. The couples laughed, mined each other's stories for the richness that exist in most people's narratives, all while breaking bread.

"So what do you two think of NYSU-Peru thus far?" asked Kesi. "I know Xavier loves it, but it was somewhat of an adjustment for me."

"Mikaela and I are enjoying our chance to positively affect the campus community," replied Felicia. "I'm still hoping for an increased budget that will allow me to be more innovative."

Mikaela added, "Perhaps it would be a good thing if you could pick Xavier's brain for some ideas as to how you might want to negotiate with NYSU-Peru for more budget."

"My brain is yours to pick Felicia," responded Xavier. "Say when and where."

"Thanks Xavier, I will," replied Felicia. "Kesi, how was NYSU-Peru an adjustment for you?" asked Felicia, recalling Kesi's earlier statement.

"Well, I haven't been around a university since I last attended one. Couple that with Xavier feeling as if he needs to be everywhere all at once, and while it's always a labor of love for him, at times it's been intense for me," Kesi admitted.

"What type of medicine do you practice Kesi," asked Mikaela.

A bit surprised by Mikaela's question, considering how quiet Mikaela had been much of the evening, Kesi replied, "I practice general medicine with my specialty being obstetrics."

With his arms draped around her, Xavier proclaimed, "Kesi is a heart doctor, a captive cardiologist. I've told her repeatedly if I ever lose her she must--in all good consciousness, tend to, if not mend--my broken heart."

The four of them shared momentary laughter as the server approached them with the option of dessert. Soon thereafter they would go their separate ways, each having enjoyed the other couple. Not surprisingly, a couple of months later Felicia contacted Xavier about meeting to brainstorm some ways for her to better situate the office she coordinated. They decided to meet at 8:00pm in downtown Peru at Naje's restaurant. Felicia said it was the time Mikaela would be returning home in time to watch their children, freeing her to hang out that evening. Xavier arrived a bit early, surprised to see Mikaela there, though apparently leaving as Xavier arrived. 20 min later he was joined by Felicia.

Felicia

"Sorry I'm late, I had to wait until Mikaela got home to relieve me of kid duty," Felicia offered in an attempt to explain her tardiness. Before she took her coat off she walked over to Xavier to greet him, hugging him, and like always gave him a kiss on the lips.

"No problem here," Xavier answered, trying to put Felicia at ease. "I'm a people watcher, armchair philosopher, and want-to-be poet. So, a few minutes of me waiting on someone go quickly. Besides, though I wasn't seen, I saw Mikaela exiting the restaurant and figured you would be here soon thereafter. So, what are you drinking, if anything at all?"

"What do you have there?" she asked, pointing to his drink.

It's an apple martini, and I feel stupid," Xavier stated, hoping to tweak her curiosity.

"Really. Why?" Felicia asked.

"Why do I have an apple martini, or why do I feel stupid?" Xavier asked.

"Both," Felicia answered.

"Okay. Cool. I have an apple martini because it is real difficult to fuck one up, so it's a safe order." Xavier revealed. "I feel stupid because they seldom put enough alcohol in these bar drinks. Hence, I may have been better situated not drinking here at all since I make stronger but just as tasty martinis."

"Oh really," responded Felicia. "What flavors do you excel at making?"

Tossing false modesty aside, Xavier answered smiling, "Chocolate Apple Raspberry, Chocolate Apple Peach, and Pomegranate Raspberry are my specialties."

"So why are we sitting here," asked Felicia flirtingly. With that she added, "Excuse me while I go to the restroom."

Xavier was somewhat surprised by what he could have surmised as Felicia flirting. He wouldn't allow his mind to fixate on this married woman whom Xavier and Kesi recently dined with. However, from the first time he met Felicia he felt a vibe that if he took half a step towards her she would not hesitate to close the distance between them.

With some time before Felicia returned Xavier's mind drifted to one of the phenomenon of the North Country that intrigued the Witts when they first moved into the area in 2000. It was how some people in the North Country greeted one another with a kiss on the lips. Xavier adopted the mentality 'When in Rome do as the Romans do,' as not necessarily bad advice, while his spouse at that time, Andrea, wasn't having it. He recalled one of their conversations on the topic.

"I just don't get it," Andrea said. Why do all these White people feel they can kiss us on the lips when they greet us?"

"Oh Andrea, not all of them do that," Xavier responded, slightly exasperated. "Why do you continue to speak about this, using sweeping generalizations?"

"Are you serious?" Andrea replied. "You know exactly what I mean. You are just playing into it because you feel you need to, Mr. Politically Correct. And your use of 'continual' is a generalization itself."

Knowing Andrea had made excellent points Xavier's response was measured, "You can look at it as negative if you choose. I choose to interpret it as a gesture of warmth, an unspoken statement of affection towards us."

"It's an unspoken statement alright," Andrea said, with a requisite amount of attitude. "They can't speak because they're lips are closed, pressed together and aimed at you, possibly contemplating whether to slip in a little tongue too. If you can't figure out that statement is wrong something's amiss."

Somewhat chuckling now at Andrea's wittiness, Xavier responded, "You don't have to kiss anyone my dear. Slavery ended in 1863 with the Emancipation Proclamation, then ended again in 1964 with the Civil Rights Act. So you have two historical events to justify your freedom."

Xavier's response had them both laughing, and helped to take some of the edge off of their conversation. Andrea then said, "It's a gender thing too. The women don't try to kiss me, and the men don't try to kiss you. I turn my cheek when a man tries to put his lips on mine. My lips are for my husband only."

"And my lips are capable of many things, like adding fullness to my face, pouting, serving as a veil that I lift to reveal my gorgeous smile (Xavier smiled as he said that), passionately kissing, and politically greeting someone. Just 30 min away is the Quebec border. When we go into Montréal and meet Québécois they greet us with a kiss on both sides of our cheeks. I know the kiss on the lips is more intimate, but both situations have us engaging different cultural norms.

"It's always about diversity to you, isn't it?" Andrea said.

"Yes," Xavier answered, "because it is always about diversity."

"You look as if you are deep in thought," Felicia said, as she returned from the restroom.

"I was, but nothing earth shattering." Xavier replied. "So, we are here to brainstorm, or do you need a sounding board? I'm cool with being either."

With that, they spent the next 45 min (between sips of martinis with not-enough-alcohol) weaving in and out on a conversation about how she could better situate the office she coordinated at NYSU-Peru for more financial support. At this time there was nothing in the wind that suggested her Office was in jeopardy, so it was more philosophical than urgent. It was a Wednesday evening, approaching 9:00pm when the conversation took a different turn.

"So you ordering another martini?" asked Felicia. "I wouldn't mind another one, but won't drink alone."

"No." answered Xavier. "I'm a lightweight and when away from home plan on staying that way. I'm paranoid about ever being stopped for a DWI. Besides, I prefer a hit of a joint over a drink any day, unless I'm thirsty."

"You have any?" Felicia asked Xavier with a twinkle in her eye and hopefulness in her voice."

"Its like my American Express card, I never leave home without it."

"Can we smoke it?" she asked without hesitation.

"Here?" Xavier mischievously and rhetorically asked Felicia. "We can take a ride and smoke, but smoking it outside in my car is not too dissimilar from smoking it in here. Both my car because of its unique color and me because of my unique color attract to much attention. We can drive, listen to some music, smoke, and then I'll return you to your vehicle. Cool?"

"Very much so," Felicia responded.

They then left the restaurant for Xavier's vehicle. Entering the car Xavier put on his favorite XM radio station, the Chill channel, which was ideal background music for lighthearted conversation. They rode 15 min, the equivalent of 3-4 modestly upbeat tunes, until arriving in Xavier's driveway. They then each hit his small travel pipe that would only yield 2-4 hits maximum.

"I'm known as a lightweight amongst my smoking friends," Xavier shared. "I'm 5'9 and I only seek a different perspective when I get a buzz, not interested in being fucked up. A nice high has me feeling about 6'0 tall, just enough to tweak my perspective. So the only way I can ensure I don't get too high is by never taking two hits back-to-back unless I'm already familiar with the smoke, know its potency, and I am somewhere safe."

If Felicia disagreed with Xavier's philosophy she didn't let on. Probably because it was his smoke, she acquiesced. So they sat there for about ten to fifteen minutes enjoying sharing a high while joking and laughing. Eventually Felicia asked if she could have another hit. Xavier was somewhat preoccupied with getting Felicia back to her car early enough to not cause her problems with Mikaela. Knowing that the pipe was probably down to its last hit, Xavier having no interest in going inside his home to get more, and not wanting her too high when he returned her to her car, proposed they share the hit.

Xavier then took the last hit of the pipe, leaned over towards Felicia where they aligned their mouths so that their lips could lightly prevent the smoke from escaping, and Xavier passed the hit to her. In retrospect, their lips touched more noticeably during their hello greeting than while sharing a hit. After completing what is known as 'shot-gunning' a hit, they yakked another moment then Xavier drove her back to her car, where she exited with a silly smile on her face.

"Thanks for a fantastic evening." She said.

Xavier responded prophetically as well as cleverly, "Goodbye Felicia."

Somehow after returning Felicia to her car, and receiving a 'thank you' text the morning after, a year and a half later Xavier was defending himself against an accusation that he exhibited inappropriate behavior with this grown-ass woman. Never mind that she lied and said they had smoked outside of the restaurant instead of in his driveway at home. Upon sharing the oddity of her lying about such a trivial detail with a mutual acquaintance of theirs, Xavier was told that Felicia may have lied to avoid another bout of domestic abuse.

More so, his time with Michelle and Felicia was now being packaged as Xavier preying on Jr. faculty. Seriously, it's impossible to make this shit up. Xavier thought that his being accused of preying on Jr. Faculty was as much a reach as the last so-called woman that would come forward during his investigation.

Jayne

It was September 2011. Dr. Witt was leaving campus when he saw Jayne Boyer walking through the parking lot. Jayne was a college junior, about 5'4, 130lbs, an ex-student of Dr. Witt's from multiple classes, currently serving as a Teacher's Assistant in his Romance, Sex, Love, & Marriage course, and White. Jayne was a Psychology major, strong writer, with an intellect she enjoyed flaunting, occasionally mindful of it being oppressive towards those less capable than her. Jayne's large intellect inflated her self-esteem, which contributed to her believing she was mature beyond her years—when she wasn't. Jayne was emotionally immature, though it wasn't easily discernible.

Pulling his car over towards the curb to get close enough to personally acknowledge Jayne, Dr. Witt extended a greeting, "Hey Jane."

Not surprised he went out of his way to say hello, Jayne replied through an enormous smile, "Hey Dr. Witt. Things are good with me. I'm just ready to relax now after a full day of activity. Where are you on your way too?"

"I'm on my way home to assemble a new desk I bought," he replied. "Considering how inept I am at doing such things, I'm not in a hurry to get home just to be frustrated."

"I'm actually good at assembling things," said Jayne. "Need some help?"

"Wow, really? Dr. Witt replied. "You would actually help me? You do know that I live 20 min away from the college. Considering it's 6:07pm now, the round trip travel time to get there and back, and the desk assembly time, which could easily be another hour or two, I may not get you back to campus until around 9-10pm. You have that kind of time available?"

"To hang out with you and help you, of course," she replied, unselfishly.

"Are you hungry?" he asked. "If so, for helping me and considering I'm hungry too, we could grab something to eat and take it to the house with us, if that works for you?"

"That sounds fabulous," she answered.

"Then hop in, let's do this." Minutes later they were on their way.

Arriving at Dr. Witt's home after picking up their to-go order, they decided to eat first before assembling the desk. 25 min later they were both sitting on the floor of the guest bedroom surrounded by parts and hardware. Before they had started assembling the desk they decided to indulge themselves with some marijuana. Xavier had already heard it through the grapevine (his student network) that Jayne was a smoker. Knowing that beforehand, he offered her some smoke to further show his appreciation for her helping him. By the time they started assembling the desk they both had a very nice buzz, though each of them had only taken one hit.

The desk assembly took approximately an hour between unceasing attempts at wit and incessant laughter, probably very much related to the buzz they both had. Jayne definitely knew her way around assembling things. Without her it would have taken Xavier twice the amount of time, if not more. Upon completing the desk assembly they returned to the kitchen, where Xavier then announced it was getting late and he should return Jayne back to campus. Upon hearing this she told Dr. Witt she needed to use the restroom which resulted in her leaving the kitchen. Upon returning a couple of minutes later she found Dr. Witt seated at the kitchen table watching the television with the volume down so the music that was playing would be discernible. Without any hint of it about to happen Dr. Witt realized Jayne had returned from the restroom when he found her two hands on his shoulders, deliberately trying to massage out whatever stress could be found within them.

"You look like you could use a massage," said Jayne.

For a moment Dr. Witt considered saying no, but instead appreciatively said, "I wouldn't turn one down." Then Dr. Witt teasingly added. "Do you have a license or references?"

"No, but if it doesn't feel like I know what I'm doing I can always stop," warned Jayne.

"You obviously can stop anytime you would like. However, what's good for the goose is good for the gander. So, after you finish it is then my turn to reciprocate. Cool?" Dr. Witt asked?

"I would enjoy a massage from you," Jayne replied.

From that point onward, Jayne massaged Dr. Witt's upper back, shoulders, and neck for 10-15 minutes. When she finished they changed positions and Dr. Witt then massaged Jayne's upper back, shoulders, and neck for 10-15 minutes. During both massages there was no talk. Some music was playing in the background throughout both massages but if anything about the evening made it more special it was the comfortable silences while being massaged. Nonetheless, when Dr. Witt finished reciprocating the massage previously given to him, they left Dr. Witt's home to return Jayne back to campus.

A week later while preparing for his RSLM course an energetic Jayne, a T.A. for that class, presented Dr. Witt with a poem that she said she wanted to share with the class. Unpacking the messages in theme related poetry or music was how Dr. Witt began many of his classes. Dr. Witt, knowing how well Jayne writes, asked her did the poem she desired to share fit the current theme of the class, which at that time was Romance. When Jayne asserted it did, Dr. Witt blindly approved the poem, trusting that Jayne, with prior T.A. experience from another of Dr. Witt's classes knew what the expectations for poetry were.

While the T.A.s usually facilitated discussions unpacking film clips and song lyrics that began the class, Dr. Witt read all the poems at the beginning of class. However, most of the time he had chosen the poem, and had time to read it. Jayne's spur of the moment request to share a poem was unprecedented. Nonetheless Dr. Witt went ahead and shared it with the class.

An Impassioned Tete-a-tete

I struggle awaiting your arrival
knowing the odds are not in my favor without you having to actually say it.
I recognize that at best we could be friends with benefits
Friends who genuinely care for one another
I want to know your pain
share it with me
even during any overwhelming emotion, or shared sensuality
because we intuit one another
we are memorialized in perpetuity,
Sexually I'll rehabilitate you flawless friend
Even acquiesce or succumb to adultery
though confused about where we are headed
along our clandestine course
it twists and turns
while unhealed scars make sure I learn
we are malleable
blemished essences in harmony
with no bread crumbs to lead us back
Time with you altered my perception
leaving me incapable of delineating devotion
though what we could have transcends time
the ardor will never be forgotten
even though you have departed
Au revoir, delectable challenge
No assignment will ever rival you
Au revoir

When Xavier completed reciting Jayne's poem, and the students unpacked it for its romantic worth, Dr. Witt approached her during the class break.

"Phenomenal poem Jayne," complimented Dr. Witt . "Students were into unpacking it."

"I was inspired when I wrote it," Jayne said, accentuating her statement with a wink to Dr. Witt.

Dr. Witt almost had a heart attack when Jayne confirmed his suspicion that the poem was a tribute to the evening they shared last week. Xavier exhaled deeply, ecstatic that he hadn't shared a sexual moment with Jayne, though wishing now that they hadn't even spent the evening together. More so he regretted even the harmless massages that may have meant more to her than they obviously did to him. Pulling himself together he knew he needed to regroup so that Jayne wouldn't be insulted for extending what was obviously an over-the-top compliment. He thought to himself, it could have been worse. She could have pulled a Glenn Close in Fatal Attraction, claiming "I won't be ignored." Though the difference in that film and this real life situation was that Xavier and Jayne not only didn't have sex, but they also didn't kiss.

This is why Xavier resisted temptations to seduce or succumb to the temptation of having sex with his students. As a grown-ass man who prided himself on his approach to sex, as well as the sex act itself, he doubted if the average 20 year old student could keep her perspective after a sensual evening with him, especially if her experience was limited to young men her age. Having never had an attraction to Jayne, the massage with her wasn't tempting at all. And not just because it didn't occur on a bed. Nor because it didn't involve any sensual body parts. It was because if he were a peer of Jayne's, her walk, talk, and air of superiority would not have been enough to motivate him to lobby for time with her. Especially in contrast to some of the other young women that would have gotten his attention even more because they were more his type.

The fact that seven years later Xavier would discover Jayne joined the other women in accusing him of inappropriate conduct—again, from one lone evening seven years prior—was the epitome of a reach by the investigators. It should be expected though since they were looking to not just determine but establish that Dr. Witt was a perpetrator of sexual misconduct.

What had Jayne experienced that evening that warranted her framing his conduct as inappropriate, especially considering the poem she wrote that celebrated the time they spent together? As well, how could anyone believe the story of a woman who not only wrote such a poem, but then also continued to T.A. the remainder of the semester?. If she had been physically accosted or disrespected in any way she had chances to distance herself from Dr. Witt as well as report it. Sure, the fact that she may have stayed on to receive the academic credit wasn't missed by Dr. Witt. Also, knowing that what is often said in defense of women who don't come forward is that the power deferential silences them. However, Xavier had an even bigger argument in support of his innocence. If anything had actually occurred with Jayne that left a bad taste in her mouth, why would she one year later once again serve as a T.A. for the RSLM class, only this time knowing she wouldn't be receiving any academic credit for it.

More so, what could possibly make Jayne claim that Dr. Witt had removed his penis, taught Jayne how to hold him, and subsequently encouraged her to masturbate him, which she claimed she did. She would tell investigators they didn't kiss, nor remove clothes during the massage, but for some reason Dr. Witt unzipped his pants to free his main man and decided to introduce him to her. Beyond the oddity of reporting any of this seven years later, considering the romantic poem she wrote about the evening that gave no impression of disdain, or approximately one year after their only shared evening Jayne approaching Dr. Witt to repeat as T.A. for the RSLM class, this time for no credit, none of it made sense.

If Xavier had wanted to have sex with Jayne that night he could have. Her after-the-fact poem confirmed that. The fact that he didn't have sex with her is the reason why he had problems with her later. She felt rejected by him. So she became distant and dastardly. Rejection by Xavier caused her to become a post-Reconstruction white woman, fully embracing her racial privilege by suggesting "nigger" without having to say it. Part of the reason she may have done this is because she may believe that Black people are overtly sensual and desirous of white women far beyond the pale or at least compliant with the image of the pale-faced White woman as the symbol of beauty in a country of people fearing Black men's sexuality.

She knew, relying on being a white woman--to suggest and through the power of suggestion—she could facilitate a story wherein once again as the far-too-often vanquished vixen is totally in-the-right to reframe a gendered exchange with a man. Xavier knew it was the epitome of abuse of gender privilege, simply because the current zeitgeist allowed her to do it.

It became apparent to Xavier, in a moment of clarity, like an American slave whom would do most anything to acquire power for the privilege of using it, women lacking power might be apt to use it, if not abuse it against someone deemed their oppressor.

Oppressors posture high moral ground because doing so is how they preserve their power and privilege. Those seldom situated as disadvantaged have the ability, if not the privilege of projecting more composure just as it is easier to judge people who have been frequently—if not systematically—oppressed as angry, or paranoid. The MeToo movement flips all of this on its head, yielding women the ability to overcompensate overcoming oppression and yet leaves some not mindful enough with their newly acquired power to avoid becoming oppressors themselves. As well, just as it doesn't make sense to believe that "all" women come forward and report, or should report, there are at least "some" women who come forward and report with an agenda.

There must be something imagined about Black people that prevents some non-Black people from seeing them as equals, thereby making it easier to not consider the humanity of the individual. Otherwise how can anyone justify playing a part in taking away someone's livelihood? How does a college reframe its negligence, its ethical responsibility to protect a man who gave his heart and soul to campus and community?

It became apparent to Xavier that perhaps he was to blame for everything that occurred to him. His inability to interpret the motivations of many around him left him quite vulnerable. His scrutiny of a *certain type of White woman* would always be incomplete until some significant consideration were given to what type of man he himself presents, regardless of his intentions.

One Evening

Alone at last, no teens around, house to themselves. Prearranged, well coordinated, the evening itself was a study in contrast. Xavier was known to be this thorough in many things he did, most when considered important, but he would never be shy admitting that sometimes shit goes wrong. This evening seemed to be counter-evident to any rising paranoia within Xavier. He and Sandy were in a nice place to enter a nice space before they planned on sharing a more intimate taste, when suddenly....

"Did you hear something?" Sandy asked, anxiously.

"I heard something," confirmed Xavier. "Probably just Vetha though. She often just drops by and outside of seeing her as one of my TAs, she's overdue for some quality time with the fam."

"I wanted to know enough to determine whether I should sit up,"Sandy said, sitting up, "or continue slouching at the kitchen table as if I live here."

Slightly smiling as if about to attempt a witticism that everyone could probably guess would eventually be said he went there anyway. "In a town of two, living under the laws of 1870 whereby you didn't even have the right to vote, whereby my vote and all my decisions would be final, I vote for continued slouching ."

"Are you fucking serious," laughed Sandy. "Was that supposed to be seductive. Dr. Diversity & Social Justice will prepare me to ensure I'm readily available for the male gaze, accessible at his convenience. Wow! Are you an ally?" she asked tongue in cheek.

"I'm an unadulterated ally, but you can just call me 'Truth.' Now, remove your tongue from your cheek and perhaps I'll answer you," Xavier affectionately answered while trying to get away with also admonishing Sandy. "I was just being silly, with my guard down completely, but now realize I can't walk intellectually naked around you," he said, sounding vulnerable. "Too revealing! My bad!!"

"You could probably get away with walking around intellectually naked," Sandy said, with an inviting shift in her body, "if you had been actually naked immediately prior, and I reaped benefits from it."

"I'm wondering, when I double gulp from a comment like that can you tell," Xavier asked. "Besides, who's being objectified now?" Xavier challenged, feeling a smidgen empowered to defend himself from what he interpreted as a lazy socially unjust comment—if not in context—from her that rivaled his.

"Who's naked now?" chimed in Vetha, to the surprise of both Sandy and Xavier. Having just arrived home Vetha couldn't resist pretending she had not heard her Father.

"In terms of our spirituality you must be poised to say all of us if one of us doesn't say it before you," answered Xavier.

"How did you know Dad?" asked Vetha so rhetorically she could have kept the question to herself. "You know me so well," she added.

"Your birthday is one day after mine, mine is one day after my Mom's." Xavier replied. "I know you as much as my Mom thinks she knows me. Hmmm, Xavier said contemplatively, "Perhaps I don't know you."

They all burst into laughter. It was easy to laugh when the mix had Sandy, Vetha, and Xavier. Vetha is Xavier's daughter, at that time 22 years of age and an extremely personable young woman. She was very intelligent, artistic, creative, athletic, beautiful and bi-sexual, though by this time she was more a full fledged non-lipstick wearing lesbian. She only met Xavier as far as she could remember at the age of 16 when they had finally reconnected after an over 15 year absence.

"Woman, are you high?" Xavier asked his daughter.

"Perhaps slightly?" she answered.

"Like a little pregnant," he replied.

"Yes, like first trimester," Vetha answered, knowing she had outwitted him.

"Aren't you the witty individual," he said matter of factly.

"One of us has to be. I nominate you since of the two of us I'm never going to be called Dr. Witt, while you repeatedly are," Vretha said convincingly.

Xavier knew he and Vetha could go back and forth all night. So as he often would do he quit while he was behind. Decisions on how friendly to be with your children are never easy. For Xavier with his two youngest whose lives he had always been in, it was a piece of cake because trust and a never ending rapport existed between them. With Vetha it was more difficult due to only recently reacquainting with her. The affection that a father and daughter might have wasn't naturally there between them, though in her first seven months of life he was actively participating in her life until her mother took her and left the state of California, relocating somewhere in the Pacific Northwest. In Xavier's mind it was a sordid case of "hell hath no fury like a woman scorned." After she swore she was taking birth control, after declining to be the family this older woman wanted them to be, after Xavier volunteered to make child support payments and made them, after he refused to let another man adopt Vetha while knowing he was being asked to relinquish his parental rights as punishment for rejecting her, Vetha's mother left with their child and no clue where she was for fifteen years, only to resurface later.

Xavier and Vetha shared a powerful Leo vibe, which is only necessary to explain to people who aren't Leos. And it isn't anything similar to a Sagittarius vibe or a Taurus vibe, beyond the fact that we're talking goat, bull, and lion. Duh!!!" he thought.

"What are you two doing tonight?" Vetha asked. "Let's go downtown!" She suggested.

"I'm cool with that," contributed Sandy.

"Let's not," said Xavier. "For me, that's just asking to have a front row seat to witnessing a number of alcohol-breathed young men and women reverting back to their adolescence as a result of being inebriated. What's fun in that for me."

"Oh Dad, it's not that bad," urged Vetha.

"Oh really, it's not?" Xavier parroted back at Vetha. "Then that one evening I was downtown by myself and was approached by two drunken good old boys who told me they didn't like how comfortable I appeared to be, essentially taking umbrage with me doing my own thing where they could see me. They accused me of thinking I was special. And all I had been doing was existing in my own world, quietly sitting at a table doing work on my IPad."

"I never heard that story Xavier," said Sandy, concerned.

"Sorry that you had to go through that shit Dad," said Vetha.

"You and me both V," Xavier replied.

"Okay, let's find some positive energy. I'm making margaritas, who wants one?" asked Sandy. 75 minutes and two martinis later, everyone was incessantly yakking when not happily laughing. Vetha left the room to take a phone call. By the time she returned Xavier and Sandy had relaxed even more and were full from having eaten too much and bleary eyed from imbibing too much.

"We're off to bed V," Sandy said as Vetha returned to the kitchen. "I have an early morning."

Picking up a camera that was sitting on the table Vetha attempted to slow their roll by appealing to Sandy and Xavier's vanity. "We have spent an entire evening together and haven't snapped one photo," she said. "It's picture time."

Xavier replied as he and Sandy exited the room, "Unless you plan on taking sexy photos of us there will be no pictures tonight, V. Goodnight," he said, slowing their exit down long enough for both to lightly hug and kiss her.

About 15-20 min later, after making love, Sandy whispered in Xavier's ear something very different from the things she often says, "You were not serious when you invited Vetha to take photos of us, were you?"

"You're not serious about the question you just asked me, are you?" Xavier asked Sandy, in disbelief that she would disrupt their flow by mentioning his daughter of all things.

"I'm only asking because there was a moment when I could have sworn she was in the room, taking pictures," Sandy stated with uncertainty. "I thought it may have been my buzz making me see things. I wasn't sure since it was so dark and we were preoccupied. I also didn't freak because it happened so quick while we were both under the covers for the most part in that always too cold bedroom of yours, but you may want to ask her. If she did, please get those pics," she beseeched Xavier.

"First thing in the morning, I'll do just that," Xavier said. "I'm too exhausted to have a conversation tonight, especially if you aren't positive."

Sandy thought to herself, I wish I wasn't positive she was in the room, and happy I'm not positive she actually was snapping pictures."

Peculiarities of Seeing and Being Black

Every time Dr. Xavier Witt exits the U.S. to enter Quebec on his way to Montreal he exhales, subconsciously experiencing nirvana. The micro-aggressions if not blatant racism that accompanies being Black in the U.S. are daunting. For example, when Xavier moved to Peru, NY in 2000, while looking into places to live, he was told by an elderly White woman that he was " a very nice colored man." Xavier was surprised that she didn't just say "a very nice man," and had to ask himself if she said it out of an expectation that he was not going to be nice because he is African-American. However, he decided, as the newly arrived director of diversity at NYSU-Peru, not engaging it at all was probably the best course of action.

As a Black man directing diversity for one of the largest employers in the area Xavier had heard that he frustrated some of the North Country Blacks due to his seeming under-serving of the African-American community. Interestingly enough if he hadn't strategically approached implementing diversity broadly the allies he has relied upon to professionally thrive—and yes—survive in this region may not have seen him as an ally, and therefore may not have become allies of his. President Obama experienced something similar when trying to be inclusive of Republican perspectives to the chagrin of Democrats. He also experienced some aspects of being considered by some Black people a sell-out for not meeting their expectations of what he would do, could do, and/or should do for Black people specifically, once in office.

Xavier always wondered why—since racially (not necessarily culturally) Obama is as much White as he is Black—didn't White people have an expectation that Obama would do something extra for them as well. For that matter, the biracial community in the United States, perhaps even globally may have had their own expectations too. After all, though they haven't coalesced as one voice yet, depending upon how much of a percentage different blood is necessary to so-called dilute one's Blackness, Whiteness, LatinXness, Asianness, or Indigenousness, the biracial people in our societies and world, who as much as anyone understand how it feels to be a problem, perhaps even more than most, could benefit from a political voice. Xavier had wondered before if Obama and Tiger Woods, both golf aficionados and biracial Black men, had ever carved any time out to discuss what that must have been like for two of the most recognized partly-Black men in the world. Perhaps engaging their intersectionality was a bridge too far.

Like a nigger...

Approximately a year prior to the NYSU-Peru "*Lynching Niggers Tonight*" drama a small gathering at OPIE of Xavier's female Teacher's Assistants asked him "Dr. Witt, do you only date women that are doctors?"

On occasion he had been asked something equivalent to whether he only dated White women. This time he answered, "Most (not all) of the women I've dated since becoming single I've met on Match.com. I was not very aggressive on Match.com so most of the women that noticed me--with the patience to read my lengthy profile--just so happened to have graduate degrees, if not their doctorate. It was not, however, a stipulation or set criteria on my part."

Searching their faces to see if the answer he gave was sufficient enough, Dr. Witt decided to continue, "I actually wonder if your underlying question, the one you would have preferred asking was 'do I only date White women?' I field that question often, almost as if in this region female doctors and white women are coterminous. In case that was on your minds, or buried in your subconsciousness, last I checked Black, Latina, Asian or Indigenous women aren't moving to the upstate New York in droves. If so, I never got the memo, nor know where they are meeting."

"Additionally," Dr. Witt continued, "contrary to the touted liberalism of Canada, a high preponderance of Canadian women, like those in often considered progressive Burlington, Vermont, do not even list Black men amongst their online dating preferences. Fortunately, the two women from out of the area I dated, one past, one present, are from different countries (New Brunswick, Canada & Morocco, North Africa) and both initiated our first Match.com conversations. One's ancestry was French Acadian with a heightened sense of social justice from the history of cultural oppression from the British. The other, now my fiancé, interestingly enough in appearance looks White, but enjoys telling me she is as African, if not more, than most African American women I have dated. Nonetheless her experiences as an Arab physician in northern Quebec better introduced her to her 'otherness.'"

"I'm so happy you shared that with us, Dr. Witt," said Yesenia, one of the best young minds Dr. Witt ever engaged in one of his students, with a socio-politically charged voice that demanded attention. "In both cases you shared it seems as if these women were able to relate to your struggle. It is too bad that there are rumors and people insisting that you as a Black man prefer White women over women of your own race."

"'It's too bad' is putting it mildly Yesenia, believe me," Dr. Witt replied. "It's no fun—to say the least—being framed as suffering from internalized oppression or self-hatred for seemingly preferring non-Black women. I now understand the frustration Jerry Seinfeld experienced when he said, "I've been 'outed' and I was never in.""

"Did I ever share with any of you the time, after giving a public presentation in the area, I received an email admonishing me for saying

'We should love our students up,' when I was only speaking in terms of supporting them?" Dr. Witt asked the young women, rhetorically. "Though my use of students was all-inclusive I was nonetheless told—if not actually reprimanded in the email—that it was inappropriate for me to use ;bedroom language.' I was incensed."

"As anyone with common sense would be," replied Yesenia. "You should have suggested they read scholar Angela Davis' "*Myth of Black Sexuality*" and "*The Myth of the Black Rapist*."

"Agreed," replied Dr. Witt, "especially since both articles challenge perspectives of Black sexuality propagated during American slavery from overtly sexualizing, and far too often brutalizing, black bodies."

Yesenia added, "They also speak to a fear of reprisal against racially privileged Whites resulting from their person-owning privilege and awareness of the sexual abuse they far too often visited upon those undervalued Black bodies."

"People by nature are not politically correct. As a result, sometimes they say whatever the fuck they want to say," Dr. Witt asserted. "For example, at a recent event attended by a Who's Who of the North Country and beyond, Kesi and I were told, with no hesitation, that a woman's husband treats her "like a Black person." We were flabbergasted. Oddly enough years ago while living in Los Angeles and attending a dinner party and the only Black couple there--My wife (a Black woman) had to endure a woman telling her, "My husband thinks he can treat me "like a nigger." In both cases I had to resist asking them to explain exactly what they meant."

Xavier never fully came to terms with what was meant by being treated '*like a nigger.*' Eventually he surmised most White people wouldn't think it is complicated being a successful upper class Black person. Besides not knowing any more about Black culture than Black people know about Jewish, Asian, or Mexican American culture, why would a White person be invested in learning the culture. This of course makes it easier for people outside of other's cultures to buy into myths, gossip, and legend while on the outside looking in. Some Whites in predominantly White communities who have bought into the myth of money buying happiness, are oblivious to the age old rhetorical aphorisms, 'What was a free Black person called in the times of slavery,' or 'what do you call a black person with a Ph.D.,' or 'what do you call a wealthy Black person,' or 'what do you call the Black president of the U.S.?' The answer has never changed, *'a nigger.'* The answer itself is an *inherited ideal,* like Independence Day. Few people question the existence of a free holiday anymore than they would daily expressions, until given a reason to consider them differently. In the North Country of New York, Dr. Xavier Witt was living with the complexity of no one wanting to be treated *like a nigger.* Far too many people don't bat an eye when the term is used in similar skinned company, with Dr. Xavier Witt being constantly reminded that-- more often than not--he was the only one, in many people's minds, that resembled one.

Xavier remembered first moving to Peru and not being able to shake his anxieties. Though he had lived in White communities before, the North Country of New York was still new territory. It may be easy for people to not pay serious attention to someone being alone, especially at a distance. When we are the one alone, or when we are one of the others who are marginalized because of our similarity to a group, it can hurt. However, there is a huge difference between being alone and being "the other," especially in terms of context. Xavier found himself constantly grappling with what happens to the person who is alone and "the other?" He wasn't accustomed to being alone when living in Southern Calif. He liked people, people liked him. His adolescent neighborhood was full of people who looked like him so his loneliness up to that point was never connected to his race. His loneliness initially stemmed from having an intense speech impediment from childhood until fourteen, while being excessively short until sixteen didn't help. These two dimensions of his identity taught him to appreciate people's struggles and to offer assistance the way he would like help extended to him. However, it wasn't until he left the confines of his predominantly Black neighborhood and entered a society disinterested in who he was or what he had to offer that he would begin to learn how it felt to be treated *'like a nigger.'*

CHAPTER FIVE
- *The Lack of Subtlety in "Lynching Niggers Tonight"*

"Today class, as a result of last week's SnapChat incident, it may seem as if you were assigned lynching articles to align our historical journey with current events that hit close to home. However, that is not the case, so let's quell the scuttlebutt. We're unpacking the not-so-subtle obviousness of lynching today because we are still in pursuit of our class theme, African-American culture today is unfortunately still a response to slave culture," Dr. Witt said, looking to see how his students processed his statement.

"Dr. Adjapong," Dr. Witt said, "please read the first passage assigned as homework." His referring to Edmund as Dr. Adjapong immediately got the class' attention, especially since Edmund was only an undergrad, though obviously an exceptional one who had made everyone in class aware of his higher education aspirations.

Edmund picked up his book and began reading:

"More than 500 persons stood by and looked on while the Negro was slowly burned to a crisp. A few women were scattered among the crowd of Arkansas planters....
Not once did the slayer beg for mercy despite the fact that he suffered one of the most horrible deaths imaginable. With the Negro chained to a log, members of the mob placed a small pile of leaves around his feet. Gasoline was then poured on the leaves and the carrying out of the death sentence was under way....

As the flames were eating away his abdomen, a member of the mob stepped forward and saturated the body with gasoline. It was then only a few minutes until the Negro had been reduced to ashes.... –
Memphis Press, Jan. 27, 1921.
This is how an eye witness described the lynching of Henry Lowry.

Upon the completion of Edmund reading the excerpt Dr. Witt then asked the 30 students in his "African American Culture class, "Who was Henry Lowry?"

"He was a victim," contributed Victoria, a bi-racial female, senior.

"He was a Black man born in the wrong era," added Joey P, a Biracial male, senior.

"He was a man accused of making an error," said Kayla, a Biracial female, junior.

"He was poor, and black, which combined made him not just a nigger, but guilty," Kate, a White female junior, offered.

"He was Henry Lowry to his family," Edmund added, "a Negro sharecropper to some whites with humane perspectives, and unfortunately just a nigger to most others in Nodena, Arkansas."

Ray, one of only two White males in the class said, "Lowry was a man who for two years had worked his ass off, only to never receive one single cent of what he rightfully deserved. So at the time of his death, his murder, he was probably a recovering angry Black man, transcending his ego because he already knew he had no true recourse."

Dr. Witt then added, "So then the next question is culturally, as ancestors or allies, should we say his name, individually and collectively? If so, why? If not, why not?"

"We should say his name Dr. Witt. If we don't, then we further perpetuate the possibility of it never truly being said," explained Natalie. "It is important that we articulate, emphatically, that he existed once."

"Why would his name not be, or not have been said, Natalie?" Dr. Witt asked.

"Because he apparently didn't have any means to defend himself, including supportive voices from whatever Black community existed in that area at that time, if any. As a result, at best he may have had friends and family that spoke about him when off the beaten path, or away from any path where they could be beaten for insinuating anything problematic about powers that be."

Dr. Witt then asked the class to take a quiet moment and imagine the fear that visited the average Black person, knowing they were vulnerable to White people's whims, similar to the Dred Scott decision which essentially stated a Black person had no rights a White person had to respect.

After a minute Dr. Witt interrupted with a question. "What was his crime? Edmund, you got this?"

"You bet. The article says:"

He went to the landlord's house and demanded wages. The landlord at first looked at him queerly, a if he did not understand what he had heard. But when he understood that one of "his" sharecroppers was actually asking for his wages, he rose in insane fury, cursing and beating Lowry with his gun. Then he leveled his revolver at Lowry's head, and fired, wounding him. Enraged at this dog-like treatment, Lowry began to fight back. In the fight the landlord was killed.

"So his crime was defending himself," Kate suggested.

"His crime was being an uppity nigger," Kayla offered.

"His crime wasn't being an uppity nigger, said Joey P. "It was stupidity for even thinking he could get away with talking to a White man like that."

"So let's continue with the story. Ed, what's next?" asked Dr. Witt.

As soon as this became known, the white landlords for miles around became obsessed with one idea – to torture and lynch this Negro sharecropper, to murder him, so that not another Negro worker on the plantation, not one of their own starving tenants dared to protest, as Lowry had done, against the brutal exploitation of the landlords. To refuse to starve, to refuse to be robbed. These were the terrible

"crimes" for which Lowry, Negro farm worker, was burned at the stake – lynched by the landlords and their henchmen. This is how the white ruling class attempts to subdue any opposition to its merciless exploitation of the Negro people.

"So was the plight of the Negro hopeless?" asked Dr. Witt.

"Yes," said Natalie.

"No, not for those born into slavery. They knew nothing," answered Damola, a Black male senior.

"No, they could run away, they could head north," offered Kayla.

"What must this have done to the Negro's self esteem?" asked Edmund.

"What self-esteem?" asked Sam, a Black male, junior. "How could any such thing develop in people who were consistently shat upon?

"Shat upon? Are you from England?" asked Damola, unable to suppress his laughter. "Seriously, I agree with Sam. "Remember, in this period the White man had no limitations on how far he could disrespect so-called Negroes."

"Like when we watched '*The Journey of August King*,' in which the Black runaway slave was cleaved in half after being hung upside down at the town's celebration," Darren said, "for having escaped with the favorite female slave of his master, who sexually desired her even though she was his daughter."

"That's some sick shit" said Bashir, an Arab male, junior.

"Perhaps. Or you can just call it slavery," said Edmund.

"What period did the White man not have limitations? Since when have Black lives ever mattered," asked Donna, a White female, senior.

"XW, I have a question for the students. Are there any historical scars passed down from their ancestors plight?" Edmund asked.

"Yes, hatred of White people every time these stories are revisited," responded Taylor, a Black female, junior.

"Wow! Does that include those of us in class who are your allies?" asked Ray.

"No it doesn't Ray." replied Taylor. "But you understand how deeply this cuts for Black people."

"Dr. Witt, it cuts deeply for White people too," Ray said. "The people doing all the dirt to Black people look like me."

"Touche Ray, touche!!!" replied Dr. Witt. "What else do you have for us, Ed?"

"I'll read the next passage Doc, but first I want to say that I feel you Ray. I have the same anxiety when we are discussing gender oppression in the Diversity class accompanied by film clips like 'Boys Don't Cry' and 'Courage Under Fire.'"

Having made a provocative point that hopefully had the students all reflecting on their roles as allies, Edmund read the next passage:

Southern liberals had begun arguing that lynching was a form of working-class violence that threatened bourgeois rationality and state authority. A fully modern system of law and order, liberals argued, was necessary to contain the irrational violence of the poor. With the implementation of state anti-lynching laws that threatened to punish law enforcement officers who participated in mob violence, some state officials agreed to expedite the trials and executions of blacks accused of defying Jim Crow racial order.

"Did you discover anything new from this passage," Dr. Witt asked the class.

"I never thought lynching was a poor White man's response to being equated to Blacks," said Damola. "I guess wealthy White men wouldn't be caught getting their hands dirty."

"Or maybe they gave the poor Whites direction as to who needed to be lynched," offered Janelle, a Caribbean female, senior.

"This fucked up shit occurred the same year as the Tulsa Race Riots, two years before Rosewood. So I'm surprised to hear there actually were laws in place to at least theoretically protect Black Lives," said Sam. "I know that the Sheriff in Rosewood wasn't held accountable for lynchings under his jurisdiction."

"XW, I'm going to read the next passage," said Edmund. "It may add something to the conversation, if not clarify some things:

But these trials, communists argued, amounted to lynchings even if "mobs" followed legal procedures. The movement to free the Scottsboro 9 thus popularized the term "legal lynching," a phrase that emphasized what was already present in the rhetorical history of the word lynching: that it was a form of establishment violence that supplemented the diffuse and ambiguous powers of policing. In 'Lynching: A Weapon of National Oppression,' Haywood and Howard used the term "courthouse lynching" to refute the legalistic approach of the anti-lynching campaigns undertaken by the NAACP. Though the Association's director, Walter White, recognized the economic dimensions of the violence (he wrote in his 1929 book, Rope and Faggot: A Biography of Judge Lynch, that lynching "has always been the means of protection, not of white women, but of profits")

"I never thought of lynching as 'a form of establishment violence that supplemented the diffuse and ambiguous powers of policing.' Interesting, in a painful, twisted way," offered Donna.

"It seems as if they're saying the trials were a moot point," pondered Kayla. "The lynchings were going to occur because Blacks weren't receiving fair trials, anyway."

"Don't sleep on just because lynchings were articulated by Walter White as a 'means of protection of profits, not White women,' that they didn't string a brother up for looking at a White woman cross-eyed," offered Dr. Witt.

"Like Emmett Till, though he was beaten to death, not lynched, for allegedly whistling at a White woman." Mark added.

"Perhaps lynching is the ultimate metaphor for a Black life meaning far less than a White life," said Ray.

"Wasn't it Supreme Court Justice Clarence Thomas who labeled his nomination a high tech lynching? asked Marquis, one of the older students in the class who took his education quite seriously.

"It was," answered Dr. Witt. "Why do you think he called it that Marquis, or anyone else for that matter who knows a bit of that story and is willing to speculate?"

"Perhaps," Marquis responded, "because he felt an unfair spectacle was occurring that would have only happened to a Black person, with Whites ultimately deciding his fate."

"Perhaps," Dr. Witt answered. However, what is important to gain from the excellent contribution made by Marquis is that lynchings still occur, or their metaphorical equivalent. Disempowered Whites or Whites who feel disenfranchised still gain power from knowing they can implement certain strategies against Black people to gain the desired results, which is often not just leveling the playing field, but creating an imbalance in their favor. Think about it. Even with videotaping by cell phones catching dirty cops doing dirty deeds, there are still far too many Black deaths at the hands of White law enforcement."

"On some level—though he wasn't hanging from a tree—Eric Garner was lynched," Ray said, "dying from being strangled from an illegal choke hold that might as well have been a rope."

Before the depth of Ray's statement could be fully absorbed Dr. Witt noticed Marquis' hand up, and a stern look on his face. Dr. Witt nodded in his direction to indicate he had the go ahead.

Marquis said, "I have a quote XW, but want to contextualize it relative to what our mentor is currently going through."

Dr. Witt was caught off guard with this verbal display of affection. He wasn't naive enough to think what was currently occurring on campus with his reputation wasn't affecting his students, but he definitely wasn't interested in converting his class discussions into a three hour session about him. Nonetheless he saw the class in its entirety assenting with Marquis that they needed this conversation. So, he humbly assented to Marquis.

"Thanks Doc," Marquis said appreciatively. "My quote is:"

***Other lynchings result from the refusal of a militant Negro worker or peasant to submit to every kind of social abuse and persecution. The lynchers themselves have admitted as some of the reasons for lynching, the following: trying to vote, accusing a white man of stealing, testifying against white men, being too successful, talking back to a white man.
— Haywood & Howard, Lynching***

"Excellent quote M," acknowledged Dr. Witt. "How are you using it?"

Marquis responded, "I want the class to help me unpack it within the context of what you are experiencing on this campus. In our study group this weekend we were obviously talking about your situation. Reading all of these post-reconstruction articles, many of them featuring lynchings, the parallels just couldn't be missed."

"Or ignored," added Donna. "I was in the same weekend discussion with Marquis."

After three other students revealed they were also a part of that same group, Marquis then said, "So I'll start by telling you we feel as if we're standing in the front row of an *academic lynching*. We know we are your crew and may be biased in our opinions, but we'll let the class be the jury if you'll be the judge.

Dr. Witt recognizing his class had just gotten hijacked, relented, saying, "Okay, do you."

"Well, to reiterate the first line in the quote:

Other lynchings result from the refusal of a militant Negro worker or peasant to submit to every kind of social abuse and persecution.

"We see you as the militant Negro worker, Dr. Witt. The work you have done on this campus and in the community, as a Black man with an unwavering voice, has undoubtedly pissed many people off," Marquis said. "You call people on their shit."

"I want to add to that the fact that we have heard that your career may be in jeopardy because of how your responded to Shalo Kloos' wack-ass allegation that she heard you disrespect women," said Tamarah. "The *academic lynching* you are undergoing parallels the above quote precisely because of your refusal to submit to Kloos' personal attack in front of 700-800 people, or as the quote says, social abuse."

"The flyers in the college center are evidence of persecution," Sam said. "No one believes that shit. The timing of flyers like that immediately following her accusation was just way too convenient for anyone with common sense."

"Well shit, on that note," Edmund chimed in, "the faculty meetings initiated by the Student government scrutinizing your job performance also reflects the persecution the quote speaks to.".

"If it is true that you have threatened to sue the college, I read this part of that quote:

The lynchers themselves have admitted as some of the reasons for lynching, the following: trying to vote, accusing a white man of

stealing, testifying against white men, being too successful, talking back to a white man...

...where the lynch mob justified one of their reasons for lynching as a Negro having the audacity to accuse a white man of stealing," Mark clarified. "I interpreted your lawsuit as you defending yourself against them stealing your reputation, if not usurping your career, which is why you are being *academically lynched*. Does that make sense class?"

"It makes sense to me," answered Donna. "The next part of the quote is "testifying against White men, which obviously would be President Utley, maybe even other non-male members of the lynch mob, since we have heard that Feminist Anthropology and Title IX are very much implicated in this too."

"It could even include NYSU if they support this move against you," said Bashir. "I was focused on the talking back to a White man part of the quote as similar to accusing a White man and testifying against him. So-called Negroes back in those days should have known better, and unfortunately your bodaciousness may be viewed similarly."

"Doc, everyone on campus knows that you are a rock star, what with your book being made into a movie and you speaking everywhere. So you may also be too successful for many of the haters on campus who probably smile in your face, all the time wanting to take your place," said Joey P.

Dr. Witt was struggling fiercely to not have his face flooded with tears. He couldn't believe how thoroughly his students had thought about his predicament. Upon reflection, he could believe it, easily. In all of his classes he consistently challenged students to think outside of the box. He realized he was reaping some of those benefits now.

"We're not done yet, Dr. Witt. We have one more quote that we felt really paralleled your situation," said Marquis. "Sam, you got this?"

"On it," Sam replied.

What is behind all this legal lynching? The answer has been given by Governor Ross Sterling of Texas. In January of 1932, Barney Lee Ross, Negro boy, was executed after a trial which took less than two hours. In denying stay of execution the Governor said, in words which no worker, Negro or white, should ever forget:

"It may be that this boy is innocent, but it is sometimes necessary to burn down a house in order to save a village."

This statement brazenly admits two things. First, that Negro workers who "may be innocent" are being murdered not for any crimes, but to "save a village."

We're not sleeping on any of this Dr. Witt," Sam warned. "The irony of our biggest vocal advocate on campus--a Black man in a position of power, who stood up for himself when unjustly accused--who is now center stage and alone on that stage seems, well, staged. How did *"Lynching Niggers Tonight'* become your *academic lynching*? You are being lynched to 'save a village,' that village being the presidency of Ian Utley. Seriously, Dr. Witt, this shit is surreal."

"The quote asked what is behind this legal lynching. We imagine there is a lot more than meets the eye here," said Kate.

"And at this moment in time I'm not at liberty to disclose too much to you, though I appreciate your concerns," Dr. Witt revealed. "I'm still trying to figure out how I want to approach this."

"Well, on behalf of the class please let us know what we can do Dr. Witt. We've already signed petitions, and written letters to the administration," said Marquis.

"I appreciate all the effort you all have expended on my behalf. It means so much to me," Dr. Witt replied, trying to fight off his emotion from the emotional support he was receiving from his students. Now, go home so I can cry alone. Class dismissed."

After literally hugging each one of his students as they left class, Dr. Witt arrived at his car an emotional mess. Sitting in silence he knew he had just entered his own personal *Twilight Zone*. On some level he had become Henry Lowry, the man who was lynched in Arkansas in 1921, for being too audacious. What was that quote that Edmund had started class off with:

He went to the landlord's house demanding wages. The landlord at first looked at him queerly, a if he did not understand what he had heard. But when he understood that one of "his" sharecroppers was actually asking for his wages, he rose in insane fury, cursing and beating Lowry with his gun. Then he leveled his revolver at Lowry's head, and fired, wounding him. Enraged at this dog-like treatment, Lowry began to fight back. In the fight the landlord was killed.

Like Henry, Dr. Witt had gone to the landlord's house (president's office) demanding wages (assistance from an unfair allegation further promoted by his Title IX office). Utley couldn't believe Dr. Witt had the audacity to threaten a lawsuit. His response was not cursing, like the landlord in the quote, but adamantly insisting Dr. Witt '*tone it down*' while his reputation was being dragged through the mud. The difference between Henry and Dr. Witt is that Xavier wasn't shot at, or wounded, literally. However, enraged at his treatment by this so-called leader, Dr. Witt fought back and is still fighting, with an end goal of not killing Utley, but exposing him for the duplicitous culprit that he is. After all, how exactly does a SnapChat post threatening *lynching niggers tonight* actually become the swan song for a Black CDO.

In his own review of the readings for class, he had stumbled on a poignant quote from one of his favorite scholars, bell hooks, which he decided to memorize, knowing it may come in handy.

"All black people in the United States, irrespective of their class status or politics," according to bell hooks, "live with the possibility that they will be terrorized by whiteness."

Knowing that FA and Title IX had moved against him in ways they could justify as ethical and moral, Xavier was left with an idiom ringing in his head, 'one country's patriot is another country's terrorist.'

Inherited Ideals - Racism as just a way of the world

As an academic who always emphasized through education the value of diversity & social justice education, an antagonist in the eyes of many, Dr. Witt was professionally inclined to push back on scholar bell hooks sentiment for its lack of inclusivity. Living with being "terrorized by whiteness" as much as one is capable of doing it, Dr. Witt would prefer to hear "most people" live with the possibility of being terrorized, not just Black people. People often probably wondered why this Black man's preference was to frame the often unique problems of identity politics in a more universal way. Dr. Witt's approach challenged people to focus on the intersectionality of their identities in a never ceasing effort to find/better develop allies. His approach to doing diversity & social justice work centered around developing allies this way. Dr. Witt was considered a community builder. Ironically, the fact that Dr. Witt endeavored to be inclusive ultimately created the situation he was incapable of extricating himself from.

There is no doubt Dr. Witt's perspective was fueled by his Blackness, a blackness that can't be separated from his surviving growing up in Los Angeles/Southern California. Xavier's perspective was tweaked by his spending most of his summers in the city of his birth, Tulsa, Oklahoma. His perspective was broadened by being an avid reader. His perspective was heavily influenced as the middle child between two strong willed girls, and more so, being the second child of four, raised by a single parent, his mother, the incomparable Yolanda Witt-Nett. Xavier's perspective may have been adversely influenced by something he wished he had. His natural father's absence from his life throughout his adolescent years gave him insight into how having an absent parent--for reasons of divorce or abandonment--feels. To a precocious child who could have used another parent, especially a male role model, divorce and abandonment or two sides of the same coin, absent father.

Xavier's perspective on women couldn't avoid being influenced by his father's rumored exploitation of women after his divorce from Xavier's mother. Xavier's father was twice incarcerated, serving his time and returning to some semblance of life as a Black person. In a very unforgiving time for Black men--the 60s in Los Angeles--Xavier's twice convicted felonious father eventually became a permanent loss, by murder.

As life would have it, Xavier would have the good fortune of a second opportunity at a father figure, one who represented the epitome of any notion of honor and authenticity within fathering. His mother's marriage to Ivory Nett, helped positively reframe fatherhood for him. Instead of immediately determining his very successful step-father's life as something unattainable, eventually after years of subconsciously seeing himself as a pawn in an already determined game of chess where seemingly the Black pieces' fate were already predetermined, Xavier figured out that all these mitigating influences aside, only he could define him.

This story offers an array of perspectives not just that of the protagonist, ranging from pearls to tidbits, both easily deemed relative. A seeming tidbit of no consequence would be that Dr. Witt enjoys being called Xavier instead of the formal "Dr. Witt" because he's convinced people don't transition from using a title to using a person's first name without some type of cognitive dissonance, perhaps due to the hierarchical consequences it suggests. He believed people eventually exhaled in relief of distancing themselves from titles, becoming less entrenched in socio-political class posturing, less entitled to fake a funk that really can't be faked. He enjoyed authentic exchanges, not posing, or even political correctness for political correctness' sake.

Dr. Witt embraced a few principles but none more so than "*perspective is the objective*." Both as a young man living in SoCal and later as a college professor/educator/consultant he realized that the key to getting people's attention to teach them anything was including them in the teaching moment as equal partners. All interactions in life can be framed in ways better understood if we only found and took the time to do it. He realized 'conversation(s) unpacking perspective(s)' or 'CUP' as he often referred to it, could be enticing enough for people to take a sip. CUP was unique in that--when facilitated well--it couldn't avoid being entertaining, informative, communal and considerate, and always offering an environment of unpacking perspectives through differing lenses, especially considering our multiple identities.

Dr. Witt often argues that perspectives are funny things in the ironic sense of funny, though always potentially funny in the "ha, ha" sense of funny too. Ironically, our perspectives are shaped by emotions we can't always control and situations/stimuli that often are impossible to fully understand, yet we hold onto our perspectives as if they are infallible. How can this be? It can't and Dr. Witt spent most of his professional life trying to convince his students and audiences that they know, logically, that their inherited perspectives, at the very least, should be challenged. Nonetheless, emotionally, spiritually, and often Dr. Witt will say, socially on so many levels we all just live out the life we were born into, further perpetuating inherited ideals.

Dr. Witt being a Black man may give people the impression that what was happening to him was only about race, and/or racism. Arguably, just as most dysfunctional situations involving identity that occur within the United States of America seem to be connected to racism and/or socio-economic class/capitalism, this sordid tale of political factions on a state college campus on so many levels transcends race and class often, but not enough to omit them.

Dr. Witt recognized that he was on a journey like no other he had ever experienced. Some people have the experience of being grossly in the minority in terms of their race, socio-economic class, gender, age, ability, religion, sexual orientation, or other defining characteristics that don't come readily to mind. Some people are oppressed by societal constructs like colorism, professional jealousy, envy, and prejudice. Some people live their lives out of fear of others different from them, anxiety about their performance, and paranoia seeded within their personality from never receiving positive strokes from approving adults. And regrettably, some people live their lives never unpacking their inherited ideals.

Arriving in the North Country of NY as one of the few Black men, not only in the city of Peru but one of the few within the entire region, the pop culture phrase "Dorothy, you aren't in Kansas anymore," became even more relative. Dr. Witt never anticipated how often he would be the only Black person dining in a restaurant, sitting in a bar, shopping for groceries, attending the movies, and unfortunately, serving as the subject for scrutiny, object to be ostracized, or person to be the community's problem.

Peru, New York, the city that is the home for NYSU –Peru is what Dr. Witt had heard would be a place that would smile at him as if he was welcome to be there. One person had cautioned him to never get too comfortable because the serenity that would be presented to him would only be a façade. He would never be welcomed into the pseudo faculty club. This became an evident truth when after spending what essentially was a lifetime working/living in the North Country of New York Xavier could count on one hand how many so-called friends and/or associates homes he had actually been invited into. Xavier, self aware enough to recognize that he himself wasn't extending many invitations to his home, he knew this type of thought wasn't productive. The city itself, the people of Peru were very cool and easy to interact with. But it wasn't happenstance that the connections he had to the academic community of NYSU-Peru felt nothing like the relationships he had developed within his immediate community with his neighbors Glen, Joe, Rob, and recently deceased but forever missed cigar smoking Jay, as well as Mary and Butch down the road. Remove race from the equation these community bonds were profound enough to provide Xavier with a sense of serenity. Nonetheless, underrepresented people always endure extra burdens from 'sometimes' inadvertently not being considered. This brought to Xavier's mind one of W.E.B. DuBois' most provocative quotes:

It is as if white people are driven by a colonial desire to possess everything. Du Bois asked, "But what on earth is whiteness that one should so desire it?" He answered, "Whiteness is the ownership of the earth forever and ever, Amen!"

While unhesitatingly embracing some of DuBois' quote as germane to his situation on campus, he couldn't attribute everything he was experiencing to race alone. No doubt his race contributed to the way some of these women saw him. He also knew his social class, misinterpreted by many as Black privilege--as if such a fragile thing could exist as long as Black lives didn't matter--was a contributing factor. Unfortunately he knew he was in for the battle of his life. Some organizational leaders conveniently convince themselves that their perspectives (often inherited) need not be checked.

Many so-called allies are clueless that at the very least they should self-reflect upon their privilege and/or ethic. Instead they comfortably look for a rope and a tree to hang it from.

Xavier couldn't reveal to anyone, especially his students that Utley had been grossly negligent in protecting him twice, at least not until he had legal representation. First when Xavier was initially attacked by Feminist Anthropology in 2009-10 and then while still under Utley's watch, they revamped their efforts to character assassinate him with an end goal of removing Xavier from his position. It brought to mind the Davis quote:

"In the history of the United States, the fraudulent rape charge stands out as one of the most formidable artifices invented by racism" (Davis, 173).

While no one had accused him of anything beyond 'disrespecting women,' he knew the whispers could easily morph into some sinister accusations.

CHAPTER SIX
- *The Useful Idiot*

To incite the white workers against the Negroes and to further build the myth of "white superiority," the white ruling class has coined the poisonous and insane lie that Negroes are "rapists." -- Haywood & Howard, *Lynching: A Weapon of National Oppression.*

"It is my immense pleasure," proclaimed Mark Sanders, the NYSU-Peru alum and ex-Student/TA of Dr. Witt's, "to introduce you to Dr. Xavier Witt, professor, author, mentor, consultant, columnist, community leader, ally, fraternity brother and most importantly big brother. Please bring your hands together, or at least find your jazz fingers and snap them to help me welcome Dr. Witt to the microphone.

As he approached the microphone Dr. Witt was honored to be introduced by his young blood Mark, who was consulting to the Canadian schools and somehow landed on a committee that brought Dr. Witt to speak. Xavier Witt imagined--from the briefing he received prior to creating the contract to facilitate a discussion with the Canadian Association of Principals--that the problems they faced within their organizations were probably about perspective. The diversity & social justice tensions that existed were the reasons why he was officially solicited to "engage" this particular audience.

Stepping up to the podium, Dr. Witt surveyed the room with a smile, acknowledging with a head nod a familiar face, acknowledging someone else with a wink and a smile. Adjusting the microphone as he began his speech, Dr. Witt asked, *"Are we limited in what we see in one another by preconceived expectations?"*

Pausing as if awaiting a response, he asked, *"Why might we be incapable of seeing the parolee as simply someone who got caught in a mistake that we ourselves got away with?"*

Without taking a breath he continued, *"Why can't we see the police officer as possibly more caring than many within the community he policeses. Perhaps it is because we are unable to imagine his intellectual or spiritual investment in social justice or unabashed love of humanity and sense of fair play? Why don't we see the homeless person as someone who lived a lifestyle similar to ours before a lost job or death of a major provider?"*

Pausing for dramatic effect while posturing as if he wasn't, Xavier continued, *"I recall thinking it was provocative to hear New York City Police Commissioner Bill Bratton's eloquent eulogy for the two murdered NYC police officers in 2014, Rafael Ramos and Wenjian Liu. He captivated my attention with words that still have not left my mind."*

"Bratton's paradoxical declaration — "We don't see each other" — still reverberates throughout my consciousness. Bratton further pushed his point beyond that excellent sound bite."

"And maybe that's our challenge...," Bratton continued.

"Maybe that's the reason for the struggle we're now in — as a city, as a nation…

"Maybe it's because we've all come to see what we represent instead of who we are."

"We don't see each other."

"The police, the people who are angry at the police, the people who support us but want us to be better, even a madman who assassinated two men because all he could see was two uniforms, even though they were so much more.

"We don't see each other. If we can…

"If we can learn to see each other ... to see that our cops are people, like Rafael Ramos and Wenjian Liu, to see that our communities are filled with people just like them too.

"If we can learn to see each other, then when we see each other, we'll heal.

"We'll heal as a department.

"We'll heal as a city.

"We'll heal as a country," Bratton said.

Looking away from his notes and back towards his audience Dr. Witt returned to his own voice, *"Bratton's comments bring to mind that often we take short cuts while articulating truths that perhaps shouldn't be abbreviated. Instead of all of us seeking profound reasons and/or responses to Bratton's statement "we don't see each other," we instead offer inadequate and/or weak responses like "it is because we see what we see."*

Xavier then asked the audience, *"Is that your excuse too? If so, then on some level, we can all do what the historical if not biblical figure Pontius Pilate allegedly did relative to owning any responsibility for the crucifixion of a reputed savior and just wash our hands of any and all episodes that threaten to get our hands dirty."*

Allowing a pregnant pause to give birth Dr. Witt took a measured sip of a water he pulled from beneath the podium, then he continued. *"People attempting to "be real" would probably answer:*
"We don't try," or "We were somewhat taught not to look," or "We somehow learned that if it is not like us, or not good for us, it must be bad or bad for us."

With an admonishing tone Dr. Witt leaned as far across the podium as he possibly could and sternly whispered into the microphone which of course still effectively projected his message,
"Just because we haven't tried doesn't mean we can't try. If we think about the fact that our world would be so much more pleasant, cooler, if everyone tried to see themselves in others, discovering energizing similarities, how invigorating that would be. If you look, you may really enjoy what you see. If you look, you may one day, along with others, see yourself in someone."

"If you don't look, your risk is minimized but so is your reward."

"Getting in the habit of not seeing people, not looking at them for their value, only makes sense if you are blind and incapable of seeing them. Even then, the blind attempt to sense others."

"We were all spoon-fed lessons about one another that we choose to continue to embrace. We need only to admit that these inherited ideals are not ideal at all. Learning to fear and believing that a certain amount of fear is both healthy and necessary for our survival only paralyzes us."

"Growing up in South Central Los Angeles, I was taught by my Mom to consider people good until they act badly. However, in the streets, I was taught that White people thought they were better than me—not just because they were white, but—because they weren't black."

"I was also taught that "two men loving one another was sinful," "a person in a wheelchair was not whole," "larger people overindulge," "smaller people overcompensate," "really smart people think everyone else is stupid," "people who think they have lower IQs are intimidated by people they think are smarter than them," "the wealthy are paranoid that those financially struggling would rob them if they could get away with it," and that "the impoverished resent feeling like charity cases."

"Commissioner Bratton was right. For the most part, we don't see each other. And won't until we look, and I mean really, really look."

"When we actually begin to see each other, we may be on the verge of hearing each other and finally ready to feel one another."

"In closing, take with you this thought from Philosopher John Stuart Mill:"

"He who knows only his side of the case, knows little of that...But if he is equally unable to refute the reasons on the opposite side; if he does not so much as know what they are, he has no ground for preferring either opinion. The rational position for him would be suspension of judgment, and unless he contents himself with that, he is either led by authority or adopts, like the generality of the world, the side to which he feels most inclination"[28].

"John Stuart Mill--in the 19th Century--was calling for a heightened level of consciousness, mindfulness, and consideration of others, challenging our inclination to only see what we see. As you leave this auditorium be mindful of the fact that what we see in others is constrained only by the limitations of our consideration."

"I appreciate your attentiveness to my thought. Thank you!!!"

The audience's response to Dr. Witt's speech was wildly appreciative, erupting in a standing ovation. Xavier surmised that the speech was probably so well received because it was timely. In the age of President Donald Trump--or Resident Rump as Xavier often referred to the United States' elected leader--celebrating if not promoting the thought of John Stuart Mill, an inclusive-minded White man as a way of closing out his keynote was a good thing, even with a Canadian audience. After all, there are no roads that one can take that will enable them to avoid an impending collision with Resident Rump.

Immediately following the cessation of the applause a lengthy line formed of audience members with an interest in having a moment with the keynote speaker. Dr. Witt was accustomed to being approached by an audience emphatically trying to discuss this, that, and other things with him. As a speaker Dr. Witt had learned how to shorten the time with unavoidable audience members who lacked concern for others also wanting to acknowledge the merits of the keynote. As he prepared to be on top of his game, determining his way out of any of those conversations that might unfold he was completely disarmed by the first person's comments.

"Dr. Witt, I really enjoyed your speech. It made me wonder if you ever read Garren M. Grafe's article, "TRUMP MUST BE A RUSSIAN AGENT; The Alternative is too Awful?" It somehow brought to mind the message of your talk tonight, that "we don't see each other."

Xavier, while not expecting a comment anything like that, especially from a Canadian, was fascinated with it. As soon as he got into his car and had a chance to google and then read the Grafe article on Resident Rump he did. One of the quotes sounded more like it was speaking specifically about President Utley. He considered whether he should send the quotation to the lackluster leader, as he read it aloud:

"Either the president is compromised by the Russian government and has been working covertly to cooperate with Vladimir Putin after Russia helped win him the 2016 election—or Trump will go down in history as the world's most famous "useful idiot..."

Somehow Xavier's mind had immediately done a word replacement, situating the quote in an Utley context:

"Either President Utley is compromised by the Title IX office and has been working covertly to cooperate with Feminist Anthropology after they both helped him overturn his vote of no confidence, or Utley will go down in history as the world's most famous "useful idiot."

Though Xavier decided against sending it, his mind nonetheless wandered, thinking about the fact that Utley has been a pawn of any group with momentary political clout or requiring political expediency, for years. The

Black students bullied him, almost into submission, during the 2015 Pigeon Messages incident. This culminated in him punishing the student editorial staff to the point of public ridicule compounded by demanding their resignations. It wasn't politically expedient for the university to see the editorial staff as students who made a mistake, in this case, a huge mistake. However, it shouldn't be confused with a mortal sin. A firm wrist slap to get their attention would have sufficed. Instead the student editors were made to feel like they had conspired to cause a racial ruckus.

The Feb 2018 Black students reacquired leverage once more with the *'Lynching Niggers Tonight'* snafu. They successfully bullied Utley again, only this time into total submission at a level where he was even worse off after they finished than he was before he started today, and he was previously in horrible shape.

Standing in front of his home, facing an angry mob, Utley was referred to by many not-so-flattering names (Old man, Stupid, a Joke, Grandpa, were some of the kinder terms used to address him that day) in varying tones (yelling, an assassin's whisper, academically critical). At one point during the process Dr. Witt considered interceding, but then decided not too. He imagined it may come off as the Black man having to rescue the White campus leader from a Black mob. He imagined further that it might emasculate Utley, if he even had anything remaining to castrate. The Black students that responded to the *"Lynching Niggers Tonight"* snafu in February 2018 were no better to this aged feckless leader, who many speculated should have been put out to pasture a few years earlier--than the White mob was to Elizabeth Eckford of the Little Rock Nine during the school integration crisis. And then, after the Black mob of angry as well as opportunistic college students verbally undressed Utley (leaving anyone who witnessed it thinking it was "once and for all), they unabashedly passed the baton to the Student Government, subsequently washing their hands of its implications.

Xavier's mind was racing so fast he realized he needed someone to talk with. Who better to talk to than his Oomboogalah, Kesi? He decided to text her first, and include within the text an article that they could discuss when they talked.

A Criminal and/or a Useful Idiot

"Hey, what you doing?" Xavier asked Kesi, as she answered the phone.

"Hoping to see you tonight. Montreal becomes Malone without you."

Smiling, Xavier replied, "Look at you! Saying what you need to get me a speeding ticket tonight. You're making me think of a Platonic quote that fits us in this moment of missing one another.

"What is it, Oomboogalah?" Kesi asked, eager for an answer.

"Okay," Xavier answered, "I think I remember it:"

And so when a person meets the half that is his very own...then something wonderful happens: the two are struck from their senses by love, by a sense of belonging to one another, and by desire, and they don't want to be separated from one another, not even for a moment" -- (Plato 20).

"Oh, my man is so romantic." Kesi proclaimed. "Who else memorizes poetry?"

Xavier always interested in sidestepping hyperbole, replied, "Only thousands of other romantics Baby. But I'm feeling you," Xavier said, flirtatiously.

"Come feel me in real time," Kesi responded, flirting back.

"Now you know we always say business first Baby, especially considering that since we aren't together it makes no sense to work ourselves into a froth."

"Oh, look who is talking," Kesi replied feigning indignation. "Where are you anyway?"

Xavier responded, "I'm on my way to Newfoundland's airport. Why? he asked.

"You know why?" Kesi answered.

"No, seriously why?" Xavier insisted.

"You know why?" Kesi persisted, while blushing.

"Okay, well then, anyway…" Xavier began to say but was cut off by Kesi.

"Anyway?" Kesi said trying to suppress a chuckle, "Don't you anyway me."

"Seriously though Oomboogalah," Xavier said, "I was thinking about Utley, and that for the court case we somehow have to communicate to our attorneys some specific things about his history or disposition so that they can begin to see him as the weak leader so many on the campus fully recognize him as such. The fact that NYSU Central doesn't see him that way is literally unbelievable."

"It's ironic too. How can the central office of one of the biggest public university systems in the country be negligent in monitoring a questionable leader they themselves confirmed," asked Kesi. "Isn't he the one responsible for a multimillion dollar budget deficit."

"At the end of the day, yes, the responsibility is his," answered Xavier.

"Baby," said Kesi, "None of us live in a vacuum. Utley knows about MeToo and the women's empowerment it represents. He was probably soiling his pants until his vote-of-no-confidence got lost in the shadow of your rumored 'disrespect of women,' your emotionally spent 'fuck that' to the campus audience, and your pushing back against ridiculous and unfounded allegations."

"I agree Kesi," replied Xavier. "Utley was well aware that the collective consciousness across the country had finally become liberal, leaning towards overcoming, as well as inadvertently overcompensating women for eons of gender oppression."

"As a survivor, you know my affection for the MeToo movement," Kesi said. "However, MeToo shouldn't have bred Him-Too, and it has."

Xavier nodded his head in agreement, adding, "And the justification for the small two-to-ten percent of men who are falsely accused or caught up in MeToo's momentum is more than some statistical collateral damage. It could be the end of the world for some of those men. It's two to ten percent of men that are falsely charged. Nonetheless that small number of men are having their reputations marred and their livelihoods lost, anywhere from partially to permanently. As a result of MeToo men around the country are dropping like flies. When it is deserved, so be it. However, it fucks me up that I'm one of those statistics now. Since College presidents have been under scrutiny as well--perhaps a bit more than usual with social media playing its part in any and all assessments--I shouldn't have been surprised that Utley would make me the sacrificial lamb he would throw under the bus to distract others from the fact that it really should have been him. However Baby, knowing it's all fucking smoke and mirrors doesn't make it hurt any less."

"I just finished reading that article you texted me a few moments ago Oomboogalah, on Trump as *a useful idiot*. You are so right in that without squinting you can see Utley in it," Kesi said. Beginning to read Xavier something she said, "I saw him in this quote:

"That's where we'll ultimately learn the truth about which scenario we face: an incredibly hapless and easily co-opted president—or an active criminal conspirator."

"Wow," exclaimed Xavier. "Great quote. I see it through my lens, but at the risk of sounding rhetorical my love, I'm curious as to how you apply it?"

"I was hoping you'd ask. If you hadn't I would've offered. It was his responsibility--as leader of the college--to protect you as much as any other professional on the campus, maybe even more since you are technically in a protected class. So his negligence should be a legal concern."

"Or at least 'could be' a legal concern," Xavier added.

"And his requesting an investigation on you that in his heart he knows isn't right is criminal."

"How so, Baby?"

"He's removing a vital resource, depriving students, many of whom may have come to NYSU specifically to study with you, from having an experience with you during campus visits or even Student Orientations. And his haplessness comes in not knowing he is being manipulated by Mothburn, Dewar, and the Student Government under the influence of Dewar's close friend, the newly elected SG president's leadership. The fact that he conspired with NYSU-Peru's Title IX office is dwarfed by his investigating you because you asked for an investigation of Linda and Mothburn, and years earlier asked a few times for a recusal of the Affirmative Action officer, because of gender bias, exacerbated by your race."

"Shit, perhaps I don't need an attorney. You could represent me."

"I'm always representing you Oomboogalah. I'm your fiancé, remember?" said Kesi mockingly, soon to be your wife. Besides, you know I come from a background in law."

"I know Baby, I know." Xavier reaffirmed, rolling his eyes though she couldn't see him.

"Kesi, it would be horribly embarrassing for Resident Rump at this point if Robert Mueller were to declare that the president isn't an agent of Russian intelligence. He then would have no excuse for having been an idiot. It would also be embarrassing for Utley if the Chancellor stayed asleep and never declared that Utley is a pawn of Title IX and Feminist Studies, in conspiracy with some attention seeking young women who know how to play him. That would make him a criminal for participating in a nonfactual smear campaign and corrupt investigation. If we deny he is a pawn, a moveable chess piece, then his decisions are all self made, and pathetically idiotic. Possibly not as much a minion as some may have imagined, but nevertheless in a panic, especially to save his ass, capable of throwing anyone and anything away. When he is stressed, it's all expendable. After all, whether or not they choose to give him the benefit of the doubt, he has been acting like it's the state's money, not his.

"An example of this is his eradication of OPIE. The parallels to Trump never end. Just as Trump came into the White house determined to erase any memory of Barack Obama, Utley has taken down a part of the college that was vibrant for over twenty years, so as to not have to face any memories, any daily shame of his dirty deed. Utley allowed, if not covertly directed OPIE staff to move without being replaced, didn't restaff OPIE, that he wrote a fat check for amidst the 2015 budget crisis, to save his ass from angry Black students. OPIE and its classes did more than anything coming out of the President's office, but slowly their dismantling some of the best practices we had on campus. The students who came through OPIE and its classes have a deep, penetrating connection to NYSU-Peru. Who is Utley really connected to? What's his legacy?"

"Breath baby, breathe," Kesi said encouragingly. "You're slipping into 'angry Black man' mode. Don't let a cowardly White man with only a posturing commitment to diversity & social justice get you going like that."

"It's not just him, it's the system too," Xavier said emphatically. "After he fucking did irreparable damage to the college the Chancellor's politically-correct ass believed what this coward said, sight unseen, even considering an 8 million dollar deficit, and chose to look the other way. Instead she got involved, choosing to support him instead of stepping into a leadership moment and just having a conversation with me. Instead of picking up a damn phone he'll have a retirement party to thank him for what, not fully sinking the ship?"

"You're not big enough Baby. And that would be too student-centered, too right a move. They would prefer to strong arm you with veiled accusations, feeble accusations, and the financial power of their privileged position."

"Well, anyway, I'm not angry. Just woke. See you soon Baby."

After hanging up from Kesi to park and hustling to catch his plane to Ottawa, to then drive to Montreal, Xavier thought that what the assemblage of people at the vote-of-no-confidence forum witnessed was an emotionally exhausted professional no longer able to maintain his cool, especially recognizing in real time that a conspiracy was unfolding amongst people with an agenda to remove someone that had become unpopular with some of them for reasons like sexism, their assertions that a man shouldn't be teaching subjects they felt were in their domain only. And the racism wasn't as veiled as they thought it was.

Utley revealed his racism early on by not responding to Xavier's cries for assistance. Thinking about Utley's negligence, Xavier got nervous when he was unsure whether or not he had the emails he had written Utley, that Utley never responded to. While waiting to board his plane he went through his old emails, feverishly looking and hoping he would find the email he recalled writing, explicitly asking for Utley to intercede on his behalf. He was elated when he found an email addressed to Utley. Hoping it was the one he was looking for he blocked out the rest of the world, and read it:

From: "Xavier Witt" <wittxw@peru.edu>
Date: February 15, 2010 at 8:05:33 PM EST
To: Ian Utley<UtleyI@peru.edu>
Cc: "Latrice Wiggins" <wigginl@peru.edu>, Helene Savoie <savoieh@peru.edu>, Malcolm Thomas <thomasm@peru.edu>

Subject: *Dysfunctional Relationships*

President Utley,

After much consideration I am approaching you to request that the affirmative action officer, Brenda Maims, be removed from the case she is facilitating regarding an accusation of my creating a "hostile environment" for two students, Dick Satton and Lacey Lyer.

I understand that the affirmative action officer appointment is one that is carefully considered and while there is nothing easy about requesting her removal, I think my request is consistent with the university's need to have someone in the position who will represent fairness. It is my contention that Brenda Maims is not ideally suited to assess my case for the following reason, I don't believe I can receive unbiased due process from Maims because of her prior and perhaps close affiliation with Feminist Anthropology (FA).

Years ago, Maims as affirmative action officer facilitated the only other complaint I have experienced in my 10 years of working here. It was an accusation of sexual harassment that was voiced, but never officially advanced. The details of the accusation we can discuss later but somehow that accusation has lingered with certain people, who in all actuality should not have been in the know at all. One of these people is Sharon Winchell, a professor in FA who I will be filing a complaint about soon. Recently, (Nov '09) Winchell posted this comment on my blog site /Wandering Witt/ under the topic heading "Girl Talk" in response to the ongoing conversation.

*I cannot discern much of a difference between verbal gossip and blog gossip. Your palpable disrespect for the "business owner," as well as your widespread reputation for disrespect toward, harassment of, and sexually predatory behaviors against women, makes the question of whether you call us girls or women a mere attempt to distract us from your more insidious, and infamous, misogyny." -- Sharon Winchell

She later followed this comment up with an apology, of sorts...

*I apologize for impetuously and inappropriately bringing up your reputation on your blog. Whatever my motives, your speculating about them does not change that reputation; only your words and actions towards women can transform your rep. -- Sharon Winchell

Winchell's public assassination of a colleague on unfounded charges notwithstanding, her assertion that my "widespread reputation for disrespect toward, harassment of, and sexually predatory behaviors against women" didn't just appear out of nowhere. While I don't know exactly where it came from, I am not comfortable with Maims conducting an investigation on me with her affiliation to Feminist Anthropology, especially when other factors are considered. Yes, I wouldn't be surprised if the information leaked out of the affirmative action office, or in veiled manners certain insinuations about my so called predatory behavior were discussed amongst the FA faculty. It isn't hard to imagine if someone actually believed the accusations how they might want to not only avoid that colleague, but also protect their students. I would feel the same way about someone I viewed uncharacteristically. As a matter of fact, that is exactly how I feel about FA faculty after all of this. The difference is, I have continued to take the high road. I responded to Winchell's blog posting, but never once publicly denigrated her and wouldn't be filing the complaint if not for the odd resemblance between her post and the students closing comments in their complaint.

The plot thickened when, after viewing a controversial film clip in my INT 426 Romance, Sex, Love, and Marriage course, the chair of FA, Ramona Saphony had a viewing of the clip in question and a lengthy discussion of my pedagogical decision to show the clip. There was no collegial exchange or announcement of this screening of my clip in her class for their discussion of my decision. There was no appropriate context established for their discussion. From what I understand it amounted to a public lynching without me present to wear the noose.

I want to file a complaint with you that Brenda Maims, Sharon Winchell, and Ramona Saphony have all exhibited various degrees of racism in the context of unflinchingly and brazenly putting forth the /myth of the black rapist/ at my expense to their students, two of whom then turned and filed a complaint that ended with this comment:

"Also, the fact that our male professor finds no fault with the coercive actions of the professor in the clip from Storytelling force us to question whether he finds fault with pressuring his current female students to have sex with him"

How do students come to that conclusion knowing nothing about me or my history of an /almost accusation/ unless it is being fostered, somewhere? Seriously, how would it make you feel knowing you were being character assassinated for something that is totally contrary to who you are and what you believe and represent? If someone would have told me that this is how mature, professional women mentor and educate their students I would have never believed it. I guess I'm the one a bit naïve here though, because in terms of the real world and a college's similarity to it, I should expect this level of immaturity. After all, professional jealousy/racism are as real as the scars that might contribute to people making these accusations.

The more significant point for this discussion is, are we serving our students best by allowing any form of character assassination amongst faculty to persist? Winchell and the students are articulating a party line that must exist in FA. Otherwise the common courtesy called "collegiality" that exists on the best campuses, especially with organizations that are supposed to be promoting the personal/civic development of their students in a context of social justice, would have Saphony calling me for some type of a discussion. I was always taught this is how mature individuals handle their differences.

My initial interview with Maims on this recent matter of my creating a "hostile environment" was somewhat hostile itself. Though Maims was the epitome of professionalism that day, the initial correspondence began with the burden of proof being on me. I was asked to provide my entire film corpus. Why would I do that? Who would do it, actually provide her 150 film clips when only 2 were in question. Easy way to acquire a social justice film collection, though dare I point out not so ethical.

I was asked to not retaliate and keep it confidential. Yet, somehow, prior to the email I received from Maims (dated Feb 5) I had sent an email out to Latrice Wiggins and Helene SaVoie (dated Feb 7) alerting them something along the lines of a complaint against me was brewing. Two students apprised me of this complaint against me over a week prior to it happening, allowing me to write the email to the provost and dean. So how confidential were these students?

Granted the two students are elected leaders on campus and we would like to think students who exhibit exemplary behavior, but that isn't necessarily the case. And what about the role I often play as a community leader and representative of NYSU-Peru? What about the 10 years I've given NYSU (including the injustice I persevered during the Jackson years) and years I will be prepared to give more to our campus while these students are long gone? Is it okay to put the burden of proof solely upon me? Is it okay to ultimately add this accusation to the other one from eight years ago that further leverages FA to not work synergistically with OPIE, but perhaps even systematically, albeit subtly I'm sure, undercut NYSU's very mission of creating well rounded civic minded leaders? Has anyone focused on the fact there were 43 students in the class and only two signed the complaint? And don't think they didn't try to entice others to join them.

On some college campuses presidents and diversity officers have very open lines of communication. That hasn't been the case for you and I. I have, however, been fortunate enough to have good and sometimes great relationships with many of our administration. Since we don't interact much, I would much rather our interactions come about over many of the positive things that occur on our campus or within our community. So, I apologize for my role in this type of interaction. That being said though, I'm hoping that you will respond to this email in the following ways:

__1.__ Recognize that Maims may have a conflict of interest in her inability to put into perspective the frame that FA has situated me in and therefore should not be the one investigating the complaint against me.
__2.__ Removing Maims from potentially investigating the forthcoming complaints by me against Winchell or Saphony.
__3.__ Take or recommend someone taking a leadership role in sitting down so-called educators and redirecting our energies towards what should be all of our bottom lines, the students in the center of our efforts.
__4.__ I would like someone to provide a list of students in Winchell's and Saphony's classes from Fall 2009 for possible interviews by an unbiased arbitrator to determine the extent of the damage done to my character.

Lastly, in the year 2010 please tell me that our FA professors on campus don't adhere to a double standard that promotes our female professors developing close relations with all their students while male professors should know their place when it comes to female students? It can't be a rite of passage for male faculty members to either withstand accusations of this sort for treating young women with the same respect and dignity they treat their male students, or have to treat young women who represent a group of people that have been clamoring for social justice, differently.

As the people I report to in our administration I am copying Latrice and Helene, along with Malcolm Thomas my HR rep.

I eagerly await your response.

X.W.

Knowing he had a few remaining moments, Xavier pulled out his IPad and searched a .pdf application. Something had been plaguing Xavier for weeks after first hearing the concept of "the useful idiot." He knew he had read something similar in concept by W.E.B. DuBois. Digging through his DuBois .pdf collection Xavier rediscovered a DuBois essay refuting assertions against him by Marcus Garvey--while reframing Garvey himself by placing Garvey in a no-win, either/or, dichotomous conundrum, by insinuating Garvey is either "A Lunatic or a Traitor," as the essay is titled. Perusing the essay, he connected with a quote that read as if it was written specifically about Ian Utley.

"Notwithstanding his wanton squandering of hundreds of thousands of dollars we have refused to assume that he was a common thief. In spite of his monumental and persistent lying, we have discussed only the larger and truer aspects of his propaganda. We have refrained from all comment on his trial and conviction for fraud. We have done this too in spite of his personal vituperation of the editor of the Crisis and persistent and unremitting repetition of falsehood after falsehood as to the editor's beliefs and acts and as to the program of the N.A.A.C.P." -- W.E.B. DuBois, A Lunatic or a Traitor

Xavier, being anal retentive at times, had to replace some of the text to better see Utley in place of Garvey in the excerpt. Now boarded and seated he texted himself the new rendering, or more precisely stated, the Utley version of "A Lunatic or a Traitor."

"Notwithstanding his wanton squandering of hundreds of thousands of dollars we have refused to assume that Utley was a common thief. In spite

of his monumental and persistent lying, we have discussed only the larger and truer aspects of his propaganda. We have refrained from all comment on his vote-of-no-confidence for fraudulently posing as a university president capable of effectively leading a university.. We have done this too in spite of his personal vituperation of Dr. Xavier Witt and persistent and unremitting repetition of falsehood after falsehood as to Dr. Witt's performance relative to OPIE, his responsibilities as the CDO at NYSU-Peru, while besmirching his character.

On some level, it was a pick-your-poison metaphor. A lunatic, a traitor, or a useful idiot all have the potential to be someone who can be co-opted to a cause without realizing it.

Assuming the assertion is valid that we want our leaders to be "smarter or wilier" like Trump going down in history as the world's most famous "useful idiot," Utley will have to face a reality of being at least a contender, for similar recognition as a "useful idiot" if not win the title itself.

Hours later, after the hustle and bustle of trying to not look at his watch in the middle of repeatedly receiving words of appreciation, shaking hands, and entertaining others semi-invitations to come speak to their organizations Dr. Witt landed in Ottawa. He knew he still had a ninety minute drive to Montréal, which could be made longer with any difficulties getting his bag. He knew it could be worse if he were arriving from the U.S. and had to go through Customs, experiencing the equivalent of a requisite border crossing from Canada to the U.S. The length of the drive itself was nothing more than a flesh wound compared to the time it would allow him to reflect. After delivering what he knew was a bomb ass keynote, he was feeling good from the reception his message received, great from the personal epiphanies he could see people had relative to certain comments they made afterwards, and better still from the level of clarity he was experiencing relative to some major problems he needed to reconcile. None any more so than not being able to escape the question of whether he was giving Dr. Utley the benefit of the doubt? He didn't know how others lived with their hypocrisy but he knew if he couldn't put into perspective something he had said and/or done that was an ethical contradiction it would nag at him indefinitely. And no moment across the span of his professional career was more provocative than trying to "see," to understand, to consider what makes a failed leader tick. As he was lost in thought his cell phone rang.

"Hello," Xavier answered.

"What's up my nigga," was the response he received.

"If I didn't have caller I.D. I may have already hung up on your black ass for calling me 'nigga.' The only thing worse than calling me 'nigga' is your applying ownership to the nigger status you affixed to my persona. When you say 'my nigga,' does that not designate me as a possession of your exploitative ass?" Xavier sarcastically replied, with a shit eating grin his friend on the other end of the line had to imagine was on his face.

"Listen, you know how your boy rolls when it is just me and my nigga about to go deep," Maurice announced. "I have no time for protocol. Instead, I'd rather dispense with all the pleasantries and cut to the chase. So, can a nigga get an update? How they treating you, Witty?"

"I'm good man, on my way to Kesi's apartment in Montréal, though still trying to get my arms around what would make this White cat throw me under the bus the way he so easily has."

"Who you talking about, your punk ass university president?" Maurice inquired.

"Yes." answered Xavier. "I sat with this guy for an hour every other week for over two years. Most of it was business as usual, but we would venture into different conversations, some covering pop culture, some political, even some personal. I always thought at the end of the day he was decent."

"I was always concerned with what appeared to be your unreserved acceptance of White people," Maurice said. "I'm cool with many of the ones I work with, but seldom if ever have I relaxed my guard the way you did with those Xanthochroids. I should not be surprised though. I remember those stories your Moms would tell us about you as a little boy. I remember her saying you trusted people way back then, to the point of walking away with strangers."

"That was then Mo, this is now. Growing up in South Central either kills you, intellectually maims you, or intellectually as well as philosophically provides you with survival instincts. I know the latter is my case. My job dictated that my approach be inclusive. Ironically, advocating for others' realities-- their struggles--their realities often became intertwined with mine. Hating or being overly cautious with people just because they're White was doing too much work for me. I wasn't trying to live like that."

"I get all of that XW. I really do," Maurice answered. "And I'm not trying to suggest that you fucked up, or necessarily say I told you so. But nigger, I told you so. Stop trusting these mutha fuckas. At the end of the day when the race revolution jumps off and mutha fuckas have to choose sides, who you with nigga? Who you with? I know that's rhetorical for you. I can already hear your black-ass saying something politically correct. In the heat of the moment though--when the decision must be quick--who you going to be with nigger? If the race riot is jumping off and you need help from a White neighbor, do you think just because you have shared a witticism while getting your mail or morning paper that he will be opening the door for you?"

"Have you talked to my Uncle Sayyid lately?" Xavier asked. "You sound as if you two had a meeting of the minds. He gave me a similar spiel the other day."

"Shit Negro, assuming your Uncle Sayyid is still a part of the Nation, the Black Muslims know that the revolution will not be televised. So they ain't trusting too many non-Black folk. But though I've said it once I'll say it again, if 9 mutha fuckas got yo back, I'm going to make it 10; and if you need anyone of us at any time or any where, know without a doubt that I'll be the first mutha fucka there! Feel me…"

"I feel your radical ass," Xavier said chuckling.

"Isn't Utley the mutha fucka who arrived on campus while interviewing with his wife, only to arrive when he started the job some months later with a different, younger, and more beautiful wife?" Maurice asked.

Surprised by what he just heard Xavier asked, "Who told you that?"

"You must be a damn fool if you don't realize that everybody who is somebody in your life is trying to figure out the different roles we can play to help you alleviate this situation. So yes Negro, someone told me, and who told me isn't as important as whether it is true or not. Is it?"

"I didn't see his first wife, and so I'm only going on hearsay, which considering my situation literally evolved from a rumor, I'm not too swift to endorse hearsay," Xavier replied. "That said, supposedly it is true."

"You are tripping if you are hesitating to endorse a truth that is easily verifiable in contrast to a rumor about you that, if it were true, would have cost you your job when the rumor first surfaced," Maurice said with a bit of impatience and consternation towards Xavier. Xavier, along with his ex-wife Andrea, are often touted by Maurice as two significant influences in his life. He was a bit younger than Xavier and Andrea, and they somewhat took him under their wings when they all worked for a Southern California aerospace company.

Maurice continued, "Nigger, you're a Black man in the fucking White world of upstate New York. Don't try to fly that "must be fair" shit with me. This shit is costing you your livelihood, even your life, relative to its quality. The mutha fucka playing judge and jury with you started his career with an ethical conundrum that made his leadership morally questionable from day one."

"I can't argue with that point. It could have, possibly should have been interpreted as an error in judgment on his part. In retrospect if the college had been on top of its game they would have rescinded his offer."

"You think?" Maurice said dismissively. "Utley pretended to still be happily married to the first Mrs. Utley, apparently at that time his ex-wife, to secure a job opportunity. Shit, most likely he was already married to the new wife, or at least fucking her before he arrived at NYSU-Peru.

"Negro, your ass is too agitated, more agitated than I am about my predicament."

"That's because your politically-correct ass would rather intellectualize your way around this shit. Nigger it may be time for some old school tactics. It wouldn't take much of an effort to get some pipe smoking mutha fuckas to don some ski masks and Tonya Harding his Nancy Kerrigan ass. It may not change the outcome but it would send a message to him and others that you're that nigger that they shouldn't have fucked with. You know, like back in the days of the Wild West when everybody was strapped. Back then no one cavalierly fucked with anyone because the consequences were clear. People were held responsible for their actions by threat of immediate retaliation, with street justice being the fastest gun."

"Damn, you went off on quite a tangent. You been smoking? If so, don't hide it, either provide it or divide it. It must be some good shit because you are all over the place."

"If we weren't on two different coasts I'd be over at your spot right now, putting my time in as your war time consigliore. And just like our indigenous brothers and sisters smoked a peace pipe, we may need to get right before we grab our pieces to handle shit."

"Your ass is just talking shit," Xavier pushed back. "Neither one of us, or anyone we know on behalf of us is going to compound matters more by doing something stupid."

"Bitch, I know that, but if you could get away with it, what then?" Maurice asked.

"First," Xavier said trying to hold back his laughter, "I'm not going to be your bitch too many more times."

"Then tell me my quota Dr. Witt, so that I don't leave anything unsaid," replied Maurice.

"How about we finish this phase of the conversation and transition into something else that has been on my mind," Xavier said. "I thought you were calling me back to discuss the Angela Davis quote I sent you earlier."

"I was Xdub," Maurice admitted. "I figured we would get to it, eventually."

"Well since I'm driving would you read it so we can discuss it with it fresh in both of our minds," Xavier asked.

"Certainly," Maurice replied. "It reads:"

"It has cooled (the Negro's) friends; it has heated his enemies and arrested at home and abroad, in some measure, the generous efforts that good men were wont to make for his improvement and elevation. It has deceived his friends at the North and many good friends at the South, for nearly all of them, in some measure, have accepted this charge against the Negro as true" ---- Davis, 188.

Having finished reading the quote, Maurice added, "That quote is heavy. Is that what you are thinking about your work friends' reaction to your predicament?" Maurice asked.

"To varying extents yes. My crew, family, friends, students who truly leaned into the work we do, colleagues, and ex-lovers who know how I roll have not been duped. Many of them believed in me enough to sign a petition on my behalf. Quite a few of them donated to my GoFundMe account, some with significantly sizeable donations. Nonetheless *the myth of the black rapist,* or in my case the alleged Black CDO who disrespects women was enough to have an allegation by an attention seeking group of women be legitimized by an administration without the courage to not succumb to something that eventually will cost the university, not so much just in terms of dollars, but in terms of what so many of my students have told me they obtained from the diversity initiative under my leadership. I was expecting that they would join me in fighting the powers that be. We have spent on legal fees over $60,000 thus far. I am absolutely positive that NYSU is counting on outlasting me, beginning with having taken away my salary while besmirching my reputation by removing me while under suspicion of an allegation that, if left unchecked, has me framed as a MeToo perpetrator. I have no interest in going out like that. My hope was that there would be enough outrage that I would have been deluged with financial assistance. recognizing that together we could possibly make this case a landmark case in terms of revealing women who would play the MeToo Card for their own ill gotten gain."

"Well good luck with that my brother," Maurice cautioned. "Men are running scared, trying to avoid having a scarlet letter attached to them. Like I said earlier, I'm one of many who has your back. People at NYSU-Peru are hesitant to endorse you out of fear something dark and dastardly is discovered that then would have blown up in their faces too if they publicly stand by you."

"I know that and understand their predicament too. They dug extremely deep and far back to try to find something on me, hoping more than anything else that I could be slut-shamed if they found just the right thing they were looking for. Idiots, I teach a Romance, Sex, Love, & Marriage class. I'm not a prude and don't hang out with them. So they can bring out whatever they choose to create or think they found, and I'll make the noise I must make about how they handle their business from womb to tomb, from the offices in Peru to the boardroom at NYSU Central. However, I'm not the guy who'll greet those who disappeared on me in my time of need as the father who welcomed home his prodigal son," said Xavier matter-of-factly. "I don't do the fair-weather-friends thing well."

"Nor should you, Xdub," Maurice agreed. "Because you don't roll like that you have an expectation that your crew wouldn't either. It's been said that we see the same people on our way up as we do on our way down. I'll twist that sentiment and say that the people who didn't make the time for you in your time of need, essentially who consciously became invisible to you, they need to remain invisible when your shit starts to jump off again. In other words, fuck them, the horse they rode in on, the mutha fuckas who shoed the horses, and even the mother fuckas who built the barn. There has always been something that turns my stomach about cowardly-ass people who don't show up."

"Well, we can unpack that more some other time, little brother. I appreciate how all my boys from back in the day, you, GJ, JB, Z, AZ, TZ, and my CGU crew, JS and TK. All continuing to show up, without invitations. I'm pulling up to the apartment now. So I'll let you go, knowing this is to be continued. Much love, YB."

"Back at you big bro," Maurice said. "Extend my best to your fine-ass fiance, Kesi."

"Most definitely. Later," said Xavier..

Upon arriving at Kesi's apartment in Montréal, before even exiting his car, Xavier searched for another email from the past that he somewhat remembered. Once again his memory hadn't failed him. Discovering an email with a subject line titled, "Response to Maims' Report on Creation of Hostile Environment," had him convinced that he may have found another email he could use to reveal both his concerns about a concerted effort to undercut his efforts at NYSU-Peru as well as Utley's negligence in responding to his requests for help. The only way to be sure was to read it. So he began reading it.

From: "X. W. Witt" <xwwitt@peru.edu>
Date: March 22, 2010 at 8:34:32 AM GMT-4
To: president_office@peru.edu
Cc: "'Latrice Wiggins'" <wigginl@peru.edu>, Helene Savoie <Savoieh@peru.edu>
Subject: Response to Maims' Report on Creation of Hostile Environment
Reply-To: witt@peru.edu

President Utley,

I received the investigation report from Brenda Maims and thought I would respond to you, and some others involved in the conversation, though none of us have ever sat down collectively to discuss it (which I believe is a mistake). I know, on some level, perhaps legalistically, procedures must advance and processes must take place, but sometimes those happenings that we think are accentuating the process are only impeding the process, especially when we substitute the process for productive dialogue/interaction.

"We must share social interactions to have the ability to share perspectives, to discuss, and to respectfully disagree, and/or change viewpoints" (Johnson & Blanchard 265).

OPIE, is the only entity on campus that promotes professional development for faculty in diversity & social justice. It is surprising that the Affirmative Action officer and chair of Feminist Anthropology (FA) are conspicuously absent from the roster of the 30 plus faculty members who have rotated through the INT404 Reconciling Otherness with Diversity Enlightenment course (including the interim provost, previous provost, three deans and numerous Morality Fellows). It is an intriguing aspect of Maims' professional development in times of budget cuts that a free and highly touted professional development opportunity has never been undertaken by her (or FA Dept. Chair Ramona Saphony for that matter). With that in mind one might assume that Maims, as Affirmative Action officer for the campus (and tenured sociologist) is steeped enough in an understanding of the literature/scholarship on social justice that it isn't necessary for her to further advance her knowledge in that area. One might even assume that all three of my so-called colleagues (including Sharon Winchell, who I will discuss later) are aware of Angela Davis' scholarship on "the Myth of the Black Rapist" and how American society has spoon fed its populace a dysfunctional interpretation of the fact that all Black men are predisposed to leveraging any and everything for sexual opportunities. However, if we make that assumption then we can also make the assumption that every professor on NYSU-Peru's campus is sophisticated enough to see their own particular blind spots simply because they have a heightened level of expertise in their valued and self-vaunted disciplines. Quite a ridiculous conclusion most would agree.

It is nothing less than a reflection of our professional inadequacies that an Office of Pluralism, Inclusion, and Equity and a Feminist Anthropology department are not co-partnering in educating dual and like minded constituencies in diversity and social justice concerns. Instead NYSU-Peru has one of these departments covertly and at times overtly undermining the other department's mission.

So, I'll begin by stating that sometimes it doesn't serve the purpose of communication well if we soft sell concerns. While I am not actually trying to insult anyone in this response, I' going to engage the topic with the same aplomb and fervor that Winchell, Saphony, and Maims have used.

Philosophically, what was the point of Maims' investigation? Was it to get the details of what occurred? Was it to seriously address two students, or perhaps more so, two student leaders; or to placate two student leaders in hopes to obtain their silence, to allow such a problematic concern to simply "fade to black," an ironic notion itself considering the circumstances.

Was it to mark an item off of the real or metaphorical checklist put in place when a faculty member has potentially gone awry in terms of the institutional ethic assumed to be in place within a so-called student centered university? Was it to ensure the ethic that abounds within NYSU-Peru remains unblemished?

I will address each of these items one at a time:

Accessing the details:
"[F]inding truth is about seeing the center from all sides" (Johnson & Blanchard 265)

I offer as evidence of Maims' inability to see the center from all sides the very clip that the students' claim started this entire investigation, Storytelling. *Maims, in the results of her investigation, claims that the professor "shoves the woman against the wall," and then commences to "have rough sex." I was flabbergasted with Maims' perspective on this and reviewed the clip again as well as with other colleagues, some women, to determine if I had missed something here. The professor doesn't touch her with his hands prior to entering her body during the intercourse. He asks her to turn around. He asks her to bend over. He then enters her body for sex (not lovemaking as Maims' naively or politically correctly claims may have been brokered between the two prior to arriving at his home). He doesn't hit her, doesn't toss her around in a menacing fashion. He has what appears to be vaginal sex with her from a rear entry point. About the only way he is shoving her against the wall is with his penile thrusts. The fact that it is "rough sex" is so value laden and somewhat difficult to ascertain. If the reviewer (in this case Maims) is predisposed to a very gentle and endearing sexual encounter, then most definitely anything that doesn't fit that mold could be construed as rough sex. If the viewer of the scene in question is lesbian and not appreciative of penile-vaginal intercourse, then the softest thrust in the throes of passion might be considered obtrusive and therefore, rough or violent. It only takes a look at this scene to know that, in terms of Maims perspective "methinks [s]he doth protest too much," if not to a greater extent "something is rotten in Denmark."*

Prior to that moment though are some other indicators that a bias might be preventing Maims from "finding truth" or "seeing the center from all sides." The Black male protagonist in the film clips from Storytelling *asks her to disrobe, though Maims' states he "orders her." It must have been an order since he didn't say please. What constitutes an order being given as opposed to a request? Is the mere fact that he violated professional protocol (sex with his student) and perhaps an unstated or understated institutional ethic enough to make the claim that he ordered her to take her clothes off? He simply said, from a somewhat distant and prone position while fully clothed, "take off your blouse." Just as we neglect to say "please" when asking a colleague to turn off the light as we leave a room there is an implied 'please' that I get the benefit of the doubt on, as I give it on similar occasions.*

If two people leave a bar on their own accord and walk in the middle of the night to a place of solitude where they can enjoy some private time, a statement from one to another to remove an article of clothing doesn't necessarily carry with it the necessary assumption of power. Maims' interpretation of that moment was value laden. I understand the power dynamic that plays out between professor and student in the scene. But it doesn't need to be further exacerbated, especially in a report that is supposed to be assessing my creation of a hostile environment.

Additionally, at what point does a woman become a consenting adult? Would we even be having this conversation if it had been a White professor and one of his adult female students engaged in coitus? Would we be having this conversation if the Black professor hadn't asked her to verbalize profanity during their sexual encounter? Would we be having this conversation if a lesbian professor or administrator was enamored with one of her adult students and said to her to take off her blouse? Would that still be considered an order, or would it somehow be different because a woman is saying it to a woman, two marginalized people allegedly without power. Let's stop playing games here, women in today's society have as much power when they play the gender card as Blacks do when they play the race card. If it is played in the proper context, you don't need an Ace (when aces or high) or King, the metaphorical Queen can easily trump them both.

She also took, at most, one step towards him, but Maims' frames her walking towards him as hesitant. Is Maims genuinely unaware of the difference in painting someone moving hesitantly with the term "walking" as opposed to the phrase "she hesitated to step" towards him? As a matter of fact, how many steps must one take to read hesitancy?

You really must see the clip to fully understand how much bias is revealed in Maims' investigation when she asserts that he "shoved" her against the wall, and had "rough sex." Some things defy description.

Taking Students Seriously:*

If the goal of the investigation was to take our students' complaint seriously, they need to experience the truth of the matter, not a "everyone can benefit from the moment" resolution. Without an unfettered dose of reality—not insinuating that there is nothing for me to learn from the events under investigation because I have acquired enormous lessons from this experience—are we really taking full advantage of an invaluable teaching moment? However, if I am the only one learning something from this incident, then the aftermath of the incident may become more traumatic in terms of residual consequences than any of us can possibly imagine.

How seriously can we take students who make the assertion these students make at the end of their complaint? What logical trail takes me from showing a film clip with a dysfunctional black professor in a very problematic sexual encounter with one of his students as a precursor for me seducing my students in a similar fashion? How does a mature professional read such an assertion and not immediately see it as possibly a complaint with more to it than meets the eye? I would imagine that you and Maims' know the extent to which she went to investigate the possible merits of the student's allegations, but I would bet nothing like asking me for all my films before any conversation with me, under the auspices of Maims' assessing them for some type of context she could discern (again, without a conversation with me, without Maims reading the pertinent articles, etc.). Seriously, am I missing something here or is this supposed to be a joke?

Real/Metaphorical CheckList

Perhaps Maims' in her part time position is adequately performing her job by being situated to check off her list of agenda items that are prerequisites to her concluding an investigation. As a result, the best that she can do with an overwhelming schedule is to try to mitigate the investigation to a conclusion that serves both parties adequately. In this case, the students got what they deemed as a transgression against them grieved to some extent, and I as the professor can breathe easier because my job is not in jeopardy and the findings were not overtly detrimental to my livelihood. Well if that is the conscious or subconscious thought surrounding the metaphorical checklist, someone bet on the wrong pony in this race. I am as satisfied with the results of this report to you President Utley as I was satisfied with Maims' telling me eight years ago to cross the street if I saw the young woman who levied the preliminary accusation of sexual harassment against me, to which my reply was I wouldn't act like a criminal then and I won't act guilty now. If I do, when is the next time I'll have to comply with Maims' efforts to "round up the usual suspects?"

An Unblemished Institutional Ethic:

At present I present to you a picture of a very tarnished effort at developing student leaders by the very existence of two professors—putatively campus leaders—who have inconsiderately blemished (and perhaps still attempting to blemish) the reputation of a colleague (me). Winchell's public attempt at besmirching a colleague with unsubstantiated allegations is an affront and an embarrassment to our university's institutional ethic. My decision, as the blog master to post it was made largely in part to force the cowards to exit the shadows and own their unwarranted gossip. But Winchell didn't act in a vacuum. And her relationship with Philosophy chair Ronald Wiener doesn't go unnoticed either. He and I have never gotten along and with the level of contempt and venom she articulated in her blog post for someone she has never interacted with it isn't difficult to imagine her being duly influenced or duped into an irrational dislike for me.

Saphony's hosting of a discussion in her class on the rationale of my showing the "Storytelling" clip is the epitome of professional immaturity, irresponsibility, and inconsideration. The interesting question about her actions and questioning of my qualifications is why would she solely rely upon the context given by two disgruntled students (and possibly one of my unethical TAs who is close to Saphony—as well as the two agenda-laden RSLM students who made the complaint—and actually gave her the clip)? Didn't I deserve a professional courtesy call? Why would I not have received one? Perhaps it is because Saphony, for all her so-called expertise in Feminist Anthropology, is more skilled at leveraging accusations against men who she deems as non-compliant with her agenda, or whom she deems as a threat to what she might see as only her right and privilege to engage these topics. This would be consistent with her admonishing a OPIE staffer, Devin Greyson, when she was a guest panelist on the OPIE Faculty Panel Discussion and he was the host. When he attempted to manage her overage of time (every faculty presenter was asked to respectfully complete their presentations within 7 minutes) her response (after presenting for in-excess of 20 minutes) was to chastise him for conforming to a Western value system. So, imbedded within her assertion is--within the 2 hour block of time designated for the event--we shouldn't have a process that regulates faculty presenter's time-of-presentation, which then doesn't ensure that every faculty presenter would be heard. With her approach we may never get to the student's voices/responses to the presenters. This was a large red flag at the time, and we did notice.

Couple these moments with Maims, who is complicit in administering this blemish by inadequately doing her job, perhaps not because she deliberately just didn't do it, but perhaps because of the blind spots she is incapable of seeing and sadly, owning.

I don't know to what extent the backgrounds of these professors include extensive study of their own socialization outside of the context of overcoming their male oppressors, but an extensive study of racism and white privilege might do them all good. I have processed how I might have been predisposed and therefore less receptive to Satton's outburst after his initial one prior to the beginning of the class. I have processed how I was angry at learning that Lyers took our class discussion to another class for support of her vision, one that is quite limited because of Lyer's inability to engage the intersections of race with power, white privilege, and the historical overtones of accusations of rape leveraged by dysfunctional white women who have no other solutions to their plight. I have processed how I need to be more vigilant of the reality of some of my students life experiences before I expose them to images that may cause them discomfort, perhaps a discomfort predicated upon emotional scars they have yet to put in perspective. But I am struggling with how our university can have a department of women, some who may be lesbian or bi-sexual, defaulting to a position of my maleness, or dare I say perhaps my blackness as sexually predatory. As if women don't prey upon women.

Goals:
I have no desire to participate in a discussion with someone that Maims' chooses who she may be elevating to a status of consultant when she as an Affirmative Action Officer can't see around her own bias[es]. If we are to have an outsider come into facilitate a larger conversation, it needs to be around the clip in question, "Storytelling." Any other type of conversation doesn't get us to the crux of the situation, and is either a Band-Aid fix, an attempt to placate the parties in question, or both. I have no interest in participating in a general conversation about sexual assault, etc that doesn't give us a fixed point of entry that includes the possibility of closure with this incident. I am as interested in attending this type of program as Maims and Saphony are in exploring their gender privilege and racism.

In receiving a copy of her report I am left with no idea of whether Maims' so-called report will be placed in my file, or dismissed summarily. I have no idea of whether the complaint is ongoing with some conditional status or has been dismissed. The findings were quite vague and general.

President Utley, I will close by sharing this last thought with you. I am prepared to play hard ball on this matter, though I would prefer not to do it. In the effort to ensure that a social injustice didn't occur to two of our students a social injustice has been further perpetuated against not only one of NYSU-Peru's most dedicated professionals (that would be me), but also against the organization that I have the privilege of leading. Deidre Bright, Robin Chris, and Devin Greyson all suffer from whatever scarlet letter has been placed upon me, if only from guilt by association, and that is not fair to them. Young women and men interested in social justice are having a bifurcated experience by looking at OPIE as inadequately doing our jobs while FA leverages such accusations to further root their relationships with these impressionable students, many of whom won't challenge the assertions of their faculty.

The two complaining students accused me of possibly not having a problem coercing female students into sexual acts for grades. How does that ridiculously unfounded assertion differ from FA cementing loyalty to their base by creating an enemy within the institution that they can all rally against? Aside from providing me a perfect example of professionals in the field of social justice) inability to see their own biases, an excellent book chapter or article framing an institution's ineptness at addressing dysfunction amongst its' so-called social justice leaders, and an exploration of how I handle being under siege and prejudged, what am I to garner from this ordeal? I know there can't be an expectation that I should be appreciative that this investigation is concluded.

Oh, and how is it that Maims' reported to you her findings before she was able to access the film clips she claimed she needed to put the problematic film clips in some sort of context? Seriously, some things are direct insults to our intelligence and her whole posturing that she would endeavor to contextualize my film clips was the height of absurdity.

I am not naïve enough to think that my not letting this incident slowly dissipate may cause me some consternation down the road, the least being that I am viewed as a non-team player or litigious. However, to the contrary, I have no interest in silently working at a university that would allow this type of dysfunction to continue on unabated. False accusations that continue to thrive and biased investigations that continue to contribute to the perpetuation of false accusations are what should be truly deemed a "hostile environment." If this matter isn't addressed or rectified in a more productive fashion, it is no idle threat on my part I will endeavor to prove I have been working in a hostile environment, and start with whatever legal actions I must take against Sharon Winchell and Ramona Saphony.

I hope the length of this letter and the passion it was written with is enough to better frame a much needed upcoming conversation. It was not my intention to disrespect you Dr. Utley, or your position, and I hope I didn't do that. On the other hand, I won't stand idly by and be disrespected any more by half-truths and veiled assertions.

X.W.

Upon completing his reading of the email Xavier knew that any sensible person could ascertain that he had effectively pleaded if not challenged Utley, in writing, to take action. He had revealed his concerns again about a concerted effort between Feminist Anthropology and the Affirmative Action officer, with a deep rooted dysfunctional connection to what would become Title IX, considering that Brenda Maims would be handing over to Molly Mothburn the Title IX responsibilities she had done for years, and the fact that Molly Mothburn teaches in the F.A. department before and during her time serving as the Title IX officer.

Xavier could imagine being a fly on the wall during a conversation between Utley, Ben Judson his Chief of Staff, Mothburn and Dewar, in Utley's office. Little did he know that one had occurred.

"Okay, thanks everyone for making it to this meeting," Utley said. "We're here to discuss what is happening on our campus after last week's forum."

"Well a big part of that discussion has to be what XW said when he came to the microphone. In my opinion he tried to intimidate potential survivors with his little speech at the Forum," Mothburn stated emphatically.

"He also was very unprofessional, using extreme profanity in front of the entire campus," Dewar added.

"He's out of control and we need to do something about him," Utley declared. "I warned him to tone it down. What are our options Ben?"

"Well, considering how he has threatened to take legal action against us, he's kind of painting himself into a corner." Judson replied.

"Did you see his Facebook post?" Dewar asked anyone listening.

"Ben," Utley said, "Is it possible his Facebook post was insubordination."

"Possibly," replied Judson. "I'll contact the central office to get their take on it."

"Linda, I hope you know you are now under scrutiny for starting an informal investigation on XW," Utley explained. "XW wants to know how an intern was conducting an investigation on him, and who approved it."

"It wasn't an investigation Dr. Utley," Dewar said in her defense. "It was just research."

Utley, being smart enough to know her "research" was still problematic didn't want to risk alienating Dewar with an opposing viewpoint, so he remained silent, allowing her inane comment to go unchallenged. Judson rescued him from the awkward silence.

"Well, XW is prepared to claim that the *"research"* was authorized by you, Molly." Judson stated. "When we met with XW a few days ago he explicitly mentioned Dewar recently asking him for a letter of reference," and then turning towards Dewar says, "and you turn around and investigate him. Do you know something? Because if not, who would do that?"

Judson may sound as if he is an ally of Dr. Witt's, but not necessarily so. While they had grown somewhat closer over the 29 month period XW was reporting to Utley, Judson knew who allowed him to pay his bills. The best he could do with Utley was push him to consider other possibilities and consequences. However, he had no problem telling Dewar what he felt she needed to hear, since he had no fear of Dewar, and probably little respect for her. Back in 2015 when she led a student revolt against Pigeon Messages that almost took out Utley too, Judson had shared with XW that it was Judson himself who absorbed most of the brunt of the impact for the president's office. Judson had also revealed that Utley had actually been terrified by the Black students in 2015 and admitted to him not knowing what to do. He said this is why he was so eager to bring Xavier on board. He essentially wanted to be rescued, but without saying it explicitly. Combine that chunk of reality with Judson planning on retiring soon, and he may have been feeling his oats. Of course, Xavier just let him talk.

Dewar answered, "I only know of the rumor."

"Who told you about the rumor though Linda?" asked Judson.

"I don't remember," she answered. "I heard it from quite a few people."

Judson decided to let Utley ask her who those people were. Utley didn't.

"What about the flyers," Dewar asked. "Doesn't he have to be investigated since the flyers indicate some silenced survivors?"

"Those flyers sure were convenient, weren't they," Judson muttered rhetorically, as he immediately looked down at his notes to avoid eye contact with Mothburn and Dewar.

"All I know is he tried to intimidate me the other day when I passed by him on campus," offered Mothburn. "I know how uncomfortable I was seeing him and being in close proximity to him. How are our students doing when they come across him? I imagine them terrified. Ian, we need to protect our students."

"I agree." said Utley. "We must look into how we can make that happen, Ben. I've already told XW he was not currently under investigation when he asked me if he was."

"I'll get started right away," responded Mothburn.

"No you won't Molly," said Judson. "Ian has already told XW that if he ever were under investigation you wouldn't be conducting the investigation."

"Seriously?" asked Mothburn. "Why not me?"

"We already made a bad situation worse when Linda did her "research" and it got back to XW. We need to show that we understand the complexities of this situation and not further complicate it." said Judson.

"Then if not me, who?" asked Mothburn.

"We're looking into it." said Utley. "We're considering bringing investigators from another campus."

"I can recommend some Title IX investigators from other campuses," Mothburn said matter-of-factly.

On March 15th, 2018 Dr. Xavier Witt was removed from campus and informed that he was officially under investigation. As a result of the investigation he would not be allowed to return to campus until the investigation was concluded.

Utley took his unethical practices to a completely different level when he intercepted a phone call from an alum calling to notify the Alumni Affairs office that as a result of Dr. Witt's treatment he would not be supporting the university any longer. When the alum informed Utley of this Utley replied, "Was Bill Cosby lynched?" The implication was horrendous considering Utley didn't really know the alum, and more so, Utley was suggesting Dr. Witt had committed a crime, essentially implying Dr. Witt is a criminal.

Swimming with Sharks -- Drowning with Dolphins

Xavier was not really surprised when he overheard a FaceTime conversation between his fiancé Kesi and his closest colleague, Nyla. They had become friends after meeting at a university event hosted by Nyla. Nyla was the director of the university's ALANA chapter. ALANA was an acronym (for Asian-American, Latino, African American, Native American). NYSU's chapter under Nyla's leadership was considered one of the strongest in not only New York state, but in the country. Dr. Witt had never had the pleasure of Nyla as one of his students, academically. However, this young woman and Xavier reciprocally mentored one another repeatedly. The fact that she had connected profoundly with Kesi, the love of Xavier's life was a spectacular occurrence, and one Xavier had to guard against over-celebrating or run the risk of jinxing a relationship between them. So he decided to attentively listen, what some would call eavesdropping to spy on how they flowed conversationally without him there to male dominate it in that way that men do.

"Girl," Nyla said to Kesi as matter-of-factly as possible, "It was President Lyndon Baines Johnson who once said:

"If you can convince the lowest white man he's better than the best colored man, he won't notice you're picking his pocket. Hell, give him somebody to look down on, and he'll even empty his pockets for you."

Being exceptionally well read, equipped with a 147 IQ, ethically energized, and with an overriding interest in global justice, Kesi replied "Then LBJ was articulating white privilege before it was popularized. He was also a forerunner to black comedian Chris Rock's assertion that racism is so beneficial to whites that "there isn't a white man that would change places with me," even though Rock added, "and I'm rich."

"How would you even know anything about LBJ or Chris Rock having never lived in the U.S., only living in Montreal for six years?" asked Nyla.

"Because your country is enough of a superpower that many if not most countries teach about your ways. Combine that with my preteen fascination with Alex Haley's television series, 'Roots,' and you'll start to understand that I absorbed everything I could about African-American culture, though it was from a distance."

"Well Kesi, I'll admit to once again being impressed. The fact you know poor whites benefit from being white while suffering from poverty brings to mind a quote from one of my previous ALANA students, Angel Acosta. Angel needing to put two classmates of his in check accused them of "swimming in privilege yet drowning in oppression."

"This is the same Angel who was NYSU-Peru S.G. President, right? The same Angel that I tease and call Xavier's guardian angel?" asked Kesi.

"None other," replied Nyla, proudly.

Kesi, an intellectual if you've ever met one, is a doctor from Morocco. Her father is a renowned lawyer, as was his father. Her mother a reputable teacher. She is the second child with three siblings, an older sister who is a doctor, and two younger brothers, both engineers of repute.

What do you think he meant?" asked Kesi. "Is it as obvious as it sounds?"

"It actually is," Nyla responded. "Angel told me he wanted them to recognize, as White women, that because of their Whiteness they are swimming in privilege, but as a result of their gender they're drowning in oppression. They had been bemoaning their gendered reality to such an extent that Angel was pushing back to force them to self-reflect.

Xavier, quietly but attentively absorbing every word, wanted to add his three cents to their conversation, but decided against becoming 'that guy.' So while trying to figure out how to reenter the room without derailing, if not dominating, their conversation, he continued to listen.

Kesi continued, "I wonder if this is why some political pundits speculate about poor white voters within the Republican Party voting against their own interests. With policies that often appear to support big business at the expense of the underclass, it isn't a stretch to see your previous President LBJ's quote as a hard-fast truth."

Nyla replied, "This is often revealed by various interviews of whites who profess disdain for Obamacare while in their very next breath articulating a preference for the Affordable Care Act, which are the same thing."

"Are you saying that it is just a case of cluelessness, or sadly, unrecognized implicit bias?" Kesi asked with sincerity.

"Many of these same pundits took Donald Trump to task during his political campaign for fanning the flames of racism with his unfounded claims about President Barack Obama's citizenry, also referred to as birtherism," Nyla answered. "Trump somehow recognized a card he could play in a society still burdened by its unresolved racial past. His confidence in how his followers would respond to his accusation reaffirms

LBJ's assertion that poor whites see themselves as wealthy compared to anyone black."

Kesi, gazing off into space suddenly looked at Nyla and said, "Trump's unfounded claims exacerbated by him playing the race card is exactly what occurred with my Baby. Linda and Shalo acted on unfounded rumors to justify the things they were saying and doing to Xavier. They knew in this MeToo climate they could successfully play the gender card to acquire the attention they both so obviously crave."

"Great connection," responded Nyla.

"I was trying to recall an Anais Nin quote that accentuates what we are talking about. I think it is "We don't see things as they are; we see them as we are.""

"I know that," Nyla said proudly. "It is one of my favorites. Great minds think alike girl."

After sharing laughter, Kesi said, "Last month Xavier and I watched a movie based upon a true story. The film is called "*Free State of Jones*" and had one of the most provocative scenes I've ever seen in a movie.

"Ooh Kesi, I really wanted to see that movie. Isn't it starring Matthew McConaughey as a confederate soldier who is considered a deserter from the Civil War? To escape, he and other deserters find refuge with a group of runaway slaves hiding out in the swamps?"

"Yes," answered Kesi. "The story is similar to one of my favorite love stories, Cold Mountain, starring Jude Law and Nicole Kidman, except minus the love story. In a scene from that film a self-liberated man—played by scrumptious Mahershala Ali—is making a plate of food after patiently awaiting Whites finishing their meal. Suddenly he is approached with hostility by a poor white who says "Put the food back, nigger!"

"Mahershala Ali's character responds: 'How you ain't one?' The poor White man is bewildered by his response and says, 'What?' McConaughey interrupts their exchange by clarifying for the poor challenged White man what Mahershala Ali meant, saying to the poor White man, 'He just picked cotton for them. You were willing to fight and die for them.' The man was left speechless knowing he was living the reality of a poor White man fighting/dying for slave owners who themselves didn't have to fight if they owned enough slaves."

You still have a copy of the book "The Nigger in You: Challenging Dysfunctional Language, Engaging Leadership Moments" from when we went to the author's book signing?

"I do," Kesi acknowledged, arising to go get it. Moments later she returned showing the book to Nyla. Rifling through her own copy with purpose, Nyla found what she was looking for. "Here it is. Turn to the introduction on page 3. I absolutely love how the author, Dr. J.W. Wiley defined the racial slur "nigger." This is so powerful. I need to memorize it."

"Okay. Having read the entire book I am curious as to where you are going. So share, share," Kesi said feigning impatience.

Smiling, Nyla read:

"A nigger isn't a person but a societal problem created through society's inability to educationally engage, to successfully integrate our differences."

"As a result, when we label someone a *'nigger*,' beyond referring to him/her as a problem, we also disrespectfully imply an expectation of behavior that at the very least borders on criminal activity, both elements of someone that society deems as a conundrum of sorts."

Kesi sat silently with her eyes closed, absorbing every word, as Nyla continued.

"We also imply that the person is a societal misfit but in the context of society's inability to have better engaged all of its citizens. This is how 'nigger' is framed within our society, yet not actually articulated, if we consider it" (Wiley, 3).

"That is very powerful. It is worthy of memorizing," Kesi admitted. Engaged to marry a Black man from America, I probably should be armed and ready with phrases and puns that will prevent people from saying stupid racist shit."

"Kesi," said Nyla with an edgier voice while looking Kesi as directly in the eyes as one can using Skype, "Nothing you ever do will stop stupid-ass people from saying dumbass shit."

"That's true," admitted Kesi.

"My social-justice instincts prevent me from blindly embracing campaigns with slogans like, "Make America Great Again," or even movements dear to me like MeToo as if everyone claiming me too status automatically becomes full of integrity while the man accused can't even defend himself without being accused of silencing survivors. It's really ridiculous."

Kesi replied, "For some reason whenever I hear Trump's slogan I imagine it'll 'make Americans hate again.' I know I'm not American, but he turns my stomach something fierce. More importantly though, as a survivor of sexual assault what's happening to my man infuriates me."

"I know girl," acknowledged Nyla. "This fucking community embraces the possibility of XW being guilty more than they will seriously consider the possibility that all of this shit aimed at NYSU-Peru's most notable social justice advocate is a hoax supported by a well woven agenda."

It was then that Xavier decided to not interrupt them with his physical presence. So, instead he decided to text both of them, something germane to their conversation, only from outside the apartment. He thought it might make him appear clairvoyant, a prognosticator of sorts.

He texted Kesi first:

Lynchings were represented as a necessary measure to prevent Black Supremacy over white people—in other words, to reaffirm white Supremacy" (Davis, 186).

Xavier wondered if it would make her think of her theory that Mothburn wanted to reaffirm her position by taking Dr. Witt down a notch. Mothburn without a doctorate, minimal attendance at her events, and a relationship with a man rebounding from being publicly, humiliatingly and unceremoniously dumped in an exceptionally hard way, not by his spouse because of any malice, but because she had a Vegas love hangover that was unequivocally a clear upgrade. The fact that he was Black probably only added to Mothburn's new man self-medicating even more.

He then texted Nyla:

"Moreover, those white women who permitted their children to witness the murders of Black people were indoctrinating them into the racist ways of the South" (Davis, 194).

He chose to send this one to Nyla knowing she would see FA and Title IX as the White women mentioned in the quote, permitting their students to witness not so much a murder, but the character assassination of a Black man, and in the process indoctrinate their students into a racist, and hence dysfunctional perspective of OPIE and its leader.

CHAPTER SEVEN
- The Investigation

"Okay class, let's unpack the following quote in terms of its relationship or relevancy to any film we've seen in class this semester," Darren requested, knowing that any stimulation of their minds in a Dr. Witt course—designed to bring out their creativity—always had the potential, the possibility of being combustible.

"The crossroads of racism and sexism had to be a violent meeting place. There is no use pretending it doesn't exist" (Davis, 197).

Darren continued, "So what clip does this quote bring to mind for you, and how does it apply?"

"Rosewood comes to mind for me," responded Jessica, a Latina senior, "in that the White woman--Fanny Taylor, who lied about being raped by a Black man--created the lie to cover her ass about an affair, or better stated, cheating on her husband with a White man who subsequently beat her after a sexual encounter."

Dr. Witt responded, "But Jessica, what does that have to do with the crossroads, essentially the intersection of racism and sexism, being necessarily violent?

Jessica replied, "Dr. Witt, her second class citizenship as a female would make her vulnerable to domestic abuse for cheating on her husband, whereas any cheating he did as a male only brought with it public shaming and ridicule. The different ways two similar acts are interpreted provide a case of textbook sexism. The racism intersects with this sexism in that to overcome the sexism she experiences daily she adeptly plays the race card. In this case, to a much heavier extent, Fanny Taylor exercises her White-racial privilege by manipulating the town's racist sensibilities with the mere mentioning of an unwanted racial advance."

Rachel, an Asian, female junior who seldom spoke up in class, contributed, "I see the quote in Woody Allen's film, 'Vickie, Cristina, Barcelona.'"

"How so, where's the racism when there are no people of color in the film?" asked Kaitlyn, one of Dr. Witt's most insightful students.

The class erupted upon hearing that two of the four main characters' identities were dismissed if not devalued as racially relative, in uncertain contexts. The film features two American White women traveling to Barcelona on vacation, where they eventually meet and are propositioned by a Spaniard. How this Spanish speaking character gets a pass--from his Spanish heritage possibly being problematic--in one of the student's minds was worthy of unpacking. How his estranged wife, a Latina--another Spanish speaking character in the film--was not seen as a person of color was just as worthy of dissecting. A rumor preceding him meeting the two White women was that his ex-wife was violent towards him. That said, imagine uprooting the Spaniard and dropping him somewhere in Mexico or Los Angeles. Until he acclimates to that environment he most certainly would be preoccupied with how others interpret his identity, if he wanted to increase the probability of surviving the experience.

The class continued to unpack the quote in contrast to varying film clips. Dr. Witt's mind continued to wander, preoccupied with the "disrespecting women" accusation that threatened to morph into an unsubstantiated MeToo taint on his reputation. Little did he know when class ended that night it would be his last time in a classroom at NYSU-Peru.

The Interview

On March 15, 2018 Dr. Xavier Witt was officially informed he was under investigation for inappropriate conduct, predicated on his passionate response to a publicly made attack on his character, a Facebook post he wrote to challenge the accusation that he was disrespectful to women, and to determine if there was any truth to an anonymous flyer posted in the Student Union that also accused Dr Witt of inappropriate conduct.

The investigation became real for Dr. Witt two weeks later when he received a series of text messages from a previous romantic interest, now close friend, Sandita (Sandy) Ramos.

"Hey X, I just received a phone call from a Lucy Renoir, asking me to partake in an interview about an investigation they are doing on you," texted Sandy.

"Are you serious?" asked Xavier, returning the text in disbelief. "I can't imagine why they would contact a lover of mine from nine years ago?"

"I have no idea," Sandy replied. "They want to meet with me on Monday at 4:00 pm on NYSU-Peru's campus.

"I am so lost as to why they would be interviewing you," exclaimed Xavier. "I'm sorry you are being pulled into this."

"No problem," Sandy said. "I'll be meeting with her and someone named Charlotte Cloudy. They must have gotten my name from Facebook because they called me Sandita Hernandez. Hernandez is my maiden name. I only use that on Facebook."

"Interesting," responded Xavier, pensively.

"They said they're interviewing me because I'm a supporter," added Sandy. "They must have seen I posted the video of you speaking at the forum."

"Perhaps," Xavier said. "Someone could've given them your name though."

"Maybe, they are trying to be fair by showing both sides."

"Well I really appreciate you telling me they approached you." texted Xavier.

"No problem X," replied Sandy. "I'll let you know how it all turns out. Please tell Kesi I said hello. Bye for now."

After hanging up, Xavier sat dumbfounded in disbelief. A few moments later, he decided to share with his fiancé Kesi his exchange with Sandy.

"Sandy just texted me, telling me she has been contacted by the NYSU investigators."

"Are you kidding me? asked Kesi. "What would Sandy have to do with an accusation that you disrespect women, on campus? Something isn't right."

"I am confused about them contacting Sandy too," Xavier offered.

"It sounds like they found nothing to support Shalo's accusation," surmised Kesi, "or found nothing supporting the existence of alleged survivors mentioned in the anonymous flyers."

"Well, you can't find something that never occurred. Anyway, no point in worrying about something we can't control."

"What are you talking about?" Kesi asked, with irritation in her voice. "They're digging around in your personal life from nine years ago. "They are fishing."

"What's even more of a trip is they are going back into the time period when I asked Utley for help with the FA program's obvious agenda against me. So, he wasn't concerned enough to take my advice and call meetings to help us reconcile our differences. He wasn't concerned enough about FA's support of the rumor to do an investigation back then." "He wasn't concerned enough back then to intercede on my behalf. So they ignored my requests for help back then and yet dig into my personal life back then nonetheless. This shit is crazy."

"Really, the same time frame?" Kesi asked.

"Yes, the exact same time period," Xavier answered.

"Is Sandy going to keep you posted about her interactions with them?"

"Definitely," answered Xavier.

"That's real cool," Kesi said. "I really love Sandy."

Xavier knew he was lucky that all the women in his life were friends, not only with him, but with each other too, though he often told people that luck is the residue of preparation. In any potential relationship he did his prep work early and often. When he first started seeing a woman he would earnestly interview them, providing them the same opportunity. He knew there were two attributes in a relationship that he couldn't handle, impatience and jealousy. Kesi was as patient as she was not jealous. So his preparation had enough residue for him to have met his Mediterranean Mango. While thinking he chose Kesi, it actually was more the case that he had been the one chosen.

A week later, Xavier texted Sandy to say hello and check on her, knowing her interview was coming up. "Good morning S. Thanks again for being in my life and having my back the way you do. I received your voicemail. It was no accident that they interrogated you. I am positive that they lied to you just to get you in a room with them. They knew what they were going to say to you when they invited you. Just saying…"

"Good morning X," texted back Sandy. "You don't have to thank me. You're welcome though. Yes. I feel violated by that woman. I believe she lied to me too. The investigators didn't ask me a single question about my support for you. Instead they asked me about some sexy pictures we allegedly took that you supposedly showed to someone at your office. I believe someone told them that such pics exist though no real complaint was made. If someone was so offended by pics from years ago they should have said something nine years ago."

"This is really a fucking fishing expedition," exclaimed Xavier, infuriated. "I almost said witch hunt, but that would sound to Trumpian. Besides, who at that office would I have shown nude pics of us? There are three people who worked at the office during the time we dated, two women and one man. The man I didn't get along well with. As far as the women, well, what man would show two women who were cool with his ex-wife nude pics of him with a new woman. For that matter, what man would even show two women who were not cool with his ex-wife nude pics of another woman? Maybe Tyrion would show some to Daenerys, but not me. The assertion is utterly ridiculous!!!"

"It gets even better, or maybe worse. They asked if I would like to file charges against you for showing nude pics of me without consent. They said they could help me file. They also treated me as if I may have Stockholm Syndrome, encouraging me to contact them if I reconsidered, or if anything else came to mind. I had an overwhelming feeling they were trying to recruit me."

Xavier's jaw dropped while reading Sandy's texts. "So they were leading the witness," he texted in reply. "They may have been hoping such a thing would flip you on me. Who the fuck do they think they are, Robert Mueller?"

"I know it is hard to believe," Sandy acknowledged in her text. "I also agree, they're fish-hunting. I hope you noticed what I did just then. Fish-hunting isn't common lingo so I can understand if you missed it."

"Yes Sandy, once again you're cooler than me," Xavier said amused.

"Of course I am," Sandy replied. "Another thing I just remembered, she said there was concern raised over your FB post "the dream" or whatever it was titled. The investigators didn't say anything other than that and they didn't ask me any questions about it."

"Darren shared with me they asked him about 'The Dream.' That post seemed to really get their attention, if not fuck them up," Xavier said impressed with himself. "How ironic they would investigate a Facebook post where I rightfully defended myself against a character assassination, when the university's leadership wouldn't take action to defend one of its own leaders now, or back in 2010 when I on multiple occasions specifically asked Utley to intervene."

"She also said you asked for an investigation when you said "bring it.""

"I wasn't asking for an investigation and they know it," Xavier texted back, irritated. "When I said 'bring it' I was speaking to women I had been rumored to have disrespected. I was inviting them to come forward, fully knowing that they couldn't since I know with the utmost certainty I had done nothing remotely close to leveraging power I had acquired for sexual favors, nor ever having spoken inappropriately towards any women on campus, or elsewhere."

"They discovered that no such women exist," Sandy said, "which is why they're reaching back into your past hoping to find anything. Oh, and the lead investigator is from Peru. She said it herself."

"Why am I not surprised that the lead investigator has a connection to Peru," replied Xavier. "She is probably also connected to NYSU-Peru. I imagine it was Molly who forwarded her name to Utley, or at the very least knows her and privately briefed her about her personal perspective on me, or the situation." I'm going to really fuck them up when we finally meet. They'll think they have the power in that moment until they realize they are dealing with an unapologetic Negro who not only doesn't give-a-fuck but is also itching for a public brawl. They're accustomed to interviewing people who operate from a position of weakness, who are guilty, who have something to hide, or are easily intimidated. There is no reason why I should act timid or afraid of them when truth is on my side. Besides, they are stepping to me wrong."

"They also asked me about some pics of us making love that supposedly were taken by your daughter, Vetha," added Sandy. "When I said to them that even if that was the case what does it have to do with the college, one of the investigators said since someone mentioned that you had shown them at work it was no longer just a personal matter."

"Well, I'll have much to discuss with the investigators then, especially considering that was almost 10 years ago and all parties were adults. My daughter at the time was 22 year old, gay, with photography as her all-consuming hobby. What I recall about that evening was Vetha asked you and I if she could photograph us making love. We were having margaritas, laughing and joking, and nothing was serious to us that evening except exchanging witticisms for us to laugh at, no pun intended. Though she repeated her request all evening to the point it became a running joke we didn't succumb to her coaxing, never acquiescing to her request. I remember you and I saying goodnight to Vetha and retiring to bed. After lovemaking you whispered to me that you thought Vetha had been was in the room with her camera. It was too late to address her violation of our privacy since she had already left the room. We had been clowning all night and that moment itself, while odd, was so quick and not evasive no one tripped over it."

"We recall the same thing. When we decided not to indulge her request she came in anyway, quickly took some photos, and left. I do recall though your response to her last request as we were leaving the kitchen to go to bed. I always thought it was the reason she came in. You said to her laughingly, if she did sneak into the room to snap some pics, she should make sure she captured your good side."

"Did I literally say that?" Xavier asked.

"Yep."

"That's a trip," said Xavier. "I do recall that the next morning she and I discussed her violation of our privacy. She was quite apologetic, which was easier for her than if it had been one of my other two children taking such liberties, because she entered my life so late. She came to live with us at 16, prior to that I had not seen her since she was 7 months old. I was always just as much trying to build a friendship with her as a father-daughter relationship, which is probably why I didn't go off on her for doing it."

"What they are trying to do is slut-shame you," Sandy said.

"I know. The investigators must think that digging up some sexy shit involving a father and daughter will intimidate me, forcing me to go away quietly. They were looking for something illegal, but decided salacious might work. It won't work here though. There is no shame to my game. My daughter and I had a phenomenal relationship during her years attending NYSU-Peru. Besides, Vetha having taken and served as a teacher's assistant in my Romance, Sex, Love, & Marriage (RSLM) class would have her perspective—from hundreds of hours spent in philosophical conversations about romantic and sexual relationships--be a perspective not easily succumbing to shame about photographing someone's sexuality. As well, as a lesbian, if anything, she would have been more interested in photographing your sexy body than mine."

"Thanks for reminding me that once you thought my body was sexy. Trying to score points, eh? Anyway, please keep me informed how this is unfolding for you. I love you and Kesi and want to see this turn out ideally for you both."

"We love you. You know your body is still hot. Shit, your number one playmate is quite a bit younger than you and I imagine he wasn't just attracted to that incisive mind.

"You are adept at saying the right thing," texted Sandy, using a silly-ass emoticon.

"Hey, truth is more than placing a 't' on 'ruth.'" Xavier replied. "I'll share our exchange with Kesi so she is up on the latest. Talk to you soon."

"Bye, clever man."

Four weeks after the investigation began, Xavier was finally about to meet with the two investigators, accompanied by a NYSU attorney. Xavier was accompanied by his newly hired attorney, Mikki Stratton. Mikki's practice was in Syracuse. NY, about five hours from Peru, and she had come highly recommended from two close friends. The meeting was for the investigators to interview Xavier while also sharing with him their findings, putatively for his feedback into other people's testimonies about his alleged inappropriate behavior. After the investigators introduced themselves to Mikki and Xavier, things got quite serious quickly.

"Do you mind if we record this session?" asked Charlotte Cloudy, the lead investigator

"Not as long as you commit to giving us a copy of it," answered Mikki.

"We can do that," assured Cloudy. "We want to start this session off with all of us viewing the forum video so we can try to all be on the same page when we start to ask you questions."

So for the next ten minutes they all silently watched the video, a video that for all intent and purposes was the beginning of the end for Dr. Witt's career at NYSU-Peru. Dr. Witt watching it again with others who had the audacity to judge him--when they didn't necessarily know the full story, or if they had discovered it, didn't really care to understand his version of it-- only served to infuriate him even more. Witnessing again Molly Mothburn stepping to the microphone and saying, 'I'm not here to make friends,' only served to lock in the fact for Xavier that she knew exactly what she was doing at the time. As the video came to an end, Xavier was counting to ten, inhaling and exhaling deeply though hopefully not noticeably, and reiterating one of his many mantras, "be cool, remain chill, you have no energy to spill."

"Now, we've been dying to ask you were you trying to be investigated?" asked Cloudy. "Otherwise, why would you say 'bring it,' as well as use profanity in a public venue, knowing at all times you should be representing the university as a campus leader?"

"Probably, looking back on it, the profanity laced tirade was me finally losing my cool after years of asking for help and receiving none whatsoever," answered Dr. Witt. "My challenge to the so-called women I've allegedly, per Shalo Kloos, disrespected was to encourage them to come out of the shadows. At that moment I was done being victimized by an alliance of women with an agenda against me. As well, I was no longer going to have an expectation that a cowardly administrator, whom, as you said, 'at all times should be representing the university as a leader,' would be riding to my rescue when it became obvious he barely saved himself, until he figured out he could save himself by using me as his sacrificial lamb, and his point of departure to escape his vote-of-no-confidence."

Ignoring Xavier's jab at Utley, Cloudy asked, "So you have no contrition about your behavior?"

"Oh, I'm contrite, and self-reflective, perhaps to a fault. So, yes, I have considered something I could have, perhaps even should have or would have done differently. I even shared them with my fiancé. However, my fiancé suggested that I consider Title IX intern Linda Dewar had started a supposedly unauthorized investigation of me days before, and that her good friend Bessie Bland, the SG president somehow decided to include me with the VPs in their vote-of-no-confidence, when initially I was one of the people leading the conversations meant to heal the campus. Shalo Kloos, another good friend of Dewar, publicly humiliated me, and then the next day took a victory lap about it on Facebook. So, second guessing my actions is ridiculous. There obviously was a collaborative effort to come after me. Why should I feel contrite for simply staring a bully in the eye."

"Do you think your 'Dreams of Reality' Facebook post was appropriate? asked Cloudy. "What type of leadership did that model?"

"Authentic Leadership! Ironically, I haven't seen that post since I wrote it and posted it. I'm surprised it is one of the topics for this investigation."

"Are you being serious with us, Dr. Witt," Cloudy asked. "Your FaceBook post could easily be interpreted as a threat, a threat to sue us."

"Do you have a copy of the Facebook post with you?" inquired Dr Witt. "If we are going to discuss it in detail I probably should reread it."

"I think I would also like to revisit it to," added Mikki.

That's fine. Would you mind reading it aloud," asked Cloudy, as she handed it to him.

Xavier was so irritated with the condescension coming from the investigators he was very tempted to say, 'Fuck you, read it yourself.' Except he knew that would be even worse than his lack of contriteness and so instead he decided to comply. "Sure I'll read it."

Facebook Post - *Dreams of Reality*:

Have you ever had one of those dreams where it felt real, so real that it had a clarity that was surreal?

Well amidst all of these troubling times recently, having not been sleeping exceptionally well, I had exactly that, either a dream that felt so real or a reality that felt dreamlike, but only in a heavenly sense.

In my dreams I'm still Black, and as a result a threat by people who easily yield to their xenophobia. I'm also male, and desirous of everyone being my friend. However, my dreams have nightmare moments within them where people who don't think for themselves will blindly impact other's lives, relationships, and careers. Ironically though in my dreams I thoroughly enjoy looking bullies directly in the eye, letting them know I've seen their type before, and as a fighter will fight for what's right, especially when they're wrong. So let the skirmish begin.

In my dreams sometimes I show up as a very short kid with bad acne and worse, with a verbal stutter. In those same dreams I was bullied, ridiculed and dismissed far too often and much too easily. In a different sense I'm a survivor with my own scars that I have been carrying for a lifetime and trying to avoid new ones.

In my dream several days ago there was a young woman who thought she could get away with defaming me publicly, only for some reason later stupidly posting on her FB account how she colluded with others to do it. Not necessarily a Phi Beta Kappa move, but thanks. No really, a lot.

In my dream a rumor existed for years that I was some type of sexual predator, yet somehow without an accuser. Understanding the silence that comes with being a survivor I now also understand the pain of being labeled something you can't refute. However, no one could ever accuse me of anything heinous, manipulative, or knowingly inconsiderate. Yes, I'm not that guy. Not that I'm perfect in or out of my dreams, but in or out of my dreams I don't float away from my ethic of building a world where my daughter can always be respected and safe. If the world I build is to be safe for her it must be safe for all women. Women in my dreamworld who know me know that I am amongst their staunchest male allies.

In my dreams any and all mistakes I've made--which I owned and preferred to not have happen because I never choose to take away another's energy--are not of a magnitude where I have ruined someone's life. So in that sense my subconscious is somewhat clear, or is it my conscious since I'm dreaming?

In my dreams none of the administrators on a college campus that has a racial incident are asked to resign for moving too slow or dispassionately, not for something they couldn't anticipate or must go through a process to handle.

In my dream I was consulting an attorney, one renowned for his work handling university cases. He seemed eager for the chance to make a tidy sum of money on a slam dunk case by bringing a lawsuit against an overzealous student government for participation in, if not contributing to, slander.

The attorney in my dreams—who is now my dream attorney—was salivating in preparation of looking to reveal the beginnings of unwarranted research conducted by someone who wasn't sanctioned to do it, perhaps empowered *by various other employees conspiring to affiliate me as a predator of "Me Too" proportions. At this point it felt like a nightmare.*

I awakened from my dream momentarily feeling awkward from the excessively wide smile on my face. It was so big it actually hurt. I realized I couldn't have written a script any better than to have a group of conspirators orchestrate an effort to situate me too as a "Me Too" predator, and botch it so badly.

In my dreams a statement was read that was easily refuted, posters anonymously posted in bathrooms conveying an over-the-top message to further exacerbate their situation, more so than mine. I was happy that this particular dream proved there was a smear campaign.

I tossed and turned a bit during the part of my dream where they continued to assert that I was out of control when defending myself being attacked against an accusation that, by itself, can be career limiting if not ending. Somehow it is okay that I'm slandered by Students not smart enough or caring enough to anticipate the consequences and as an employee of that university—within my dreams—I'm just supposed to take it. Too bad, in this dream they went after the wrong Negro. More so, it's on.

In my dreams I am really happy that my friends care enough about me to have one of the best lawyers in his field to actually initiate the call.

In this dream I was devastated to discover how easily some lost faith in me. Perhaps it was easy because they never really believed in me anyway.

I'm going to awaken and immediately return to sleep to look for the answer to how people can actually take it upon themselves to be judge n' jury.

In my dream a few days ago I was excessively pleased with how much love I received from others. I hope when I awaken that I remember to have a big party at my Timeshare in NYC for all my supporters who can attend to thank them for having my back. Of course it will be paid by the winnings from the different lawsuits I'll win. Got to love America!!!

Even in real life, perhaps more, I wouldn't stand for such treatment, like initially being framed as professionally inadequate when it is far from the truth. So it was cool that I'm not having any part of that in my dreams too. It was refreshing to discover that in my dreams I don't go quietly in the night as my reputation gets worse and worse.

In my dream my fiancé—who originates from a family of privilege consisting of lawyers - judges - notaries, insisted I promise I would sue the parties involved to reinforce the fact that the "Me Too" movement isn't something to play with. Women have been exploited, abused, ridiculed, and relegated to lesser status at the whims of men. Anyone using the movement for their own ill-gotten gain must be punished, a statement must be made. After all, appropriating the movement for your personal reasons or vendettas is again using women.

In my dream it was nice people recognized how important it is not to rush to judgment. When people you think you know—say negative things about people you don't really know—you don't have to believe them. It is a choice.

In my dream the one person who tried to avoid being implicated in the dirty deed overplayed her hand and was revealed for exactly who she is.

In my dream my attorney is known for cases like this having served as legal counsel for a University System. He knows his way around a college. I almost awakened from my slumber when told that my case of slander against the student government will be a slam dunk, with so many witnesses present to corroborate the slander. Also my lawsuit against an underhanded, deceptive individual—who endeavors to be involved in every single thing occurring at the college of my dreams—will be a simple thing to prove in terms of a violation of the policies of that office, especially with solid evidence available.

It must be an interesting thing watching a train barreling towards you, you're strapped in your car, and it won't start. Then my alarm went off and I realized it was just a dream, or was it? Oh well, how could they know that the nice man that most people like when they get to know him was the wrong Negro to defame. How could they know? I didn't know until I awakened. Fortunately, I'm woke now.

"Is your question a serious one, or are you just fishing?" Dr. Witt asked, unabashedly. "Even before revisiting it I thought my Facebook post was appropriate considering the circumstances. After reading it I have no regrets about posting it. If I had not defended myself who would have? Utley certainly would not have. And as to your question as to who I was modeling leadership? I was demonstrating to all my students in the room that someone who teaches social justice and yet won't defend himself-- when a blatant miscarriage of justice is playing out--isn't modeling well for his students at all. I was also modeling that I wasn't going to be anyone's house nigger, content with having more access than others, nonetheless groveling, begging Utley to help me survive, hoping the good people in the room who believe in me would fight for me, perhaps find it in their good graces to argue on my behalf with the people in the room who believe I'm guilty, essentially forming an opinion of me from a distance since they don't know me."

Dr. Witt, added, "As to whether it was a threat or not, there's an old saying, 'if you throw a rock in a pack of dogs, the one that howls, is the one that got hit.'"

"I'm getting the impression you aren't taking this interview serious," Cloudy asserted.

"No, I'm taking it more seriously than you could have anticipated. I thoroughly enjoy looking bullies directly in the eye. They send three White women, one with a connection to Peru, possibly even knowing the Title IX officer who claims to not have known what was happening in her own shop, and I'm not the one taking it serious, really?"

"You think threatening your employer and its governing system with a lawsuit is appropriate behavior?"

"If they deserve a lawsuit, yes I do. Why wouldn't anyone consider a lawsuit if treated unfairly." Dr. Witt answered with no reservation. "The post was titled '*Dreams of Reality.*' As I said in it, "I awakened from a dream enlightened and didn't fight the urge to articulate my dream."

"You expect us to believe it was a dream?" asked Cloudy, rhetorically.

"With all due respect, I could care less what you believe. However, am I here with you right now with my attorney?"

That's kind of obvious Dr. Witt," replied Cloudy, itching to call Xavier an asshole, definitely thinking it.

"Perhaps not so obvious, considering that in my Facebook post all references to attorneys are male references. As you can see my attorney is not male. So as I said, the dream post was me sharing a dream I had."

Nevertheless, you don't expect us to believe it was a dream, do you?

"Listen, you came in here already believing something about me. I'm not naive," replied Dr. Witt. "So I'm really not overly preoccupied with what else you have chosen to believe. When I said in the post that," looking down at the paper in his hand to read from it, "I couldn't have written a better script than one revealing a group of conspirators committed to orchestrating an effort to situate me as a 'Me Too' predator, only to have them botch it so badly," I wasn't exaggerating. Your job as investigators, ethical investigators I would hope, would be to fact-find, not clean up their mess by digging so deep in my past that you found a girl in the second grade who I pushed off the slide. You've seen the flyers, but my question is, has anyone come forward to validate the flyers existence, to validate the message in the flyers?"

"We're asking the questions," Dr. Witt, "Not you."

"You're asking the questions because I'm still on the payroll, which somewhat purchases my silence if I want to remain employed. That's convenient isn't it?" responded Dr. Witt, while mentally editing to nothingness his desire to say 'You may be asking the questions today, but I'll ask my questions eventually.' Instead, he complied, "Okay. I'll let you do your job. But I hope your job isn't such that you will adopt the party line mantra, 'He's out of control' when I'm totally in my right to defend myself from being character assassinated to the extent it could be career limiting, if not ending. It is sad that somehow Utley thinks it is okay--that I'm slandered by students not smart enough or caring enough to anticipate the consequences--and as an employee of that university I'm just supposed to be the consummate professional and just take it."

"We appreciate if you allow us to do our jobs," Cloudy said, with anxiety written across her face. "So your reference to a lawsuit in the dream post wasn't a threat?"

"It was a dream I decided to share," elaborated Dr. Witt. "However, the dream may have been only a vision, because look at us now, all lawyered up." "May I ask you a question though, before we go any further?"

"Sure."

"In the dream post I mentioned how my fiance, as a survivor, made me promise to sue the parties involved to reinforce that the "MeToo" movement isn't something to play with," Dr. Witt stated. "Women have been exploited, abused, ridiculed, and relegated to lesser status at the whims of men. Anyone using the movement for their own ill-gotten-gain must be punished. Have you given any consideration to the possibility that this thing I'm going through could be trumped up charges?"

"Of course, we're professionals. We enter investigations with open minds."

Xavier didn't believe her for a single moment. Other questions she would ask later, and her responses to questions Xavier asked solidified his concerns that he was swimming upstream with these two investigators. They would go back and forth for hours, taking a break for lunch, then resuming the interview.

Slut Shaming

"So can you tell us about your evening with Dr. Michelle Boone?" asked Cloudy.

"It wasn't an evening, it was lunch, and that was seven years ago," answered Dr. Witt.

"Appreciate the correction," Cloudy said. "Please continue."

"Not much to tell. We had lunch, it lasted about ninety minutes. We were both single at the time, had met at LeAnn Prey's home and a week or so later decided to have lunch."

She claims you shared an inappropriate poem with her," Cloudy offered, "that made her feel uncomfortable."

"I told her I was a want-to-be poet. She asked me to share my poetry with her. I specifically asked her what category of poetry she would prefer." Shifting his weight, Dr. Witt continued, "She preferred to hear something romantic and as a result I shared a romantic poem with her. She didn't think it was inappropriate at the time. As a matter of fact she probably didn't consider it inappropriate until the MeToo crusaders on campus recruited her to their cause."

"She claims you tried to hug her. She said it made her feel uncomfortable."

"It would have made me more uncomfortable than her. Of the two of us she was the negative Nancy, not me. Why would I want to hug a woman who looked as if she enjoyed scowling? First off I would assume she wouldn't want to hug anyone, me included. Even a tree would avoid such a hug."

"Ask her if she was so uncomfortable with me why she didn't mention it to her current boyfriend of approximately 5-6 years. He and I hang out at least once or twice a year, visiting each other's homes, drinking, sharing brotherhood smoke. He is my H.R. rep and wouldn't hesitate to broach the topic if he had any problems with what he heard. We both have reputations as straight shooters."

Writing something down quickly, Cloudy abruptly looked up and said, "So can you tell us about your evening with Felicia Priest?"

Unfettered, Dr. Witt replied, "Which one, the double date we had with both of our partners joining us, or the meeting we had a couple of months later to brainstorm situating her office?"

"The time you two dined alone."

"We didn't dine. We just had drinks."

"Is that all you did?"

"What did she tell you happened? As far as I'm concerned you're asking questions of me about my personal time."

"She claims you tried to place your lips against hers, making her uncomfortable."

"Are you serious?" Dr. Witt exclaimed. "Every time I see this woman she greets me with a kiss on the lips. I figured she did it to expedite our level of comfort with one another, if not posturing as the new kid on the block that she's connected to the campus' movers and shakers. She isn't shy about it either, even doing it right in front of my fiancé. So now when it suits her duplicity the greeting kiss she has always initiated is a problem. Think about it. I'm a Black man. Do you think I'm arbitrarily running up to White women and putting my lips on them?"

"She also said you two smoked weed immediately outside the restaurant. Is that true?"

"If it is true why would it be your business?"

"We have a concern that you are preying on Jr. Faculty."

"What, preying on Jr. Faculty. Are you serious?"

"There appears to be a pattern of behavior that supports our concern," asserted Cloudy.

"There appears to be a pattern of lies by White women who are all connected, many of whom have similar reputations. Have you investigated that, investigators? I mean, oh my god, this is unreal," said Dr. Witt, thrown somewhat off balance by Cloudy's declaration. "First off," decried Xavier emphatically, "I would never, ever smoke weed in downtown Peru. That evening, after we discussed our various ways of escaping North Country doldrums Felicia asked me if I had any marijuana on me. When I said yes, in my car, she expressed an interest in getting a buzz before she returned home. So when we left the restaurant we took a drive out to my home, about fifteen minutes from the restaurant, where we sat in the car and shared a hit, since I didn't have much in my pipe. I did not invite her into my home. We were in my driveway no more than ten minutes, and then I returned her to her car."

"Did you try to kiss her?"

"No way, our lips touched lightly when I passed a hit to her, but our lips touch much more intimately when we greet."

At this point there was a pause in the interview while they were all feverishly taking notes, even though the session was being recorded. Eventually the other investigator shifted her weight in her chair as if she was about to speak.

"Tell us about the evening you spent with Jayne Boyer?" asked Renoir.

"Sure," Dr. Witt answered. "She joined me at my home one evening after classes to help me assemble a desk. We stopped by an AppleBee's to get some food. We were out to my home about 2-2.5 hours. We successfully assembled the desk and then I returned her back to campus."

"Were there any romantic moments shared between the two of you?"

"Not one."

"She says there were."

"Romance is about the possibility of the thing. In my mind there was never any possibility of anything happening because I didn't see Jayne like that."

"She claims you gave each other massages."

"We did?"

"You don't think that was romantic?" asked Renoir.

"Not compared to massages that I give to take an evening to another level," Dr. Witt said unapologetically. "The massages took place in my kitchen, which is not where I give my sensual massages. If you think airport or mall massages are sexy or romantic, then you may think it was romantic. I don't. Jayne initiated the massages, putting her hands on my upper back and shoulders as she asked me if I wanted it. I said yes because it felt good. She massaged my upper back, shoulders, and neck for 10-15 minutes. When she finished we changed positions and I then massaged Jayne's upper back, shoulders, and neck for 10-15 minutes. During both massages there was little talk. When I finished reciprocating the massage we left my home and I returned Jayne back to campus."

"So she didn't masturbate you?"

"What?"

"She said after the massages you took out your penis and showed her how to masturbate you."

"She's lying. Did she say we kissed?"

"Did you kiss?"

"No. And I've never been masturbated by a woman I didn't kiss."

"She actually said you didn't kiss, but said she masturbated you."

"So somehow I pulled out my penis and said, "Would you hold this for me?

For the first time during the interview the investigators looked like they were suppressing a smile. My attorney Mikki however was as gangster as she alway is. No smiles there, probably thinking to herself, '*He doesn't pay me to smile.*'

Dr. Witt then asked, "Did she tell you she wrote a poem about our evening?

"No," answered Renoir.

"I'll make sure we get it to you," Mikki offered.

"Did she tell you she finished the semester as my T.A. and a year later returned to T.A. for me again, for no academic credit?"

"No."

"Well then you have some more work to do. Jayne is lying. You won't know that unless you ask her to reconcile a few things. When you read the poem you'll know she came forward to testify as a survivor seven years after that evening for reasons other than being disrespected. However, for at least a year after that evening she was conveniently still around me, by choice. How could anyone believe the story of a woman who not only wrote a romantic poem about the evening, one that was a flight of fancy, she wasn't kissed, claims she masturbated me, then also continued to T.A.

the remainder of the semester and for free a year later. If she had been physically accosted or disrespected in any way she had chances to distance herself from me as well as report it. Having never had an attraction to Jayne the massage with her wasn't tempting. It didn't involve any sensual body parts. Jayne experienced nothing that evening that merited her writing a poem other than me being cool with her."

Not seeming to be too pleased with my refutation of their weak-ass testimony from Jayne, the investigators regrouped, asking, "Did you smoke marijuana with her."

"Yes."

"Was that appropriate for you to do with a student?"

"She was a T.A. and it was more appropriate than sharing martinis with her. Who assembles a desk at the end of the day without some type of libation or buzz?"

"Well while we are on the topic of appropriate behavior, do you think it was appropriate for your daughter to have taken pictures of you and your lady friend having sex?"

"That was quite a segue. If any such thing occurred, how would it be your business?"

"It became our business when you showed those pictures at the office."

"When I showed them, not if?" Dr. Witt stated defiantly.

"When he *allegedly* showed them at the office," Mikki said, correcting their overstatement. Unless you have video tape that corroborates your assertion all you have to support that is someone's word against my client's word."

"And we know how much they think my word is worth, don't we," added Dr. Witt. "Nonetheless, I didn't think it was appropriate and I let her know that. The fact that my lesbian daughter who is into photography somehow misinterpreted me and as a result thereafter stealthily entered our bedroom to take pics of us, is not enough for you to try to slut-shame me into silence. For the record, that won't work with me but nice try."

"Someone on your staff reported to us that you shared some inappropriate images from a phone app. Is that true?" asked Renoir.

"I have no idea what you are talking about," Dr. Witt answered.

"Deidre Bright told us you shared some Kamasutra images on your cell phone with her."

"Startled to hear this, Dr. Witt responded, "Why wouldn't I share them with her. She was my assistant director, who had input into many things I was designing. Considering I teach a Romance, Sex, Love, & Marriage class why wouldn't I ask her opinion?"

"Did she tell you about the time she grabbed my ass one day in the office, or what she said when I questioned her about it," Dr. Witt asked frustrated.

The investigators looking perplexed as to what to say, had no response. So Dr. Witt continued, "I said to her, 'Hey, if I did that to you I would be in all types of trouble.' Deidre responded by saying, 'You certainly would be.'"

Though he put up a good front, this testimonial of inappropriate behavior by him hurt much more than others. He and Deidre had always been close. Never in his wildest dreams would he have thought she would have contributed to a court case against him. They had co-taught classes for almost a decade together, co-facilitated workshops, co-presented at conferences all over the country, and essentially co-directed OPIE. They had vacationed together with their significant others, dined alone often, and talked openly and honestly about topics both light and heavy. The fact that she turned on him was a surprise, but once done he didn't struggle imagining the reason. She had essentially adopted Devin. She hoped when she retired in 2013 that Devin would be hired as her replacement. However, that just wasn't going to happen. Hiring Devin as assistant director of OPIE would be perilously close to inviting LeAnn Prey into the inner sanctum. So, this left Dr. Witt with no recourse other than imagining Deidre betrayed him out of loyalty to Devin, or LeAnn, a close friend of

Deidre. Ironically, a few weeks later while discussing with Oliver (an ex-student of Deidre & XW) the investigation Dr. Witt was surprised to hear that Deidre had confided in Oliver about her testimony. She told him she didn't know why she testified against Dr. Witt. She acknowledged she had been recruited to testify, but if she could take it back she would have.

Devin also had a chance to contribute to the investigation, which wasn't surprising at all. The last time Dr. Witt had seen him was when Devin attended Dr. Witt's book signing, which actually did surprise Dr. Witt. However, the exchange with the investigators concerning Devin's input was disconcerting. It wasn't because of what Devin said, but the fact that the investigators thought it was worthy enough to even discuss.

"Someone in your office found on the copier a Montreal Swingers article."

Dr. Witt didn't alter his breathing one iota. Looking directly in the investigators eyes, he said, "If it were mine, so what?"

"You think it is appropriate behavior to copy a Montreal Swinger's article on the company printer-copier?

"I imagine that would depend upon the reason someone does it, though I know you bring it up to try and suggest something about me," Dr. Witt said exasperated. "If it were mine, I wouldn't be ashamed. My reasons could range from using it as research for my Romance class, to researching it for mentoring of a student or colleague on the topic, to genuine interest in what that could be about. Why is your investigation so preoccupied with over-sexualizing me, so focused on insisting there is some problem with what you must consider as my overactive libido? If I do have an active libido--or an overactive libido--is it stated somewhere in the Chief Diversity Officer manual that we must be asexual?"

Xavier knew he was antagonizing investigators who were trying to antagonize him. More so, like the evening when he lost his cool at the forum, he had once again entered into 'fuck that' territory. He was not going to overly defer--out of some misguided sense of respect for their position--to investigators that he deemed dirty. Ethical investigators would have pretended to care about his answers to their questions. The entire time he answered their questions he felt they were just checking off questions they needed to ask him to justify doing their jobs fair and impartially.

"Can you tell us, from your perspective," asked Renoir, "what started the rumor about you disrespecting women?"

"Certainly, it was the false accusation of sexual harassment by an ex-student of mine back in 2002-03."

"You are speaking of Kathleen Kline."

"Yes."

"She declined to speak with us, but we have the report detailing her accusation against you," announced Renoir. "Are you aware of what was in the report?"

"Other than her being upset over grades and fabricating a reality around her inadequacy, she accused me of saying something she deemed after the fact as sexually inappropriate."

"Do you recall what that was?"

"Yes," said Dr. Witt, "She said a comment I made about her arms one day when she was wearing a short sleeve blouse made her uncomfortable."

"Do you recall what the comment was?" Renoir asked.

"I told her she had nice arms, then asked her if she worked out." Dr. Witt responded. "I should add that I extended that compliment to her the first semester she took classes from me. So it's odd that she would follow me into two other classes and lobby me for an opportunity to be my Teacher's Assistant if she was offended by that comment. I mean on some level does that not sound like someone reaching to have a problem with me?"

Renoir, unimpressed with the point Xavier made, replied, "In that report she made some even stronger allegations. For example, she says one evening she came out to your house with another female student to watch some film clips you were considering using in one of your classes. She reported you saying—after a scene in the film showed a well-endowed Black football player—something along the lines of 'Wouldn't you like to play with a big black dick like that."

Dr. Witt, totally unprepared to hear such a thing purported to have been said by him, responded, "First off the comment is nonsensical. It's like calling a Black person a Black nigger. The term nigger is universally applied to Blacks so associating Black with nigger is redundant. If I ever would say something about someone playing with a Black dick I wouldn't need to say 'big' because that is already implied."

Dr. Witt knew he had made the investigators uncomfortable but at this point didn't give a damn. They brought up black dicks, not him. He just took their conception of black dicks to another level, possibly embarrassing investigators committed to embarrassing him. He knew they were seeking to advance their agenda and he wasn't going to be duped into thinking he could say anything that would change their minds.

"Besides, I have never heard anything about 'black dicks' before, which makes me wonder why I never received that report. There is no way I would forget such an incredulous accusation. If I lived alone that wouldn't have occurred because I respect women and myself too much to say anything like that to anyone. More so, anyone who actually knows me would not begin to believe I would say something so racially charged, sexually problematic and sensually titillating to two young women, especially White women, who could be inclined to run back to share it amongst their circle of friends. More so, anyone that would believe that—in my home, with my children and wife at the time moving throughout the house, including the fact that at anytime my wife could have joined us—I would say something like that is an unequivocal idiot."

"Listen," Dr. Witt said pointedly, "Do you think I just awakened in this world, or that I have lived my entire life with my head in the sand?"

Without awaiting an answer Dr. Witt continued, "Or do you think I was born with no ability to discern the bigger pictures life insists we pay attention to, if we want to be successful and/or happy. I'm a Black man living and working in a predominantly White community. I also happen to teach, amongst other courses, *African American Realities*. Do you actually believe that I would be so stupid as to say to young impressionable White female students such things—not to mention have sex with them—and not have those words and deeds take on a life of their own? I know American history. I teach about Angela Davis' *Myth of Black Sexuality'* and the *'Myth of the Black Rapist.'* Those lessons weren't lost on me. Nonetheless, my very existence as a progressive educator—who has done nothing close to what is repeatedly being alleged—has resulted in this web of lies that it seems you are apt, like so many others, to believe."

"You do know that for us to believe you we would have to think that all of these women are lying and you alone are telling the truth."

"That's it exactly," Dr, Witt replied, unapologetically. "All of these women amount to what, four that you have mentioned to me, two of which are close personal friends with the woman who once hoped to have the CDO position and would try for it now if it wouldn't be so obvious. Those same two, if you looked into their disposition you would discover two of the more likely candidates to fabricate an untruth."

"I'm wondering if you will actually follow up with any of these witnesses against me and include not only my responses in your final report but their responses to my rebuttals. I'm wondering why you didn't ask Deidre and Devin what Dr. Witt may say in defense of their accusations. Will you take my responses to them for their reaction, or am I guilty in your minds and you're already so far out there you can't find your way back?"

While receiving no bona fide commitment they would, when we concluded the interview Dr. Witt was surprised to hear that within two weeks Charlotte Cloudy would no longer be employed by NYSU, moving on to another career opportunity. This minimized greatly his confidence that the two investigators would do any follow up. More so, he was disappointed in himself for not asking them to reconcile Linda Dewar's actions while reporting to Molly Mothburn against one of the stated Title IX mantras:

"No person in the United States shall, on the basis of sex, be excluded from participation in, be denied the benefits of, or be subjected to

discrimination under any education program or activity receiving Federal financial assistance."

Dr. Witt and his attorney Mikki spent a few moments unpacking the interview and the merits as well as demerits of the investigators, and then went their separate ways. With a three-hour long drive home from Albany, N.Y. to Peru, N.Y., Dr. Witt had plenty of time to reflect upon some of the various things discussed throughout the five-hour interview. He revisited Shalo's problematic statement of what she had "heard" followed by his impassioned reply. First only a rumored whisper existed. Then flyers were created, and posted in multiple places, flyers that oddly suggested a potpourri of problems with Dr. Witt, not just predatory behavior. Suffice it to say, beyond a smear campaign, the move against Xavier was as clear as it was political.

Additionally, considering the meeting with the investigators it was intriguing how little was discussed about the flyers as evidence of a smear campaign. Was it not worthy of investigation? Most likely it was amongst the fuel that ignited if not conveniently legitimating the investigation. Xavier however would have bet his life on the fact the investigation on him began to take shape on February 29 after he informed Utley that he was going to sue to defend his name.

Yet, the investigators only mentioned three women coming forward, one (Jayne Boyer) alleging a sexual encounter (2010) at his home, one (Michelle Boone) alleging an attempted hug and inappropriate poem (2011) after a first and only lunch meeting, and one (Felicia Priest) suggesting an attempt by Xavier (2016) to place his lips against hers while smoking marijuana together. While all of these accusations sadden him in terms of the extent some pathological white women will lie to advance their cause, were any pertinent questions asked? How about two simple questions each for Boone and Priest? Why didn't they ask them what their status with the campus currently is? And ask them if they aren't both close associates of LeAnn Prey, a professor rapidly losing respect amongst her peers because she was becoming known more for her duplicitous behavior than any social justice efforts. A private interview with the current Dean or the previous one (now interim Provost) would reveal much of this. However, that would mean that a legitimate investigation was underway, not one to corroborate years of inadequate administrative activity wanting to be swept under the rug.

Xavier then reflected upon how the Jayne Boyer testimony could be revealed as a flight of fantasy by simply asking her to describe his penis. If she actually saw it, held it, and masturbated him she shouldn't have any problems describing it. Under oath she would have to state its size, thickness, curvature, and style of cut. He was absolutely positive she wouldn't take a lie detector test either. He thought that he should have insisted that the investigators ask her about her failed sexual relationship with a student close to Dr. Witt a month later. She was visibly upset over her relationship with that student not working out, revealing to enough students that she felt as if she had been abused due to how lacking it was in romantic intimacy. Nonetheless she writes Dr. Witt a poem about their time together within a week after assembling the desk. If he had any remote interest in a sexual relationship with Jayne, it would have only happened that one night. Her poem's flight-of-fancy would have dramatically prevented it from ever occurring a second time.

Dr. Witt then thought of how friends of his had forever teased him about possibly being tempted to have a sexual fling with his students. As a very sensual man who is romantically inclined and who has taught many about *romance, sex, love, and marriage* in his similarly named class, the average college aged student—who obviously would have had to consent to a sexual interaction with him— would probably lose her perspective considering the differences in experiences and privilege existing between Dr. Witt, an accomplished man, and the garden variety college male.

Xavier hoped the investigators would reconnect with one of Jayne's witnesses, Hai Foo an Asian-American student who once was a student of Dr. Witt, to ask him what his rapport with Dr. Witt is currently like, and why. Foo asserts it changed because of Boyers revealing Dr. Witt's alleged intimacy with her. Dr. Witt has always adamantly disagreed with this as the reason he and Foo drifted apart. Foo had an axe to grind with Dr, Witt over Witt not rehiring his mentor to return to campus on OPIE's budget. Foo, also once a T.A. of Dr. Witt's, was upset with Dr. Witt forgetting to write a reference letter for him, and felt embarrassed with his mentor from

NYC when he promised something he couldn't deliver, and subsequently blamed Dr. Witt and never forgave him.

Xavier wondered if the investigators ever interviewed campus police about the flyers. He found it odd that the flyers stated "Dr. Witt please stop touching us," while no one who allegedly was touched ever came forward, other than two Jr. Faculty from years before. Xavier surmised that is why they came forward to be interviewed. Without these two lying White women, both known across the campus as malcontents, their case would be even more frivolous than it actually currently is. Both of these two unethical women knew they could hide behind the cloak of survivors while the campus investigation was underway. They both probably figured out, in cahoots with LeAnn Prey, that their first priority was getting him off campus. After that they would let the chips fall as they may, never anticipating that Dr. Witt would take it to the next level. NYSU had no true grounds to terminate him based upon any recent evidence so they went back as far as necessary to have something they could spin against him.

Confirmation Bias

Dr. Witt asked himself aloud, almost screaming it, "How does a university president initiate an investigation of an employee on the recommendation of a Title IX officer he explicitly stated couldn't objectively conduct the investigation herself? This couldn't be any more fucking unbelievable."

Catching his breath a bit, Dr. Witt wished he had offered to construct a timeline that beyond a reasonable doubt would prove there was a smear (defamation) campaign against him, supported by the S.G. and FA/Title IX, and further supported by a couple of incidents of public humiliation, which all together fostered a hostile environment from the S.G., the FA/Title IX, and the administration. Bullying in terms of character assassination occurred throughout. Student letters Xavier received in support of his defense against FA/Title IX are documentation he could provide upon request. However, would the investigators care about looking at them.

Dr. Witt second guessed not having given investigators a copy of FA professor Sharon Winchell's post to his Wandering Witt blog on the

Democratic Perspectives website, Nov 19, 2009. In that post Winchell unequivocally labeled Dr. Witt as a sexual predator. He wished he had engaged them about the accusatory February 5, 2010 letter from two FA minors who were both very close to the Dept. chair at the time, Ramona Saphony. He wanted to kick himself for not insisting they take time to discuss the email he wrote to the University President requesting that the Affirmative Action Officer recuse herself due to potential bias and Dr. Witt's early articulation of a smear campaign underway, orchestrated by FA. As well, he should have discussed the email of April 25, 2010 that was proof of an ongoing effort to discredit him, accentuated by a correspondence with the Dean of Arts and Sciences regarding tactics implemented by the Chair of FA, revealing exactly how lacking in collegiality, if not pathological, the behavior towards him was by various colluding factions.

When the investigators asked him why he didn't follow up on his early complaints against Feminist Anthropology he didn't want to tell them that his divorce and defending his doctorate were dominating his life during that period. Ultimately he decided to not beat himself up too much. He didn't write the letters for writing sake, but was genuinely requesting help. While he recognized now how very different his life might be if he had forced Utley to take action to resolve tensions between OPIE and FA, he also knew that hindsight is 20/20.

Later that smear-flyer Monday evening, around 9:15pm the Student Government held a meeting to discuss their resolutions and vote on them. The meeting was considered a sham by the large number of students attending, specifically in support of Dr. Witt. However, towards the end of the meeting the S.G. allowed a young woman to publicly read a statement that further attempted to paint Dr. Witt as sexually inappropriate, if not a sexual predator. Within the statement were assertions that he just showed up to a woman's job unannounced, loitered, and upon receiving some time with her asked her about her sexual orientation amongst other comments that were allegedly inappropriate. What people wouldn't know is that she initiated their first conversation with a Facebook message exchange, followed by an invite to visit her job. What is unbeknownst to all who heard this statement is that Dr. Witt had the transcripts of all their written exchanges, beginning with the first so-called problematic exchange of

August 5, 2014, which included her twice inviting him to drop in at her job. The other further exchanges, most of which she initiated, all occurred in 2014, on August 20, Sep 3 & 4, October 7, and Nov 5. It wouldn't be much of a reach to suggest she also may have been colluding with the FA program considering she was also close to Ramona Saphony.

Immersed so deeply in thought, Dr. Witt almost missed a phone call since he hadn't taken his phone off of silent from the meeting with the investigators. Fortunately, he heard it buzzing. It was his fiancé, Kesi.

"Hey Oomboogalah, how did it go today."

"Hey Dr. Mahila, it went well, I think. Mikki thought so. She said they had nothing. She said they were reaching."

"Were you surprised by anything investigators asked, or said?" she asked.

"Actually, I was a few times, "Xavier admitted. "Deidre Bright came forward with statements suggesting I had been inappropriate at the office. Devin weighed in with whatever he could to pay me back for not hiring his petty, always pouting ass."

"Wasn't it Deidre who playfully grabbed your ass as you passed by."

"Yes, and I told them about it. They left me with the impression they could care less what I had to say. Baby, you know me, I pride myself on being respectful. But I was consistently edgy with the investigators. I didn't enjoy it, but would have felt stupid giving them authentic respect when their respect for me was non-existent, when it wasn't fake as hell."

"I'm sorry to hear that Oomboogalah," Kesi said. "Fortunately, it is them who will discover how not fake hell is when they arrive there for conducting a one-sided investigation. At least they won't be alone though. They'll have plenty of company when Michelle, Felicia, and Jayne all arrive there for lying."

"Kesi, I know I'm not a saint? I have a few things in my background that I am ashamed of relative to women, but nothing criminal, nothing abusive.

There is nothing I'm ashamed of that borders on disrespect or harassment. Once, and only once I misread a woman, thinking she was green lighting flirting with me, and I flirted back. Though she took our conversation down that road when she asked me about the RSLM class, which lead into her sharing with me that sexually, she liked her hair pulled. It turned out she was offended by me flirting with her. My entire lifetime I have always prided myself on being a gentleman. Whenever I have fallen short of that ideal it has bothered me"

"Baby, since I've known you that is the only moment with a woman you've ever mentioned you were ashamed of. I remember you described how the evening that went awry with her as more like a congratulatory meal with a young woman graduating nearly a decade ago."

"Yes, we launched into a flirtatious conversation she started when we talked about the Romance, Sex, Love, & Marriage course . Over a meal and two drinks each we spent approximately 90 minutes together. At the end of that time I returned her to campus. Days later I discovered that she was bothered by the conversation. I immediately apologized for my role in her discomfort."

"Xavier, baby," Kesi said as endearingly as she could, "when you first told me that story I assumed--from the shame you revealed while telling me about it--that you had actually been involved with her sexually."

"You would've wanted to know I rocked her socks?" Xavier asked.

"If you had sex with her, I assumed you handled your business," Kesi said with as complimentary a sultry voice as she could muster. "I couldn't reconcile how you could be ashamed just from a conversation. I finally figured out you were ashamed because, as an ally, you had no desire to take away anyone's energy. However, a conversation between two adults that went south isn't enough to paint you as a sexual predator, even if you are seen as having more power than the woman. Obviously it wasn't the most intelligent thing you've ever done, but there was no coercion, threats of retaliation, violation of physical space, drugging, harassment, or stalking."

"It means a whole lot to me Baby that you believe in me."

"I not only believe in you," said Kesi, "but I believe some glory seeking women decided to make a name for themselves at your expense by attempting to reveal some things that don't exist. They were fishing for their MeToo moment, thinking if they manipulated or collaborated with the SG to make it happen, it would happen. During the process of trying to find survivors to justify having your name on the list they publicly defamed you as professionally inadequate, as well as an incompetent CDO."

"And Utley conveniently took the most politically expedient action," Xavier added, "His specialty. With no hesitation he colluded to take my career away as a CDO, looking the other way as my character was sledge hammered, while oddly somehow trying to save face from taking me down, if not out, even possibly agreeing with the Student Government that I'm quite good as a college professor, good enough to be retained in that capacity, but not as his CDO.

"Baby, how the S.G. and its insipid advisor came to the conclusion that they could publicly humiliate you is crazy," Kesi said. "Just as long as they complimented you intermittently. All of this is rationalized against an underlying assertion that you are a "MeToo" perpetrator."

"Shit I knew I should have had you with me at the interview with the investigators," Xavier said. "No one knows my story as intimately as you do. You would think we are fucking or something."

"We don't fuck baby. We make love," Kesi said, playfully admonishing Xavier. "Well, maybe we kind of fuck, sometimes," she admitted.

"Kesi, I do know this though, I ignored the whispering for years because I know who I am. I couldn't ignore the whispers any longer when they became connected to political machinations designed to sully my reputation and undercut my worth to my immediate employer and/or future employers who have unhesitatingly hired me as an educational consultant and committed ally. Besides all of that, the "MeToo" movement is not only an idea whose time has come, but was long overdue. For me it parallels moments when some Black people used unwarranted, unnecessary violence or terrorist tactics while flying the flag of Black Lives Matter. The movement is too valuable for one person to use them as personal whims."

"I agree Baby," Kesi said supportively. "MeToo wasn't designed for the selfish use of some ambitious women with a misinterpretation of someone predicated on a legacy of whispers. As both a battle-tested womanist and survivor my life was at risk as a Mediterranean physician often speaaking about women's rights when I practiced medicine in Morocco and Germany. That is why from the beginning I insisted you sue NYSU for blatantly usurping—for their own purposes—such a critically important platform."

"And we are suing. The role the system played in supporting Utley needs to be scrutinized. I know the Chairman of the Board, personally. We're not crew in the sense of doing coffee when I'm in town. But we have conducted business over the phone. We have shared a stage, professionally (Unpacking MLK's I Have a Dream Speech). Supposedly we are both Alphas, though I have never found him in our membership directory. Most importantly, we are both Black men. He knew of the work I was doing at NYSU-Peru, and around the country. How he let what happened occur under his watch is inexplicable. He chose to allow two White female investigators to perpetuate the *Myth of the Black Rapist* against a diligent brother who had given his heart and soul to NYSU."

"What about your students Baby?" asked Kesi. "What happened to NYSUs student-centeredness? Utley's focus when under pressure is always his own self-centeredness. I would bet anyone that you have had more of an impact on students, expanding their intellectual horizons, influencing their perspectives, than Utley, by leaps and bounds. You impacted the North Country by raising its consciousness. Yet NYSU chose Utley over you, on his word that you were out of control, a problem. Ooh, it infuriates me just thinking about it."

"The Chancellor and I had just met when we took a photo together a year prior, when she visited NYSU-Peru," Xavier said. "I followed her on Twitter, having sent her the pic of the two of us posing with some students. Assuming she probably didn't remember me, the Chancellor almost gets a pass, almost. I imagine the Chancellor will finally awaken, only too late, and then have to admit that she made a bad call in how she supported

Utley, essentially nothing more than a straw man in contrast to the measurable impact I had on the campus and surrounding community."

Xavier continued, "Utley for years has been the Emperor wearing new clothes. Most whispered of his ineptness. I studied how Ryan Coughman and Morgan Mark manipulated him, did their equivalent of a Vulcan mind meld on him, to which he was highly responsive. This is why I know what Molly is doing. He's malleable, not breakable, but spineless and bendy."

Same Here/HimToo - Creating Male Survivors

"Mothburn should be ashamed." added Kesi. "The misappropriation of MeToo discredits the entire movement on another level, by creating male survivors that are often dismissed because of the low percentage of them in contrast to the larger percentage of perpetrators facing justice."

"So true Oomboogalah," Xavier said. "Male survivors are dismissed without consideration because of some MeToo code that allows for the most unethical male attrition. As a result of protecting MeToo survivors, wrongly accused male survivors become lepers relegated to a lifetime of people wondering, and whispering, with a membership in the HimToo movement, their application being nothing more than having been accused. Is that justice?"

"That is nowhere close to justice, Kesi agreed. "Since when is it okay for women to begin to attain equal status and improve our lives, but while doing so sacrifice the lives of men that may be innocent, regardless of how inconsequential some find the percentage to be."

It must be a case of 'the king is dead, long live the king," Xavier speculated. "Only in this scenario men were perennially king, dominating women by taking their voices away. Finally though, that abusive, sexually inappropriate king was slain, by women. And now as the monarchs themselves, women do similar things when they exercise their newfound power and dominate or control the lives of innocent men, taking their voices away too. That must have been what rap artist Snoop Dogg meant in the Dr. Dre Song 'Imagine,' when he said, *'but just imagine if the rabbit got the gun.'"*

Xavier continued, "I do not begrudge women their day in the sun, nor want to detract from all women as a species being recognized as survivors of misogyny. Who knows how many of them are MeToo survivors. Yet there is something troubling about silently accepting any person's allegation against someone without proof. An example of how problematic this can be is the *Susan Smith* case where she was believed by many who chose to believe, to invest in her story. Instead it looks like she set the whole thing up because it benefitted her to do so. Her reasons for choosing a Black man are as evident as NYSU's trying to build a case against me as a sexual predator. The moment the allegation was levied, for some in the audience I was no longer the CDO, or even Dr. Witt. I morphed into a *nigger* for many in that crowd, or like Aunt Sarah said in the film Rosewood, 'nigger, just another word for guilty.'"

"Obviously Oomboogalah, it was politically expedient for Utley to remove you." Kesi said. "In removing you he allowed himself another day of life."

"I wonder how many people will say, 'Oh shit, now that makes sense,'" said Xavier, "when they hear the story behind my impassioned video response that most saw but couldn't understand."

"Which is why we are going to sue NYSU/NYSU-Peru for creating and ceaselessly perpetuating a hostile environment, including the public humiliation you had to endure," Kesi stated emphatically. "They covertly as well as overtly defamed your character and reputation. I'm also looking for you to sue the Student Government of NYSU-Peru, their gangly, snake-in-the-grass, advisor for the role he played in it, along with the Title IX office in conjunction with Feminist Anthropology for their collusion, and that two-faced heifer Molly."

"Breathe Oomboogalah, breathe," Xavier said. "My threat of a lawsuit, which prompted NYSU to investigate, regardless of my cries for help being ignored for years, is now literally a pending court case as a result of their sham of an investigation. Now I plan on doing whatever it takes to make a huge statement on behalf of the misappropriation and misuse of the

"MeToo" movement. NYSU-Peru conducted a retaliatory investigation with the hope of embarrassing me into quietly going away. That won't happen. I'm not ashamed of any of my actions in the context of any allegations or even insinuations of abuse of power. I'm totally okay with all the details of my story coming out along the way to publicly reveal NYSU-Peru's ineffectual leadership, and it's dysfunctional Title IX Office overly influenced by a pathological FA department. I am planning on using every resource available to fight for financial awards/damages that address the ruination of my career after 18 years at NYSU-Peru. I have no desire to attempt to rebuild my career this late in life. I'm looking for financial compensation for the impact to my consulting business *Xamining Diversity*, which was largely predicated upon my impeccable reputation as an ally and social justice educator/consultant, I'm looking for a financial penalty large enough to awaken academic institutions to the responsibilities they must accept in protecting their employees."

"I'm curious Baby if any other NYSU-Peru faculty/staff have had flyers posted in the Student Union defaming them?" Kesi said. "I spoke today with your two young bloods that are attorneys, Nick and Aaron. They both called to check up on you. I don't recall which one mentioned it, but one of them said you should sue NYSU-Peru for 'Mobbing.' Supposedly it is a malicious attempt to force a person out of the workplace through unjustified accusations, harassment, and emotional abuse. It involves rallying others into systematic and frequent "mob-like" behavior against a target, and 'ganging up.'"

"I looked into that Kesi. Nick practices law in Massachusetts and Aaron in California. So they are not necessarily speaking from the legal perspective of New York. I was informed a mobbing lawsuit isn't feasible in New York State. I'll check it out again anyway," Xavier promised. "I do have something I want your opinion on that I was considering mailing to the investigators after the fact. I call it a:

RECIPE for a Misappropriated Serving of MeToo

1 Successful Man, preferably *Black*
1 ounce of a Rumor created by an unhappy person (*preferably a White woman* if the man is Black and you want it believed).

30-50 Impressionable, vulnerable female students who are semesterly manipulated into absorbing a diet of myth seasoned with misandry (preferably FA majors or minors).

1 Environment wherein so-called Allies are easily receptive to dubious/obvious allegations made anonymously in a Flyer under the pretense of protecting survivors.

2-5 Attention Addicts duped into believing the rumor true

1 Attention Addict *'researching'* the Black man without researching how legally vulnerable she may be due to the consequences of her actions

1 Attention Addict taking a victory lap after mentioning a rumor without realizing—when the case is legally resolved contrary to her expectations—she will forever be associated (by name in Internet searches) with being on the wrong side of history.

2-3 women believing they are willing to perjure themselves to further advance their cause until actually faced with a subpoena.

1 Leader known to sacrifice anyone to cloak his professional inadequacies/save his own ass.

4-5 Other so-called leaders who prefer to look the other way, whisper that their leader is wrong, and/or fall on their sword for such a leader, and yet believe they aren't complicit, subconsciously hoping the allegations are true so they can feel validated for distancing themselves from someone they once claimed to care for.

2 ropes for the sole purpose of lynching, in case one snaps.

1 Student Government (S.G.) to publicly critique the Black man for his inadequate leadership and performance, which is contrary to NYSU's acknowledgement of his facilitation of the campus' Diversity Plan, or never having a blemish on any performance evaluations.

1 S.G. President who is close friends with two attention-addicts.

1 S.G. Advisor who failing elsewhere when exploring career options was left with no other place he could be the big man so he returned to NYSU-Peru, hopeful that he could at least impress 19-22 year olds.

1 Title IX Officer who (must be a FA professor) conveniently if not incompetently knew nothing about research being done by her Title IX Intern.

1 Questionable Investigation incapable of generating anything related to posted flyers, so then reaches far into the past for anything to justify not defending a Chief Diversity Officer who won't "tone it down," or better stated take one for the team.

1 Academic Community who consider themselves allies while actually bystanders waiting for someone else to make the difference

Shake, stir even, do something to mix it all up. Let it sit for however long it takes to remove the students (Summer vacation) who might have an angry response to losing someone they valued on obviously fabricated charges. Serve cold or hot, perhaps to taste, if you have an appetite for such a dish. I recommend a glass of red wine to get the taste of this dish out of your mouth or to wash it down if you are incapable of digesting it.

PLEASE NOTE: It is an acquired taste, putatively preferred by people scarred from previous relationships or who blindly *inherit ideals* from others they think have their best interest at heart.

"Baby, you shouldn't send this," Kesi said. "I love it. But it serves no purpose."

"I knew you would deny me my fun. I'm just so pissed off at how backwards NYSU-Peru is. I should have anticipated this all could occur when I received that email a year ago after I doing my first Chief Diversity Officer presentation and the HR director sent me that email I forwarded to you last night. Can you read it to me so I can get more pissed off?"

"If you are going to get more pissed off I won't read it to you," Kesi said.

"I was just kidding baby. Please read it to me now, since I know you haven't read it yet."

"How do you know that? Maybe I have read it,"

"Have you?"

"Okay, I'll read it:

From: Lou Menard <menardl@peru.edu>
Date: November 16, 2015 at 4:30:21 PM EST
To: "X. W. Witt" <wittxw@peru.edu>
Subject: Inappropriate Language

Hello Dr. Witt, I thought I would share with you this excerpt from an email I received today.

Newly appointed CDO in his Diversity forum used inappropriate sexual language in relation to students when he said a few times we should "love 'em up". Bedroom talk does not belong in the workplace, or in relationships between faculty and students. He should have said "show the students we care".

Lou

Xavier said, "Oomboogalah, read me my response to that email. It should be at the bottom."

"Your response was:"
"What I actually said was "love them up" not "em up." Discarding the potential racial implications of someone hearing broken English when it wasn't broken, the larger point is how my saying "love them up" could be considered "inappropriate sexual language." Which word was sexual, 'love,' 'them,' or 'up?' Which words hints at "bedroom talk."

The person who should be insulted is me. If I were a woman would this have even been broached? More problematic is what this says about how I am seen by this individual. Scholar Angela Davis names this way of seeing in her book "Women, Race, and Class." In her chapters "The Myth of the Black Rapist," and "The Myth of Black Sexuality" she speaks of certain types of people who struggle with not sexualizing Black men. I highly suggest you direct the person who sexualized me to read these articles."

Even a year prior to all of this drama Xavier was dealing with the myths.

CHAPTER EIGHT
- *Allies, All Lies, Alibis, & Bye Byes*

To incite the white workers against the Negroes and to further build the myth of "white superiority," the white ruling class has coined the poisonous and insane lie that Negroes are "rapists." -- Haywood & Howard, *Lynching: A Weapon of National Oppression.*

"Although the cry of rape was invoked as popular justification for lynching in general, most lynchings took place for other reasons" (Davis, 189).

Waking up one morning in mid-May, it being 3-months that he hadn't set foot on campus, Xavier was reflecting back on so much that had transpired as his career at NYSU-Peru continued to go south. The unsanctioned investigation by a Title IX intern; being added to the students votes-of-no-confidence list; the public accusation about an unfounded rumor; Xavier's unfiltered, very real response to the hostile environment fully revealed at the Forum; the 800 signature alumni petition; the anonymous flyers in the Student Center; the all-faculty emails announcing public lynchings disguised as all-faculty meetings wherein Xavier's performance was scrutinized; the university president telling Xavier—whose problems were much more than votes-of-no-confidence—to "tone-it-down XW; Xavier's removal from campus; the Intern who investigated Xavier receiving a seat on President Utley's Social Justice Task Force; and the Investigation. There had been not one dull moment. But there had been plenty of moments where he saw people—that he thought he knew—for what really felt like the first time.

It was intriguing how Xavier's mind had not landed before in the space it was currently in. He had a conceptual epiphany that left him seeing self-proclaimed allies as literally the *allies* they claim to be, or *all lies* about what they have postured to be, or people who have *alibis*, excuses for not showing up (while nonetheless expecting others to be there for them). He realized he experienced *allies, all lies,* and *alibis* at a level he never would have fathomed. Most have. Ironically he also realized that he must be prepared to say '*bye bye*' to many relationships as a result of his situation.

Thinking back on it, perhaps the beginning of the end began that October, during the Fall semester of 2015. Xavier had taken the day off to have an extended weekend with his paramour, Dr. Kesi Mahila, a Moroccan medical doctor he had only recently met on Match.com. Match.com as a dating website had contributed so much to his love-life that it felt more like his home away from home. More importantly, it was the conduit used to give him his opportunity with Kesi, his North African love(r), his "Oomboogalah." At that time Kesi was immersed in completing her residency at a hospital in Amos, Quebec, a small town seven hours above Montreal. Amos was far enough North that it makes more sense to describe its proximity more in terms of the North Pole and Santa Claus since they both may be closer to Amos than Montreal is to them. Amos was 8.5 hours from Peru, which is one of the last stops in New York state.

That day a phone ringing interrupted light morning banter between the two lovers. Xavier removed his hand from Kesi's and answered, hearing his close colleague Nyla Earlford saying, "Hey XW, you got a minute?

"Sure Nyla, hold on for a moment though," Xavier said, arising from the sofa to go into a separate room away from noise or distracting Kesi.

It's funny how our minds work. In the moment it took Xavier to situate himself for a conversation with Nyla his mind raced. He thought of how he always had a minute for Nyla. She was interesting, funny, smart and cool. He thought randomly about how most conversations would be better served if people began them with a commitment to sharing a quality experience with someone. He always had those types of conversations with Nyla.

He thought about how he almost didn't even answer the phone, especially since he believed that answering to just tell someone you'll call them back was wasted time. Since the evolution of caller I.D. Xavier seldom answered the phone, instead he would just call back, or relegate the caller's desire for a conversation to an unfulfilled whim that caller would experience that day.

He thought about how many calls are returned by texts and scrutinized as to the reason why. On some level he knew he was guilty of that with certain people who he considered long winded. Sometimes a brother just didn't have the time. His mind returned to the fact that he always answered Nyla's calls, and not because she was the only other Black professional at NYSU-Peru. They often broke bread together, and they actually hung out with others, including Kesi, from time-to-time. As a matter of fact, the only time Xavier wouldn't answer a Nyla call would be if he was indisposed, unavailable due to being immersed in a conversation already, enthralled in a sexy moment, or necessarily engaging a toilet. And nowadays who doesn't take their phone into the restroom. Xavier chuckled, saying to himself, "It's the perfect place for such shit." He then thought there is something satisfying about indulging in self-indulgent laughter.

Xavier thought about the depression he had been battling for a while now. He recognized he hadn't enjoyed thinking lately. He had even considered recording his eccentric thought so he could possibly revisit it later. After all, there may be something worthwhile that will come out of all this. Xavier thought, "Even a broken clock is correct twice a day,"

As Xavier closed the door to the bedroom he entered, he thought, Perhaps it is acting out what my mind encourages that I need to manage, by engaging my thoughts thoroughly before they can be put into action. Sometimes it happens so fast anyway. If you haven't experienced anything similar to what you imagine you are about to experience, you can only shoot from the hip trying to anticipate what you are about to experience.' He wondered if he shared the thought he just had with Nyla now, Kesi later, Angel eventually, and others in his crew (George, Julius, AH, Martha, Tim, Edmund, Nick, Darren, AnnaE, ER, Edmund, HR would any of them get it, or would they be concerned about his mental health. Almost as if snapping out of a trance he then realized that if he took too much more time thinking instead of acting Nyla may be wishing she never called. Shit, he thought, I'm on vacation,albeit forced, trying to enjoy everything available for me to enjoy. Hence, Xavier's mind had been shut off, intuitively regulating all thought to a later moment. Nyla's call made later now.

Xavier recognizing something different in Nyla's voice replied, "Sorry that took a moment. Of course I have time for you, Nyla. What's up?"

"It's getting crazy Xdub," Nyla said. "This week is homecoming and on the front page of the school newspaper is a racist image that is inexplicable. The campus is turning upside down, Black students protesting, a national newspaper got wind of it so now it has gone national."

"Do I need to head South?" Xavier asked. "I just got here last night, but if I leave now, what is it, 11:00 am, I could be in Peru around 9:30 pm."

"Don't sweat it. Just know it'll probably get crazy here next week," Nyla added. "Students are tired of shit on our campus and around the country. It's bigger than our campus and when the megaphone is handed to a campus nowadays they take advantage of their opportunity to make noise."

"As we would have to varying extents when we lacked any sense of power or position, right?" Xavier asked, not really expecting an answer.

"You know it!" Nyla added, with Xavier imagining her warrior visage creeping across her face.

That specific call ended but they would stay in touch by texting across the weekend. The anxiety didn't lessen any on campus, but the weekend passed uneventfully, which was a good thing, all things considered. Monday was the last day of Xavier's extended weekend vacation and he had planned on spending Friday recovering from Thursday's drive, Saturday as his one true vacation day, Sunday as their "let's get sad out of impending loneliness" day, and Monday another travel day, returning to work on Tuesday. Nyla's call made Xavier hustle to get back to Peru for Monday morning, just in case, making Saturday necessarily divided between being his one true vacation day and also their 'let's get sad out of impending loneliness' day, with Sunday now his travel day, though no one expected him at work Monday.

On Monday morning, now back in Peru, Xavier awoke to a text from the Associate Provost, Dr. Morgan Mark. "Where are you," it read. "Why aren't you at the staff meeting in Utley's office?"

"What staff meeting?," Xavier replied.

"Are you serious? Man, hustle up and get here. We need you," Dr. Mark texted with an urgency that couldn't be ignored.

Twenty minutes later Xavier was walking into the presidential suite, attired in Calvin Klein jeans and a pullover sweater, something he just grabbed to wear as he practically ran out the door. As he entered the room he noticed the room was packed, every seat at the 10 person conference table was taken and the chairs on the side were mostly full. He also noticed a distraught look across every single face. All the Veeps were in the room, all of the Deans, Utley's Chief of Staff, the campus' Public Relations person, the campus Police Chief and his Assistant, the director of Recruitment/Enrollment, and the Assoc VP of Student Services (the person more responsible for racially underrepresented students than anyone else, who was also Nyla's boss).

"Okay, XW's here so let's get started." President Utley announced.

Xavier thought, 'what the fuck have I just walked into that would have them waiting on me. I thought this meeting was about the racist article.'

"Dr. Utley," said Ben Judson, Utley's Chief of Staff, trying to gain his attention, "Are you going to ask XW what we discussed earlier?'

"Yes, I am." replied Utley. Turning to Xavier in front of the entire room, Utley asked, "You thought about our offer for the university's Chief Diversity Officer (CDO) position?"

Again, it is so very interesting how quickly one's mind can race in front of a room of people all staring down your throat, awaiting your reply. The shock of Utley's question completely threw Xavier off balance. The room all of a sudden seemed to be moving in slow motion. Xavier imagined he was probably under some type of scrutiny by every single person in the room. He scanned the room and could almost hear what they were probably thinking:

"What's he going to do?"
"I wouldn't accept under these conditions."
"Utley shouldn't have asked him that question in front of all of us."
"I don't want him as my CDO."
"I can't wait to tell Feminist Anthropology about this."
"That would be interesting, someone of color in the senior administration. We can possibly benefit from this."

Xavier regained his composure in time to take stock of Utley and what was really occurring in this moment with this so-called campus leader. Wasn't this the man who offered him the CDO position, without going through the prefered search process. That is a cool thing and some type of statement about how he values Xavier. However, isn't this also the same man who told Xavier to write a detailed proposal for the budget he would like to have for this newly created position, amidst budget cuts addressing a two million dollar deficit? And now he's asking me to accept the job unconditionally. Shit, that's not happening. I'm not going to be pressured to accept a job that will have its inherent headaches already. I'm not going to add headaches to my reality I don't need. Fuck it. If he can ask me a serious question like that in front of a crowd of people he can handle a real answer in front of them too.

"Dr. Utley, I can't accept that position until I know I have the budget to do the job I'm capable of doing." Xavier said, matter-of-factly.

The room looked as if it was in disbelief, suffering from some mind-numbing cognitive dissonance. Xavier felt anxiety creeping in for a moment, until he reached for whatever intestinal fortitude he developed out of a necessity to survive. Of course all of this happened so quickly. While he felt like the room experienced an awkward silence for a lengthy amount of time--primarily because he knew he left Utley hanging--it was really only a matter of seconds before Utley responded.

"We'll discuss your budget needs immediately after this meeting, Dr. Witt." Utley said. "We want to announce you as Chief Diversity Officer within the press release being emailed to the paper, which includes our actions in response to the newspaper snafu."

Xavier thought to himself what a trip this all was. He imagined himself having a bit more leverage now, thanks to the newspaper debacle, than he would have had without it. Amidst the rest of the hustle and bustle occurring in the conference room was a half dozen other conversations starting/stopping from one moment to the next. Xavier chimed in on this or that one, but none prevented him thinking he really needed to have his shit together later when the time finally came for him to speak with Utley.

Xavier remembered the meeting in Utley's conference room ending and President Utley motioning to Xavier to wait for him in his office. While awaiting Utley's return to his office for their budget negotiation, Xavier remembered revisiting those moments that had just occurred. The CDO position, if he chose to accept it, would have him often being the only Black person in higher level conversations about the campus. Anticipating turbulent times in the near future made him remember darker days working at an aerospace company in Southern California, Rockwell International. Though the situation was different in terms of an end result, it was similar with Xavier being the only black person in the mix in a room full of White folk with varying expectations of him. Though it was just this one day at NYSU-Peru that was immediately in his mind, it would recur often since due to his promotion he would now be reporting to the university president and working closely with Vice Presidents and Deans, none of whom were racially underrepresented.

As a young man just starting to earn his way he had been hired by Rockwell International as an expeditor, someone who moved parts and blueprints from one building to another, as required. It was a thankless job, but a necessary one, though it didn't necessarily require anyone with heightened initiative. It was however Xavier's initiative that provided him the opportunity to transcend the limiting confines of the expeditor pool.

Being in the House Isn't Always a Privilege

The eventual promotion Xavier received to the salaried position of Materials Planner for Rockwell International could be attributed as much to his mother's wisdom as to his implementation of her idea. In a conversation about appropriate attire in the workplace Xavier's mother advised him to 'dress for the job you want, not for the one you have.' Implementing her philosophy, and as such becoming the only expeditor (essentially a "gofer," go for this, go for that) who daily wore a tie (which was not required) came with its own burden. Add to that always being the one asking questions--which demonstrated his intellectual curiosity, though he had only been working for the company for six weeks--and no one should have been surprised. Eventually Xavier was noticed by the Project Planner on the Leasat satellite program, and extended the opportunity to join the planning team. Little did Xavier know that he was about to be introduced to the word "nigger" in ways he could not have anticipated.

Xavier was excited about being promoted in only his seventh week on the job. He was looking forward to working in a new, all-male professional environment, where ties were mandatory, and eight encircled desks were not shared. He wasn't sure how he would feel being surrounded for the first time by all white co-workers, but he figured it couldn't be that bad. Of course Xavier always knew he was black, but he would soon realize that he was perhaps blacker in others' minds than he ever imagined before.

Nevertheless he naively believed that the cultural climate should not be that different for a young man who grew up in a predominantly black community and who never interacted with whites before, outside of athletic endeavors, but who generally likes people and gets along with most.

A few hours into his first day in the new office space one of the most brilliant minds in the group, a man named Mike, approached him after first making sure he had the attention of all the rest of their office mates.

"I have a joke that you will all enjoy," Mike said.

Everyone turned around from their desks to view him--with Xavier as his hapless Black victim standing next to him like a deer in headlights--with Mike poised to entertain their colleagues with his wittiness. It was then he shared with them his first amongst a seemingly never ending repertoire of racist jokes featuring the N-word. He went on to tell a racist joke almost every day for the next 18 weeks (90 working days).

Sadly, those jokes were told unopposed. The other six White men in the planning group--from one day/joke to the next--at best rolled their eyes at the unrelenting jokester. At worst, they laughed with him, perhaps unbeknownst to them that their support emboldened him to continue.

No one in the group ever interceded on Xavier's behalf. There never arose an actual moment where the not-so-veiled attack was lessened by a caring soul. No one checked in with the young man behind the scenes to see how he was holding up from the unfair onslaught against his blackness. None of them knew he had been told by his Mother that he needed to transcend any turmoil to successfully reach the end of his probation period, and to prevent that from happening he probably would be tested, if not provoked.

So as a result of not risking the consequences of verbally challenging any of them, Xavier eventually took to self medicating everyday prior to his arrival at work and then on his lunch break. Searching for an escape from his tormented state he was processing how to rationalize six adult men looking the other way while one of their colleagues indirectly insulted his reality--as well as culture--simply because he was different from them.

Over time Xavier eventually realized that those White men didn't exit the womb wanting to disparage him, or support others efforts at doing so. Like Bill Maher's inexplicably using the word 'nigger,' they were victims themselves, uneducated and/or lacking empathy about situations they hadn't experienced and unfortunately as a result exacerbating the situation.

Maher's assuming house Negroes had real priveilege only revealed his lack of insight into the horrors of slavery, no matter where someone was situated on the plantation. These inconsiderate White men green lighting their duplicitous colleague's insidious attempts at humor revealed them as far worse than Maher's inconsideration, instead depicting them as pathetic human beings, knowing full well that what they were doing was not kosher, nor cool.

At that moment the president entered his office. "So, what do you need to accept the position XW?" asked Dr. Utley?

"Nothing has changed Dr. Utley," answered Xavier unabashedly. "I still need the financial resources to staff the office to get the job done."

"I understand that much," Dr. Utley said impatiently. "I mean in terms of dollars and cents, what do you need?"

Xavier knew this was his moment. Taking a deep breath he went for it. "I need Lori Flee's salary at the level of full time, 12 months instead of her current 20 hrs per week for 10 months.

Utley replied, "Got it, what else?

Xavier was momentarily caught off guard by Utley's matter-of-factness concerning his casually coughing up $25,000. Xavier gathered himself to further negotiate, "I need to have on my staff another full time, 12 month person...", he began to say, but before he could finish Utley interjected, "Do you have anyone in mind?"

Xavier answered, "Yes I do. His name is Darren Shultz and he volunteered for two years at OPIE."

Without a moment's hesitation, Utley continued scribbling and without looking up said, "You got it. What else do you need?"

Xavier thought to himself, "He must be fucking with me." After all, Xavier had been working on the proposal Utley and his Chief of Staff (COS) had said was necessary for them to consider his budgetary needs, a condition for his acceptance of the CDO position. He had been pulled to the side and somewhat coached by the COS to not expect much, because amidst a 2 million dollar deficit at that time back in 2015 anymore than $15,000 was like wishing in one hand and spitting in the other with an unrealistic expectation of which hand would be filled first. Nonetheless he responded to Utley accordingly, "And I need a $10,000 travel budget. My staff is young and will need some professional development that they can't get in the North Country."

"Okay, it's all yours if you are accepting the position," Utley stated, sounding a few moments away from being in a panic.

"Once I have all that in writing President Utley," Xavier said, "I'll feel comfortable about accepting the position."

"We really need to get this Press Release out, XW. I'll make sure you get our agreement in writing ASAP. In the interim I'm hoping a handshake can seal our deal," Utley said hopefully while extending his hand.

Xavier took the high road and shook hands with his new boss.

Moments later, after leaving the confines of Utley's suite of offices Xavier thought to himself, Utley essentially didn't ask him for rhyme or reason as to why he wanted to increase Lori's hours, or create a new position. He now realized that the university leadership was possibly if not probably posturing, posing, and pretending. The best classes taught by the best professors, the best organizations facilitated by the most passionate student centered staff are all mirages without hard money, institutionalized funding. With soft money, grants especially are here today and then gone so quickly you disbelieve what they funded was ever really there. Leadership has to make the real call and live with it, or not. But you can't fake the funk. At NYSU-Peru when the President doesn't have any sense of a budget in mind when he offers the Chief Diversity Officer position—without a search— and then shows no interest whatsoever in even seeing the budget proposal he himself requested, something is amiss, wrong in Denmark, and problematic at NYSU-Peru.

When a problematic racial incident occurs on campus in the middle of budget negotiations and as things are heating up even more the university president drops $70,000 into your budget so you can save his ass, what do you do? No, his fearful financial deposit of budget into Xavier's account was not a commitment to diversity, its risk management on his part. He coughed up financing the campus' diversity initiative only when Xavier seized upon the opportunity to further bend someone who was close to breaking. Within two years Xavier had no doubt--with things continuing to advance unevenly under Utley--in no time this combination of the Wizard of Oz's Tin Man and Lion, a man lacking heart and courage would revert back to the diversity center having no true meaning for him that wasn't politically expedient.

Xavier wondered if Utley considered the consequences of his actions, that he could be ruining a person's career and seriously damaging an organization and many lives attached to it. He and/or NYSU had choices in terms of paths to take. The fact that they chose to treat the person—who led their social justice movement for almost two decades—as a criminal speaks volumes itself.

Their meeting concluded, as Xavier walked across the campus back towards his office, his mind wandered further, somehow revisiting his negotiations with Utley, somewhat rewriting Utley's return to his office with a similar spiel to that of Ving Rhames' character aimed at Bruce Willis' character in Quentin Tarantino's "Pulp Fiction," when Rhames had an expectation that Willis would throw the fight. Rhames asked Willis the question, "You my Nigger?" Xavier knew Utley would never exhibit that type of racism/classism. Utley wasn't an active racist, someone actively practicing racism. He was instead a passive racist, to the extent of being in denial of exhibiting any type of racism, whatsoever. Xavier nonetheless pondered whether Utley subconsciously cogitated over having somewhat purchased Xavier, with his $75,000 budget increase, though in this specific situation, with NYSU's money.

"XW, you my nigger?" he imagined hearing Utley ask him, the exact same thing Rhames asked Willis. Willis' response was, "it appears so," knowing he had plans to usurp Rhames' authority when convenient. In other words, he wasn't trustworthy. Unlike Willis, while never owning to being Utley's nigger or anyone else's for that matter, Xavier wasn't looking to undermine Utley, or the university. He prided himself on being committed to the university, and being an ally to the socio-politically disenfranchised.

Allies, All Lies, Alibis, & Bye Byes

Some time ago Dr. Xavier Witt had a conversation with White colleagues forming a North Country chapter of "Showing Up for Racial Justice," (SURJ), a national organization of White allies against racism. Finally, he thought, a gathering of White people where he wouldn't be overtly concerned about being the only Black person as he often had been in

President Utley's meetings. The reason he felt uncomfortable as the only Black person was more about the White people he was in the mix with. The VP of Student Affairs, Ryan Coughman, would have been described as square as a pool table and twice as green if he had grown up in the hood with XW. Essentially a good man, Coughman may have become too indebted to Utley when Utley chose him, without a doctorate, as his VP. However, over the years Coughman and Xavier had actually grown closer, though not close enough for Xavier to let his guard down with a tried n' true company man. It wasn't that he had anything to hide from him, but Ryan always seemed to be prominently positioned upon the moral high ground, though perhaps rightfully so.

The VP of Academic Affairs, Dr. Morgan Mark, was the closest VP to Xavier. For years they had collaborated on projects, workshops, sponsorships, and classes. They had some of the same mentors and shared many of the same mentees. Most importantly though, Xavier believed Morgan was a good man, one step better than Coughman in that under no circumstances could he imagine Dr. Mark goose-stepping behind a severely flawed leader just to keep his job, whereas he was uncertain of Coughman.

The other two VPs were women. The VP of Institutional Advancement, Suzanne Ransome was quite intriguing. Always trying to close the deal she never left Xavier with any sense of authenticity when they brainstormed this or that. As a result of her posture as the ultimate gift-getter she unfortunately wasn't believable when drama hit the campus involving racially underrepresented students. Always her voice would soften, eyes too, as if she was so invested in being an ally, while her staff was all White, mostly women with one White gay male. Xavier was never convinced by her posturing as a concerned colleague. He anticipated if he ever fell out of favor she would not be accepting his calls.

The VP of Finance & Budget, Rose Katt, was the newest senior administrator to join this illustrious crew. She was chosen more by Utley and the power-seeking contingent of women on campus. There must have been a memo circulating stating Utley had a hole in his back which required a hand to manage this aging man. Utley must have surmised her hand would be less obtrusive. In the short time at NYSU-Peru Katt had successfully alienated quite a few of the not easily irritated. Xavier definitely saw Katt as a strong person, capable of intimidating men not so easily intimidated. Xavier marveled at how she had figured Utley out and was in the process of making him do dances as if he was a dunce.

As CDO, Xavier could have been situated on a VP level or slightly below, or on a Dean's level or slightly above. From one campus to the next that would depend upon the president and the university's commitment to diversity & social justice, which weren't always one and the same.

The problem with this crew and their leader was no real skin in the game, beyond financial support when under scrutiny. Most of them were allies when it was convenient to be, at least in Xavier's mind. Allies don't blindly accept one of their own being removed from the academic equation simply because a failed leader hints that a moral transgression may have occurred, based upon a rumor. Only one of these VPs reached out to Xavier after his outburst at the S.A. Forum where the votes-of-no-confidence were officially announced. They were obedient soldiers to an unremarkable leader. Somehow it didn't occur to any of them that the cool customer many of them had grown up with professionally might have been pushed too far. Not one of them had the capacity to imagine what it must have felt like for a person who does social justice work to be accused of such a grievous act. Instead, like roaches feeling at home in the dark of a kitchen until the lights come on—sending them scurrying for cover—they all chose to stay in the dark, essentially keeping their heads down, opting to believe that something highly problematic had been found while investigating Xavier. As Xavier suspected, and had even been warned, these campus leaders weren't progressive leaders. They were appointed leaders, which aren't necessarily allies, nor necessarily perpetuating all lies, but their excuses for not showing up were hard to not see as alibis, inadvertently in support of a useful idiot.

However, if it walks like a duck, yet has rabbit's foot luck, someone should give a fuck, at least enough of one to not buy into the prevailing narrative.

His concern about being "the only" could easily make Xavier seem paranoid to the uninformed observer. However, the battles he recently fought over office moves, budget cuts to staffing lines, and angst from local conservatives about his liberal messages created an undercurrent that in retrospect one day Xavier would kick himself for not recognizing, and unfortunately that day had come.

Gangsta John Brown

Xavier was fortunate (or so he thought) to have the pleasure of working in the community with dynamic White allies for decades, though none more satisfying than a decade spent as a board member of John Brown Lives. The organization itself provided him with a network of allies from different walks of life. He had an appreciation for the JBL crew, heightened even more by the way some of the membership revealed themselves as allies in the truest sense of the word when the shit hit the fan for Xavier.

Many years prior to that, ironically, while doing some extensive research on Dr. W.E.B. DuBois at Harvard and Yale back when Xavier lived in California he recalled seeing a biography DuBois wrote on an abolitionist named John Brown. Xavier wasn't familiar with the name at the time and dismissed it as irrelevant. It wasn't until he met Bertha Fawn an extraordinary community leader, the founder of, and catalyst for, John Brown Lives, a non-profit social justice organization of enlightened activists that he became more aware. Xavier was invested in discovering more about Brown, as well as situating in his mind this ultimate ally and American hero. Never one for hero worship, he knew an original gangster when he came across one.

With aims of enhancing diversity & social justice education across and throughout the North Country, while challenging wrongs within correctional facilities amongst many other things, John Brown Lives completely rejuvenated Xavier's energy in the possibilities of the NYSU-Peru community doing work to improve the region. Xavier then started teaching for NYSU-Peru a class that addressed the plight of the so-called Negro/often called nigger, which prompted the purchase of the DuBois biography on Brown. While preparing to teach the class Xavier discovered these words by Brown that would forever reshape his attitude as an ally, after first overcoming his shame and embarrassment from not having known of Brown previously.

If it is deemed necessary that I should forfeit my life for the furtherance of the ends of justice, and mingle my blood further with the blood of my children and with the blood of millions in this slave country whose rights are disregarded by wicked, cruel, and unjust enactments-I submit; so let it be done." – John Brown (Nov 2, 1859) during his sentencing where afterwards he would be hanged.

Like many, Xavier had heard something of the Harper's Ferry raid led by John Brown. However, his discovery of this White man's passion for social justice completely revolutionized Xavier's approach to it. Not only did Brown sacrifice his life, but he also sacrificed the lives of many of his sons as well. He did this for disenfranchised people who needed allies, while struggling with being seen as fully human at a time that was more understandable than it is now. He, along with his two allies Harriet Tubman and Frederick Douglass were the Black Lives Matter movement before Black lives actually legally mattered.

John Brown died so that Black people could live. From the moment Xavier discovered Brown's commitment to the struggle for social justice Xavier's passion for other people's struggles elevated. From the exposure Xavier had witnessing and working with White people who had the John Brown mentality towards racism he further cultivated a John Brown mentality towards sexism, heterosexism/homophobia, ableism, classism, privilege, ageism, and any form of unearned privilege that benefitted some unjustly at the expense of others, or the so-called 'Other.'

Xavier was invested in helping more people discover John Brown's commitment to those without privilege. He believed most would appreciate Brown's sacrifices for people who could have easily been seen as not a part of his community. Xavier had to admit to himself that as a Black man leading a university's diversity effort he sometimes hesitated to be too involved in Black facilitated organizations within the predominantly White community of Peru. For reasons of professional survival Xavier's strategy for implementing diversity & social justice was casting out a very broad net that would be inclusive of many other groups' struggles. He knew the consequences of being seen as any professional version of the Black guy who is only about Black causes. He also wondered what John Brown, the patron saint of social justice allies would think of his NYSU-Peru colleagues' response to his plight.

Allies or All Lies

In 2010, during Dr. Witt's fall Romance, Sex, Love, & Marriage (RSLM) class it became necessary that he intercede in an in-class altercation involving two male students over a controversial film excerpt from the movie "Storytelling."

"Okay class," Dr. Witt said, knowing he had to do nothing to gain their attention after they had just witnessed arguably the most provocative film clips of the semester, "Again let me apologize for the necessity of you viewing such painful, yet poignant film clips. It isn't easy getting to some of the complexities we discover in life that exist but are seldom discussed. Here is our chance to discuss at least those presented in the 'Storytelling' clips. Your reactions?"

"It was a mind game the Black professor was playing with his White student," Kim, a White female senior, said with a twinge of exasperation in her voice. "Why else would he be asking her to say 'Fuck me nigger?'"

Martha asked, "Why would she have gone to his home with him? He was an asshole."

Derek, a White male senior, perhaps answering Martha, said, "She wanted to fuck the Black professor to get back at her boyfriend for their breakup."

Dorhani, a Latina junior, replied, "What is more interesting is how some of you felt it necessary to use race identifiers when he was the only professor in any scenes we saw, and he had no Black students, they were all White."

Dr. Witt had to decide in that instant whether he would leave Kim and Derek hanging after Dorhani's undeniable observation. Kim's comments hinted at the possibility that what many of the students processed viewing the film clips were interracial sex, a power dynamic between a professor and his student, and perhaps a professor who--while in the middle of a sexual encounter--was nonetheless testing a young woman's commitment to social justice, if not her morality, by what she wouldn't say during an extremely vulnerable moment. Before he could articulate his thoughts, more comments were made.

"The pictures of young White women in bondage that were in his bathroom for anyone to see intimidated her," said Katie. "After all, the pictures revealed a dimension of the professor that hadn't been previously seen."

"At least not by her," chimed in Nick.

Dr. Witt then inserted his voice into the conversation to diffuse the growing tension, "I knew this clip would exacerbate some racial anxieties. It always does. The question I must ask now that no one has gone anywhere near it thus far is how many of you thought it was rape?"

Many hands went into the air immediately, unflinchingly committed to what they saw. A few hands slowly lifted after seeing enough hands in the air to feel safe about joining that contingent. Of the 40 students in the class about half demonstrated their belief they had just witnessed a rape.

Dr. Witt then followed up the first question with another one, "The question now I must ask that many of you may have already anticipated is how many of you thought it was NOT rape?"

Ironically, and again without much hesitation the majority of the hands that raised went into the air immediately, steadfastly committed to what they saw. Again, a few hands slowly lifted after perhaps being reassured that they wouldn't be the only dissenters. Of the 40 students in the class about half demonstrated their belief that they had NOT witnessed a rape.

Dominic, a young man of Italian heritage offered his opinion, "I didn't see rape at all Doc. Her actions throughout the evening demonstrated willing consent to what occurred that evening."

Suddenly voiced contempt blurted out, "If you don't think that was rape you're an idiot."

The student who blurted out disrespectfully in response to Dominic's opinion was Dick Satton. Dr. Witt was left with no choice but to chastise Dick for not only yelling his answer, but also for insulting another student.

"Uncool, totally uncool Dick," responded Dr. Witt, who appeared to be getting irritated. "In what world do you think I would let you takeover my class by yelling in it, and insulting another student. You have a choice, either leave the class immediately, or sit quietly and never, ever act this way again."

Dr. Witt knew full well that Satton at that time, was the Executive Vice President of the Student Government (SG). To complicate matters more the young woman he sat with in every class was the President of the S.G. They also were both Feminist Anthropology minors. The scene under scrutiny by the class featured a Black male Professor involved in a sexual interlude with a White female graduate student. Historically, the class was always divided in their opinions of whether or not it was a case of rape. However, in that year's class the two elected student representatives considered the mere showing of the film a personal affront. As a result, they filed a hostile environment complaint against Dr. Witt. In their complaint against Dr. Witt they stated that:

"Also, the fact that our male professor finds no fault with the coercive actions of the professor in the clip from Storytelling forces us to question whether he finds fault with pressuring his current female students to have sex with him."

After a minion of Ramona Saphony provided her the film clips of Storytelling a larger controversy arose regarding Dr. Witt's ability to teach such a class.

One thing that was certain to Dr. Witt, upon reflection of that one eventful class and its ensuing discussions, was that he had become a marked man, only now not just with FA but now also within the NYSU-Peru Student Government. The two elected SG officers who took umbrage with that particular class, in their official complaint attempted to make two things very clear:

1. Dr. Witt found no fault with the coercive actions of the professor
2. The students were "forced" to question whether Dr. Witt would coerce his female students to have sex with him.

Dr. Witt upon receiving his copy of the report was left curious about who *forced them* to question his motivations. Certainly not Dr. Witt, who rationalized that the force was probably their consciousness, acting off of their instincts about this one particular Black man they really didn't know. That mattered little though in the academic environment of NYSU-Peru, where there was an abundance of allies, or at least people who would say they are allies. It brings to mind the Michael Cohen congressional hearings that featured Lynne Patton, a Black woman, as a prop for a Congressman attempting to prove that Resident Rump isn't racist. The congressman, Mark Meadows was infuriated that someone had insinuated he was racist, if not outright accusing him of it. Xavier wouldn't necessarily label Meadows a racist no more than he would call someone stupid for doing a stupid act. Meadow's cluelessness about his actions might save him from being considered a racist, but don't negate the racist act. NYSU'S Feminist Anthropology Department could have and at times tried to dress up their actions, but those with any consciousness, in their quiet moments, know that they made a choice to believe a rumor, and then become complicit to varying extents in how that rumor impacted their community. One of the consequences of their complicity was the sharing of their contrived tribal knowledge with incoming colleagues and impressionable students.

Nonetheless, not knowing that the rumor would one day become an amorphous myth, and inevitably an overdue act of justice, or a grossly misinterpreted social injustice, this crew of White female allies were comfortable carrying around negative energy towards someone they didn't even know. Similar to the chicken-egg phenomenon the students concerns may have fed the Faculty concerns, which became more sustenance for whatever incoming class of students would arrive and filter through Feminist Anthropology lessening their chances of becoming better citizens. Both the students' perspectives (influenced by dysfunctional faculty) and the faculty perspectives, (influenced by students who feared Dr. Witt, due to their conditioning by their faculty mentors) probably became circuitous rumors without an ending, for most providing no sense of how they began.

On top of whatever other rumors branched off those, these rumors never died, fueled by the pathetically infamous couple, Winchell and Wiener.

When life or events within it seem to unravel in any given moment we are apt to believe that the moment sits alone, uniquely. This episode however could be traced back to so many contributing factors like Karen, the White wife of the interracial couple. She had an axe to grind with Xavier for not being interested in intimacy with her or a foursome with her and her husband. Subsequently she communicated her axe to grind with a creative spin to Feminist Anthropology professor Sharon Winchell. Winchell, obviously as gullible as her husband was touted about being monotone and self-indulgent, would later in defense of her friend post this comment on Dr. Witt's blog page in a discussion titled, "Girl Talk," just a few months prior to the Storytelling incident:

"I cannot discern much of a difference between verbal gossip and blog gossip. Your palpable disrespect for the "business owner," as well as your widespread reputation for disrespect toward, harassment of, and sexually predatory behaviors against women, makes the question of whether you call us girls or women a mere attempt to distract us from your more insidious, and infamous, misogyny."

At the time he first read Winchell's post Xavier was as dumbfounded then as he has always been reflecting on the sheer audacity of the post.

Years later, In May 2016 during a search committee meeting for the director of the Center for Morality one of the committee members, Dr. Erin Yeast, said, "This is why no one wants to work with you, XW." Having never worked with her before Dr. Witt found her comment quite perplexing. Then it occurred to him that she taught in Sociology with Dr. Brenda Maims, the Affirmative Action officer who heard the initial complaint about Xavier in 2002-03. As well, the FA and Sociology programs on NYSU-Peru's campus were closely aligned, with Maims consistently teaching classes for both departments.

In terms of *allies* or '*all lies*,' eight years later these prominent negative influences that had been unceasingly affecting the perspectives of impressionable young minds developed into a collective voice with assistance from their advisors, complicit faculty, some who must have convinced themselves their crusade was justified, influenced by a co-opted *useful idiot* leading the Administration. After Dr. Witt's name was somehow conveniently added to the list of administrators they desired to see resign the table had been adequately set. Friday evening, Feb 23, 2018 the Student Government in collaboration with the disgruntled students protesting the SnapChat image facilitated a meeting in the ballrooms to discuss their shared resolutions, asking for the resignations of those facing votes-of-no-confidence. After the resolutions had been shared with the audience of approximately 850 students/faculty/staff the students then had another chance to voice their concerns. About twenty comments deep into the discussion, most of them reaffirming Dr. Witt's name should not be on the list of resignations, a female student named Shalo Kloos spoke, saying,

"I would like to have a Chief Diversity Officer that I haven't heard disrespects women."

The room momentarily fell eerily silent after a collective gasp. Then voices exclaiming how improper it was for an accusation of that magnitude to be cavalierly tossed in the air abounded.

Eventually about twenty minutes later, following some vacuous comments from the virtually vanquished President, which did nothing to quell the crowd, Dr. Witt approached the microphone immediately addressing the not-so-veiled student slur. His anger and hurt were apparent in his comments especially the fact that someone could feel it appropriate to comfortably slander him. Dr. Witt's comments ultimately would be framed more as him silencing "survivors" instead of Dr. Witt having the right to engage such an allegation passionately. Stated differently, the pain, anguish, frustration of 15 years of working in a hostile environment--rife with negligence by a president twice informed that Dr. Witt was being racially harassed, and a FA department of White women responding fearfully, emotionally and perhaps strategically to a rumor—would not have been easily visible from Dr. Witt's profanity laced tirade.

Dr. Witt's comments were followed by solicitous comments by the Title IX Officer, herself a FA professor, who ultimately encouraged anyone and everyone to not be afraid to come forward, but only after prefacing her tirade with "I'm not here to make friends." Dr. Witt, upon hearing that almost choked. Who that was meant for he didn't know, but she couldn't think that his guard had ever dropped low enough to be surprised by anything this maneuvering manipulator could do. He knew that her motivation was an increased probability of being able to solicit survivors as well as eventually urging Utley, her pawn, her personal minion, to initiate an investigation of Dr. Witt. These actions and not so veiled allegations essentially went unquestioned since in the MeToo era, in the minds of one-dimensional feminists, any man accused is "probably" guilty and any woman accusing is "probably" not lying. Every time Xavier heard that rationale it took him to a similar ridiculous rationale, the one about the slaves who actually enjoyed slavery. All the people forced into slavery didn't necessarily abhor it, with some in the big house fortunate enough to have masters with more decency than others, preferring slavery over struggling on their own. But they were going against the prevailing sentiment for their own personal gain. All women that claim a MeToo incident have more likely than not endured a MeToo moment, but that doesn't mean that every claim aligns with every moment they may have been victimized.

Molly Mothburn - Opportunistic Ally

The Title IX office under Molly Mothburn's coordination was a study in disorganization. Mothburn, actually a highly intelligent person, had street cunning, but no street smarts, unless you want to acknowledge some of the moves she made as gangsta-as-fuck. The empire she set out to build for herself was impressive and she did much of it in broad daylight, like Resident Rump as a candidate--during a stump speech--calling for the Russians help with Hillary Clinton's email. Not many women working as hard as Mothburn does, with an abundance of children to take care of, had time to be as manipulative and deceptive without it adversely affecting her family in terms of lost time. Xavier actually, upon fully realizing it, had to admit it was impressive. Ironically though, she wasn't smart enough to avoid marrying someone touted as an alcoholic. Xavier, never one to perpetuate such talk unfounded knew this scuttlebut had more than a grain of truth to it. On a personal level Mothburn's second husband, a grown-ass man who went by the adolescent moniker of John-John, just so happened to be the ex-husband of one of Dr. Witt's very close ex-students, Maude Harrold, now one of Xavier's dearest friends. Xavier had even attended Maude and John-John's wedding, spent some time with them trying to salvage their marriage after being invited to join them and a couple of other friends in what amounted to a counseling session. Xavier also knew many of the sordid details of Maude's leaving this older, emotionally dependent, yet affluent white male for a much more grounded, just as affluent male, who happened to be Black. The fact that Maude met her future husband in Vegas on a female road trip didn't help John-John's public profile. Because of Xavier's friendship with Maude, Xavier and John-John had actually met for drinks on occasion, both while Maude and John-John were still a couple and after their divorce. As a result he had first-hand repeatedly witnessed John-John already inebriated by the time he arrived, only to have three more drinks to every one Xavier might have (which was never more than 2 over a period of 3 hours) which would leave John-John staggering about the establishment.

Xavier marveled at how Mothburn chose as a second husband a man rebounding from being unceremoniously dumped, who from an outside perspective could pass for impressive, definitely pleasant enough, and physically probably would receive many more compliments about his looks than negative comments. However, unless her love can solve all their possibly impending problems in ways that other couples haven't figured out yet, Mothburn, already owed a nice healthy serving of some negative karma, was soon going to be served and it looked like that serving would also come from a slice of her personal life. Unfortunately for her, the last thing she needed was more calories, metaphorically speaking.

The Title IX office had abysmally poor attendance at most of their events, poor evaluations for their summer orientation workshops, and with a notoriously abrasive Black woman as her assistant--known for often spewing racism towards whites--was the laughing stock of the campus in regards to any consistent professionalism. Mothburn had style but when paired with her assistant, her assistant would even go after her, leaving Mothburn looking rather hapless trying to recover from a monster she herself created. The word around campus itself would have had her office under severe scrutiny by any leader invested in eliminating problems in their early stages, which considering also Xavier's cries for help, proved

Utley was either adept at not doing something, or inept at doing something, essentially six in one hand, half a dozen in the other.

Dr. Witt saw Utley as incompetent when it came to any serious problem solving ability that required more than money as a solution, or passing the buck to resolve this or that.

Mothburn's decision making should have been challenged after she hired and retained a caricature of a strong Black woman. However, Mothburn's poor judgement was never more apparent than when office assistant once told a room of professional colleagues, approximately 100 people, that she hated White people. Dr. Witt was in the room when she loudly proclaimed her enmity for Caucasians. Dr. Witt thought to himself that for the most part the White folks he had met in the North Country of New York were relatively cool. Xavier experienced few good ol boys in the sense of them being racists as he moved around upstate NY. Xavier also didn't hang out, especially in bars, so he had little to draw on.

Xavier saw Mothburn as 'one of those.' Someone who wanted Black people around to legitimate her cool, as long as they remained entertaining, and deferred to her in some way. Mothburn and Xavier actually got along fairly well professionally, except she couldn't hide her hating on his celebrity and chose to believe to varying extents given her political motivation, a rumor that ultimately became self-serving to the Feminist Anthropology department and Title IX office. Mothburn's resentment was as much a result of professional jealousy, or good old fashioned player-hating as it was the choices she continued to make. Dr. Witt's success off campus (and around the country) as well as OPIE's on campus success had Mothburn often making comments about Dr. Witt not being present on campus to give the campus what Mothburn's omniscience deemed as the proper amount of attention. With all this brewing and to Xavier's chagrin he then got wind of some gossip that John-John had been asking if anyone knew whether Maude and Dr. Witt had ever been sexually intimate with one another. Furthermore, by asking he was somewhat insinuating that they had, which in his limited mind was the only reason why Maude and XW could possibly be close, John-John never fully examining his own inadequacies. Supposedly it was the only way this Neanderthal could rationalize the affinity his ex-wife had for Dr. Witt. Once again, *the Myth of Black Sexuality* meets *the Myth of the Black Rapist*.

Combine all these factors together and Mothburn's comments that evening take on a different flavor. The next day, Saturday, February 24, 2018 Dr. Witt's energy, understandably at an all time low, was resurrected when he was introduced to how bonafide allies react to another allies duress, by being inundated with texts, emails, Facebook messages, and phone calls in support. Dr. Witt was also notified that student-allies had begun to mobilize on his behalf with letter writing campaigns and petitions. By the following Monday, in only three days, a petition in support of Dr. Witt was signed by approximately 800 alumni, many asserting disassociating with the Alumni Relations office as a result of Dr. Witt's treatment. Additionally another petition by current students, created to challenge the S.G.'s assertion they represent the entire student body, was signed by over 200.

Monday morning Feb 19, 2018 it is discovered that the below attached flyer had been taped to walls all over the bathrooms of the Student Union.

Text of Flyer Posted in the Student Union

Dear XW,

We are hurting from the racism, sexism, and sexual harassment on this campus. It is not safe to use our names, but we will not be silent anymore. We've found power in numbers.

We have lived with our shame, guilt, and blaming ourselves. We thought we were responsible for your unwanted comments and sexual touches . We have cried, lost sleep, been alone. We have watched people cover up for you. But we are no longer alone.

We saw the video. You didn't even talk about the snapchat. We need a Chief Diversity Officer who will protect us. But you can't do that when you're too busy sexually harassing us. You don't stand up for us. We're asking you to step down. Do the right thing for all of us. Until you do, we will not feel safe."

The obviousness of this flyer aside, it was probably the only justification Utley needed to have a reason to investigate Dr. Witt. After all, in all good conscience how could Utley not take every available measure to protect his students? Xavier was sure if it had been Utley's son that a flyer was describing he would have investigated him too. Did this progressive so-called leader ever once calculate the difference in succumbing to the whims of a fanatic group of protestors--the same ones who humiliated him in front of his own home--instead of protecting his Chief Diversity Officer, a professional whose problems with another fanatical group (FA) he had been made well aware of years before. It just wasn't possible for the flyer to have been more convenient than it was.

Student Government (SG)

Dr. Witt, for years recognized the importance of a healthy relationship with the student government. In his first few years at NYSU he had a professional relationship with almost every president and a personal relationship with some. This all went south with the Storytelling' incident in RSLM class, further fueled by Ramona Saphony's elected student cronies, when they weren't being manipulated as Saphony's minions. Couple that with the young woman serving as SG President while attending Dr. Witt's class, being madly enthralled with one of Dr. Witt's closest students. Their tryst didn't turn out ideally in terms of what she wanted, so not being able to lash out at him when he eventually walked away from her, perhaps she leaned in against Dr. Witt a bit more than she was going to already, considering the company she was keeping. However, that she would forever frame Dr. Xavier Witt as someone who 'may find fault with pressuring his current female students to have sex with him' will always be unfathomable to him. Dr. Witt's perspective on her yes man Satton however was never more than Satton being an attention seeking clown.

No one should be so naive as to think that a chosen belief with a glaringly different option available couldn't be culturally nourished until it just felt like 'a truth,' though false, with the truth then itself depicted otherwise. Xavier thought of the world being flat. He thought of the idea of the U.S. becoming post-racial with the election of President Barack Obama. He thought of the lie about George Washington never telling a lie. Washington was the first big name politician in the U.S., hence, the father of the country and hence the father of lies, with Resident Rump an obvious descendant. So the SG inheriting and nurturing a venomous perspective on Dr. Witt made sense in a nonsensical way.

Enter Linda Dewar, one of the in-your-face students at NYSU during the newspaper incident. Dewar demonstrated political astuteness when she realized Utley could be useful to anyone who figured out he was a not-so-complex, under-qualified leader. With him in tow she went out of her way to build a relationship with OPIE as well, even taking an OPIE offered course. Ultimately, she landed an internship in Title IX after serving two years as NYSU's SG president. The word around campus was that she essentially served as campaign manager for the next SG president, Bessie Bland. So it isn't rocket science to see Dewar's investigation earlier that week, along with Kloos' public pronouncement against Dr. Witt at the vote-of-no-confidence forum; Kloos' victory lap on Facebook; and bathroom flyers, all aligning nicely for so-called campus allies, who took it upon themselves to know what was best for the college. Utley, shrewd enough to know Dr. Witt could be his red herring or sacrificial lamb took the leap of faith with Dewar and Mothburn's hands up his back, helping him attain a lift his aging knees would have prevented.

Dewar gained a reputation of playing dirty ball when she relentlessly bombarded with emails and texts the student editor of the campus newspaper during the Pigeon Messages incident of 2015. Now, serving as an intern in the Title IX office (remember, run by a FA professor) Dewar approached Ms. Robin Kris, Dr. Witt's previous Office Assistant from 2000-2014. Dewar didn't identify herself as a Title IX intern, under the auspices of doing research, and asked Robin if Dr. Witt had ever sexually harassed her or ever made inappropriate comments towards her. Later when Dr. Witt asked the university President about this he was satisfied with the Title IX Officer Mothburn's reply that she had no knowledge of the investigation. Dr. Witt wasn't satisfied, at all. He asked himself how would an intern—that isn't qualified to do an investigation—have known Dr. Witt may be investigation-worthy without it being whispered to her? Dewar had just finished a class with Dr. Witt and asked (Oct 2017) for, and received (Jan 2018) a letter of reference from him. Who would ask for a letter from someone they know to be a "sexual predator?" Dr. Witt was convinced that Dewar wouldn't have if she had heard the rumor. Oh, and two months later, almost as if a reward, Dewar was appointed by Utley to a position on the newly formed Social Justice Task force. Xavier shrugged his head and thought, if these moves were written in a screenplay no one would believe them.

The initial S.G. announced resolutions in support of a vote-of-no-confidence were as indefensible as a three year old stopping a Kyrie Irving crossover, very difficult for Dr. Witt to read with a straight face. He either was apt to laugh emphatically about how ridiculous they were, or scream loudly how wrong this all was.

Nonetheless Xavier took the time to study them and decided to actually directly refute their assertions in an attempt to challenge the image of incompetence the SG was trying to suggest about him. He then posted it on his Facebook page:

"I know most of our students, in their youthful exuberance, can sometimes find themselves moving in a direction that may feel correct until it is too late to change. However, facts are facts. As such, here is my response to the SG resolution that specifically articulated reasons why I should resign my position. (Their comments are announced in a bold font. Xavier's are italicized).

SG STATEMENT: As the Chief Diversity Officer, Dr. Xavier Witt has an inadequate 5 year diversity plan that does not specifically indicate any upcoming actions in regards to the current events on our campus.

Really? First, the plan is for 3 years, not 5. As well, why was it specifically stated the NYSU Peru Diversity Plan was exemplary.

SG STATEMENT: Despite Dr. Xavier Witt's 17 years of experience as a diversity educator and since stepping into the position of CDO, he has not taken any initiative to improve the campus as well as the safety of the student body.

Really? So how did the SG reconcile my:

1) Creating an environment that endeavors to inclusively educate all of our students, working with Greek letter organizations to challenge them about embracing inclusive language;
2) Working with Border Patrol and the local police Academy to minimize the possibility of implicit bias while growing their understanding about diversity & social justice;
3) Adding to the Reconciling Otherness with Diversity Enlightenment course a professional development component that has had over 100 faculty rotate through at least one of the six themes of the class, conjoined with over 300 students who have benefitted from the leadership component by serving as TAs;
4) And it seems writing a monthly column that provokes the community to consider other perspectives did nothing to improve the campus and isn't contributing to the safety of our students at all.

5) And the diversity class (INT404 RODE) that we use as a Gen Ed, professional development opportunity for faculty/staff and leadership development for returning students (TAs) is being taught at four local high schools. Since they all provide us local students why not have them arriving to NYSU-Peru with a heightened level of sophistication of knowledge about diversity & social justice may provide them with a prior understanding that social media posts that use slanderous and threatening language like 'lynching niggers tonight' are inappropriate and definitely not cool.

SG STATEMENT: As the head faculty member for the Office of Pluralism, Inclusion, & Equity (OPIE) he has done exceptional work. As a professor, he has worked diligently to educate the students on issues related to diversity and inclusion and we believe he works well in that position.

Really? How nice of you to acknowledge that amidst all the negative, unfounded things being said.

SG STATEMENT: However, after the racially motivated incident occurred within the first six months of his role he took no immediate action against the hideous article and image publicized by the Pigeon Messages.

Really? Well considering that when I was appointed to the position (Nov 3, 2015) I'm surprised they would have any detailed insights into what I did/didn't do since many of them may not have been on campus. Additionally, since the majority of the SA who wrote the resolution don't appear familiar to me I highly doubt they would have a working knowledge of what transpired. Perhaps there are some faculty on campus, disgruntled because they didn't become CDO, who have unethically influenced (or are manipulating our students). Anyway, I didn't look for a raise and instead negotiated to increase Ms. Lori Flee's hours from 20 hrs/10 Month appointment to 37.5 hrs/12 months and brought Mr. Darren Schultz on to the OPIE staff at 37.5 hrs/12 months. I guess that action wasn't immediate enough, though it did immediately allow us to better facilitate our campuses diversity efforts. Oh, and would someone please explain to me what the Chair of the Faculty Senate was writing about in the letter, dated Nov 9, 2015, thanking me for developing guidelines for our faculty days after the PM incident. Oh and a copy of the actual letter you'll find below.

SG STATEMENT: Since then, there have been both minor and major incidents where he was there but didn't appropriately advocated the student body's stand. The NYSU Diversity, Equity and Inclusion Policy states the appointed CDO must "implement the best practices related to diversity, equity and inclusion in such areas as the recruitment and retention of students and senior administrators, faculty, and staff hires", as well as "serve as part of a system wide network of CDOs to support NYSU's overall diversity goals.

Really? Who determines what is "appropriately advocating" the student body's stand?" Is the student body all of the same mind set?

Aside from being a part of the CDO network I am left to imagine that "implementing the best practices related to diversity...in such areas as recruitment and retention" doesn't include my collaborating with Admissions in initiating the CDO going to NYC (Nov 18, 2017) to present to the Culturally Based Organizations that assist us in recruiting students? Or the visit scheduled for March 22, 2018?

And I also struggle to imagine how my being in an ongoing dialogue with the NYSU Chairman of the Board's office about the possibility of the

Reconciling Otherness with Diversity Enlightenment course (INT404) isn't a best practice except perhaps because what I've recommended as a model can't be a best practice since it has never been tried before and if I dared to anoint it as a best practice those jealous of the innovativeness would probably find a way to have my pride in this accomplishment framed as overt smugness, ultimately leading to another resolution.

SG STATEMENT: As such, Dr. Xavier Witt has done an admirable job as an educator on our campus and as the head of OPIE but we as a student body voice feel that he has failed to meet the expectations as the Chief Diversity Officer.

Really? How nice of them to say after undercutting an abundance of my efforts throughout their unfounded resolution.

4. The female student who leveled the not-so-veiled "Me Too" accusation against me, Shalo Kloos, approximately 24 hours later posted the following statement on her FB Timeline:

"As a leader at NYSU-Peru, I hear and have had some tough conversations. To be an EFFECTIVE leader, I believe that you can not just listen, you have to speak up, and take action. I have preached that I am here for ALL students. As a confidant, I have been urged to speak up for those who felt uncomfortable coming forward. Though I understand the argument that it was not the right place to mention the situation; it was an unified agreement that I speak up for those who felt silenced. I have my facts straight, and please understand, that I am unbiased in the situation of speaking in front of my university.

Thank you SG for doing your part."

Some of what Kloos meant was impossible to understand. Some could be interpreted broadly. Dr. Witt imagined a thorough investigation would ask her to clarify her post. Who was she representing? How did she "hear" about Dr. Witt? However, it is clear she came to the Friday, Feb 23, 2018 SG Forum as part of a planned attack upon Dr. Witt.

"As a confidant, I have been urged to speak up for those who felt uncomfortable coming forward. Though I understand the argument that it was not the right place to mention the situation; it was an unified agreement that I speak up for those who felt silenced."

When she says she was "urged to speak up for those who felt uncomfortable" she could have only meant speaking up for those who heard the whispers and yet hesitated articulating an unfounded rumor. There were no survivors found on campus because there never was a person who could honestly allege sexual harassment or sexual impropriety against Dr. Witt.

5. In response to the student forums and S.G. resolutions the presiding officer of the faculty facilitated 3 meetings, Tuesday, Feb 27, 2018 at 12:30pm, Tuesday, March 6, 2018 at 3:30pm, and Friday, Mar 9, 2018 at 2:00pm. In all of these meetings Dr. Witt's job performance was one of the things being scrutinized by others than his immediate supervisor (the College President), prompted by student leaders ill-equipped to assess Dr. Witt, and not authorized to do it. Every one of these community gatherings generates another series of local newspaper articles wherein Dr. Witt's competency is again under consideration. How this affects him with current students and with future students due to the problematic whispering it obviously causes in this environment can't be accurately determined, but is difficult to dismiss. Actually, Dr. Witt just recently received correspondence shared with him about a conversation between two potential students. Apparently the word on the street is Dr. Witt was being investigated for possible rape, which was the furthest thing from the truth.

The fact that the SG was no longer in a healthy relationship with its diversity office could have blame spread all over campus, but it has to be affixed to the university president who for years knew of the undercurrent and never took proactive steps to mitigate the oncoming storm.

Advice or Adverse

Some attention needs to go to the not-so-successful professional politician. An unsuccessful stint with a losing political campaign had one of NYSU-

Peru's previous semi-stars return back to town humble, and spinning his reality. Years earlier Conan Labelle, as a NYSU-Peru student held the position of VP in the SG, under two previous presidents that Dr. Witt had solid rapports with. The first president, and engaging young woman and Labelle fell into a relationship for a short time, until both discovered something was missing. She solved her dilemma by stepping into a lifestyle that more suited her, and now is married to her lovely partner, another of Dr. Witt's previous TAs. Labelle discovering he was bi-sexual, began visible relationships with high profile young women. These relationships with women lasted as long as it took them to realize that Labelle was a mile wide and an inch deep. His relationships with men were clandestine. Dr. Witt knew because Conan shared that he was bisexual.

Labelle as an undergrad had been a T.A. for Dr. Witt. After almost a ten year absence Dr. Witt welcomed Labelle back with open arms. Labelle then, amongst other administrative duties elsewhere, co-taught classes with Dr. Witt and the OPIE teaching contingent, while also serving on the OPIE task force.

Labelle's relationship with Dr. Witt took a turn for the worse when Dr. Witt, in conjunction with accepting the position of CDO, also was tasked with responsibility for creating the campus' Diversity Plan (DP). This document, due October 2016 was supposed to provide essentially the details in support of each NYSU campuses Diversity Plans policies and procedures. With a working body already in place Dr. Witt doled out various actions to the newly conceived OPIE Task Force Diversity Plan committees. It was during this assignment that Labelle began to reveal his pettiness, ego, and immaturity to colleagues paying the slightest attention.

After months of committees submitting work on the document Dr. Witt published a draft for the OPIE Task Force to review. Labelle didn't agree with Dr. Witt's approach to articulating and displaying much of it. Dr. Witt had previously written two unsolicited diversity plans for NYSU. Labelle had written none. Regardless, his approach towards critiquing the draft was incredulous, obnoxious, and very disrespectful in terms of the egotistical approach he took towards challenging Dr. Witt's vision. Ultimately—in protest of Dr. Witt's draft—Labelle resigned from both the OPIE Task Force in conjunction with his role of teaching the one OPIE offered class he was qualified to teach. The irony of the situation, which probably exacerbated the assault on his fragile yet too large ego was that the OPIE led Diversity Plan was celebrated by NYSU Central as one of its dozen exemplary plans. As a result though, as the advisor to the NYSU SG, Labelle is the one who fed the SG leadership the interpretation they used to argue that Dr. Witt was inadequately performing his duties as CDO, as was previously discussed.

Embarrassed Himself

Dr. Witt recalled a conversation he had in his office with OPIE assistant director, Lori Flee, about Labelle.

"Did you see Conan's email?" asked Lori.

"Not yet I guess," answered Dr. Witt. "What did it say?"

"He's resigning from the Task Force and no longer teaching the class with us."

"Really," Dr. Witt said while shaking his head and smiling in that way a parent smiles when their child storms out of a room angry they didn't get their way, taking their toys too, to avoid sharing them with others. "So he is also hurting himself while trying to say 'fuck you' to me. Classic"

Lori looking perplexed asked, "How is he hurting himself?

"Because his immature ass, in trying to hurt me, is depriving himself of teaching a class he loves, with the woman he has a ridiculous crush on," Dr. Witt said while closely monitoring Lori's reaction. "You choose to ignore it, but you know it, don't you?"

"Maybe, but I'm married," she replied, as if marriage was her salvation. "Besides, he's my husband's friend too."

"Is he, really? Okay, perhaps. But he was devastated when you got married," Dr. Witt said. "He was the first person to exit your wedding, but he didn't get away before I literally said to him, lightly teasing him though it was real talk, "Well Conan, Lori is both legally and morally unavailable to you as a romantic interest. I hope you see that now."

Dr. Witt then told Lori, "Conan's response was, 'It does seem that way, doesn't it.' His expression was insidious, indicating that the limitations I was imagining he would respect, while real, were not daunting to him."

At that moment Lori was conveniently notified she had a phone call. "I need to take this. I'll be right back," she said.

While awaiting Lori's return Xavier admitted to himself that he had suspected all along Labelle was not an ally, but more all lies, that he wasn't trustworthy, a reaction Xavier had not dissimilar to how he interpreted and as a result kept his guard up with Molly Mothburn. Except his caution about Labelle first came from a warning he had received from Oliver, the SG President he had served under, upon his hearing about Labelle working closely with Dr. Witt and OPIE.

"XW, when Conan and I were undergraduates and I was NYSU-Peru's SG President, he was my second in command as a SG VP," Oliver stated, adding, "I never felt as if he could be trusted back then, and doubt he has changed."

"I'm kind of remembering you sharing some of the problems you had with him," Xavier recalled. "Remind me."

"Oh shit, that's easy enough. He was highly opinionated and hypercritical. He thought his shit didn't stink and somehow thought since he had served as VP under the previous SG president that he knew more about running the SG than I did. He couldn't see it at the time but his White privilege had him struggling with deferring to me on any level, as if he thought he could be a puppet master with me as his marionette."

"Interesting," Xavier responded pensively, ruminating over Oliver's comments. "Conan often told me I was the first Black teacher-professor he had ever had. Perhaps there is something to enlightened White men subconsciously believing that they are superior to Black men. I have told you on numerous occasions that it wasn't only his diminutive status that prevented your boy Devin from having a decent relationship with me. Until he unpacked his own shit relative to his bantamweight size he was going to always flirt with succumbing to being a hater. Nonetheless you were present that time I called him on his White privilege relative to his struggling to defer to my approach. This is one of the reasons he became a pawn for LeAnn Prey. While she knew nothing about running a diversity center, and was struggling with being respected in her own department, Devin was so ecstatic to be rescued by this White woman whose diversity credentials were never inseparable from her being married to a Black man. Thinking about it, Conan is gaunt and gangly, Devin is miniscule and melancholy. What they have in common though is their unchecked, shared White privilege. Fascinating."

Lori returned to Xavier's office looking as if she was trying to be cavalier, prepared to readily dismiss Xavier's concerns, but she wasn't convincing when she said, "Well, I just wanted to make sure you saw Conan's email. I have a meeting across campus and must go."

"Cool, have fun," Dr. Witt said to her as she left his office. He had known Lori on multiple levels, with her younger sister and Dr. Witt's daughter both on a girls soccer team that Lori also assistant coached. As a result of being soccer parents together Dr. Witt grew to know Lori's parents too, eventually actually becoming friends. He was very pleased when Lori joined Opie, though the talent pool was phenomenal to draw from (AnnaE, Rachel Berggren, Jasmine Washington, and Robyn Edghill) to replace long time staffer Deidre Bright upon the announcement of her retirement. Most things being equal what had been in Lori's favor over the others was her being local. This also turned out to be detrimental as well.

Xavier had always viewed Lori as his ultimate ally, personable, outstanding initiative, highly competent, reliable and trustworthy, actually believing that the relationships he had with her, her husband (who also had a seat on the OPIE Task Force), her parents, siblings, grandmother, and even her aunt and uncle from Georgia were as real as they come. So the realization he had one evening—amidst all the professional turmoil he was experiencing—that Lori may have betrayed him cut him like a knife. He had to share it with someone other than Kesi who could talk him out of it, someone who would tell him that he was tripping. So that evening he made a phone call to his colleague Nyla.

"Hello," Nyla answered.

"Hey Nyla," greeted Xavier. "I've got some heavy shit on my mind. You got a minute."

"Always for you big brother," Nyla responded. "What's up?"

"Lori knew," Xavier said.

"Knew what? What did Lori know?" asked Nyla.

"She knew that they were coming after me, that Linda and Shalo had something up their sleeves." Xavier asserted confidently.

"No way, wait, what makes you think that?" Nyla asked, anxiously awaiting an answer.

"Because if Linda approached my previous assistant, Robin Kris, asking if she had ever been sexually harassed or knew of someone who had been, why wouldn't one of them have approached Lori with similar questions. Both Shalo and Linda know Lori much better than either know Robin. If they were looking to construct their MeToo moment on this campus the easiest route to accomplishing it was to have Lori as their ally."

"Are you saying she turned on you?" Nyla asked, hoping otherwise.

"Not at all, well not exactly. It's just I now know that some of the other young women that could have joined my staff would have never silently assented to being approached by Shalo and Linda. Just as Robin Kris let me know she had been approached by Linda, Lori could have told me to watch my back.

"You're disappointed. Or, are your feelings hurt?" Nyla inquired.

"How about both," Xavier admitted dejectedly. "Kesi tells me often that in her culture there are moments where you can't remain neutral and must choose a side. Lori's silence, perhaps a byproduct of her fear of supporting someone who could be guilty—speaks volumes about her as an ally. Anyone can be an ally when it is convenient."

"Last week I called to check on you and instead spoke with Kesi," Nyla said. "She mentioned to me how appreciative you and she were of the many young women you had once considered as potential candidates for the job Lori now has, because of how they consistently reached out to show their belief in you. That must have been rewarding."

"It was very rewarding. I'm also not naïve about the fact that Lori probably had many opportunities to throw more firewood on the flames, and didn't. It is unbelievable that I'm in a situation whereby I'm also celebrating women that told the truth. Lori at least appears to have done that with everyone, except me. Not that she lied, she just silently witnessed my demise. Regardless, Lori's inability to even privately acknowledge my pain, even if not publicly step up, has taught me one of my biggest life lessons. I now have more insight into what a seriously committed to social justice ally looks like, and they look nothing like Lori. I now have four categories framing people's responses and never would have dreamt that Lori would have been in any category other than the first."

"The first being…," Nyla wondered.

"The first category is fairly obvious, 'ally.'" Xavier answered. "The other three are 'all lies,' 'alibis,' and 'bye bye.'

"Wow, now that sounds interesting," Nyla said approvingly. "Are these not-ally categorizations your original thought? If so, please break them down for an unknowing Sistah."

"They are my original thoughts that organically took shape as people who postured like allies either showed up, were *'all lies'* about truly being my ally, had an all-too-convenient *alibi* as to why they didn't show up, or by their actions or lack thereof either chose to say *'bye bye'* to avoid getting caught up in my drama, or their inaction told me our relationship was only a fair weather one, leaving me no choice but to say 'bye bye' to those relationships."

"And Lori is where in these categories?" asked Nyla.

"Not that it would make her a bit of difference," responded Xavier, "but she's now somewhere floating between 'all lies' and 'alibis,' considering her knowing about this and not mentioning it is what is often referred to as a lie of omission.

Nyla's only response was "Damn."

"Listen Nyla," Xavier said, "that situation was further exacerbated by the fact that we are a few weeks into my removal from campus and I haven't heard a peep out of her. Her alibi could range from a fear of losing her job, to anxiety over being too closely associated with someone like me, considering the bad rap I've acquired that she did nothing to correct. Even though she had no problems being associated with me during the good times, even traveling with me to do consulting work and as a result picking up some serious extra funds. I also haven't heard anything from her husband either, not even a Facebook like from either of them. Even her aunt—for whom I risked and lost a significant relationship with the hospital—now has a convenient alibi for her disappearance too. It breaks my heart, especially considering how her sister and Mom have actually publicly supported me from time to time, here and there."

"That's too bad Xdub. It hurts to hear Lori disappeared on you like that."

"Hey Nyla, my Mom used to paraphrase a Maya Angelou saying that went something like this, 'When people tell you who they are, believe them.' On the other hand, everyone isn't everyone else's cup of tea. There are a lot of good people in the world and we often meet them but don't connect with them, or not profoundly. And everybody has their own shit going on. Lori was cool, real cool, but like they say on *Game of Thrones*, *'and now her watch is done.'*

"I thought you were going the Niemoller route," Nyla mentioned, . "To some extent that would apply here too, even though after all this conversation we had about her she could wake up tomorrow and call you."

"She may call, her and her husband may also once again start to 'like' my Facebook posts," Xavier explained. "Her aunt and I probably never were going to collaborate on projects we once discussed prior to my being accused. For many people they couldn't risk being associated with someone contaminated by a MeToo allegation. I doubt if these relationships with people I once considered my North Country family are salvageable, unfortunately including Lori's mother and younger sister McKenzie. Her mom Priscilla posted on FB, in the middle of all the drama, that I had their support. Though I only knew McKenzie as a soccer teammate of Autumn's she donated $50 to my GoFundMe campaign. Those expressions of support meant so much to me at a time when subconsciously I was in dire need of validation. Anyway, what is the Niemoller quote you were mentioning. I know the gist of it, but don't recall it exactly.

"Oh," Nyla said, "the poem is:

"First they came for the socialists, and I did not speak out—
    Because I was not a socialist.

Then they came for the trade unionists, and I did not speak out—
    Because I was not a trade unionist.

Then they came for the Jews, and I did not speak out—
    Because I was not a Jew.

Then they came for me—and there was no one left to speak for me."

"Oh shit, said Nyla. Sharing that poem with you brought to mind something Kesi said to me, and now I'm thinking she may have been thinking of Lori when she said it.

What was it?

"She said, 'The fact some people have remained silent in your defense, who know you well, could be interpreted as them believing the rumor as true.'

Allies

Having experienced some of the most debilitating moments of doubt a person could ever encounter, Xavier was reaching quite far in an attempt to acquire the perspective he would need to survive his precarious plight. Xavier was living in limbo. Unemployed but not really fired, engaged but not yet married, off campus but still working, and in between Peru and Montreal, nothing in his life was clear cut. In the process of existing like that, along with searching for some evidence he might be able to use in court, he discovered something inspiring.

Xavier was almost euphoric revisiting his students cultivating their voices, one advocating for him, and the other one owning her shit about him.

From: *Oliver Costa <olivercosta16@gmail.com>*
Date: *Thu, Feb 18, 2010 at 9:03 AM*
Subject: *Oliver Costa: Concerning Allegations Against Professor Witt*
To: *maimsbj@peru.edu*

Dear Brenda Maims,

I hope all is well for you this academic semester. It was brought to my attention that a few students are attempting to file a complaint against one of our professors, Dr. Xavier. Witt. To my understanding the allegations are that Dr. Witt "established a hostile environment in the course based on sex, specifically by belittling particular students and mocking analyses of gender oppression. I am baffled by these claims when the essence of the course RSLM is partly to challenge the constricting notions of gender oppression and allow students to look at sex, romance, love and marriage through different lens.

Personally, I have been a student and a teacher's assistant for RSLM. I was present when Mr. Witt facilitated discussions. I was present when Mr. Witt selected the films clips for each specific theme. These experiences provide me with the impetus to write this letter in order to assure you that the allegations mentioned above are groundless. But of course, these charges must come from somewhere. If I had to hypothesize about their origins, I would say they come from the mouths of students feeling threatened by individuals who challenge their ideals. From my perspective, this is about more than just the film clip from Storytelling and the grievances coming from a few wounded egos. Underlying all of this, there is the fact that Dr. Witt has consistently challenged WHITE privilege with a strong BLACK voice. I wonder what levels of discomfort stem from this?

Regardless, this letter is more a statement of support than analysis of the situation. If you have questions, you can contact me at 646-538-1205, or email me at: olivercosta16@gmail.com. Thanks for your time.

Sincerely yours,

Oliver Costa

"I want to answer questions and question answers in the quest to self-enlightenment. My whole life will be a question and an answer until I cease to exist" --Unknown

At the time this young man wrote in support of Xavier he had recently completed his term as the SG president. He wasn't asked to write it, and stood to gain nothing from it. However, on some level his actions were not a surprise at all. Anyone and everyone who really knew Oliver saw him as one step away from god sent. Oliver's email also revealed his knowledge of what Dr. Witt was fighting eight years ago as well. Xavier, like most people in his orbit, appreciated an unexpected, unanticipated ally.

Personal epiphanies are few and far between, but not difficult to attain. We only need to open our minds. This ex-student of Dr. Witt's models that:

From: "Clarice Best" <cbest@gmail.com>
Date: July 29, 2009 at 11:22:39 AM GMT-4
To: wittxw@peru.edu
Subject: An Apology

X.W.,

I have been postponing writing this letter for a while now. Why? Probably to lick my wounds and boost my ego a little. But at some point I needed to swallow my pride and realize my wrong doings. It was wrong of me to post anonymous comment on your blog in April. Very wrong of me. Furthermore, if I had something to discuss with you about your character, etc., I should have done it in person, not anonymously through the internet.

I think you are an incredibly sharp and witty man. I like that you are trying to broaden the minds of North Country folk and I appreciate most of what you have done in this community.

Yes, through the grapevine, I have heard promiscuous things about you. Unfortunately, instead of approaching you (face-to-face) or, better yet, minding my own business, I decided to slam you on your blog. My point of the blog comment was, at the time, that I felt like you were subconsciously disrespectful to women. And, I couldn't understand how the Director of the Office of Pluralism, Inclusion and Equity at New York-State University-Peru and a Lecturer in Intellectual History & Interdisciplinary Studies could boldly disrespect women.

Now, again, everything I have heard about you has been through second, third, maybe even fourth-told ears. So, instead of simply believing everything I heard about you, I should have been optimistic and stopped the gossip. I am normally not a gossiper, but I listened and believed in some of the things that were told about you. I am sorry for that, sincerely.

I have done some messed up things this past year because of my insecurities, but I certainly want people to believe in me and listen to what I have to say before taking the gossip of several people around me. I am sorry I judged you.

I am not going to go into what I have heard about you and why it once made me think you were a womanizer, etc., but if you ever want to discuss this further, you know how to reach me.

Again, I am sorry for sinking to a low and anonymously posting that comment. I am sorry for the stress it likely caused you and for the pain. I do not like to inflict pain and stress onto people, so I don't know why I thought it was fine to attack you. If I could go back in time, I would change the way I handled things. But I cannot time travel, I can only learn from my mistakes and hope they make me into a better person.

If it helps, I do not talk, gossip or spread rumors about you to anyone. And I have learned to tell people to stop talking if they are going to accuse you of things while you are not around.

Like I said, you are a brilliant man and you deserve the respect that you have earned. I consider myself a liberalist, but I was once stuck in the dark ages when it came to homosexuality. Spending a few months with you and reading your recommended materials helped to change my mind about homosexuality, entirely. I am now a staunch supporter of same-sex marriage and I see no fault in being homosexual.

You have a powerful gift, X.W. You can help educate the most closed minds in this world. That is amazing and I encourage you to keep on preaching and teaching!

So one more time, I am sorry for violating any trust you may have had in me and for hurting you.

Hopefully one day you can forgive me.

Sincerely,

Clarice Best

Xavier was humbled discovering he was the catalyst for someone's personal epiphany. Clarice Best's email, though an echo from the past, was invigorating in terms of validating his approach and substance. It was also intellectually invigorating. Clarice apologized to Xavier thinking he was a womanizer. It must be a default interpretation of a man comfortable with women enough to be in their company often, to be seen as always on the prowl. A good question would be why would anyone want to be the person on the prowl, crowding someone, being that guy, instead of being around a lot of beautiful people, many of them women comfortable about being around you? Xavier's entire life he has been the guy with the group, not the guy trying to grope. These two emails energized him because one was of an ally putting in some work for him. The other one featured someone who thinks she is ready to put some work in, perhaps unaware she already started by invigorating Xavier.

This wasn't the first time Xavier had heard some version of this story. In support of his struggle with Feminist Anthropology, Xavier received many similar statements of support from students who would not stand by silently acquiescing to rumors and lies.

In addition to sending these below statements of support to his attorneys, Xavier decided to post them in a Facebook album he titled, 'Feminist Anthropology Testimonials.' The letters were unsolicited, supportive and quite revealing:

*** STUDENT EXCERPTS ***

Bringing down someone like Dr. Witt is not the equivalent of bringing down the Donald Trumps and Harvey Weinsteins of America who have been accused of sexual assault and have gone years never facing consequences. Dr. Witt is not this person. Not even close. Marking him as the symbol of injustice at NYSU-Peru does NOTHING for the larger community of Peru OR future students of color who choose to attend NYSU Peru...*Where is the evidence that these allegations are true?* Without that evidence, I cannot generalize and wrong a Black man. If you feel that Dr.Witt is getting away with something, this is the time to use your voice to say something, otherwise, don't use your voice to negate the work of a man who has been hundred percent dedicated to students of color at Peru for decades.

The purpose of this letter is not to discredit a woman's voice, but *the paper posted in the ACC today has no signatures, no trace of WHO or what group wrote that letter,* so for me to believe in that voice, *I* *need to know various factors...*In today's society, *we cannot be foolish, believing everything written down on paper* or posted on social media.

In my time at NYSU Peru I was very active in the women's movement, but as a woman of color, I need to say that *the feminist movement at large needs to be more aware of how allegations* (because that's what they are!) *against men of color impact professional lives and reputations* in the long run.

I took Romance with Dr. Witt in the Fall of 2011 and although it is just my perspective and experience with Dr. Witt, never did I feel he was inappropriate in any matter...Even through difficult conversations about romance, sex, and love and their relationship to race, I never felt that Dr. Witt was trying to take advantage of me or my classmates. I remember watching a clip about a white woman who believed she was raped by a Black man in his Romance course, and I remember the way he facilitated these conversations and DID not generalize people or races because of their varying perspectives of the clip.

I remember Dr. Witt being honest about his vulnerability as a Black professor on campus teaching Romance to a large room filled (at that time) with mostly white students. I praised his bravery in facilitating these hard conversations even with white women in the room. I say that because *historically, white women have viewed Black men as violent, sexual abusers, which is important to recognize and discuss* as a student body. Without Dr. Witt in Peru, who will facilitate those difficult conversations and put themselves in such a vulnerable positions just to reach a larger goal of understanding and tolerance?

There are so many political games that continue to emerge in Peru, that it also would not surprise me that this message was and is meant to discredit a Black man's work and make him a scapegoat.
— **Rasa Adjapong '12**

****

I was shocked to hear of the allegations towards you. I will be the first one to admit that I left NYSU-Peru with a little bit of saltiness towards you. All of which was none of your own doing, and a lot of it came from my peers and mentor (Ramona Saphony).

I was assaulted by a student while taking your [RSLM] class. Someone who I had to see in class every week. There was a film that you showed that teetered the line of consensual sex and rape, I had to watch it with my attacker in the room. At the time I felt like I deserved it, I put myself in an unsafe environment. I now know different. I only shared it with one person at a time, another student in the class who was also part of the Feminist Anthropology major.

The night of that movie, We were able to really have a conversation regarding the video but those of my peers who were in my Feminist Anthropology major insisted it was rape. They then discussed it in all of my gender studies classes the rest of the semester. I remember the anger I felt towards you for the film and my peers for the constant reminder of what happened. Reflecting back as an adult now, *the time they spent attacking you interrupted everyone who went to that department to seek a safe space. Many of us were very traumatized by having to live a conversation over and over.*

I have moved on and forgiven my attacker, though I have had no contact with him since Peru.... To this day though I do not disclose my gender studies degree, *I have not forgiven that department for the mockery that made of a cause so dear to my heart and how they spent more time creating a hateful environment towards another faculty member* then [a] safe space for a student.

I am very grateful to you for all that you have taught me, especially being a white woman raising a young man of color. I wish you the best in your legal endeavor. I hope what I've shared with you if nothing helps shed some light on what really happens in that department.

— **K.E. Carreras**

As I got older I saw the group of women for what they really were. I can't speak to what the department is now *but I know with Ramona* it was always a "who has the worst struggle" conversation. *She was threatened by someone else who could engage students and impact a larger group of people than she could.* I don't know Sharon well but I do recall her being very upset by us bringing up things in her [F]eminism in the [M]edia class that you taught us in diversity.

In the end my saltiness was not towards you at all it was towards the situation I was in and it took me a few years to see it. I owe a lot of my successes in life to you, you opened my very privileged Upstate mind... I use so much of what I learned from you.

You have the ability to impact so many people, with or without NYSU-Peru. It is the University's loss. <u>You are definitely not paranoid</u> though because in the spring of 2010 <u>there was a crusade against you</u> in that department. That was the year I graduated. I remember them holding a group after you showed the film for people who were bothered by it in the gender studies department. She had students write statement to give to the university.— **K.E. Carreras**

I have the pleasure of knowing Dr. Xavier Witt since the day he came to my high school and spoke to my 9th grade class. I remember being floored by the presentation as he opened my mind to new ideas and entirely new perspectives. I didn't see him again until 4 years later when our diversity teacher took us to visit the man who created the class ours was based upon. I went on to be the first freshman to take NYSU-Peru's diversity class.

A major difference in the way his classes are taught is the discussion that takes place. No topic is off limits, because the hard conversations we don't have are part of the systematic "-ism" (sexism, racism, ableism, etc.) culture we see everyday. He taught us our racist thoughts were not abnormal, rather conditioned; we had never even thought about these things before. These conversations lead my roommate at the time to get into a heated argument about one of the film clips we watched in our class. At the time she was a FA minor. During her class that day they watched a clip about a professor who engages in sex with his student. She knew at the time I was in Dr. Witt's class. *We had discussed before the hatred the FA department had for my professor, she reconfirmed it on this day.* The exact details of the clip are unnecessary for me to tell you;... *From my understanding Dr. Witt was torn apart due to the parallels of the clip to him. The professor in the clip happened to be a black male.—* **K. Marie**

I feel a bit guilty in this situation because during my college career (2011-2015), *two of my RA's told me the rumor about you and called you a "Hypocrite."* In my disbelief, *I might have indirectly helped spread this rumor* to fellow students. I apologize for not coming to you and telling you of these encounters, but I did not know the severity of the situation and I was irrationally afraid that you would think I was questioning your morality. Lastly, I want to say that you are a good, brave and generous individual. *It takes a lot of courage to live where you live* and do what you do; especially, being a person of color. — **Joey P.**

I just wanted to say hi and send some love and support your way since I know you've been getting some undeserved flack for being a so-called sexual predator to women. I was shocked and appalled when a friend informed me of your termination from NYSU. When I learned of the reason, I was confused, doubtful, and disappointed. Mind you, I did not harbor these feelings because I thought you were "guilty," but rather because *I could not understand how the college could allow such rampant rumors to get so out of hand;* I could not view you as a predator of any kind, much less a sexual one inappropriately touching women; I was stunned that the college would allow one of their most influential and coveted professors to leave due to what has occurred. Since initially hearing of your end at NYSU, I have read newspaper and online articles, etc. Now I am just...flabbergasted!

I was told by a former student a number of years ago that you were, to paraphrase, a pervert who hit on female students, especially white blondes, and that you either had sex with students or tried to. At the time, I had taken a couple of your courses and I had never heard such things before but it's sometimes hard to read how people truly are and so I took it with a grain of salt, but I still took it as a possibility. Since that time, I have taken all of your courses except for one (and a couple of them multiple times...☐) as well as served alongside you as a TA. I have known you for around 12 years now, taking classes on and off and going to lectures and the film wrap series. That amounts to a significant amount of time observing you (especially given my anthropological nature and tendency to study people), as well as time in which I feel that I've truly gotten to know you as a person and your character. During these last 12 years, I can honestly say that I NEVER perceived you as a predator towards women. I never once observed you inappropriately conducting yourself with any students, whether it be physical interactions or verbal ones. Of course I noticed your charming, joshing, flirty personality. It's one of your most endearing and attractive qualities to both women and men.

This makes me surmise that *these students who have hopped on the academic lynching* bandwagon have either done so *because of rumors* and not firsthand experience with you, or have misinterpreted your actions or words and vilified you in their minds. The unfortunate truth of the situation is *this is undoubtedly due to the myth of the black male rapist*. I cannot help but feel the same attention from another professor of a different skin tone may be interpreted differently.

I spoke with a friend familiar with you from a few courses concerning your current predicament. This particular person already had preconceived notions about you and did not like you as a person. When discussing the validity of the allegations, *this person said to me that it most likely was true. This struck me as odd because this person did not have any personal inappropriate experiences with you nor had they heard from anyone who claimed to.* So I realized in that moment people assume these allegations are true, simply because they do not like you or may not agree with your approach to things! I suppose it was simply naive of me to not have already come to that conclusion, but *to hear it from a friend who I think of as open-minded and as having reasonable common sense was alarming*. It's simply not fair or right. It's persecution. It's injustice. It's a deplorable example of a modern-day witch hunt with racial and gender-related undertones (or should I say overtones?).

I cannot believe that you are accused of such inconsiderate and predatory attitudes towards women. You may have stronger convictions in teaching about racial injustice because of your personal experiences, but you teach equality and embracing diversity. I never saw you as one to subjugate women in general, especially not female students that you have a rapport with.

And lastly, I wanted to touch on the controversy surrounding the viewing in Romance of the scene from "*Storytelling*". *It's preposterous to claim that you showed that to students with the intent to somehow suggest all white female students should have a sexual relationship with all black male teachers.* It's not even a sound argument! It literally does not make any sense, especially considering the context in which the clip is shown. *If anything the clip proves your lack of intent to sleep with students; since many students DO view that scene as rape, and you are very much aware of that, by preying on students, particularly white ones, you would be implicating yourself as a rapist essentially.* It's just complete nonsensical thinking! Also, *I loved that clip.* I thought it was one of the most <u>enlightening and provocative</u> (not in a sexual sense of course) scenes that we watched and *it was the precursor to a very important and eye-opening discussion* that should be had. Honestly, it seems to me that anyone who viewed showing that clip as predatory on your part is either too ignorant or too unwilling (or too immature) to understand its relevance. — **A. Velsi**

...As you know the lack of diversity within the FA department as well as *the unsubstantiated accusations made against you is the reason that I started taking your classes* in the first place. It is one of the best academic decisions I could have made.

There are a number of good professors within the FA department, however they are overshadowed by the individuals that are promoting their own agenda by willingly repeating slanderous gossip to their students. I hope that in addition to light being shed on the truth of your dismissal from NYSU-Peru, that the FA department is scrutinized and made to take stock of the tunnel vision of some of their colleagues. The climate in that department has left a bad taste in many alumni's mouths. — **D. Kellard**

Support from students of Dr.Witt's from years past was enormous in lifting his spirits. Their articulation of the overriding sentiment of FA towards Xavier had him truly believing he would reap dividends when it came to establishing in a court of law that *a hostile environment* had been created against him.

More Lies - More Alibis

Not too dissimilar from Dr. Lee Jones' 'energizers,' 'energy stealers,' and 'energy impostors,' were the four categories of allies organically appearing to Xavier during the first months of his staving off allegations of him being 'disrespectful to women.' Allies, like energy impostors can be wolves in sheep's clothing, but when found in their natural state are all lies, not allies, like energy impostors posing as energizers until they are discovered.

One of the most prominent energy impostors who could also don the distinction of being 'all lies' when the rubber meets the road was Dr. LeAnn Prey. LeAnn was a faculty member who rotated through all five components of the Reconciling Otherness through Diversity Enlightenment class, later co-teaching the same class with OPIE staff. She served on the OPIE Task Force for several semesters and frequently required her students attend OPIE events. For all intent and purposes she resembled an energizer and ally. However, it didn't take long before the wolf came out of the lambskin. Within a relatively short span of time she was seen as a pariah within her academic department, with her calling card being that she suffered from thinking she was the smartest person in the room, believing she could spin anything in her favor. After years of watching her Machiavellian moves, Xavier decided to end the charade, calling a spade a tool, or better yet making sure she knew that this spade was no tool, or no one's fool.

He was blown away when he opened his email a week after the Pigeon Messages snafu to find a correspondence from LeAnn Prey:

On Nov 9, 2015, at 12:05 PM, LeAnn Prey <preyl@peru.edu> wrote:

Hi XW,

I am forwarding you a copy of some correspondence I had last week with President Utley and the Provost. Let me know what you think.

LeAnn

---------- **Forwarded message** ----------
From: Le Ann Prey <preyl@peru.edu>
Date: Thu, Oct 29, 2015 at 12:11 PM
Subject: Some Thoughts on Actions
To: Provost <provost@peru.edu>, J Utley <utleyj@peru.edu>

Dear President Utley and Provost,

I am writing to express my concern over the recently published image in Pigeon Messages and to offer a possible direction for taking action.

I am personally and professionally very appreciative of the responses to this horrible event. These responses demonstrate an ability to take ownership that this image is in fact racist and to apologize for its publication. I am grateful the responses were not those of denial or excuse.

These responses do little to ease pain and hurt caused by publication of this image, nor do they capture the work that still needs to be done. I frequently ask myself f"how could this happen?" My students are echoing this same question. It is a question that demands a deep look into who we are as a community.

A few years ago I was deeply honored when invited to participate in the creation of the NYSU-Peru Campus Plan. As part of my role in that initiative, I convened the committee working on Strategic Goal #7 - Increasing Diverse Experiences and Cultural Competencies. This group was comprised of several faculty and administrators around campus. We worked with enthusiasm and hope and were ready and willing to continue the work as the Strategic Plan was rolled out to campus. This did not happen. My understanding is some of this work was taken on by others.

My suggestion is that you reconvene this group of committed and enthusiastic members of our community and give us the charge of increasing multicultural competencies for faculty, administrators, students and staff at NYSU-Peru. Our conversations, rich and thoughtful as they may be can not be where this work ends. Without deliberate and direct attention to developing multicultural competencies history will repeat itself.

Thank you for your time and consideration.

LeAnn
--
Dr. LeAnn Prey
English Dept.
NYSU-Peru

Very much caught off guard by what was obviously LeAnn attempting to situate herself for an opportunity, what really annoyed Xavier was the fact LeAnn must have thought she might be discovered jockeying for position, Xavier's CDO position. As a result she forwarded to him, four days after she wrote it, the letter that she just as easily could have copied him on in real time, as well as copy her boss too. After considering her forwarded email she shared with him over a few days, Xavier finally responded:

On Wed, Nov9, 2015 at 10:01 PM, Dr. Xavier Witt <wittx@peru.edu> wrote:

Hello LeAnn,

What do I think? Frankly I'm surprised to hear that you would all of a sudden care about my opinion. But I'm sure you must have your reasons.

Since you asked though, I think it is admirable and collegial that in a time of crisis you would offer your services. We will need all the talent we can muster to right the ship. However I don't agree with you that we have to ask ourselves profound questions about who we are as a community in response to the incident. From my perspective the pertinent question is, more so as a community, how do we respond to it.

Regarding the reconvening of a committee to advance multicultural competencies, it has been done under my leadership. The Office of Pluralism, Inclusion, & Equity's Task Force met twice this semester and is rapidly advancing the campus' diversity initiative, under the charge from our President, whom as Chief Diversity Officer I now report to.

Thanks for taking the time to make sure we are making positive things happen for our campus community. Rest assured we are.

XW

Dr. Xavier Witt
"Perspective is the Objective"
***Author:** The "Other" Within Us:*
Reconciling Identities with Leadership Moments

****

On Nov11, 2015, at 8:14 AM, LeAnn Prey <Prey@Peru.edu> wrote:

Dear XW,

Thank you for taking the time to look over my suggestion. I appreciate your honest response, as it has provided me with great clarity on the direction you will be taking as Chief Diversity Officer for NYSU- Peru.

It should come as no surprise to you that I want to engage in the work of social justice in as many ways as possible. This work is deeply personal and it has been the core of my professional life. I remain committed and willing. It is my sincere hope that as Chief Diversity Officer you will tap into the diverse group of people on this campus who are already engaged in social justice work.

I wish you the best,

LeAnn

*Dr. LeAnn Prey
English Dept.
NYSU-Peru*

****

On Sat, Nov 17, 2015 at 4:53 PM, Dr. Xavier Witt <wittx@peru.edu> wrote:

Hello LeAnn,

I'm happy that you appreciated my response. It always feel good to be appreciated. However, I must admit I am a bit clueless as to how the honesty of my response--honesty which could only be in question by my opening remark to you about being surprised that you might care about what I think--somehow "provided [you] with great clarity," or revealed anything else to you about the direction I'll be taking as CDO.

Why is it I can hear your voice softening as you essentially counseled me about what you may have surmised as a symptom of my professional immaturity or my insecurities. Please don't conflate things simply because my response to you may not have been what you anticipated. I haven't decided the direction I'll be taking as CDO because I won't be making that decision alone. I had already (as you suggested, albeit after the fact) tapped into "the diverse group of people on this campus who are already engaged in social justice work." There are many people eager to bring an open mind to the conversations, eager to try new approaches along with traditional ones, to raise the collective consciousness of our town and gown community. As well, there are many people seldom given the opportunity to contribute who will learn how to engage and educate themselves and others in our never ending effort to enhance consideration of the so-called "Other" while developing leaders and allies.

The email you chose to share with me on Nov 2, four days after You originally sent the email to our President/Provost, accentuates my point. Professional courtesy would have been exhibited on your part by a call asking me about the possibilities of the task force reconvening. Even copying me on the letter to our executive leadership, especially as the director of OPIE--the closest thing we had on campus to a CDO--would have been a professional courtesy. Instead you chose to take a different route. What does that say about your thoughts about my leadership of the campus' diversity initiative up to that point? I guess it's moot now because the CDO position was offered to me, followed by a deluge of emails of acknowledgement and support. That was more than enough validation that I am doing the director of OPIE job more than adequately or I would not have been offered the job on October 16, one week before the Pigeon Messages incident and about eleven months prior to when that position needed to be filled.

But your not-so-veiled implication that as CDO our lack of much of a past as colleagues--and your seeming lack of genuine respect for my style of leadership and different approach to implementing diversity & social justice education--would have me not appreciate you or anyone else who wants to lean in and contribute to the campus' diversity initiative is incorrect. It only reveals you really have no idea who I am and what I'm about. I hope you will contribute to the enhancement of multicultural competencies in the array of ways that you do. I don't begrudge you any of the success that I imagine you will continue to have doing what you do. I wish you the best in that regard.

XW

Dr. Xavier Witt
"Perspective is the Objective"

Author: The "Other" Within Us:
Reconciling Identities with Leadership Moments

****

From: LeAnn Prey <preyl@peru.edu>
Date: November 11, 2015 at 7:48:48 AM EST
To: "Dr. Xavier Witt" <wittx@peru.edu>
Subject: Re: Some Thoughts on Actions

Dear XW,

I have been thinking about your last e-mail to me for several days now. I remain puzzled by your response.

Although you and I have not always been in agreement, I took our disagreements as learning experiences. As a firm believer in democratic living, I see disagreements as important aspects of learning and growth for individuals and society as a whole.

I am not sure where to go from here. Your words indicate to me that you do not have a desire to continue working with me or anyone else who you perceive to have "a lack of genuine respect for my style of leadership and different approach to implementing diversity & social justice education." This too, surprises me as I have often heard you speak about the importance of working across differences for social justice.

It is certainly true that working relationships grow apart – perhaps that is what has happened to us. That's fine. What is not fine is the picture being painting of me as someone who has not been supportive of the work OPIE has done and the contributions it makes to NYSU-Peru and the community at large.

Sincerely,

LeAnn

Dr. LeAnn Prey

English Dept.
NYSU-Peru

On Sun, Nov 19, 2015 at 10:24 AM, Dr. Xavier Witt <wittx@peru.edu> wrote:

Hello LeAnn,

I'm surprised that after a few days of reflecting upon my thoughts to you that your response didn't address one of the most significant points we both discussed, 'professional courtesy.' So I'll try again. As previously stated-- but not addressed--in the email you replied to, that prompted this response from me, I once again am stating/asking you:

"Professional courtesy would have been exhibited on your part by you calling me about the possibilities of the task force reconvening. Even copying me on the letter to our executive leadership, especially as OPIE director--the closest thing we had on campus to a CDO--would have been a professional courtesy. Instead you chose to take a different route. What does that say about your thoughts about my leadership of the campus' diversity initiative?"

So LeAnn, if you choose to respond to this email please start with a response to the above. Because I imagine you did not decide to just ignore my assertion about your lack of extending a professional courtesy to me, after you had no problem implying I did not extend it to you?

No doubt we have a history, a productive one. Once upon a time you were much appreciated at OPIE. I also don't recall ever having a difference of opinion with you. However, feigning dismay at any sense of impropriety or duplicity on your part must get tiresome. Perhaps you'll discover this side of yourself as you respond to my thoughts of the hypocrisy of your assertion towards my lack of extending you professional courtesy.

Regarding your use of a quote of mine, I'm perplexed you could interpret it this way:

"I am not sure where to go from here. Your words indicate to me that you do not have a desire to continue working with me or anyone else who you perceive to have "lack of genuine respect for my style of leadership and different approach to implementing diversity & social justice education." This too, surprises me as I have often heard you speak about the importance of working across differences for social justice."

I said nothing specific about not having a desire to work with you. I am astonished as your not responding to my accusation about your lack of professional courtesy. As I said in my last email and apparently must repeat again, you really don't know me and what I'm about. We do similar work for the same cause. Our professional paths will most likely cross and that is not problematic for me. However, any expectation that I would reach out to someone who appears to have little respect for me/my approach/my work is naïve, coy, or both. Contrary with how you choose to interpret me, I surround myself with colleagues that push me. It's how I grow. My colleagues don't have to see the world, nor articulate it, as I would. However, I must trust them. I do not trust you. Your lack of professional courtesy by not copying me on the letter to the President/Provost, even the omission of copying your Dean in that email-- are quite revealing. Are those the actions of someone trustworthy? What was your purpose in asking my opinion? Was that a preemptive strike, an empty gesture, a preventive measure anticipating the President/Provost forwarding me your message?

If I didn't know better I could mistakenly surmise that you were jockeying for another position, perhaps as my boss, with me remaining OPIE Director, reporting to you, the Chief Diversity Officer. While this is now a moot point, perhaps you can educate me as to what you were trying to accomplish in that email and why your offer to assist the campus in recovering was not an "inclusive" one. Ironic isn't it when people who claim to be doing social justice work "seemingly" aren't practicing what they preach. I put "seemingly" in quotes this time to make sure you didn't miss it, since until I receive your response educating me about your omission of Dean Mark and I, I can't be certain of your motives, can I?

You will no doubt share these emails with your campus crew as evidence that I'm professionally immature and perhaps insecure, two cards that *some people in similar situations play far too often and not as well as they think. We both have been on this campus for awhile. We both have reputations. I am quite confident that my reputation has me situated well as a campus leader capable of being a major player in turning this campus around. I have never sought career advancement at NYSU-Peru because my attitude has always been if I'm doing my job well opportunity will find me. It has, over and over again off campus and now finally, before our campus crisis arose, it found me on campus. I imagine your reputation is serving you well too. Since it is more than likely that our diligent work ethics and well earned reputations are taking us where we deserve to be I don't discount the possibilities of our professional paths intersecting often. As well, as the Chief Diversity Officer I will be receptive to ideas to advance the college's commitment to diversity and the campus' diversity initiative/plan. This would definitely include your ideas, even if you prefer to believe that because we had some real conversations recently that it would probably be otherwise.*

So, I'll patiently await your thoughts on professional courtesy and any other responses to this email.

XW

Dr. Xavier Witt
"Perspective is the Objective"
Author: *The "Other" Within Us:*
Reconciling Identities with Leadership Moments

If Xavier miscalculated anything at all, it was the enemy he made out of LeAnn Prey. This would eventually make him regret letting his guard down with her from thinking she was a vanquished opponent, instead of a worthy one.

Scarred Perspectives - Ally Objectives

"Hello Class," said Dr. Witt in his most welcoming voice, "Today is the day that you have all been waiting for, final presentations. Is the first group ready?" he asked.

"Yes, we are," answered Bashir. "We'll start by introducing ourselves, and then our presentation. So, I'm Bashir, a 5th year senior, an Arab, heterosexual male, from an upper-middle class reality."

Gabby, never shy, described herself too, "I'm a senior, a White heterosexual-female, from a lower-middle class reality."

Jasmine described herself. "I'm a junior, Black, bi-curious-female, from a upper-lower class reality."

Donta then described himself, "I'm a senior, a Black heterosexual-male, from a middle class reality."

And today, my colleagues Jasmine, Gabby, Donta and I will be unpacking the topic '*Scarred Perspectives and their relationship to Ally Objectives.*' Our approach is conversational, with you as flies on the wall observing."

All of them were situated shoulder to shoulder in front of the room with somber, yet focused faces, silently staring back at their classmates before the silence was broken by Gabby.

"We sometimes disrespect one another's differences," Gabby said. *"We insult using humor, dismissing the things we say as not racism, sexism, heterosexism, or other "isms."*

Donta added, *"When we consciously or cavalierly are caught using "isms," we claim innocence, though intuitively we knew it wasn't cool."*

Jasmine then took a step towards the students seated in front of her, perhaps to guarantee their attention, and said, *"It takes a while to figure out that life is easier when we create alliances, are patient with one another and have* open-minded conversations leading to profound relationships. Projecting ill will is, and will always be, ill advised."

"*Scars are the results of projecting ill will,*" Bashir added. "*Feeling devalued, mocked, some aspect of your identity scoffed at; all these situations result in permanent pain and/or lingering hurt, residual scars.*"

Gabby further added, "*We all have scars. Big ones, little ones, scars that others see that we ourselves don't, and scars that some of us hide. Some people are even able to put scars in perspective; our scars embarrass us, contribute to our impatience, unruliness, invisibility, even make us unbearable, and/or irascible.*"

Donte chimed in, "*If you were socialized in the U.S., how could you not have scars? There is always something about our identity (even in terms of height, weight, neighborhood, attire, family members, etc.) that serves as a target for someone else. No one escapes unscathed.*"

If verbal attacks are artfully aimed at us when we are vulnerable, even the most resilient amongst us can be scarred," stated Jasmine. "*Dr. Witt--in all of his classes--emphasizes that those of us who grew up in U.S. culture are biased, prejudiced and intolerant but, more so, heterosexist, racist, ableist, classist, ageist, sexist and yes, jingoist.*"

Jasmine continued, utilizing the power of the dramatic pause, "*Unless the surface of our subconscious is slightly scratched, or our perspectives provoked, we don't necessarily unpack the reasons we act woefully childish with one another. As a result, we far too often immaturely assault one another in an inconsiderate pursuit of cute, cool, clever or collateral.*"

Assenting with an affirmative head nod, as if in passionate agreement with Jasmine, Gabby said, "*Many of us after high school continued acting like middle schoolers. We blame our neighborhoods, our opinionated uncle, mom/dad not in our lives, overheard conversations, repetitive messages in songs/movies, books we read, including the so-called good book.*"

"*We are slow to own it ourselves.*" declared Bashir. "*We are slow to take responsibility for inherited ideals we don't question.*" Abolitionist John

Brown, a white man, risked it all at Harper's Ferry for people different from him, Black people, because he felt it was the right thing to do. Who does that nowadays?"

Jasmine said, "*It was Dr. Martin Luther King Jr. who said that " Cowardice asks the question 'Is it safe?':*

Donte added, "*Expediency asks the question 'Is it politics?'*

Gabby said, "*Vanity asks the question 'Is it popular?'*

"*The conscience asks the question 'Is it right?'*" said Bashir,

Jasmine then redirected the presentation, saying, "*Yet, in not doing the right thing, are we hypocrites? We want to answer no, but then we reflect on the prejudice we may have in contrast to prejudicial treatment we prefer to avoid, and our hypocrisy is undeniable.*"

"*Can we have certainty it will ever change if we aren't the catalyst?* Gabby asked the class, rhetorically. "*It's not rocket science, only common sense.*"

"*Ironically,*" said Donte, "*most of us have a chance to avoid social injustice and hypocrisy through our actions, modeling the ally we want to see riding to our rescue.*"

Bashir, then looking at Jasmine instead of the students in the class, said, "*The primary thing preventing our being socially just without hypocrisy is our ego.*"

Jasmine responded, "*Which trumps the other: ego or logic?*"

The entire groups as one responded, "*Why did you have to bring him up?*"

The class chuckled at the presenter's creativity, regardless of their political affiliation, they seem to appreciate the corny jab at President Trump.

Gabby got the class back in serious mode by asking, "*How many of you have taken Dr. Witt's diversity class?*" Over half of the class of 40 students raised their hands to indicate having taken the class. Gabby continued, "*So then most of you have heard Dr. Witt's spiel about how seldom or often any of us outside of the transgendered community actually intellectually engage the challenges of being transgendered.*"

"*Dr. Witt then hits us with this provocative thought,*" Bashir said, adding, "*Hypothetically, once upon a time, our parents themselves may have been faced with the decision to select our gender due to some form of anatomical ambiguity at our birth. Armed with this knowledge, our reactions to the transgender community could change. We may have even momentarily imagined ourselves as part of that community.*"

By momentarily imagining ourselves a part of that community, are you saying we considered them?" Jasmine asked Bashir.

Bashir answered, "*Yes, or we may have actually considered that our parents may have made the right decision for us, while many others parents probably did not. The more important point is, are our egos so large, and yet so fragile that we need not consider how hypocritical we are, enjoying the comfort of our bodies without imagining the discomfort we would experience if born a man trapped inside a woman's body, or born a woman trapped inside a man's body?*

Donte poignantly and somberly concluded by saying, "*Ironically, we may have laughed at or dismissed others in the throes of figuring out who they are, or can be, without realizing, if not for the grace of God, there go I.*"

Standing shoulder-to-shoulder, the presenters absorbed the adulation of their classmates for their unique style of presenting their perspectives. Dr. Witt stood along the side of the wall silently, realizing how very difficult it actually is getting people to consider how their scars have them interpreting and acting out those interpretations. He knew he was living through some of that with his campus drama.

Father & Son - Mutual Alliances

The impact of scandal upon a family is something very difficult to anticipate. Xavier didn't realize how adverse his campus drama and the assault on his reputation was impacting his now adult children until he overheard his 21 year old son on the speakerphone, passionately defending his father, a few weeks after the scandal hit the newspapers.

"Anybody believing an accusation framing my Dad as someone who would abuse his power or position to gain favor with women either doesn't know him, is predisposed towards wanting to see him as a culprit or criminal, or is a fucking idiot," Justin declared to Peter over the speakerphone.

"Honestly though Justin," said Peter, "No one would have ever anticipated Bill Cosby's dark side either."

Knowing Peter wasn't equating his Dad with Bill Cosby, but instead was playing devil's advocate, Justin replied, "I get that too. However, Cosby as an actor, comedian, and legend wasn't known for fighting for the disenfranchised across the board. Most of his work was associated with improving the plight of Black people. My Dad's focus was much more expansive, or as he would say, more inclusive. I'll share two stories that you've never heard. Hopefully they will further enlighten you to the man I grew up watching."

"Peter, don't you remember how very concerned my Dad was about me when, as teenagers, my sister Autumn and I moved to Brooklyn to live with our mother after they divorced. We were very fortunate that their divorce never got ugly. Somehow they reconciled the end of their marriage by committing to keeping their children in the center of their relationship. They were trying to minimize the drama, and it worked."

"I remember." Peter said. "I also remember how respectfully your parents treated each other while divorcing."

"They were nice to each other," Justin added in agreement.

"I also remember your Dad having mixed emotions about you two leaving. You told me he wanted you to have a taste of city life without you getting devoured by it," Peter added.

"Our Dad anticipated that Black kids from predominantly White rural areas could get bullied by some ignorant-ass kids either with too much time on their hands, or out of jealousy of two kids with self respect who appeared to be quite different," Justin said. "He had encountered something similar when he went to high school in Tulsa, Oklahoma. Within our first few weeks in Brooklyn all of his concerns about preparing us for big city living had come to fruition. Autumn, then 13 years old was jumped on by three girls at school. Fortunately some other girls she had made friends with came to her rescue. Besides, Autumn could fight her ass off, and the word on the street was that she was initially holding her own with the first two girls who jumped her. The third girl entering the fight is what prompted the other girls to help Autumn.

Justin then shook his head as a slight grin formed across his face, and said, "I hate to admit that I was being bullied too. This 20 year old, basically a grown-ass man, who hung out at the basketball courts and was friends with some of my new friends was always overtly fouling me, or verbally threatening me. I've always been close to my Dad and so I turned to him for advice. He taught me how to box and sparred with me for years, so I knew he would have some words of wisdom. I remember that conversation like it was yesterday."

"Hey Son, How is Brooklyn treating you?" asked Xavier with concern.

"Dad, It is all good for the most part, though this kid Reggie has been bullying me at the basketball courts," Justin said. "He's not much of an athlete and gets physical with me since he can't stop me from schooling him on the court."

"Have you considered changing courts?" Xavier asked. "Do you have to play with him?"

"Dad, he is part of the crew," Justin replied. "Either I get an entirely new set of friends, or stand up to him, fight him, and make a statement to all by hopefully whipping his ass, or…

"There is no 'or' Son. Can you take his bullying ass?" Xavier asked? "What's his size?"

"He's a little shorter than me." Justin answered. "Probably outweighs me though, but slow, and kinda stupid."

"If you start to win the fight would he pull out a blade, or a gun?" Xavier asked, hoping to hear the answer he desired.

"I don't think so," Justin responded. "The fellas would break it up before it got to that point. I'm telling you all of this because the other day he slapped me while we were all over a mutual friends house. I couldn't fight him then or we would have broken some furniture."

Infuriated with what he heard, Xavier said, "You're probably then going to have to fight this clown. If so, don't let him get you in a brawl. Box him, keep your distance, stick and move. If you are successful peppering his face with jabs he'll eventually lose his cool and blindly rush you. When he does that, side step him and drop his ass like a bad habit."

Justin then told Peter, "Little did I know after that telephone conversation with Dad, he took action on my behalf. Though he never mailed it, I found a copy of a letter he wrote Reggie in my mother's bedroom in Brooklyn. He must have shared it with her when he was thinking of sending it. I took a picture of the letter so I would have it forever."

Looking through his phone, he eventually found it. "My Dad never fails to amaze me. Check this out."

Adjusting his phone to a landscape position, Justin began reading the letter:

"Hey wannabe gangsta, it doesn't take much energy to bully someone who is younger than you and not as connected as you are. Justin, my Son, is new to Brooklyn still and comes from an environment where

people didn't make themselves feel better by beating down others. But I grew up in South Central LA, where my Father was murdered when I was 15. I had to deal with stupid ass, worthless, pieces of shit like you all through my adolescence. I know your punk ass would never have approached Justin if he was 6'5 225. You would never have approached him if you heard he had three Black Belt degrees in karate. So why do you do it now? Are you are a bully with no life? Stupid ass! Aren't you even smart enough to know that people don't respect you when you do shit like you do. They fear you, and most silently hope you one day get yours. And ironically you want to start a fight with someone younger than you who may just whip your ass if he realizes you are a loser trying to get a reputation off of fighting someone younger than you because you see him as an easy target. You are a real tough guy, aren't you?"

Pausing to check in with his friend, perhaps to make sure the call hadn't dropped, Justin said to his friend, "That's intense, isn't it?

"Intense as fuck," Peter said.

Apparently receiving the response he desired, Justin said, "There's more, that was just the foreplay." He then continued.

"Real talk: I know real hard asses who would just as soon fuck someone up for exercise as say hello to them. It has been brought to my attention that your worthless ass has been bullying my Son. REAL TALK: If anything else, ANYTHING, happens to my Son you will be looking over your shoulder the rest of your life wondering when payback is coming, because it will be coming, guaranteed. The only thing I despise more than racists, rapists, and child molesters are people like you who have no lives trying to make a life by fucking with others. So show me exactly how stupid and pitiful you are, fuck with my Son again. I'll have you unable to sleep peacefully ever again. I know you may be too stupid to understand the consequences of what I am saying so take the time to ask someone to explain this message to you. Maybe then you'll realize how much more sense it would make for you to be threatening and menacing people who are real threats to you and your community than a kid who only each day wants to be a

better person. What a joke, a 20 year old man hanging out with younger men and probably getting an erection when you bully them. Save that erection for when your stupid ass ends up in prison as somebody's bitch because of the stupid shit you are doing."

"Damn! Your Dad went in deep on that fool," Peter said, endorsing what he just heard.

Justin's response to Peter was more celebratory than before. "I know, my Dad is the fucking truth."

"Do you think your Dad would actually go after Reggie?," Peter asked.

After thinking about Peter's comments Justin replied, "I don't know if he was bluffing, but don't doubt that if something had actually happened to me he would have taken some type of action. I hope not as a vigilante. Anyway, this is how he finished the letter."

"Justin doesn't know I wrote this to you. You can tell him if you choose, and obviously you can share it with others too. But the bottom line is what it is. People have choices. Most of us spend our time in life trying to make it, trying to improve our lives and the lives of our loved ones. But there are always those in life who aren't happy unless they can fuck with others. You are obviously one of those. It is sad that I had to take time out of my very busy day and life to even write this to a 20 year old Black man who somehow thinks he is cooler because he can terrorize younger men new to the community. Yes, you are a real winner. Or is it loser? A smart person would read this and realize that there is some serious truth in what I am saying. A smart person would interpret it as a wake up call and go deep, eventually realizing how more beneficial it would be for them to reinvest their energy in turning their life around. A stupid person would get mad and want to retaliate against someone defenseless who had nothing to do with this message. My Son would have been as stupid as you if he hadn't shared his snafu with you with his Father. He hesitated sharing it with me for fear I would be disappointed in him not ATTEMPTING to kick your ass. Instead I applauded his decision of respecting his friend's home, something your stupid ass didn't even think about. He also probably hesitated because he knows my temper and my background. I may be well educated and living a successful life now, but you don't survive the streets of L.A. without being a shrewd mutha fucka. My brother was a twice convicted felon because he didn't use his head. Most of my homies are dead or in prison because they didn't use their heads. But I survived because I refused to be a statistic, someone the White man could count on to brutalize other Black people, making racist white people's jobs easier. Take that shit down South to the Klan. Find yourself some skinheads to fuck with. Menace some assholes that truly mean you harm. Grow the fuck up and find some way to be a credit to your race instead of a liability. Stop living up to stereotypes of black criminality, which only makes it harder for every other Black Man in this country to have a life free of being stereotyped."

Justin inhaled, exhaled, then continued:

"I don't know you, and from what I've heard about you don't care too. But I would like to think that like most people in this world you must love someone. Why don't you keep those who love you in mind before you go out and do stupid shit. I am a college professor who teaches young men and women, many coming from neighborhoods similar to yours and mine. I know the struggles we have to overcome. Shit, my Mom was 22 and had four kids while her husband, my Dad, was in prison. We were laughed at, teased, bullied. I can still taste those days. But I chose to not let that shit define me. I believed I could be better than the streets and poverty insisted I had to be. You can too. I seriously encourage you to read, and then reread this message. It will either be the start of a new Reggie with endless potential if he just took a deep breath and reinvested his time and energy in himself in positive ways, or the beginning of the end of the old stupid ass Reggie who has no life and so constantly invests his misguided time and energy in hurting others without realizing the irreparable damage he is doing to others and his community. You can be better than you are now. I hope you choose that path. But if not, and you choose to continue to fuck with others, especially my Son, I will show you how an OG handles his business if no one else beats me to it."

"Shit Justin, your Dad is probably one of the most understated original gangstas there ever was," Peter declared.

"Like I told you earlier Peter, there is another dimension to my Dad that I'll share with you, which puts him in a very different light," Justin said. "Like the time we were riding on the A-train towards Brooklyn a few years ago while my Dad was on vacation in Manhattan. About 10 minutes into the 30 min ride it became obvious that something was amiss. Though we were immersed in a project of transferring data from my new IPhone (Dad's old phone) to his IPad we were still checking everything out. After all, one of the first rules of engagement Dad claimed he learned growing up in South Central Los Angeles was that while many Black Folk in America share in the lack of certain privileges, all Black Folk lacked the privilege of being 'clueless.' He told me that Black people in America couldn't afford the luxury of not being aware of their surroundings."

"Consequently, people on the train were all of a sudden anxiously moving, stealthily whispering, and yet interestingly enough many of them were also smirking, chuckling, or even laughing. It all of a sudden had us wondering what could contribute to so many strangers all being on the same page? Eventually we discovered it was a very tall woman, who looked disoriented, perhaps under the influence of drugs, perhaps with some form of mental disability, perhaps both. We noticed her as the person under scrutiny more so when all eyes followed her as she left her seat and walked down past my Dad and I."

"Later my Dad would refer to W.E.B. DuBois to articulate how the woman could be seen as a "problem" for most around her, simply because she represented something excessively different. Within that actual moment she passed by us we felt her pass by but neither of us was giving her any serious attention, both being focused on our technology. 5-10 seconds after she passed we both detected a very offensive odor, confirmed by our eye contact with one another, without any conversation. We couldn't attribute it to any one specific person at the time. However, about 30 seconds later we noticed her once again gathering herself for a move. This time we were more attentive to her movement and as a result realized that the disarming stench we had smelled earlier was coming from her. Then we noticed what appeared to be some type of large brown stain (that looked like dried feces) upon the back of her dress. At this point we realized what all the earlier commotion had been about. Sitting next to her would have been torturous to say the least. More than a minute had passed and yet the scent was lingering powerfully enough to make you nauseous. Remembering the range of reactions people were giving her Dad turned to me and said 'Let's make sure we don't contribute to embarrassing her any further.'"

"I nodded my head in support. It was immediately after that when Dad noticed a family of four, a woman/mother, man/father, and two children all huddled together in their seats. The woman/mother, holding a boy, was laughing and whispering something in the boys ear which had him smiling, smirking, and chuckling. Often she glanced towards the man, their eyes would simultaneously gravitate towards the tall woman, then back towards one another with something that felt like a shared wink and a smile. This same woman/mother with boy/Son had earlier been searching for eye contact from Dad and I when our seating area of passengers all experienced her scent. Dad chose then to not nurture what he surmised as her insensitivity. I of course followed his lead. But now it seems as if Dad was left with no choice. In his mind, because of the combination of watching people laughing at this woman whom they knew nothing about, combined with possibly modeling behavior for me, had him trying to figure out the best course of action. It was then that he appeared to fully realize he needed to make a statement to more people than just the smiling woman with a child."

"'Excuse me Miss, but do you speak English?'" he asked in a voice loud enough to reach others without his voice and perhaps more importantly his message reaching the tall woman.

"'Yes, I do,' she said."

"'Good,' Dad said. 'Then I must say that I hope you or anyone else who may be apt to laugh at an unfortunate person must know that the person they are laughing at would prefer to be immersed in a different reality." "I doubt very seriously if her reality today is by choice."

"The woman, surprised to say the least, muttered that she wasn't laughing, but completely lost any semblance of a smile thereafter."

"After Dad said that it appeared as if his anger dissipated, while respect for what he did emanated from others on the train. As his son I was in momentary disbelief, recognizing quickly that I shouldn't have been surprised. This is how my Dad, more often than not, rolls. I then leaned into him, my shoulder against his hoping he would understand I was trying to let him know how pleased I was with him. Later at our hotel room he shared this story with some of his visiting students and in the middle of telling them the story I was caught off guard by his reaction. In telling them the story he became so overwhelmed with emotion that it was very difficult for him to hold back the tears. I wasn't emotional at all until seeing my Dad get emotional, then I guess it became contagious."

"The next day I returned with him to Peru for summer vacation.. On our train ride homeward I saw Dad interrupting whatever he was writing by wiping away tears. He could barely see his keystrokes from the deluge of tears welling up in his eyes as he attempted to chronicle the events on the Subway the day before, probably to ultimately share the story with others.

"I asked him, unsure exactly why at the time he was so emotional, 'Why are you crying, Dad?'"

"Dad replied with an answer that I'll never forget."

"'Because I don't understand how we can laugh at each other's pain, or be entertained by each other's struggle, Son,' he said with tears now flooding down his face." He continued, 'That woman is, or was someone's daughter, sister, mother, lover, cousin, niece. She is a sentient, human being. My tears are not just for her, but for the human condition. We are far too often inconsiderate cowards when we need to be considerate leaders on our way to being the best allies we can be.'"

"Continuing on Dad said, 'Son have you asked yourself what you would have done in the same situation if I hadn't been with you? If you are unsure how you would have, or better yet should have acted ask yourself if you would REALLY appreciate someone riding to your rescue?" Son, my tears are probably also related to all the times I could have, or should have said something and didn't. I'm not afraid to admit shame for at least some of those times, fully aware that different contexts dictate different realities. My tears may have also been for my actions, which could possibly be construed as bullying by some. I hate we live in a world where I feel the need to have to challenge someone like this.'"

"Dad then said, 'Perhaps my tears are symbolic of the hope of creating a world of allies who'll help that woman, other women, and anyone else deemed a problem, while consistently challenging others to be more considerate of others' realities, by stepping into their leadership moments.'"

"I remember telling him, 'Damn Dad, now you've got me crying too.'"

"He responded with a hearty chuckle, saying, 'Excellent Son. Empathy for others is a good thing.'"

"I know when my Dad is dead and buried I will never forget and always appreciate having witnessed him stepping into what he calls *a leadership moment* for a stranger. More to the point, when I look back upon those two train rides with my Dad I am absolutely positive that while the man I know has always had a healthy appetite for an intelligent, attractive, consenting woman, he would never do anything sinister or inappropriate to gain a woman's favor."

"It seems as if everyone in the North Country is talking about it now, though most people who know your Dad don't believe any of that shit. Your Dad has always been cool."

Though slightly ashamed for his eavesdropping, Xavier was happy to know that Peter, his Son's best friend in the North Country, thought he was cool. He especially enjoyed hearing Justin's response to Peter.

"I know," Justin said. "He is kind of cool."

A Daughter's Love

A week after Xavier was terminated by NYSU-Peru he was sitting in Hopkins restaurant in Peru, NY with his recently graduated from high school daughter Autumn and her friend having breakfast. Xavier handed her $80 dollars, cash, attempting to contribute financially to her traveling in support of his wedding weekend in Montreal. Autumn pushed it back to him saying, "Donate it to your GoFundMe campaign Daddy."

Xavier slid the money back towards her, saying, "You do it, and it doesn't have to be the full amount BabyBaby." "It can be $25, $47.18, whatever you feel."

Autumn relented, saying okay. Her friend Nardia and XW talked while Autumn had her head down. Xavier was thinking she was still texting her guidance counselor about her decision to change her mind and not attend NYSU-Peru since Xavier was no longer working there. Autumn had planned on spending a year there taking classes from him and some of his colleagues he was always boasting about (Stan Rivers, Darren Schultz, Lori Flee, Clay Arman, Joey Torrey, to name more than a few). She also had some concern about reprisals against her as the daughter of Dr. Xavier Witt. Xavier reminded her that he had a large crew still remaining at NYSU-Peru who don't live in fear of haters against him, believers in rumors, or leadership within an administration that will do whatever it takes to appease a small group of disgruntled students even at the detriment of the larger student body. All of a sudden Xavier received a text.

Xavier looked up from his phone in shock. The text he received alerted him to the fact that his little girl, now an 18 year old woman, parted with some of her legendary wealth (savings from years as a restaurant server) to help her Dad fight a necessary fight. Thus far he had quite a few people contribute and anticipated more help. If Xavier had to guess how much Autumn would have contributed to the war he was brazen enough to wage against NYSU it would have been $50 - $150 max. When he first saw the text his mind convinced him it was less than it was. Then it hit him. She had donated $1,000. The woman who once was a little girl who had no compunction asking Daddy for anything and everything with an expectation she would get it, was now not interested in receiving. She only wanted to give her Daddy some financial support, and of course, love. It was then Xavier's tears began to flow. The little girl that he adored all of her life was trying to now carry her Dad. Xavier placed his hand over his eyes in the restaurant and openly sobbed. He then heard her crying too. Nardia probably thought, "Damn! What have I gotten myself into."

Autumn didn't want to hear anything about the amount being too big, or Xavier trying to give her money back. She looked at him with that very understated intellectual look she has perfected and said, "You'll pay me back with a victory against them, Daddy."

Xavier thought, "My BabyBaby! Damn I'm glad I tried to give her $80 today."

CHAPTER NINE
- *A Hostile Environment*

A Time to Kill

The Scene: An attorney (portrayed by Matthew McConaughey) presents his closing arguments for a case wherein a Black Father is on trial for the murder of two White men who raped, beat and attempted to murder his daughter.

I want to tell you a story. I'm gonna ask you all to close your eyes while I tell you this story. I want you to listen to me. I want you to listen to yourselves. Go ahead. Close your eyes, please.

This is a story about a little girl, walking home from the grocery store one sunny afternoon. I want you to picture this little girl.

Suddenly a truck races up. Two men jump out and grab her. They drag her into a nearby field, and they tie her up, and they rip her clothes from her body. Now they climb on. First one, then the other, raping her. Shattering everything innocent and pure with a vicious thrust in a fog of drunken breath and sweat.

And when they're done, after they've killed her tiny womb, murdered any chance for her to bear children, to have life beyond her own, they decide to use her for target practice. So they start throwing full beer cans at her. They throw them so hard that it tears the flesh all the way to her bones.

Then they urinate on her.

Now comes the hanging.

They have a rope. They tie a noose.

Imagine the noose coiling tight around her neck and a sudden blinding jerk.

She's pulled into the air and her feet and legs go kicking. They don't find the ground. The hanging branch isn't strong enough. It snaps and she falls back to the earth.

So they pick her up, throw her in the back of the truck, and drive out to Foggy Creek Bridge, and pitch her over the edge.

And she drops some 30 feet down to the creek bottom below.

Can you see her? Her raped, beaten, broken body, soaked in their urine, soaked in their semen, soaked in her blood, left to die. Can you see her?

I want you to picture that little girl.

Now imagine she's white.

Dr. Witt only lectured once per semester in his classes, cherry picking the topic he would force his students to silently process and hopefully digest. In his Societal Dilemmas-Moral Problems class he had a love-hate relationship with this scene from the movie "A Time to Kill." He wanted to make sure he left nothing on the table from this invaluable lesson. He knew the weekend discussions would provide the students their opportunity to voice their opinions.

He knew he wasn't alone hating atrocities forced upon the little girl, hating the scars she'd carry for the rest of her life, appreciating the conclusion of Matthew McConaughey's closing argument for its creative assault on implicit bias.

"I hope this story brought to mind *philosopher John Corvino*'s quote:"

'Condemning people out of habit is easy,
  Overcoming deep seated prejudice requires courage.'

Corvino's quote frames the message Matthew McConaughey makes with his closing argument. He challenges the jury to muster up the courage to do the right thing, with the right thing being for them to not be racist-hypocrites. It is hard for Xavier Witt to imagine that the jurors weren't already empathetic, but then he has on occasion been labeled naive.

Dr. Witt then asked, rhetorically, "How many people sitting in the jury do you think needed to hear such an evocative statement to muster the courage to rise above the prevailing sentiment of their provincial community, a community dominated by racists. Please don't raise your hands to answer my rhetorical questions during my only lecture to you this semester. Just think about it. That is why I'm pausing, to give you time to reflect upon the question."

"I'm hoping Matthew McConaughey's speech brought to mind Aristotle's virtue ethics, including his theory of the Golden mean. Aristotle's postulation of virtue—the mean between the two extremes, also known as the two vices, deficiency and excess—provides a vivid example of how the virtue, courage, can be interpreted within a community."

"Courage sits between the extremes of recklessness and cowardice. For an all-White jury in a racist town to convict two White men for an assault on a defenseless black girl should be prima facie evidence of guilt, especially given the depiction by McConaughey of how the crime unfolded that day. However, going against the prevailing sentiment of your peers requires courage, which isn't as easily accessed as one might think."

"In the movie '*A Time to Kill*' if we focus on the jury's courage we will see their options are to choose the excessive extreme of *recklessness* and free the men with a consequence that they may or may not rape and/or attempt battery or murder again. If the deficient extreme of '*cowardliness*' is succumbed to, then the jury won't convict because as locals they are apt to feel intimidated by reprisal from the families or friends of the men on trial. If the *mean* between the extremes '*virtue*' is achieved then the jury is hung or deliberates a very long time before becoming hung. Perhaps since it is a murder case the virtuous act becomes finding the courage to preserve the perpetrators lives, of course unless something sinister is around the corner." (Dr. Witt decided to not share with his students that he knew if it were his daughter he couldn't guarantee what would have happened to those two men, but like the little girl's father it wouldn't have been a virtuous or cowardly reaction).

"A few weeks back you saw courage on display in the film '12 Angry Men.' In that movie the lone juror, portrayed by Henry Fonda, didn't just conform to the overriding sentiment of the other jurors who chose to believe they were deliberating an open and shut case. In that classic film—that I firmly believe every potential jurist should see—Fonda's character was the lone dissenting vote that prevented the boy—on trial for the murder of his own father—from being found guilty."

"Some of the other jurors were too afraid to speak up on behalf of the rush to judgment occuring, situating them with the deficient vice of cowardice."

"Some of the jurors for their own dubious reasons warmly embraced the excessive vice of recklessness in wanting to essentially check off having done their due diligence, enabling them to get back to their own lives."

"Only one person amongst the twelve resisted the excessive vice of recklessness and the deficient vice of cowardice to truly, better yet, justly determine the accused's fate. Ironically, my personal mantra which you may be tired of hearing by now, "perspective is the objective' is quite appropriate here," Dr. Witt said with a mischievous twinkle in his eye.

"From a reckless jurors' perspective Fonda, initially the only virtuous juror, was seen as a coward because reckless jurors believe they're virtuous."

"From the perspective of the cowardly jurors, Fonda, was seen as reckless because the cowardly jurors believe they are being virtuous."

"In both cases they can be seen as hypocrites. If the boy on trial was their child, and they had an expectation of a fair trial, they would be appalled at the actions of eleven of those 12 jurors, prepared to admonish their actions, while clueless as to the damage they were about to do to the life of someone else's child."

"Corvino's quote, *'Condemning people out of habit is easy, Overcoming deep seated prejudice requires courage,'* sounds so simple, so doable. So why then is it so seldom done?" Dr. Witt anticipated this eager group of students wanting to contribute to the conversation, especially since he had conditioned them to carry the classroom conversations. Nonetheless, beyond the lessons of the subject matter at hand was also a lesson in patience for them, and the way Dr. Witt kept his own game tight by engaging a captive audience the way he would when providing an organization with a keynote.

Continuing on he said, "Perhaps that type of courage is seldom found. Perhaps people go along to get along because if the context considered features a so-called, self-appointed leader or leaders, and easily intimidated and/or duped subordinates, you've got the recipe for enough of a hostile environment to adversely affect someone's livelihood, if not their life."

"Let's change the specifics of the "A Time to Kill" story from a truck to a street corner, change the two men to a multiplicity of police officers, and the little girl who was raped to the never ending brutalizations of Black bodies (Rodney King, Sandra Bland, Amadou Diallo, Trayvon Martin, Eric Garner, Sean Bell, Oscar Grant, John Crawford, Lamar Jones) and the same bottom line exist. If Eric Garner, a man who died of a chokehold for selling single cigarettes was White how different would his arrest have been? Would he be alive instead of being swarmed upon by a host of zealous law enforcement officers eager to show they were in control? Yes, he died while declaring "I can't breathe,' while a rambunctious officer using an illegal chokehold, possibly enjoyed demonstrating for all available to see how kick-ass a cop he was. Garner died because of *a hostile environment*, one often created by the circumstances of living life in an inopportune America where it is easier to mindlessly succumb to our implicit biases than receiving education to mitigate them."

"But is that the reason it was as easy to choke him as it would be to shoot a target at the rifle range, or shooting cans out in the backwoods or fields. In America shooting cans is probably easier since their value is slim to none, with Slim seemingly always absent from the room. No one is going to raise a ruckus in the United States about someone shooting beer cans, Pepsi cans, and/or tomato cans. As a matter of fact it often feels as if no one blinks when it is Mexicans, or Puerto Ricans being shot either. Shit, shoot an African American and you get two cans for the price of one."

"That slice of witticism from your own Dr. Witt aside, a deliberating jury, a classroom propagating micro-aggressions, a non-inclusive work situation meaning something far different from exclusive, can all be interpreted as *hostile environments* if/when certain variables align in certain ways."

"We are now going to watch some film clips from the movie, 'The Philosophers [After the Dark].' Dr. Witt said, hoping to entice the movie-loving students. "This movie is set at an international school in Jakarta, where a philosophy professor challenges his class of twenty graduating seniors to choose which ten of them would take shelter underground and reboot the human race in the event of a nuclear apocalypse. It is my fervent hope that this film and subsequent discussion will enhance your ability to recognize implicit bias and confirmation bias as contributing factors to the creation and maintenance of *a hostile environment*, as well as any other moral problems - societal dilemmas that come to mind while watching it."

Dr. Witt then motioned to one of the T.A.s to start the film clips. Having seen the movie countless times and knowing he had approximately 40 min available to him before he had to finish his lecture he whispered to a T.A. that he would be back and left the class.

Taking a walk to clear his head Dr. Witt would eventually gravitate back to his career threatening drama. It had been two weeks since he had been loud talked by loudmouth Shalo Kloos, with growing concerns that Dr. Witt had created *a hostile environment* by intimidating potential witnesses. It had been seven years since attention addict Dick Satton had his profane outburst in Dr. Witt's Romance, Sex, Love, & Marriage (RSLM) class and along with another representative of the Student Government filed a charge against Dr. Witt for creating *a hostile environment* in his class. In the recent incident he was deliberately publically humiliated. In the incident from seven years ago Dr. Witt and a student from the class were both verbally assaulted. The student was directly assaulted by being called an idiot. Dr. Witt was indirectly assaulted by the student's outburst after Dr. Witt and the attention seeking, emotionally immature student had agreed before Dr. Witt admitted him to the class that he would never attempt to assert his voice over others. What these two incidents had in common was him being accused of creating *a hostile environment*. Beyond blaming the victim it was a glaring instance of the pot calling the kettle black. As if that wasn't bad enough, it somehow prevented those accusing Dr. Witt of seeing him as someone justifiably defending himself. Since when does a lion doing lion things get blamed for defending itself from attacks by hunters.

A *hostile environment* resulting from identity politics can be found in the classic film, The Wizard of Oz. Within the film the so-called Wicked Witch of the West, Elphaba, a green woman, is vilified for her anger at discovering her sister Evanora has been killed by an allegedly random series of events. A house dropped out of the sky onto her, crushing her to death. Making matters worse, when Elphaba arrives upon the scene she is denied her rights to her siblings ruby red slippers, obviously too expensive an item to walk away from. Yet, somehow Elphaba is chastised for even daring to defend herself. She easily was seen at fault, yet for what? Isn't she entitled to anger over her sister's untimely death, followed by the theft of her inheritance. Nonetheless, Elphaba is essentially blamed for intimidation and creating *a hostile environment,* though she was the only one victimized at that point in the movie (the slippers) and immediately upon her arrival suffered from *a hostile environment* created by the so-called Good Witch, Glinda.

Aside from the implementation of one of the oldest tricks in the book—not naming or reframing by renaming someone—accusations against Elphaba for creating *a hostile environment* were as preposterous as those levied against Dr. Witt for firmly ending a volatile situation in his class seven years ago, and recently defending himself against direct accusations of being disrespectful toward women, with even more not-so-veiled implications. The *Wizard of Oz* parallel accentuated further the eerie similarity between Molly Mothburn's posturing as an ally while propagating *all lies* and the tale of the so-called Good Witch who unabashedly created *a hostile environment* for Elphaba by reinterpreting Elphaba's anger into a narrative similar to Mothburn's declaring '*I'm not here to make friends.*' (A month prior to Mothburn's declaration she had been chastised by the legal system for denying a young man his rights during an investigation).

Xavier imagined if it had been asserted the little black girl had eventually been lynched because of how she treated the two rapist throughout her ordeal, implying she may have never suffered a noose around her neck if she had willfully assented to--(tone it down)--all of the other horrendous treatment. While what Xavier was considering is incredulous, it is nonetheless compatible with a general definition of lynching:

Lynching is a premeditated extrajudicial killing by a group. It is mostly used to characterize informal public executions by a mob in order to punish an alleged transgressor, or to intimidate a group.

Without dickering back and forth as to what group the two White hate mongers may have been attempting to intimidate, per the above definition (Black girls, girls, women, Black women, or Black people), the question as to whether she was lynched for some transgression against them was the larger concern for Dr. Witt, trying to comprehend how whatever actions of resistance the defenseless little Black girl may have offered up against her oppressors were interpreted as transgressions against them, or whether her very existence transgressed them.

Paralleling his current snafu at NYSU-Peru, Dr. Witt was initially seen as a transgressor based solely upon a rumor. However, daring to defend himself, vociferously voicing vindictiveness towards his accuser(s) and anyone else in the room that was participating in the organized one-two punch confirmed the biases of many in attendance, misappropriating and reframing Dr. Witt's words as a transgression against alleged survivors in general, with an interest in seeing if Dr. Witt was trying to silence his alleged survivors.

Looking for the definition of *hostile environment*, Xavier surprisingly discovered it was:

In United States labor law, *a hostile* work *environment* exists when one's behavior within a workplace creates an environment that is difficult or uncomfortable for another person to work in, due to discrimination.

Beyond the events that unfolded at the controversial forum to discuss the votes-of-no-confidence and '*Lynching Niggers Tonight,*' Dr. Witt had evidence that *a hostile work environment exists when one's behavior within a workplace creates an environment that is difficult or uncomfortable for another person to work in, due to discrimination.* "The Feminist Anthropology department had repeatedly targeted Dr. Witt as incapable of teaching his romance class, with bold pronouncements that transcended mere insinuations that he was a predator from a FA faculty member; with bold pronouncements that transcended mere insinuations that he was not above choosing and using film clips that would allow him to prey upon his female students; with veiled insinuations that he was worthy of investigation for having possibly sexually harassed his staff; and with bold pronouncements that he was inadequately doing his job though he had never once been informed of inadequate performance by his supervisor, the easily manipulated President Utley. The *hostile environment* against Dr.Witt became even more untenable when the presiding officer of the faculty called for all-faculty meetings to discuss the votes-of-no-confidence, with Dr. Witt the only one accused in explicit detail by the SG of being professionally inept in emails that were distributed campus wide.

Label Him, to Disable Him

Frederick Douglas described the catastrophic impact of the fabricated rape charge on the movement for Black equality in general:

"It has cooled (the Negro's) friends; it has heated his enemies and arrested at home and abroad, in some measure, the generous efforts that good men were wont to make for his improvement and elevation. It has deceived his friends at the North and many good friends at the South, for nearly all of them, in some measure, have accepted this charge against the Negro as true" (Davis, 188).

The ultimate move made to create and perpetuate *a hostile environment* against Dr. Witt were the flyers, which forced the hand of an extremely weakened leader, along with Dr. Witt's refusal to 'tone it down.' If it seems as if Xavier is obsessed with Utley's audaciousness in telling him, in the midst of the most horrific character assassination a social justice activist could be subjected to. 'Tone it down' is the last thing that should be said to someone Utley never 'turned it up' to defend. The flyers took Kloos' accusation to another level, essentially labeling Dr. Witt as sexually deviant. Douglass' quote accentuates Dr. Witt's plight. Many of the

NYSU-Peru faculty, fearful of being targeted by a president grabbing at anything to stay afloat, steered clear of their once upon a time valued colleague, if not friend. It gave the haters more fuel for their fire, because of course it isn't enough to humiliate someone, they must be destroyed.

Ironically John Brown came to mind for Dr. Witt. At NYSU-Peru, approximately an hour away from Brown's gravesite, only a few colleagues and campus friends dared to publicly associate with Dr. Witt. Brown, known in many Black communities as the ultimate ally was a bad ass White abolitionist who sacrificed his life and the lives of his family for a community of people he barely knew because it was the right thing to do. Dr. Witt's work, due to social media, was well known throughout the region. It mattered none though to a faculty that was averse to any attempts at virtuous behavior in defense of the indefatigable Black diversity & social justice advocate. Nor did anyone exhibit outwardly reckless behavior on his behalf. But cowardliness as the deficient extreme was in abundance, even with previous colleagues whose careers Dr. Witt had advocated for, or whom Dr. Witt had assisted in ways that others would not have.

Some scholars suggest John Brown lit the fuse on the Civil War when he dared to take up arms in defense of Black people's rights, creating the penultimate hostile environment. Xavier knew his situation was nowhere near as dire as all that. However, his situation was very real in its own way. NYSU adopted a Goliath posture in trying to bully Dr. Witt, relegating him to a David role because it controlled the bully pulpit. Nonetheless an unrelenting David squared off against the Leviathan that is NYSU, with no holds barred. Resembling Game of Thrones' Jon Snow as the cause looked lost during the Battle of the Bastards, Dr. Witt continued to fight when, for all intent and purposes, it may have been easier to silently if not stealthily walk away and reinvent himself. Instead, after beginning to exit his own personal *Twilight Zone* Dr. Witt publicly called the bluff of this pretentious financially struggling university. What NYSU found in their investigation, no matter how boring, interesting, academic, sexy, or salacious (dependent upon your morality/perspective) it was totally unrelated to the university's implied position that Dr. Witt was culpable for inappropriate conduct, sexual misconduct, and sexual harassment. Instead the investigation relied on weak-ass witnesses whose stories would fold like a house of bent cards under the slightest scrutiny or cross examination. Instead, Feminist

Anthropology (and by association the Title IX office) left themselves glaringly vulnerable to litigable charges for creating and fostering *a hostile environment* predicated upon their veiled attempts to hide their obvious racism/sexism. This includes FA/Title IX's illicit affiliation with the Student Government--revealing them all complicit in this not-so-well woven tale. That all of this could be supported by the university's leadership is almost unfathomable, until it is revealed that the biggest culprit in creating *the hostile environment* was President Utley for his negligence in not stepping into his leadership moment, resolving tensions that existed between OPIE and FA years ago when the drama was in its infancy. Considering that Dr. Witt had even literally spoon fed Utley the steps he could take to lessen the hostility within the campus environment:

I'm hoping that you will respond to this email in the following ways:

1. Recognize that Maims may have a conflict of interest in her inability to put into perspective the frame that FA has situated me in and therefore should not be the one investigating the complaint against me.
2. Removing Maims from potentially investigating the forthcoming complaints by me against Winchell or Saphony.
3. Take or recommend someone taking a leadership role in sitting down so-called educators and redirecting our energies towards what should be all of our bottom lines, the students in the center of our efforts.
4. I would like someone to provide a list of students in Winchell's and Saphony's classes from Fall 2009 for possible interviews by unbiased arbitrator to determine the extent of the damage done to my character.

Utley didn't take the actions Dr. Witt recommended. The *hostile environment* against Dr. Witt that permeated the university since 2004, surfaced again in 2009-10, poked its head up in 2016, and erupted in 2018 is a direct result from Utley's negligence, as well as his aiding and abetting an agenda driven by misguided so-called allies.

Racism Nourishes Sexism

Many within Dr. Xavier Witt's inner circle of friends, bona fide allies, and war-time consigliore cautioned him to not make too much of a stink about how NYSU-Peru unceremoniously treated him in response to his vote-of-no-confidence, in conjunction with veiled accusations of his disrespecting women. Dr. Witt refused to go quietly, preferring to elevate the discourse to a level that would allow him to prove his innocence. Knowing full well it would be an uphill climb he preferred people openly discussing his situation than whispering in the back halls of the academy things they really knew nothing about.

"...the racist cry for rape became a popular explanation which was far more effective than either of the two previous attempts to justify mob attacks on Black people" (Davis, 187).

Dr. Xavier Witt always knew he needed allies capable of looking beyond the hype. He also felt that anyone who knows his NYSU story and can't see a conspiracy isn't looking. From smear flyers in bathrooms to slanderous comments in newspaper article's feedback sections—including the repetition of copy-cat occurrences of flyers carrying MeToo allegations from one campus to the next—the written thought in most revealed contempt for him and not because of anything inappropriate. It was never about Dr. Witt harassing or touching anyone. It was always about power, White privilege, and now in 2018 the misappropriation of a vital movement for the ill-gotten gain of a disjointed group of dysfunctional women. Fast-forwarding, eventually the White privilege and misappropriation became too exaggerated. How dare Dr. Xavier Witt, a black man we are not comfortable with, be successful in a predominately White environment, when we struggle to sustain interest from anyone in our classroom conversations about sexism. Oh, and he is also a predator? How dare XW fight against a movement taking down much bigger people. Who does he think he is?

Xavier's response to similar questions about his confidence, often interpreted as arrogance because of his courage to say what others hesitate to say, is almost formulaic in terms of its consistency. 'Who am I? The not-so-easily intimidated Black male ally who recognizes this small fight I am having in the North country has bigger implications. Not too many people are situated to stand shoulder-to-shoulder with NYSU. Not many people are bold enough to stare NYSU in the eyes without blinking because if you are guilty it would be a stupid-ass move. Xavier knew he was not guilty, and wouldn't be punked by NYSU's concerted effort to reach here and there and find a few people with an axe to grind, or to spin something. Utley, Mothburn, Dewar, Kloos, and Labelle, along with LeAnn Prey, and her prone-to-perjury crew, Boone, Priest, & Boyer all misread whom they chose to victimize because they didn't really know Xavier. If they did they would not have gone after him. Xavier was difficult to intimidate because of knowing himself. And other than the obvious goal of at least having his version of the story told--if not getting his name cleared as much as possible --was to reveal the snakes in the grass."

What's ironic is if someone was to visit NYSU-Peru and inquire about the character of all those named above, its conceivable more would agree than disagree with Xavier's assertions, finding a plethora of corroboration. Nevertheless, Dr. Witt's work was always about preparing students for leadership within a global society, hence his concept of environment has never been limiting. That doesn't bode well for conspirators who may have thought their collaborative and individual efforts to bastardize his character was a one-and-done effort. Oh no! The work of removing wolves from lambskins has just begun. Dr. Xavier Witt is bound and determined to redefine, at their expense, the concept of *hostile environment*, by speaking truth to misused power.

Suddenly, Dr. Witt is cut off by a car invading the crosswalk. Witt having his concentration broken reentered full consciousness in time to realize something significant, "Oh shit, my class. I have 5 minutes before that film finishes." And with that thought, Xavier went into full stride.

CHAPTER TEN
- *The Twilight Zone*

"There is nothing in the dark that isn't there when the lights are on."
--- Rod Serling, creator of The Twilight Zone

"Hey XW, how you doing?" asked George.

"Hey Jorge," answered Xavier, devoid of energy.

"You didn't answer my question," George said. "How you holding up?"

"I'm okay GJ. Just feeling deflated. My head feels as if it has been in a neverending fog. It's ironic when I saw the film 'Get Out,' I processed it as a creative escape. Now I see it as art not just imitating life, but in my case also predicting it, which is peculiarly poignant as a parallel to my predicament. I'm in that sunken place, an eerily dark space without light."

"Well Xdub, one of my favorite quotes is 'There is nothing in the dark that isn't there when the lights are on.'

"I like that. I really do, GJ. What does it mean to you?"

"Shit man, only you would ask me to break it down."

"Okay, but still, what does it mean?" asked XW, insisting upon a response.

"What's that saying you always use," George asked rhetorically. "'Perspective is the Objective?' Well, recognize Negro though your funk, if not depression can be combated with medication, it can also be fought with your mind."

"Who said I was depressed?" asked a slightly perturbed Xavier. "And I'll admit I'm feeling you about not letting my situation define me. But it's so bizarre that at times I have to ask myself if I'm going crazy. This is the most inexplicable experience of my life. I've had many opportunities to be the person at the podium, the keynote, the consultant. Never could I have imagined I could be the center of attention while also being a curiosity, monstrosity, martyr, perpetrator, predator, educator, bully, victim, fiancé, father, and yet somehow invisible, especially to myself."

"I know it must be tough now. But you've also been the man of the moment, the mudslinger, gunslinger, and if deemed crazy at all it would have to be like a fox."

"You're funny 'G.' I haven't heard my tennis nickname in a while, Gunslinger. I always liked that compliment to my backhand being as strong, if not stronger than my forehand."

"I enjoyed adapting Gunslinger from your college nickname, Mudslinger. I still haven't met anyone who can talk shit the way you do, while in professional mode or personal mode. Not too many people can break someone down or off the way you do Xdub."

"And no one is as adept at trying to fill someone up with positive energy when they obviously are depleted--like you do. I appreciate you GJ. You're such a good salesman you could sell me, me."

"You're funny. How are Kesi, Justin and Autumn?" George asked.

"Well I'm sure you can imagine that it rocked Justin to actually live in the same town where this shit is going down in real time. But the message he has received from me his entire life about respecting women has always been consistent and clear. So more than anything he had a rude introduction to the ways of the world. Nevertheless, he has worked diligently to have my back."

"And Autumn?"

"Autumn was planning on coming to NYSU-Peru, excited about taking classes with me, and some of the other professors I had told her would intellectually challenge her. Instead, Andrea and Kesi--who by the way considering they are the only two members in the been-married-to-Xavier Witt-club, and nonetheless have an excellent rapport with one another-- convinced Autumn that she didn't want to attend a university that would allow someone who gave his heart and soul to the university to be publicly maligned and character assassinated. In some ways the immediacy of it has forced her to intellectualize social injustice instead of just default to emotional responses."

"Kesi?" George asked.

"She's my unadulterated, unrelenting truth. I have never experienced a woman, or anyone for that matter, who is literally proactively unpredictable when it comes to things that I would have anticipated unfolding otherwise. She's the most mature partner I've ever had and I've been fortunate enough to share moments of my life with some amazing women. She is the catalyst for both my perseverance and resurgence. Her love has made my courage unwavering."

"You know X," George said solemnly, "I'm so happy you are suing them. Anyone who knows you knows this is fucking bullshit. However, anyone who doesn't know you should have figured out by now that you aren't stupid enough to throw good money out the window. You wouldn't be paying exorbitant amounts for legal defense if you didn't feel you had a strong case."

"You would think so, right. However, now that I've ventured down litigation road instead of only visiting it on T.V., I know how real it can be, and that I'm still a Black man in a predominantly White community who has the stink of inappropriate behavior on me. I also know we've got a third of the U.S. population that believes Fox News is the truth, and as a result they also believe Resident Rump is unjustly maligned, no matter how credible the evidence presented to them is. So expecting some people to default into a belief about me that is so counter to what I am about and counter to what I have exemplified my entire life makes sense in the most bizarre of ways.

"They believed a minion instead of my brother," George said curiously, "I wonder what their return on that investment will look like. I do know this Xdub, I'm sure everyone aware of what you're going through now knows how much of a fighter you are."

"I have always put my work in for social justice, never anticipating one day I would have to fight for myself."

"Well you also know that you are not alone."

"It feels like it at times George. To have eight hours a day that you once took for granted now available again is a mind-fuck. Disciplining yourself to accomplish this and that, that or this, and trying to convince yourself that it has meaning in contrast to the meaningful things you once did, it has been a challenge, my brother."

"I don't doubt it. But not insurmountable for you Xdub. You've got this."

"Fortunately I have had another career I've been interested in my entire life that I now have time to pursue."

"What is that? Writing? I remember your poetry in college, and the book you wrote a few years back. Please tell me you are writing about this shit that is going down."

"I'm writing about this shit that is going down."

"My brother, that is probably one of the smartest things you could do. Break this shit down for these mother fuckers."

"Can I break it down for the father fuckers too?" Xavier asked, impressed with himself.

"He's got jokes! Anyway, look man, I only had a quick minute. I'll get back to you later, but was just checking on you real quick."

"Cool. Much appreciated. Please tell Lorraine I said hello. The next time we talk it will be for you to update me on what's happening in your world."

"Bet!!!" George said. "I'm out!"

George has always been good at injecting Xavier with energy. They met at CSULB in front of the campus bookstore, through a mutual friend. They often laugh at the fact that they immediately connected, profoundly, while neither one of them is friends any longer with the person who introduced them. They were both conscious about social injustices like racism and not shy about engaging it directly, had tennis in common, similar appetites for female companionship, likeminded notions regarding morality in general, similar music interests, and an affection for non-accessible heroes, like Bruce Lee and Malcolm X. They also both saw the social significance in icons as centerpieces of stories, or better stated, moral tales.

Xavier as a boy in South Central Los Angeles (often referred to as the hood) was a comic book collector. As such, with an absentee father, he reached to find his male cultural references, which ranged from Spiderman to Richard Pryor to Daredevil to Humphrey Bogart to Shaft, John Shaft more so than Bond, James Bond, though Bond actually was cool too. All were positive male role models for a young man in need of one.

Richard Pryor was the street smart, shit-talking comic genius who introduced a very young Xavier into the power of profanity, the hypocrisy of hypocrites, and the ironic as well as irreconcilable laughter at black lives not mattering before the ignominy that fosters Black Lives Matter. He demonstrated to Xavier how powerful and strategic a good sense of humor and quick wit could be, when packaged with inner city instincts.

Xavier interpreted Bogart in most of his leading man roles as a type of 'cool' inseparable from affiliation with both smooth and edgy, which essentially are two sides of the same coin. Bogart played more often than not the role of a reluctant hero, drafted into situations requiring an unflappable intellect. No one framed Xavier's notion of cool better than Bogie. And he was as dynamic away from the camera as he was in front of it. Not only did he stand up to McCarthyism, but also served as a mentor to a group of future stars known as the Rat Pack, all seen as cool to most, though not necessarily above succumbing to being men of their day, mindlessly objectifying women.

Shaft, though a movie character, was like Bogart with his attitudinal cool, except he was Black like Pryor, which made him Black Cool long before a younger upstart, Barack Obama would completely reframe its meaning. Obama just looked like he always had Sade singing to John Coltrane playing in his backdrop. Just as Obama isn't alone in representing contemporary Black male cool, with shout-outs to his peers Sam Jackson, Eric Holder, Kyrie and LeBron, Drake, Dr.Dre, Trevor Noah, and Jay-Z, Shaft the film character had Nigger Charley and Superfly as his metaphorical road dogs, while the actor who played Shaft, Richard Roundtree could be thought to have kept company—to a lesser extent and out-of-character—with Sidney Poitier (who was never better than in 'A Patch of Blue' & 'Paris Blues'), Harry Belafonte, Walt Frazier, Gale Sayers, Billy Dee, Sammy Davis Jr., and yes, with full disclosure, William Henry Cosby Jr., also known as Bill. In some form or fashion, rhyme or reason, they all captivated Xavier's attention long enough for him to reflect upon what their roads to success must have looked like.

James Bond possibly more than most had another type of cool that Xavier went out of his way to study, without realizing it at the time. While many of these role models were popular with women, none were repeatedly celebrated for their implied sexual prowess more than Bond, James Bond. After all, there were the Bond girls. Enough said.

Xavier especially liked the understated cool that Peter Parker displayed until transforming into Spidey, where he became comfortably immersed in his hipster cool. Peter Parker was the respectful, on-point, open book, nondescript, boy-next-door, kind of guy. He also had anxieties and doubts. Parker's cool came from—considering all of his complexities—never overreaching for cool. Spidey was the complete opposite in many ways, but not in his ethic. The morality of Peter Parker and Spidey may have been the second thing they shared, the first thing being the same body. They both, at all times were going to do the right thing. The differences in how they acted out their ethic were the opportunities, good fortune, and privilege(s) one may have had over the other. In this regard Spidey had more light to leap into than Peter, though until his Uncle's death he still had more privilege than many.

Xavier recognized a similar alter ego phenomenon in Batman and Superman, but until Christian Bales' performance as the Dark Knight they always seemed like clownish caricatures of campiness. Nonetheless while noting the differences between this comprehensive list of pop culture role models, somehow, perhaps to transcend his own dark nights, it was

Superman's dichotomy with Clark Kent that inspired Xavier to write a poem about it:

Modern Day Hero

How I marvel at this super hero,
soaring high so all may see
that he's the man of steel
and no one flies as high as he.

With a birds-eye view of life,
I wonder if he stares
when someone who doesn't wear a cape
is brave enough to dare
to be himself
and not run to a booth to change
every time he is faced with problems
he can't rearrange.

Probably not, for he is Superman
with his own astrology sign,
and he feels if he can't sweep you off your feet
his kill will blow your mind.
Then he's back in the saddle again,
air current as his mare
knowing fully that any speed he travels
cannot muss his hair.

Why, he has even convinced himself
that Clark Kent is a square, a clown,
and that no one will give Clark the time of day
when the man in the cape is around.
When will he finally realize
that in this day and age
as the hero
he couldn't get a ticket
to see Clark on the stage.
For Clark is the man that is super,

it is Clark who is down to earth,
and Clark who would not be flying around
if he knew how much he is worth.

Xavier's inspiration for the poem was people's pretentiousness and their often unrecognized or duplicitous reasons for being fake. He knew people who would wear what they deemed as the appropriate face to win someone over, perhaps effecting a cool persona when what was needed was more in line with whom they usually were when no one is around. It was about being accessible and down to earth. In his adolescence though no one fit that description better than Matt Murdock, also known as Daredevil.

Daredevil's sense of social justice as an attorney, and his abilities as an ass-kicking superhero, both while being a differently-abled man was matter-of-factly cool. Both personalities took you into a different space, more than any of the other role models. For all intent and purposes connecting with him was vicariously venturing into the *Twilight Zone* for the first time. Though Daredevil couldn't see in traditional ways, he inspired empathy, and was savvy and talented enough to overcompensate without missing much in an essential message. More so though, Daredevil saw things others didn't and couldn't.

A couple of days after talking with George, Xavier reflected back on the quote that George had shared, "*There is nothing in the dark that isn't there when the lights are on.*" He searched on Google to see whom if anyone might be the owner of the quote and was pleasantly surprised to discover it was Rod Serling, creator of "*The Twilight Zone.*" He concluded that George must have known that, when Xavier mentioned feeling as if he was in his own shadowy corridor.

Somehow this time the quote brought Daredevil to mind. It was Xavier's perspective of Daredevil's never-ending loneliness that helped him interrogate his own dusky domain. The only thing capable of more indescribable loneliness than Daredevil's world was this *Twilight Zone*, where at all times all bets were off. In this shadowy space you couldn't predict a damn thing, and heroes could become zeroes regardless of how fear grows, courage goes, and highs or lows.

Xavier entered his own personal *Twilight Zone* when he heard this young woman who didn't know him, express some familiarity with his story. Who would do that? What would be the motivation to deliberately impact someone's life. That thought would perplex Xavier for months though there is a good chance she did it on a whim. And the second guessing, reconsideration of words/actions he couldn't take back, inability to put into perspective the entire experience, and/or justify the things that he couldn't change. It was as if he had awakened as he did every morning, and then, where normally his daily script would start to unfold, there was nothing. The paper was blank, 'tabula rasa' in full effect. All of a sudden, each day he was thrust into a completely new experience, being in spaces he wasn't accustomed to being in.

Xavier had always been prideful without slipping into obnoxiousness. Always a leader, he seldom was not at least a co-captain on athletic teams he was on, one of the smartest kids in class, and somehow able to negotiate that space where he had popularity with others his age, while still being cool with his teachers. He always tried to take full advantage of opportunities that came his way. He was one of those people that when working with a friend or more so, for a friend, he would overcompensate in his efforts to make sure he wasn't taking that friend for granted. Now however, Xavier was dodging doubters, hiding from haters, and pivoting away from pity. Some mornings he awakened asking himself why even awaken. Some nights he didn't want to sleep.

Eventually he re-acquainted himself with an old strategy he had implemented during one of his most trying times in his earlier days, exercise. So he started walking. Then he walked. Then he walked some more. He walked listening to jazz which gave him flow. He walked listening to hip-hop which woke his ass up, if not also providing him some needed edge. He walked listening to the cool channel on XM radio, mindful that being cool is chill, until heat is needed. When heat is sought, chill alone won't get it done, instead becoming cold, leaving cool undone, flirting with being uncool. That's when Xavier would go from the 'The Chill' channel on XM radio to 'The Heat,' or 'HipHopNation.' His favorite thing though was talking on the phone, hands free, while walking. It always felt like he had company—especially when his head was right— though people on the streets of Montreal would wonder who the Black

American--walking down the street gesticulating--was talking too. Oh, yes, because Xavier couldn't do Peru, New York anymore, except in cameos. As one of the few Black men in the area he couldn't scratch his ass in public without it being noticed. That along with now feeling like anyone who knew what he was going through, who didn't really know him, may want to keep him, as an unregistered predator, at bay.

"One morning having just thought about the drama that went down with his now infamous Facebook posting that he titled "Dreams of Reality" Xavier decided to reframe the sentiment within a poem cogitating existence, as indicated by the title, only in a different way. Just as he finished writing another piece of philosophical poetry meant to chronicle his joyless journey, the phone rang. It was his other college roommate, Julius.

"Hey Xavier, how are you doing man?"

"Hey Stone. I'm actually doing better than the last time we talked."

"That's good to hear. Any specific reasons?"

"Well, my fiancé is the biggest reason. Thank god she is a doctor. "If not, I would probably be deeply immersed in depression. I've never been one for taking medication, or even going to doctors or psychologists for things that fuck with my head. Her powers of persuasion and my trust in her however make me putty in her hands. So, I end up doing whatever she tells me, whenever she tells me, and don't feel any lesser.

"Now that's great news Xavier. I can't wait to meet Kesi. Perhaps during your wedding this summer in Montreal. I'll be there."

"Oh man, that is so cool," Xavier said excitedly. "I'm looking forward to all my people meeting my soulmate."

"I know how you feel. I've been married and in love with mine forever."

"And who introduced you to her?" Xavier asked rhetorically.

"Here we fucking go again," Julius bellowed, feigning exasperation. "Will I be indebted to you for the rest of your life, or worse, the rest of my life?"

"Yes! No! I tell you what. The debt is paid if you let me share a poem with you, and then give me an honest reaction."

"Is it a long poem? I know your long winded, loquacious ass can get going and I could be at risk of having to listen to you all day."

"Damn best friend, thanks for the support," Xavier said, then intentionally whispering loud enough for Julius to hear, he murmured, "Selfish fuck."

Playing along, Julius said, "I heard that. What's the poem manbrat."

"It's titled, Dreams of Reality."

"Hey," Julius said, surprised. "Wasn't that the name of that controversial Facebook post you shared with me?"

"Kudos you selfish fuck," Xavier said, "for actually remembering something other than your own shit."

"Just read the fucking poem, buddy boy."

Okay," Xavier said, trying to act nonchalantly:

Dreams of Reality

It's okay to dream
for dreams are silver lined hopes
and if we have wisely learned the ropes
we will not dwell on them upon awakening
yet in the not forsaking of our dreams
for what we deem
for what society deems is reality
perhaps we will come to the finality of the fact that maybe
just maybe
we are sleeping through our reality

and awake in our dreams
and things are never what they seem
which makes it even more okay to dream.

"Wow! Xavier, that's nice, very nice. It is however also quite dark." said Julius. "What I heard in your redo of "Dreams of Reality" is the implication that you may have slipped into a deep enough funk that you entertained thoughts you were surprised had entered your mind. Are you finding solace in your sleep?"

"I don't know if I would call it solace. I feel as if I've become a shell of myself, not too dissimilar from a Game of Thrones Wight-Walker, essentially dead but still somehow advancing. Unlike a wight that tends towards violence I have never been one to wish violence upon anyone. However, I now better understood the Eminem line from his hit song, 'Superman' wherein he indicated he wouldn't urinate on someone to extinguish them if they were on fire. I wouldn't throw my life away hurting someone and subsequently risking becoming a criminal, but I would do nothing to prevent a crime against the people who have unhesitatingly impacted my life.

"Jesus would want you to turn the other cheek."

"Should I care about what some Mexican dude named Jesus, whom I've never met, would want?

Chuckling Julius responded, "Your ass is going to hell for selling your soul just to be witty, and playing around with God's son's name. You do know that, right? Hey, can you hold on a minute. I have an incoming call, but want to finish this conversation. It may take a minute."

"No problem Stone. Do you."

While waiting for Julius to return to the phone Xavier reflected back upon another time during his college days when Julius, whom he also called JB, and Stone had been there for him, big time. Xavier was dating a woman he really loved who was away at dental school. He lost his job just as she was returning home for the holidays. Since Xavier was only working part-time, living paycheck to paycheck, his job loss was devastating. Without asking for it, Julius showed up to his door with a few hundred dollars, loaning it to him without an expected date of return. Across the years, in an array of ways, they would have each other's backs. Ironically, these two lifelong friends met the first week of school when they were both first semester first-year students. Julius was waiting at a bus stop and Xavier recognized him from the political science class they were both in. Pulling up to the bus stop, he offered Julius a ride. They've been riding ever since.

Eventually Xavier's mind drifted back to earlier moments in his conversation with Julius about Dreams of Reality-revisited. He reconsidered the line in the poem, "*maybe we are sleeping through our reality, and awake in our dreams.*" Though he didn't want to accept Julius' suggestion that he may be finding solace in his sleep Xavier couldn't deny that his reality was nightmarish as evidenced by the months that followed his being removed from campus. During that period Xavier recognized he was self-medicating, smoking more marijuana than he ever did before, drinking more than usual too. His awake moments weren't pleasant. He found himself enjoying slumber more than before. Perhaps it was because he either wasn't dreaming, couldn't remember his dreams, or subconsciously didn't want to recall them. Perhaps that is why he wrote a poem inspired by a previously used title. In comparison, he knew the pain he was in when awake, especially having prided himself on being 'woke.'

Xavier lived between the worlds of dumbfounded disbelief that 'Lynching Niggers Tonight' would be his swan song with NYSU-Peru, awkward awe at how he was caught in such an imperfect storm, perhaps naivete that in the end the truth would prevail, sad at how much of a charlatan as well as a coward Utley turned out to be, and mad at how much of a charlatan as well as a coward Utley turned out to be. He somehow even felt sorry for each person that had participated in his demise, be it a supporting comment that just fueled the fires of the lynch mobs, the persons who would claim they didn't do much, though they knotted the noose, and the person who would look away from him while he was being hung, or hanging, and yet feel good about not having participated in his demise. This sorrow surfaced sometimes, but even then it didn't erase the feeling that one day karma would visit each of them.

The so-called friends and allies that were present more so to feel better about themselves by being designated as someone's ally, were either all lies or alibis, and sadly, sometimes both. He was totally prepared with a standard response for those days when he would encounter someone that fit the description. He imagined himself saying, "*No apologies necessary for your delayed response. Your response time has always been reasonable, so it's definitely no biggie. Besides, everyone has their shit to deal with. Don't sweat it.*

Xavier was confident that he could say some version of that sentiment. He didn't want to put anyone on the spot, though he had concerns about hiding his disappointment. He couldn't ignore or deny that this one time would be the most glaring time for someone to not show, or say 'bye bye,' just when he needed them most. Just then his phone clicked and Julius was back.

"Xavier, sorry about how long that took," Julius said apologetically. "Where were we?"

"You were preaching from your illustrious glass house about me turning the other cheek."

"Seriously though, how are Justin and Autumn through all of this?" Julius asked concerned.

"Whatever innocence the kids may have had relative to this thing we call life is gone. They have instead discovered some tough truths about life."

"I'm sure they have also discovered how much of a fighter their father is," Julius said, complimenting his best friend.

"If they have or haven't, they haven't seen anything yet," Xavier affirmed.

"How is the book coming along. I remember you saying you were going to write a novel based upon the shit that went down."

"I started it. I've got to figure out how to make a dark tale interesting. My natural inclination is philosophical, but I'm also a want-to-be comedian.

Merging those two while necessarily having to articulate romance, sex, love, and marriage will be the challenge."

"I hear you XW. Let me know if you need me, in any way. I need to get back into my day. We'll rap soon, sooner if need be."

"Later JB."

Many times calls like the two Xavier received that morning would jumpstart his energy for the day. At times he wondered if his crew had put together a schedule whereby they took turns to make sure he was staying afloat. Something akin to a suicide watch, though he hoped none of them were thinking he could be anywhere close to considering such an act. Not that it didn't enter his mind. After all, when for a moment it feels as if everything has been taken away from you, what else do you have to control except your own life. But Xavier would never leave Kesi second-guessing what more she could have done, especially since she is doing it all, and then some. He would never allow Autumn and Justin to go the rest of their lives with unresolved questions about what they could have done differently.

Xavier thought of other people who had overwhelming obstacles to overcome. He thought of his close friends, the Stewart family, and the unexpected challenges they had to manage. He thought of friends who unexpectedly lost a partner, children who lost a parent, people who lost the ability to provide for themselves, and people who were born severely underprivileged. The adage he had used most of his adult life never had more meaning than it did now. Perspective is truly the most pressing objective he should hold onto.

At times Xavier slipped into a deeper funk, mad at himself, for having allowed the duplicitous Utley to prevent him from saying goodbye to his big brother, the retired university historian, Fred Copps, and his little sister, Nyla Earlford. Fred had been sick for quite some time, yet having outlived the first predictions of his demise. He and his lovely wife Evonne were behind the scenes mentors who were there for Xavier in ways that most could not imagine. Missing the tributes to this man were indescribably painful. He was happy to be able to have seen Fred a few times within the last couple of weeks before he ascended upward.

Nyla's death was not anticipated, and probably as far from anyone's mind as it could be. She was an inexorable intellect, an organic force of philosophical femininity that afforded her the opportunity to adeptly transcend gender roles. Nyla was intimidating to some who only heard her bark, and feared what her bite might be like. Those that knew her though had the experience of being entertained by her, illuminated by her, and the fortunate ones, loved by her too.

Fred and Nyla were pillars of morality at the university, two voices that couldn't be silenced, that wouldn't be silenced. And now they were gone. At that moment, ironically, Xavier realized that there may be some people on campus who still held him in a similar regard to the way they held Fred & Nyla, probably making their healing from the loss of three close and/or valued colleagues feel insurmountable.

Xavier had little time to regret that those who felt as if they understood his situation were not close to comprehending the multifaceted ways in which Black men are interpreted in current society. Most of them somehow were sleeping on the fact that Xavier--because of the work he had put in for years--was more prepared than most men to understand the extent of the historical transgressions and wounds women have had to endure. The MeToo implications attached to Xavier's situation are real and painful, and he is not naive. It didn't help that he often wondered if he would believe his own story if he were on the outside looking in.

Xavier hadn't given Kobe Bryant the benefit of the doubt at the time Kobe went through his shit. Whether Kobe was guilty or innocent was inconsequential contrasted to the pre-judgement he had endured in Xavier's head. Xavier had already made up his mind, without a thought as to Kobe's context. It was the Wizard of Oz lesson he taught his Diversity students all over again. It was too easy for Xavier as a youngster to watch the Wizard of Oz and never stop to consider how it must have been for a green person to live in a world that had no qualms articulating her as evil. Now as an adult he may have become, in the eyes of some, the Wretched Warlock of the North.

It was after reading the book followed by seeing the play 'Wicked' that Xavier was affected as much subconsciously as professionally. Wicked the play is based upon the Wizard of Oz, but retold from the perspective of the so-called Wicked Witch of the West. Xavier is never shy asserting that if you do social justice work it is a must see. The play reinforced the fact that Dr. Witt probably was not alone thinking he naturally had everything figured out. Then Xavier turned a corner and almost instantaneously it became apparent that all the logical thought he thought he had situated logically was illogically situated in a context so loaded with pretext that it was hard to even consider the subtext. Suffice it to say, when you start to consider how the Wicked Witch of the West was not an evil bitch to detest but a person that challenges us to be our best, it becomes apparent that we failed again to see an 'Other.' It is all too easy seeing someone who is unceasingly framed as a perpetrator as a criminal and nothing more. Postulating what motives others have for accusing someone verbally under siege as being defensive when they have every right to defend themselves, is akin to not considering the reasons a so-called criminal who has been systematically disenfranchised might have a criminal response.

People who don't know anything about someone, professing insight into their reality based totally on hearsay and hype (if there aren't other motives in place) could be using diversionary tactics to keep the focus off of them. Or may be suffering from an overinflated sense of worth, thinking they have an inherent right to critique others, or 'the Other.' We should just ask them the simplest of questions, like "if you do not know this rumor is a fact why repeat it?"

Only caring about the welfare of those related to us, or only caring about news that directly impacts us, finds us assisting in the construction of a world so desensitized that nobody cares. If we don't care about what's happening outside of our homes, down the street, or around the corner, why should anyone else?

It would behoove all of us who posture as if we know ourselves, or care about making this world a better place to imagine being the only Green person in the country. No one wants to be framed as inadequate, aberrant, deviant, different, even wicked just because someone can label us, knowing others will buy into it. One day perhaps after experiencing the hype of being the unfathomable prototype we will, through self-reflection recognize the assault on our psyches we must engage before we can see how we see. Additionally, perhaps we will all see who is going out of their way to invite us into their world, not to mention caring enough to understand ours.

At times understanding the risk involved to his reputation and career--if not the irreparable damage already done--was daunting. Xavier understood that all of his efforts could all be done for nothing. Already and for awhile he had to forgive himself for not being optimistic enough. On other days he struggled to forgive himself for perhaps subconsciously being too reticent, cautious, and not receptive to counseling.

Kesi convinced Xavier litigation was an integral component of his journey of redemption, instead of a road to perdition. Timing being everything, one could argue that the uniqueness of Xavier's legal case, which makes it so provocative, may have been more destiny than destiny itself would prescribe. His awkward employment situation challenged him in some very unique ways, with an unpredictability attached to its outcome. Xavier's Twilight Zone left him with a sense of dread randomly varying in intensity.

Xavier attributed his being a philosophy professor to his inability to not allow illogical things to further exacerbate his mood. However, the sentiment that some women in support of the MeToo movement insist that we must believe every survivor was preposterous to him. It presumes that most women are true survivors. But what about those who have a personal agenda and use the movement as an opportunity to implement it?

Reconciling false allegations as somehow negligible in the utilitarian calculation that situates anyone accused as guilty is hypocrisy waiting to unfold. Xavier was curious as to how the same women who are okay believing self defined survivors over the men they accuse would shift their opinion if the accused was their father, brother, son, or close friend. What about real survivors who become pathologically consumed with hate and decide to despise and/or destroy all the men they meet in their life? What about the women who never saw their aggressors, and yet their desire to have justice served has them rounding up the usual suspects. After all someone must be designated as a criminal, arbitrarily penalizing further the unfortunate man who most closely resembles an attacker?

Some survivors just want to transfer their shame and guilt to a convenient suspect, giving survivors the right to say it is not their fault, as if it is the fault of any survivor, instead of it being the fault of perpetrators. What about racists constructing opportunities to put Black men in jail because they refuse to defer to white supremacy? Consequently, they're punished for nonconformity, thereby creating a convenient victim, achieving their hate-filled agenda. Thinking about the rationale he was going to have to combat to obtain justice was enough to push Xavier beyond the *Twilight Zone* to the Outer Limits.

To help extricate Xavier from his prison of platitudes Kesi never ceased offering theories as to why women come forward with false allegations. She shared with him that some women, who have been oppressed in ways other than sexual abuse, are also victims. But they don't know how to find their voice to allege, report, charge, and/or defend themselves as victims. She would offer as a reason their fathers who physically or psychologically abused them, spoke over them, took away their voice since childhood. An abused child seldom only hates their abuser; often unknowingly hating themselves too. It might be a lover who psychologically or physically abused them. It also need not be sexual. But regardless of situations they never learned how to speak up for themselves with dignity, how to be proud of their lives. Kesi proffered them seeing themselves as victims, and lacking any sense of pride they often seek to confirm it.

The MeToo movement's rise gave voice to sexual survivors. Suddenly survivors of non-sexual abuse see other victims have a voice and a safer space than usual. Suddenly their hope of being recognized as victims is within their reach. So they don the attire of a sexually abused woman to assume the role of victim, not knowing that through their deception they are creating a male survivor, if not a monster, by transferring their victim status to the falsely accused man. In their desire to obtain their moment of glory they forsake considering consequences.

The Twilight Zone, as a television show, always left the characters in the stories wondering if what they had just witnessed was real. That feeling of visiting an inescapable void reoccured more often than it did not. However, Xavier, even as a pre-teen had begun to understand that he had the ability to turn off his television set and step into life. Like Dorothy in the Wizard of Oz who always had the ability to return home, though she didn't know it, Xavier had the ability to manifest his own destiny. His commitment to social justice had never waned. He was all in, and always has been. Xavier saw no other way for the world to change than people with open minds sitting down and examining their differences by examining diversity. For years he taught that learning to be more mindful leads to a more considerate perspective. More consideration leads right back to mindfulness. Two sides of the same coin, consciousness. All it ever takes to achieve that level of consciousness is enticing solicitation of a necessary conversation, conversations involving real talk, open minds and authentic people.

For months Xavier was embarrassed about how he obviously had misread NYSU's inconsistency and inadequacy, regardless of the student-centered work he and others had put in. The university leadership postured, posed, and pretended to be down with its underrepresented students. The best classes taught by the best professors, the best organizations facilitated by the most passionate student centered staff were mostly mirages, especially without institutionalized funding. This was his first clue. With soft money, or short term grants here today and then gone so quickly it wouldn't be far-fetched to doubt if what was putatively funded was ever really there. Leadership needed to make the call and live with it, or not. But you can't fake the funk.

This was best evidenced by Utley's disinterest in ever participating in the 'Reconciling Otherness' course, to which he had been repeatedly invited. Once a requisite amount of time passed and we returned from racial-incident-distress-mode back into financial-distress-mode Utley's readiness to start gutting the diversity center was as predictable as it was expected. Once again crisis management at its very best. Utley further proved his lack of a commitment when after removing Xavier from campus within weeks he had begun the necessary measures to eliminate the OPIE without looking back. Why were they mutually inclusive?, Xavier's termination didn't have to mean the end of an extremely vibrant operation.

Xavier's *Twilight Zone* experience had him unfortunately in a dubious situation, unfolding within the context of one of America's most unique movements/moments. Was his termination precipitated only by Kloos' sharing a concern over a rumor and his passionate response to it? Or perhaps the university's president shame throughout the vote-of-no-confidence process that had him tiptoeing and whispering in response to students who insisted that he was inadequately performing, in contrast to Xavier's calling bullshit to any such allegation about his own performance. Perhaps any idea of transparent courageous leadership in the face of social injustice was intimidating in it being something Utley may have been incapable of.

A lawsuit which Xavier believes increases his ability to reveal the co-opted leadership, uncover covert alliances, and punish any and all political expediency that contributes to a hostile environment is pending. Xavier's belief that he will win this lawsuit is steadfastly evolving and slowly enabling Xavier to exit the darkness. Oh, and the book he is writing that will tell his version of the story helps quite a bit too. Family, friends, exercising to reduce/remove stress, and time eventually provided enough light to find a way out of his own personal *Twilight Zone*.

"Albert Camus once said, "There is no sun without shadow, and it is important to know the night." The 'Other' in all of us has often been a dark experience. It is nice that so many of us are working diligently for our day(s) in the sun" (Wiley, 278).

CHAPTER ELEVEN
- *In the Rear View Mirror*

One of Dr. Xavier Witt's favorite coaches, college basketball's 'the Wizard of Westwood,' UCLA's John Wooden is attributed as saying, "It is better to be lucky than good." No pun intended, but Coach Wooden couldn't have given legendary baseball manager Branch Rickey a better assist, especially when considering their compatible philosophies on luck. It was Rickey who was as daring as he was responsible for providing Jackie Robinson the national stage on which he would prominently and superbly perform after Robinson stepped across the color line. Robinson would go on to become a MLB Champion & MVP, a baseball legend, Hall of Famer, a sports icon, and Civil Rights activist. Was Robinson more lucky than good? The very question brings back to mind the chicken-egg debate.

Branch Rickey stated, "Things worthwhile generally don't just happen. Luck is a fact, but should not be a factor. Good luck is what is left over after intelligence and effort have combined at their best. Negligence or indifference are usually reviewed from an unlucky seat. The law of cause and effect and causality work the same with inexorable exactitudes. 'Luck is the residue of design'."

Dr. Witt spent the bulk of his life believing in a similar sounding sentiment, 'luck is the residue of preparation.' He should be the last person to deny he is, and has been lucky most of his life. However, the gradations existing between designing his own luck and preparing for opportunities to become lucky, while subtle, are nevertheless significant. Xavier imagined the feasibility of someone designing their own luck, someone making things happen the way they desire them to occur. Could something so far-fetched be attainable?

Preparation is situating yourself in a state of readiness in case lucky opportunities are made available to you. There is no doubt designing your life with luck being the residual effect may be seen as more proactive. Who would not want to orchestrate much if not all of their opportunities at luck? However, it may not be the most prudent path to pursue.

Xavier Witt, like many Black youths growing up in South Central L.A. had dreams, aspirations, even fantasies about what his adult life would look like. Imagining designing a life that would have him partnering with an earth walking angel to create beautiful life, finding and fostering forever friendships, meeting awe inspiring personalities, developing profound relationships with young minds destined to be leaders, and searching for a soul mate that upon discovering her provided Xavier the luck of loving as well as liking the most lovable. This type of design is beyond the capabilities of mortal men. However, fantasizing, wondering, cogitating about possibilities begins the preparation. After all, imagination is only a bridge away from reality.

Coincidentally the cultural capital Xavier developed across his lifetime while teaching about diversity & social justice served him well enough to not completely dissipate or disintegrate upon his being professionally denigrated. Xavier having had his share of daunting experiences was well equipped, or to state the obvious, 'prepared' to handle the next one that came his way. There is no way in hell he would have designed such a series of events.

As luck would have it, all his dreams culminated in a reality of Xavier sharing his consciousness raising journeys with others the way he always appreciated others sharing with him. Perhaps Xavier's fixation on examining 'otherness' originated through these exchanges. One thing is certain, the vehicle he intuitively knew was his destiny was storytelling. The irony of one of the reviewers of his first book telling the publisher, 'This guy is a storyteller' was never lost on Xavier, though it didn't initially resonate. The fact that Xavier would lose his first career as a result, amongst other things, of choosing a film titled, "Storytelling" for use as a point of departure to teach his classes about the problematic intersectionality of race, gender, social class, and privilege, is not something he would ever design. However, in retrospect it was something for which he was definitely prepared.

As a younger man playing and teaching tennis in L.A. Xavier firmly believed it was the extra push-ups, the 5:30 am Saturday morning runs and training sessions with his tennis partner extraordinaire, 'Z,' the meticulous carbohydrates loading before a match, and studying of tennis greats as well as hours of viewing taped recordings of his own performances that ultimately made the difference between a tennis ball striking the net cord and landing on his side of the court. If Xavier *designed* anything to make this happen it was the plan to be prepared for whatever comes. He recognize that his athleticism, intellect, lifestyle, even personality were all engineered to varying extents by portions of privilege mixed with at least a little luck if not a lot.

Xavier realized somewhere in the middle of his extended stay in a *Twilight Zone* of his own design that it could instead be a more short lived visit than anticipated. Somewhere during an early moment of clarity Xavier saw that his journey thus far had been only about him finally arriving at this destination. You are, at this very moment, reading his destiny. Everything up to this point are stories shrinking in the distance, disappearing in the rear view mirror as he advances further down the road. Some stories are to be remembered, some forgotten, but all appreciated for their once upon a time catalytic effect. So stay tuned for more stories.

Oh, and perhaps your paths will intersect again. He'll be the guy at the party that is often discussed across the duration of the evening, people whispering to one another when looking at him from afar, saying:

"Isn't that Dr. Xavier Witt, the protagonist in Dr. J.W. Wiley's novel, inspired by a True Story?"

Only to hear different versions of, "That may be Dr. Wiley himself."

"Well, which one of them is the social justice guy who was fired for inappropriate conduct, and other allegedly questionable behavior?"

"Neither. Both. Either one, depending upon who is telling you the story."

"How did his trial turn out? Maybe knowing the outcome of his court case could enlighten us."

"Maybe, and maybe not. Remember, *this is America*."

* Dr. Xavier Witt was terminated from NYSU-Peru in late June. He misses many of the souls of good folks that he grew to know rather well, but doesn't miss the soulless place that turned out not to be such a safe space. Like how Trump's 'make America great again' brings to mind the question, 'for whom?' NYSU-Peru's safe space begs the same question and pleads the same proposition, essentially six in one hand, a half-dozen in another. With no interest in signing a non-disclosure agreement that would have had silence as a condition for payment he knew that large entities like NYSU bank literally as well as figuratively on the fact that at some point they can negotiate with litigants in similar situations, basically buying them. What they didn't figure out was this social justice thing that Dr. Witt has been doing his entire career was never a passing fancy. Fun was just the way it worked out for him. XW is serious as hell about the work he does, knowing he makes a difference. Once he left the *Twilight Zone* and started writing about what went down it was energizing for him in ways impossible to describe.

Early attempts to arrive at an amicable settlement failed when Dr. Witt's attorney responded to NYSU Central's attorney that their offer was only off by a couple million. When it comes to offers to shut down his voice, like NYSU did when removing him from campus, all he had to say to himself, or to them if they made such an offer once his book was in his mind was 'Fuck that!'"

Considering the pending litigation looming large on the horizon, all Dr. Xavier Witt had left to say is, "Let's do this."

REFERENCES

Alexander, Michelle, The New Jim Crow, (New York, The New Press, 2012).

Armstrong, John, Conditions of Love, (New York, Norton & Company, 2002).

Blumenfeld, Warren J., (2004), "How Homophobia Hurts Everyone" in Maurianne Adams, Warren J. Blumenfeld, Rosie Castaneda, Heather W. Hackman, Madeline L. Peters, & Ximena Zuniga (Eds.), Readings For Diversity And Social Justice: An Anthology on Racism, Antisemitism, Sexism, Heterosexism, Ableism, and Classism, (pp. 9-14) N.Y., Routledge, 2000

Churchill, Ward, (2004), "American Indians In Film: Thematic Contours Of Colonization," in Jun Xing & Lane Ryo Hirabayashi (Eds), Reversing The Lens: Ethnicity, Race, Gender, and Sexuality Through Film (pp. 43-111) Boulder, Colorado, University Press of Colorado, 2003.

Corvino, J. (1997). Homosexuality: The nature and harm arguments. In Alan Soble (Ed.), The Philosophy of Sex: Contemporary Readings (pp. 135-144). Lanham, MD: Rowman and Littlefield.

Davis, Angela (1981). Women, Race, and Class. New York, NY; Vintage

DuBois, W.E.B. (1997). John Brown: A biography. Armonk, NY: M.E. Sharpe, Inc.

DuBois, W.E.B., (1907). The Souls of Black Folks (1986) Vintage Books, Library of America

DePalma, B. (Director). (1989). Casualties of war [Motion picture]. Hollywood, CA: TriStar Productions.

Fleming V., Cukor, G., Leroy, M., (Directors). (1939). The Wizard of Oz [Motion picture]. Hollywood: Metro-Goldwyn-Mayer.

Haywood H., Howard M., (1925) Lynching. a Weapon of National Oppression, International Pamphlets

Helgeland, B. (Director). (2013). 42 [Motion picture]. Hollywood, CA: Legendary Pictures

Huddles, J. (Director). (2013). The Philosophers [After the Dark] [Motion picture]. Jakarta, Indonesia: SCTV.

hooks, bell, We Real Cool: Black Men and Masculinity, (New York, Routledge Publishing, 2004).

Katz, Jackson (2004), "Pornography and Men's Consciousness" in Maurianne Adams, Warren J. Blumenfeld, Rosie Castaneda, Heather W. Hackman, Madeline L. Peters, & Ximena Zuniga (Eds.), Readings For Diversity And Social Justice: An Anthology on Racism, Antisemitism, Sexism, Heterosexism, Ableism, and Classism, (pp. 247-251) New York, Routledge, 2000

Keith, Thomas, Masculinities in Contemporary American Culture, (New York, Routledge Publishing, 2017).

Loewen, James W., (1995). Lies My Teacher Told Me, New York, NY. Touchstone Publishing.

Mill, John Stuart, (1988) The Subjection of Women, Edited by Susan M. Okin,
(Indianapolis, Hackett Publishing Co., 1988), P.23.

Schumacher, J. (Director). (1996). A Time to Kill [Motion picture]. Hollywood, CA: Milchan, Grisham

Seinfeld, Season 4, Episode 16. (1993). The outing [Television episode]. New York: SONY Pictures.

Singleton, J. (Director). (1997). Rosewood [Motion picture]. Hollywood, CA: Warner Bros.

Solomon, Robert, C., About Love, (Maryland, Madison Books Publishing, 2001).

Solonoz, T. (Director). (2002). Storytelling, Fiction [Motion picture]. Hollywood, CA: New Line Production.

Taylor, Marianne, The Book of Cool, (Philadelphia, Running Press, 2009).

Witcher, T. (Director). (2013). 42 [Motion picture]. Hollywood, CA: Wechsler, Samuels, Stern.

Wiley, J.W., (2013). Intro (3), The NIGGER in You: Challenging Dysfunctional Language, Engaging Leadership Moments - Sterling, Va, Stylus Publishing.

Wiley, J.W., (2009)."Affirmative Actions at PWIs: Explicating the Glass as Half Full, While Pouring Something They're More Apt to Taste" in Darrell Cleveland (Ed.), When Minorities Are Strongly Encouraged to Apply: Diversity and Affirmative Action in Higher Education (pp. 241-278). New York, NY., Peter Lang Publishing.

ABOUT THE AUTHOR

Dr. J.W. Wiley is an accomplished writer/poet. His book "The NIGGER in You: Challenging Dysfunctional Language – Engaging Leadership Moments" was published by Stylus in May 2013 and now serves as the inspiration for the upcoming film '*How Does it Feel to be a Problem*' by renowned educational filmmaker Dr. Thomas Keith (The Bro Code, The Empathy Gap) scheduled to complete in Summer 2019.

Dr. Wiley is the president and owner of Xamining Diversity whereby he keynotes, consults, facilitates cultural competency workshops and day/weekend retreats or presents his interactive workshop "Diversity Enlightenment." His client list is as diverse as his message including the Canadian Association of Principals; National Center for Atmospheric Research; University of Notre Dame; Midwest Athletic Conference; Pfizer Pharmaceuticals; Vermont National Guard; Los Angeles County Fire Department; Princeton Jr. Scholars; Univ of San Francisco Medical Center; New York State Nurses Association; Homeland Security; Norwich University in Vermont; PACE University; University of Vermont; Champlain Valley Physicians Hospital; Wyeth Pharmaceuticals; Southwoods Summer Camp; Bombardier; Zone 9 Police Academy; Joint Council for Economic Opportunity (JCEO); North Country Legal Services; and the Plattsburgh New York Mayor's Office, City Council, and Police Department; various school districts, high/middle schools; and countless other businesses, universities, and colleges.

Dr. Wiley's previous leadership experiences include serving as Chief Diversity Officer at State University of New York – Plattsburgh and a Lecturer in Philosophy/Interdisciplinary Studies from 2000-2018. Prior to his academic career, Dr. Wiley worked for three Fortune 100 companies: Hughes Aircraft Co., Rockwell International, and McDonnell Douglas Corp. His doctorate is in Educational Leadership from the University of Vermont in Burlington.

CLASSES TAUGHT:
Examining Diversity through Film
African American Culture from 1865-Present
Moral Problem - Societal Dilemmas

Examining Dimensions of Cool - A Study of Social Class
Philosophies on Romance, Sex, Love, & Marriage
The Philosophy of W.E.B. DuBois

From 2007-2018 his thought was shared monthly beginning with a blog titled, "Wiley Wandering," followed by a column on diversity & social justice titled "Justice for All."

**** JUSTICE FOR ALL ****
 Newspaper Columns
http://www.pressrepublican.com/opinion/columns/

WE SHOULD START TO REALLY SEE EACH OTHER
http://www.pressrepublican.com/opinion/we-should-start-to-really-see-each-other/article_fa75a74c-266d-5c5e-a6a8-8a2325a03be1.html

SO FAR RIGHT THERE IS NOTHING LEFT
http://www.pressrepublican.com/opinion/justice-for-all-so-far-right-there-is-nothing-left/article_fb84fa69-5735-5040-990a-1e5ceab328d1.html

UNMASKING OUR HEROES ISN'T EASY
http://www.pressrepublican.com/opinion/justice-for-all-unmasking-our-heroes-isn-t-easy/article_23a17026-d792-56be-813b-a1bab56b7203.html

SCARRED PERSPECTIVES - ALLY OBJECTIVES
http://www.pressrepublican.com/opinion/scarred-perspectives-ally-objectives/article_2807973e-377e-556d-bbe9-daecc40e2816.html

BLACK LIVES LOST IN AMERICA
http://www.pressrepublican.com/opinion/black-lives-lost-in-america/article_29cba00f-dd01-50f5-852c-2e8cc8f6b063.html

IMAGINING AN AWAKENED CONSCIOUSNESS
http://www.pressrepublican.com/opinion/justice-for-all-imagining-an-awakened-consciousness/article_40333550-efa9-52a2-b2e2-45033072eeda.html

WOMEN AND THE CLUELESSNESS OF MEN

http://www.pressrepublican.com/opinion/women-and-the-cluelessness-of-men/article_9ec4019b-bba2-5ab8-b236-28f7cb86c569.html

PREJUDGING AMERICANS IS UNAMERICAN
http://www.pressrepublican.com/opinion/justice-for-all-prejudging-americans-is-unamerican/article_8779b708-c4a8-5478-9a94-d7358c369c8e.html#.Vmfv76uR8uU.mailto

PROBLEMS WITH PLAYING CARDS
http://www.pressrepublican.com/opinion/problems-with-playing-cards/article_9ddf4900-0cb9-5904-8802-d93f4d365a13.html

BEING IN THE HOUSE ISN'T ALWAYS A PRIVILEGE
http://www.pressrepublican.com/opinion/justice-for-all-being-in-the-house-isn-t-always/article_6cd7ebdc-d0a9-557e-92b6-7e0fd3d2af6c.html

SUCCESSFULLY SWIMMING WHILE UNDENIABLY DROWNING
http://www.pressrepublican.com/opinion/justice-for-all-successfully-swimming-while-undeniably-drowning/article_1bade6a1-da9a-5153-8efe-23773a793f28.html

THE PRIVILEGE TO NOT CONSIDER OTHERS
http://www.pressrepublican.com/opinion/justice-for-all-the-privilege-to-not-consider-others/article_99024c7f-22b4-5f3b-a17f-b6fa58503ac4.html

RELATIONSHIP, EGOS, AND INHERITED IDEALS
http://www.pressrepublican.com/opinion/justice-for-all-relationships-egos-and-inherited-ideals/article_f6a38f22-6189-5651-855f-82140401b898.html

AVOIDING THE POLITICS OF HYPOCRISY
http://www.pressrepublican.com/opinion/avoiding-the-politics-of-hypocrisy/article_28e70d74-b8da-54f3-ba97-4b621f3bfc9e.html

DEMOCRATICALLY SUPPORTING THE PRESIDENT-ELECT
http://www.pressrepublican.com/opinion/democratically-supporting-the-president-elect/article_cdfd0e3a-1e21-594e-b4a4-b8949a732b12.html

TRUMP IS MAKING AMERICA HATE AGAIN
http://www.pressrepublican.com/opinion/justice-for-all-trump-is-making-america-hate-again/article_448353dc-026a-5b66-9aac-94bee9cecde1.html

TIME TO EMBRACE OUR LEADERSHIP MOMENTS
http://www.pressrepublican.com/opinion/time-to-embrace-our-leadership-moment/article_34197bcc-99da-11e5-bb1d-e76af64226fd.html?mode=jqm

STANDING UP FOR LESS FORTUNATE
http://www.pressrepublican.com/opinion/in-my-opinion-standing-up-for-less-fortunate/article_8b077435-01df-5f90-a35b-56324396f624.html

SOCIAL MEDIA LINKS

MANTRA: "Reconciling "Otherness" with Diversity Enlightenment"
WEBSITE: http://xaminingdiversity.com/

SUNY Plattsburgh 2017 Summer Orientation
https://youtu.be/aO8OUGNfyVA

TNIY Film Outtake: The SUBWAY Story
https://youtu.be/dWCs9FkGEyg

XAMINING DIVERSITY (XD) CONSULTING WEBSITE:
http://www.xaminingdiversity.com/

ON THE MEANING OF THE N-word
http://youtu.be/lq9VS7S3RyM

FILM - DISSED RESPECT:
The Impact of Bullying
D-Respect 30 min movie
https://youtu.be/6xAXAaNai8E

UNPACKING MLK's I HAVE A DREAM SPEECH
http://wamc.org/post/dr-martin-luther-king-jr-i-have-dream-speech-h-carl-mccall-and-dr-jw-wiley

YouTube Presentation Video Clips

SMIDGEN EDGY (:34)
https://www.youtube.com/watch?v=E3I2qfw_-k0

WE SEE THINGS AS THEY ARE (5:03)
https://www.youtube.com/watch?v=tl7rFRMgU2k

IMPLICIT BIAS - BENEFIT OF THE DOUBT (1:26)
https://www.youtube.com/watch?v=WxRiPSsTlEA

SPEAKING TRUTH TO POWER (1:23)
https://www.youtube.com/watch?v=V8g87cyCZQM

LM - SOCRATIC METHOD (2:42)
https://www.youtube.com/watch?v=wxxOqJ9XVLc

LEADERSHIP IN CONTEXT (4:49)
https://www.youtube.com/watch?v=Dv6W_Y5IcKo

HOW DOES IT FEEL TO BE A PROBLEM? (1:20)
https://www.youtube.com/watch?v=7wkgyXpAGjA

PROBLEM = CRIMINAL = NIGGER = RETARD = BITCH (1:39)
https://www.youtube.com/watch?v=lOIk1wWndls

HOW COURAGEOUS ARE YOU (2:12)
https://www.youtube.com/watch?v=DQraX1lr6FQ

HVCC Version of "The Subway Story" (10:00)
https://www.youtube.com/watch?v=xrve6v9bjGE

****

On Smiling
[YR, KS, SJ, RS, KCo, IW, ER, KP, TS,
https://youtu.be/e01nl50dwDU

The Complexity of NIGGER (4:27)
https://youtu.be/hFh-egyXGkk

The Elite Group (2:42)
https://youtu.be/eR6lDZaN6Fg

Inherited Ideals - Perspective (1:58)
https://youtu.be/BM7vGquD4Ok

Puppets - Responsibility (2:27)
https://youtu.be/DPtrLqsjfIg

Leadership Moments
http://youtube.com/watch?v=61EWCEeGUMk

Leadership Moments II
http://youtu.be/biHZlWO80oM

White Males
http://youtu.be/nvHzLvLGuw0

Hostages
http://youtu.be/umHoVB3jg34

Allies Making a Difference
http://youtu.be/9z8zcvpDU-8

Unpacking Baggage
http://youtu.be/7MQDqkposiA

Seeing Things Differently
http://youtu.be/Ts8PUC9Llco

You Guys
http://youtu.be/pRfsLax3QOM

Ugliness & P=C=N=R=B
[JM, KS, SJ, EDi, YW, HR, DL, BE, HF, BM,

http://youtube.com/watch?v=XOZCbo5Zpzs

Finding Your Voice
[JM, VD, ED, JH, JB, GJ, AE, EDi, YW, CP, CL, TS, RW, BE, BM, SH,
http://youtube.com/watch?v=BmfvoezDT_M

Awareness of Disrespect by Allies & Colleagues
http://youtube.com/watch?v=iLQQC4E1Uu4

Consideration
http://youtu.be/I0ZQZ9-mLAw

Socratic Approach
http://youtu.be/9fkAOChO86s

Scarred by Language
http://youtu.be/v_X2HnQraDA

EXAMINING DIVERSITY THROUGH FILM
http://theodysseyonline.com/suny-plattsburgh/more-than-meets-the-eyes/226512

POLICE OFFICERS IN DIVERSITY CLASS
http://cardinalpointsonline.com/officers-participate-in-diversity-class/

CONTRIBUTED BOOK CHAPTERS

AFFIRMATIVE ACTIONS AT PWIs:
Explicating the Glass as Half Full While Pouring Something They're More Apt to Taste in **When Minorities are Strongly Encouraged to Apply**

RETAINING AFRICAN AMERICAN ADMINISTRATORS:
A Subconscious Deluge of Neglect, Or a Conscious Subterfuge to Reject

INSTITUTIONAL ETHICS:
Forty Acres of So-Called Morality and Still No Mule
in **Brothers of the Academy**

UTILIZING FILM to INSPIRE ALLIES to ENGAGE LEADERSHIP MOMENTS in 'Theory to Practice: Fostering Diverse & Inclusive Campus Environments'

CONTACT EMAIL /
Please contact me at:
drjwwiley@xaminingdiversity.com

Made in the USA
San Bernardino, CA
27 June 2019